MOUNTAINS

Other books by the author

Action, Emotion and Will
Wittgenstein
Will, Freedom and Power
The Aristotelian Ethics
The God of the Philosophers
Aquinas
The Computation of Style
Thomas More
A Path from Rome
The Logic of Deterrence
God and Two Poets
The Metaphysics of Mind

MOUNTAINS

An Anthology

Compiled by
Anthony Kenny

JOHN MURRAY

Introductory text and compilation © Anthony Kenny 1991
Illustrations © Paul Kershaw 1991

First published in 1991
by John Murray (Publishers) Ltd
50 Albemarle Street, London W1X 4BD

British Library Cataloguing-in-Publication Data
Mountains: An anthology.
  I. Kenny, Anthony
  796.509

  ISBN 0–7195–4639–7

Typeset in 10½ / 12½ pt Garamond by Colset Pte. Ltd., Singapore
Printed and bound in Great Britain at the University Press, Cambridge

Contents

◆

Illustrations

◆

Wood engravings by Paul L. Kershaw

O ye Mountains and Hills, bless ye the Lord:
Praise him and magnify him for ever.

Canticle *Benedicite*

Thy mercy, O Lord, is in the heavens;
Thy faithfulness reacheth unto the clouds;
Thy righteousness is like the great mountains.

Psalm 36: 6–7

Ye mountains of Gilboa, let there be no dew, neither let there be rain upon you, nor fields of offerings; for there the shield of the mighty is vilely cast away.

2 Samuel 1: 19

See one promontory (said Socrates of old), one mountain, one sea, one river, and see all.

Richard Burton, *Anatomy of Melancholy*

Night's candles are burnt out, and jocund day
Stands tiptoe on the misty mountain tops.

Shakespeare, *Romeo and Juliet*, Act 5, Scene 9

Each cloud-capt mountain is a holy altar;
An organ breathes in every grove.

Thomas Hood, 'Ode to Rae Wilson'

'Tis distance lends enchantment to the view
And robes the mountain in its azure hue.

Thomas Campbell, 'Pleasures of Hope'

Great things are done when men and mountains meet;
This is not done by jostling in the street.

William Blake, MS Notebooks

Separate from the pleasure of your company, I don't much care if I
never see another mountain in my life.

Charles Lamb to Wordsworth, 1801

Mont Blanc is the monarch of mountains
They crowned him long ago
On a throne of rocks, in a robe of clouds,
With a diadem of snow.

Lord Byron, *Manfred*, I, 1.

Many an Alpine traveller, many a busy man of science volubly represent to
us their pleasure in the Alps; but I scarcely recognise one who would not
willingly see them all ground down into gravel, on condition of his being
the first to exhibit a pebble of it at the Royal Institution.

John Ruskin, *Fors Clavigera*

It is a fine thing to be out on the hills alone. A man can hardly be a beast
or a fool alone on a great mountain.

Francis Kilvert, *On the Black Mountain*

Introduction

◆

The love of mountains is no new thing, no fad of an industrial era. Human beings have loved mountains since history began, but their love has taken different forms in different ages. The Psalmist looked to the hills for help, and rejoiced that the mountains stood around Jerusalem as a guarantee that the Lord was with his people. The Greeks, when they tried to imagine a region of the greatest felicity, fit for Gods to live in, placed it on top of their highest mountain.

Mountains have always been admired for their stability, revered for their antiquity, feared for their mystery. The writers of the Old Testament set forth the eternity and omnipotence of God by proclaiming that He surpasses even the mountains in age and strength. 'Before the mountains were brought forth, or ever Thou hadst formed the earth and the world, even from everlasting to everlasting, Thou art God' says the ninetieth Psalm. When the prophet Habbakuk wants to describe the majesty of the presence of God, he says 'The everlasting mountains were scattered, the perpetual hills did bow; the mountains saw Thee and they trembled.' At the Exodus from Egypt, the foundation event of Israel's history, 'The mountains skipped like rams, and the little hills like lambs' and at the coming of Messiah in the future, 'every valley shall be exalted and every mountain and hill made low'.

Strength, rather than beauty, is the aspect of mountains most hymned in the Old Testament; but already in classical antiquity men knew that mountains were beautiful to look up to and beautiful to look down from. The poet Horace, having admired Mount Soracte white with the winter snow, preferred to stay at home with his friends; but the Emperor Hadrian was prepared to make a mountain ascent before sunrise for the sake of the view. Ovid, describing how Phaeton lost control of the chariot of the sun and scorched the earth beneath him, takes the opportunity to list the great summits of the ancient world:

> The moon in wonder sees her brother's team
> Running below her own; the scalding clouds
> Steam; the parched fields crack deep, all moisture dried,
> And every summit flames; the calcined meads
> Lie white; the leaf dies burning with the bough

And the dry corn its own destruction feeds.
These are but trifles. Mighty cities burn
With all their ramparts; realms and nations turn
To ashes; mountains with their forests blaze.
Athos is burning, Oeta is on fire,
And Tmolus and proud Taurus and the crest
Of Ida, dry, whose springs were once so famed,
And virgin Helicon and Haemus, still
Unknown, unhonoured. Etna burns immense
In two fold conflagration; Eryx flames
And Othrys and Parnassus' double peaks;
Cynthus and Dindyma and Mycale
And Rhodope, losing at last her snows,
And Mimas and Cithaeron's holy hill.
Caucasus burns; the frosts of Scythia
Fail in her need; Pindus and Ossa blaze
And, lordlier than both, Olympus flames
And the airy Alps and cloud-capped Appenines.

This passage is not only the earliest known warning of the dangers of global warming, but also prefigures that roll-call of summits seen from above which is the essential feature of every Victorian mountaineer's description of his latest conquest.

The Christian era began with a sermon on a mountain, just as it was from a mountain that Moses had brought down the covenant of Israel. In its first centuries, however, Christianity was an urban religion, and mountain folk were paradigms of paganism. But there came a time when Christians fled the corruption of the cities, and many chose to live their lives in mountain solitude. It was the loneliness and severity of the mountains that attracted the ascetic; but several legends of the saints show that such asceticism was not held incompatible with an appreciation of the beauty of mountain landscape. The nature mysticism of St Francis has antecedents which go back to the hermits of late antiquity.

In the Christian Middle Ages many a famous monastery was founded among the mountains, some of which survive today and have been objects of pilgrimage for centuries. St Bernard of Aosta, a contemporary of William the Conqueror, devoted himself to the service of Alpine travellers, for whom he built hostels on the passes still called after him the Great and Little St Bernard. His name is recalled also by the well-known breed of dog, and in 1923 he was proclaimed patron saint of mountain climbers by the mountaineering Pope, Pius XI.

The writing saints of the Middle Ages, however, showed little interest in the mountains, even when, like St Anselm and St Thomas Aquinas, they were born in mountainous regions. The computerized concordance to the eight million words of St Thomas's writings reveal that in almost every one of the many places where the Latin word for 'mountain' appears it is in a symbolic sense. Only rarely is he forced by the duty of commenting on Aristotle or the Old Testament to make a literal mention of a mountain.

On the other hand, Dante, for all his didactic purpose, describes the Mount of Purgatory in very concrete terms, and his vivid accounts of some of the difficult climbing which he and Virgil undertook could almost persuade one that he was a mountaineer in the flesh as well as in the spirit. As, for instance, at the beginning of the Fourth Canto of the *Purgatorio*:

> Climb to San Leo, drop to Noli, try
> > to scale Bismantua to its crest one might
> > with only feet; but here was need to fly:
> I mean, with the swift wings and feathered flight
> > of great desires, following his guidance, who
> > both was my source of hope and gave me light.
> We toiled up by the chimney cloven through
> > the rock, which grazed us on both sides, the ground
> > not feet alone but hands requiring too.
> When we had scaled the cliff and reached, beyond
> > its topmost verge, the open mountain-side:
> > 'Master' I said 'where shall a path be found?'

Whether or not Dante's description of this tricky pitch is based on experience, his friend's son Petrarch, a few decades later, left us an account of an ascent of a specific peak on a specific day. Mont Ventoux, which he climbed, is only 6430 feet and is not a difficult climb, but a higher and much more difficult mountain, Mont Aiguille near Grenoble, was ascended in 1492 by the chamberlain of King Charles VII of France, who has a solid claim to be the first serious rock climber in history.

The age of the Reformation and Counter-Reformation was in one way unfavourable to Alpine exploration: an age which saw witches and demons everywhere was also happy to people the mountains with dragons and hobgoblins. None the less, a number of new ascents were made, of which the most spectacular was the expedition which ascended Popocatapetl, at the orders of Cortez, in 1521. By the end of the sixteenth century several of the lower Swiss peaks were quite commonly ascended, in particular the Stockhorn (where an inscription in Greek was placed reading 'the love of mountains is best') and Mount Pilatus (where the climber had to brave the danger of meeting Pontius Pilate's ghost). And already in mid-century, a Professor at Zürich, Conrad Gesner, had made a resolution to climb one mountain every year.

Marti, a friend of Gesner, ended a description of the view from the terrace at Berne with these words:

These are the mountains which form our pleasure and delight when we gaze at them from the highest parts of our city, and admire their mighty peaks and broken crags, that threaten to fall at any moment. Who, then, would not admire, love, willingly visit, explore, and climb places of this sort? I should assuredly call those who are not attracted by them dolts, stupid dull fishes, and slow tortoises . . .

A traveller quoted in Coryat's *Crudities* in 1611 asks his reader a series of questions:

What, I pray you, is more pleasant, more delectable, and more accept-able unto a man than to behold the height of hilles, as it were the very Atlantes of heven? To admire Hercules his pilers? To see the moun-taines Taurus and Caucasus? To view the hill Olympus, the seat of Jupiter? To pass over the Alpes that were broken by Annibals Vinegar? To climb up the Appenine promontory of Italy? From the hill Ida to behold the rising of the Sunne before the Sunne appears? To visit Pernassus and Helicon the most celebrated seates of the Muses?

If this traveller had visited all the sites which he commends, mountain tourism must already have been thriving.

However, it cannot be denied that for most travellers between Britain and the Mediterranean, the Alps presented themselves first and foremost as an obstacle to be traversed. Almost every account of the Grand Tour in the seventeenth and eighteenth centuries dwells on the discomforts and dangers of the Alpine crossing. None the less, many a traveller, in haste to reach the artistic and architectural treasures beneath the Italian sunshine, discovered that the mountain passes could offer inspiration and delight no less than inconvenience and terror. John Dennis, having described the wonders and the perils of his Alpine journey in 1688, summed up his sentiments thus: 'The sense of all this produc'd different motions in me, *viz.* a delightful Horrour, a terrible Joy, and at the same time, that I was infinitely pleas'd, I trembled.'

The terrors of mountain travel before the nineteenth century were real enough, and it is easy to understand those travellers who were too weighed down by them to look up with delight at the beauty of their surroundings, and preferred to pull down the blinds of their carriages or wished that their chairs were closed instead of open. But even those best known for their complaints about the horror of the Alps were capable of enjoying mountain scenery in regions less alarming. Thus George Berkeley, writing from Ischia in 1717, told his correspondent that 'Nothing can be conceived more romantic than the forms of nature, mountains, hills, vales and little plains, being thrown together in a wild and beautiful variety'. And he commended to Alexander Pope the ascent of its central 2000-ft peak: 'Its lower parts are adorned with vines and other fruits; the middle affords pasture to flocks of goats and sheep; and the top is a sandy pointed rock, from which you have the finest prospect in the world, surveying at one view, besides several pleasant islands lying at your feet, a tract of Italy about three hundred miles'.

It was Sir Leslie Stephen who convinced the world that until the closing decades of the eighteenth century mankind in general hated mountains. The contrast which he drew between the old perception and the new was greatly overdrawn; both before and after the onset of the romantic era the relation of the human race to the mountains of its planet was a mixture of fear and love.

There is no doubt, however, that as the eighteenth century drew to its close interest in mountains took on a new intensity and expressed itself in novel forms. The savant De Saussure, in 1760, offered a reward to any peasant who could find a way to the summit of Mont Blanc. He went himself on many scientific expeditions in the lower Alps. When his wife complained of his frequent absences from home, he retorted 'You would sooner – God forgive me for saying so – see me growing fat like a friar, and snoring every day in the chimney corner, after a big dinner, than that I should achieve immortal fame by the most sublime discoveries at the cost of reducing my weight by a few ounces and spending a few weeks away from you'.

De Saussure's reward was not claimed until 1786, when the physician Michel Paccard, and the peasant Jacques Balmat, reached the summit of Mont Blanc from Chamonix. Saussure himself followed in their tracks a year later, and before his death in 1799 he had explored also the lower regions of the Matterhorn. As the nineteenth century developed, the best-known peaks of the Alps were climbed, beginning with the Ortler in 1804 and the Jungfrau in 1811, and ending with the Matterhorn and two other peaks in 1865.

Simultaneously with the flowering of Alpine exploration in the wake of Saussure came the explosion throughout Europe of literary romanticism. The two movements had separate origins, but they were capable of fusing to produce a novel intensity of mountain vision. The concept of the Sublime played a key role in the Romantic sensibility, and according to a writer like Burke the mark of the Sublime was its capacity to generate emotions of awe and terror. The high mountains, in their power and vastness, with their mysteries and perils, became for many romantic writers the very paradigm of sublimity.

Wordsworth and Coleridge, Shelley and Byron all found poetic material in mountain landscape; though they shared a common inspiration they give it expression in very different ways. Wordsworth, though he breathed the Alpine air before the others, was more at home in description of British hills and fells than in grand set-pieces about the Alps. Coleridge and Shelley each produced odes to Mont Blanc, but whereas for Coleridge one vast mountain will proclaim the same message as any other, Shelley attaches importance to the accurate description of scenic detail. Like Coleridge, Byron often captures the feel of the mountains in prose better than in verse. Following in the wake of the great romantics, many a lesser poet served up his ration of mountain verse. As Arnold Lunn has said, 'Too often Byron and his contemporaries saw in the hills yet another peg on which to hang their philosophy of life. The mountains are made to utter one man's revolt against the social order, and to vindicate another's unshaken confidence in the Thirty-Nine Articles'.

Romantic motives were not the only ones that drew men to the mountains in the early nineteenth century: in the half-century after Saussure scientific researchers also went up into high places. Volcanoes had stimulated the interest of philosophers and scientists since ancient times, and curiosity about their nature and operation was rumoured to have been responsible for the death of Empedocles in Greek and Pliny in Roman times. Charles Darwin carried out a scientific exploration of the Andes in the 1830s, and in the later decades of the century many scientist-mountaineers sought to discover the true nature of the glaciers which had fascinated tourists since the 1740s.

Part romantic, part scientist, but also a wholly individual historian and philosopher, John Ruskin, whose life spanned the nineteenth century, proved himself to be, in the most varied of contexts, the greatest mountain writer of all time. His love of the mountains knew no bounds: all natural beauty, all moral goodness, was to be judged by its proximity to or distance from the ideal serenity of the high peaks. He described the mountains as the 'great cathedrals of the earth, with their gates of rock, pavements of cloud, choirs of stream and stone, altars of snow, and vaults of purple traversed by the continual stars'. Ruskin's best descriptions of mountain scenery remain unsurpassed, but his passion for the mountains remained Platonic: he was a mountain lover, but no mountain climber, and indeed he deplored the efflorescence of mountaineering in his lifetime.

One thing was common to Ruskin and to the athletic climbers who aroused his disgust: they both valued the mountains as the antithesis of the city. The Victorian businessman, no less than the Desert Fathers, sought in the solitude of the mountains release and purification from the bustle of commercial and competitive life. Just as a third-century hermit might treasure the biblical texts which urged flight from the world, so too the nineteenth-century mountaineer would remind himself of Byron's words:

> I live not in myself, but I become
> Portion of that around me, and to me
> High mountains are a feeling, but the sum
> Of human cities torture.

The hermit, however, went to the mountains for life, the Victorian went for a holiday. The novelty of the mid-nineteenth century, which Ruskin hated, was the emergence of mountaineering as a sport. Early mountaineers, if they were not to be thought frivolous or reckless, felt obliged to emphasize that their climbing was – like Petrarch's – an act of piety, or – like Saussure's – a pursuit of science. With the foundation of the Alpine Club in 1857 there were more and more Alpinists who were willing to admit frankly that they ascended the mountains for pleasure, in the pursuit of challenging, invigorating, and increasingly competitive physical exercise. The Alps, once inaccessible, once forbidding, once sublime, turned by degrees into the 'playground of Europe'.

Sir Leslie Stephen, editor of the *Alpine Journal*, who coined this description, was a better writer than most of the Victorian climbers, and a better climber than the best of the Victorian writers. He is well known as the author of *An Agnostic's Apology*, and the title of that work reminds us that there were links between the Victorian passion for mountains and the Victorian ambivalence about religion. The mountain monasteries were no longer objects of uncritical veneration, and Matthew Arnold used the Grande Chartreuse as the setting for the most famous poetical expression of the Victorian crisis of faith. The geologist's hammer which was no less essential than an ice-axe as a tool for the early nineteenth-century mountaineer was also the instrument which undermined the cosmic chronology of Biblical fundamentalism. Those who abandoned Christian belief were anxious to exhibit, in the stoic traits of character essential for success above the snowline, that loss of faith need involve no diminution of moral fibre. Those who gave up belief in the eternal God of Abraham, Isaac and Jacob were glad to retain a sublime object of awe in the everlasting snows of Mont Blanc, Monte Rosa and the Matterhorn. John Tyndall, the agnostic President of the Royal Society, thus describes the view from the summit of the Weisshorn: 'An influence seemed to proceed from it direct to the soul; the delight and exultation experienced were not those of Reason or Knowledge, but of BEING: I was part of it and it of me, and in the transcendent glory of Nature I entirely forgot myself as man'. There was something incongruous, if not profane, he felt, 'in allowing the scientific faculty to interfere where silent worship was the "reasonable service"'.

Whether or not mountaineers felt close to God on the high mountains, they could not help but realize that even at their most skilled and most confident they might find themselves close to death. The tragedy which so immediately succeeded the long-delayed triumph over the Matterhorn was the most spectacular of Victorian mountain fatalities, but there were many more during the years of Alpine conquest. In the year 1882, when three English dons fell to their deaths in less than a month, Queen Victoria felt moved to ask her secretary to write to Mr Gladstone 'to ask you if you think she can say anything to mark her disapproval of the dangerous Alpine excursions which this year have occasioned so much loss of life'. Gladstone replied:

'My dear Sir H. Ponsonby, – I do not wonder that the Queen's sympathic feelings have again been excited by the accidents, so grave in character, and so accumulated during recent weeks, on the Alps. But I doubt the possibility of any interference, even by Her Majesty, with a prospect of advantage. It may be questionable whether, upon the whole, mountain climbing (and be it remembered that Snowdon has its victims as well as the Matterhorn) is more destructive than various other pursuits in the way of recreation which perhaps have no justification to plead so respectable as that which may be alleged on behalf of mountain expeditions'.

As the nineteenth century drew to its close mountaineering became in one sense more professional, in another sense more amateur. It became more professional in that the resorts from which climbers and their guides started their expeditions became fully commercialized. It became more amateur in that many climbers now foreswore the use of professional guides altogether, and a generation of guideless climbers ascended more and more difficult routes unaided. These amateurs themselves then became professionalized in the sense that their routes became codified, their standards more competitive, and their technical apparatus more sophisticated.

Because of the expense of even guideless climbing in the Alps the amateur climbers of the Victorian era tended to belong to a comparatively small elite. In the twentieth century mountaineering became a more universally popular sport, particularly once the rock climbing routes in the Welsh and Scottish mountains had been explored and docketed. The centre of interest for the really venturous mountaineer moved from Europe to the Himalayas, and the series of unsuccessful attempts on Everest between the two World Wars fired the imagination of many who themselves preferred to stay close to sea-level.

In this book I have tried to illustrate, by quotation from writers of many different periods and styles, the significance of the mountains for human beings across the ages. The great majority of the passages I have selected concern the mountains of Britain and Europe, and when I have followed mountain explorers in Asia and in the New World it has been from a European viewpoint: I have not attempted to illustrate the significance of mountains for Chinese, say, or for American Indians. And I have chosen to end the story with the arrival of Hillary and Tenzing at the summit of Everest in 1953: the high point in history of the response of frail humans to the challenge of the everlasting hills.

It now remains for me to express my warm thanks to the many people who have helped me in compiling this anthology by suggesting pieces for inclusion, in particular Margaret Kenny, Janet Adam Smith, Adam Roberts, Jennifer Barnes, Roger Lonsdale, George Band, Marigold Johnson, and especially Hugo Brunner, most encouraging and helpful of publishers.

CHAPTER 1

◆

The Mountains of God

The ancient Greeks, though reluctant to scale mountains themselves, were very willing to place their Gods there. The chief abode
of all the Gods was Mount Olympus, as described by Homer in
the Odyssey. Homer's description of the windlessness of the divine
home reappears, taken in full literalness, in the medieval account
in a travel book ascribed to Sir John Mandeville. In Pope's
eighteenth-century version Olympus has become totally etherialized, and no reader would guess it was a mountain at all. Pope has
preserved the flavour, however, of another famous mountain set-
piece of Homer's: the description of Zeus descending to Mount Ida
to watch the battle between the Greeks and the Trojans.

The Hebrews, like the Greeks, attached religious significance to
the mountains, but of a different sort. Jahweh does not live in the
mountains, but is a distant creator, who may manifest himself upon
them for particular purposes. The greatest event in the history of
Israel, the giving of the Law to God's chosen people, took place on
Mount Sinai. An account of a pilgrimage by a fourth-century nun
from Spain shows that Mount Sinai was already by that time a centre
of devout tourist attention. The narrative in Deutoronomy of
Moses' death on Mount Pisgah was glossed by Ruskin in terms that
would please mountaineers but might surprise biblical scholars.

◆ ◆ ◆

The Abode of the Gods

So saying, the goddess, flashing-eyed Athene, departed to Olympus, where,
they say, is the abode of the gods that stands fast forever. Neither is it
shaken by winds nor ever wet with rain, nor does snow fall upon it, but the
air is outspread, clear and cloudless, and over it hovers a radiant whiteness. Therein the blessed gods are glad all their days, and thither went the
flashing-eyed one, when she had spoken all her word to the maiden.

Homer, *Odyssey*, VI

Olympus Explored

In this country be right high hills toward the end of Macedonia, and there is a great hill that men clepen Olympus that departeth Macedonia and Thrace. And it is so high that it passeth the clouds. And there is another hill that is clept Athos that is so high that the shadow of him reacheth to Lemnos that is an Isle and it is lxxvi miles between. And above at the top of the hill is the air so clear that men may find no wind there. And therefore may no beast live there so is the air dry.

And men say in this country that philosophers sometime went on these hills and held to their nose a sponge moisted with water for to have air for the air above was so dry. And above in the dust and in the powder of those hills they wrote letters and figures with their fingers and at the year's end they came again and found the same letters and figures which they had written the year before without any default. And therefore it seems well that these hills pass the clouds and join to the pure air.

The Travels of Sir John Mandeville

Olympus Etherialized

Then to the Palaces of heav'n she sails;
Incumbent on the wings of wafting gales;
The seat of Gods, the regions mild of peace,
Full joy, and calm eternity of ease.
There no rude winds presume to shake the skies,
No rains descend, no snowy vapours rise;
But on immortal thrones the blest repose;
The firmament with living splendours glows.
Hither the Goddess wing'd th'aethereal way
Thro' heav'n's eternal gates that blaz'd with day.

Pope's Odyssey, VI

Zeus on Mount Ida

The Cloud-compelling God her suit approv'd
And smil'd superior on his Best-belov'd.
Then call'd his Coursers, and his Chariot took;
The stedfast Firmament beneath them shook:
Rapt by th'aethereal steeds the chariot roll'd
Brass were their Hoofs, their curling Manes of Gold,
Of Heaven's undrossy Gold the God's Array

Refulgent, flash'd intolerable Day.
High on the Throne he shines; His Coursers fly
Between th'extended Earth and starry Sky.
But when to *Ida*'s topmost Height he came
(Fair nurse of Fountains and of Savage Game)
Where o'er her pointed Summits proudly rais'd
His fane breath'd odours, and his Altar blaz'd,
There, from his radiant Car, the sacred Sire
Of Gods and Men releas'd the Steeds of Fire
Blue antient Mists th'immortal Steeds embrac'd
High on the cloudy Point his Seat he plac'd.
Thence his broad Eye the subject World surveys
The Town, the Tents, and Navigable Seas . . .

Long as the Morning Beams encreasing bright
O'er Heaven's clear Azure spread the sacred Light;
Commutual Death the Fate of War confounds,
Each adverse Battel goar'd with equal wounds.
But when the Sun the Height of Heav'n ascends,
The Sire of Gods his golden Scales suspends
With equal Hand: In these explor'd the Fate
Of *Greece* and *Troy*, and pois'd the mighty Weight.
Press'd with the Load, the *Grecian* Balance lies
Low sunk on earth, the *Trojan* strikes the skies.
Then Jove from *Ida*'s Top his Horrors spreads;
The Clouds burst dreadful o'er the *Grecian* Heads;
Thick Lightnings flash; the mutt'ring Thunder rolls;
Their Strength he withers, and unmans their Souls.
Before his wrath the trembling Hosts retire;
The God in Terrors, and the Skies on fire.

Pope's *Iliad*, VII

The Law Given on Mount Sinai

In the third month, when the children of Israel were gone forth out of the land of Egypt, the same day came they into the wilderness of Sinai.

For they were departed from Rephidim, and were come to the desert of Sinai, and had pitched in the wilderness; and there Israel camped before the mount.

And Moses went up into God, and the Lord called unto him out of the mountain, saying, Thus shalt thou say to the house of Jacob, and tell the children of Israel;

Ye have seen what I did unto the Egyptians, and how I bare you on eagles' wings, and brought you unto myself.

Now, therefore, if ye will obey my voice indeed, and keep my covenant, then ye shall be a peculiar treasure unto me above all people: for all the earth is mine:

And ye shall be unto me a kingdom of priests, and a holy nation. These are the words which thou shalt speak unto the children of Israel.

And Moses came and called for the elders of the people, and laid before their faces all these words which the Lord commanded him.

And all the people answered together, and said, All that the Lord hath spoken we will do. And Moses returned the words of the people unto the Lord.

And the Lord said unto Moses, Lo, I come unto thee in a thick cloud, that the people may hear when I speak with thee, and believe thee for ever. And Moses told the words of the people unto the Lord.

And the Lord said unto Moses, Go unto the people and sanctify them to day and to morrow, and let them wash their clothes,

And be ready against the third day: for the third day the Lord will come down in the sight of all the people upon Mount Sinai.

And thou shalt set bounds unto the people round about, saying, Take heed to yourselves that ye go not up into the mount, or touch the border of it: whosoever toucheth the mount shall be surely put to death:

There shall not an hand touch it, but he shall surely be stoned, or shot through; whether it be beast or man, it shall not live: when the trumpet soundeth long, they shall come up to the mount.

And Moses went down from the mount unto the people, and sanctified the people; and they washed their clothes.

And he said unto the people, Be ready against the third day: come not at your wives.

And it came to pass on the third day in the morning that there were thunders and lightnings, and a thick cloud upon the mount, and the voice of the trumpet exceeding loud; so that all the people that were in the camp trembled.

And Moses brought forth the people out of the camp to meet with God; and they stood at the nether part of the mount.

And Mount Sinai was altogether on a smoke, because the Lord descended upon it in fire: and the smoke thereof ascended as the smoke of a furnace, and the whole mount quaked greatly.

And when the voice of the trumpet sounded long, and waxed louder and louder, Moses spake, and God answered him by a voice.

And the Lord came down upon Mount Sinai, on the top of the mount: and the Lord called Moses up to the top of the mount; and Moses went up.

And the Lord said unto Moses, Go down, charge the people, lest they break through unto the Lord to gaze, and many of them perish.

And let the priests also, which come near to the Lord, sanctify themselves, lest the Lord break forth upon them.

And Moses said unto the Lord, the people cannot come up to Mount Sinai, for thou chargedst us, saying, Set bounds about the mount, and sanctify it.

And the Lord said unto him, Away, get thee down, and thou shalt come up, thou, and Aaron with thee: but let not the priests and the people break through to come up unto the Lord, lest he break forth upon them.

And Moses went down unto the people, and spake unto them.

And God spake all these words, saying,

I am the Lord thy God, which have brought thee out of the land of Egypt, out of the house of bondage.

Thou shalt have no other gods before me . . .

And all the people saw the thunderings, and the lightnings, and the noise of the trumpet, and the mountain smoking: and when the people saw it, they removed, and stood afar off.

And they said unto Moses, Speak thou with us, and we will hear: but let not God speak with us, lest we die.

And Moses said unto the people, Fear not: for God is come to prove you, and that his fear may be before your faces, that ye sin not.

And the people stood afar off, and Moses drew near unto the thick darkness where God was . . .

And Moses went up into the mount, and a cloud covered the mount.

And the glory of the Lord abode upon Mount Sinai, and the cloud covered it six days: and the seventh day he called unto Moses out of the midst of the cloud.

And the sight of the glory of the Lord was like devouring fire on the top of the mount in the eyes of the children of Israel.

And Moses went into the midst of the cloud, and gat him up into the mount: and Moses was in the mount forty days and forty nights.

Exodus, 19

In the Footsteps of Moses

As we walked we arrived at a certain place, where the mountains between which we were passing opened themselves out and formed a great valley, very flat and extremely beautiful; and beyond the valley appeared Sinai, the holy Mount of God. This spot where the mountains opened themselves out is united with the place where are the Graves of Lust [Numbers 11:34]. And when we came there those holy guides, who were with us, bade us, saying:

'It is a custom that prayer be offered by those who come hither, when first from this place the Mount of God is seen'. So then did we. Now, from thence to the Mount of God is perhaps four miles altogether through that valley which I have described as great.

For that valley is very great indeed, lying under the side of the Mount of God; it is perhaps – as far as we could judge from looking at it and as they told us – sixteen miles in length. In breadth they called it four miles. We had to cross this valley in order to arrive at the mount. This is that same great and flat valley in which the children of Israel waited during the days when holy Moses went up into the Mount of God, where he was for forty days and forty nights. This is the valley in which the calf was made; the spot is shown to this day, for a great stone stands fixed in the very place. This, then, is the valley at the head of which was the place where holy Moses was when he fed the flocks of his father-in-law, where God spake to him from the Burning Bush. Now, our route was first to ascend the Mount of God at the side from which we were approaching, because the ascent here was easier; and then to descend to the head of the valley where the Bush was, this being the easier way of descent from the Mount of God. And so it seemed good to us that having seen all things which we desired, descending from the Mount of God, we should come to where the Bush is, and thence retrace our way through the middle of the valley, throughout its length, with the men of God, who showed us each place in the valley mentioned in Scripture.

So then we did. Then, going from that place where we had offered up prayer as we came from Faran, our route was to cross through the middle of the head of the valley, and so wind round to the Mount of God. The mountain itself seems to be single, in the form of a ring; but when you enter the ring you see that there are several, the whole range being called the Mount of God. That special one at whose summit is the place where the majesty of God descended, as it is written, is in the centre of all. And although all which form the ring are so lofty as I think I never saw before, yet that central one on which the majesty of God descended is so much higher than the others, that when we had arrived at it, all those mountains which we had previously thought lofty were below us as if they were very little hills. And this is truly an admirable thing, and, as I think, not without the grace of God, that although that central one specially called Sinai, on which the majesty of God descended is so much higher than the others, yet it cannot be seen until you come to its very foot, though before you are actually on it. For after you have accomplished your purpose, and have descended, you see it from the other side, which you could not do before you are on it. This I learned from the report of the brethren before we arrived at the Mount of God, and after I had arrived there I perceived it to be so for myself.

It was late on the Sabbath when we came to the mountain, and arriving at a certain monastery, the kindly monks who lived there entertained us, showing us all kindliness; for there is a church there with a priest. There we stayed that night, and then early on the Lord's day we began to ascend the mountains one by one with the priest and the monks who lived there. These mountains are ascended with infinite labour, because you do not go up gradually by a spiral path (as we say, 'like a snail shell'), but you must go straight up as if up the face of a wall, and you must go straight down each mountain until you arrive at the foot of that central one which is strictly called Sinai. And so, Christ our God commanding us, we were encouraged by the prayers of the holy men who accompanied us; and although the labour was great – for I had to ascend on foot, because the ascent could not be made in a chair – yet I did not feel it. To that extent the labour was not felt, because I saw that the desire which I had was being fulfilled by the command of God. At the fourth hour we arrived at that peak of Sinai, the holy Mount of God, where the law was given; i.e. at that place where the majesty of God descended on the day when the mountain smoked. In that place there is now a church – not a large one, because the place itself, the summit of the mountain, is not large; but the church has in itself a large measure of grace.

When, therefore, by God's command, we had arrived at the summit, and come to the door of the church, the priest who was appointed to the church, coming out of his cell, met us, a blameless old man, a monk from early youth, and (as they say here) an *ascetic*; in short, a man quite worthy of the place. The other priests met us also, as well as all the monks who lived there by the mountain; that is, all of them who were not prevented by age or infirmity. But on the very summit of the central mountain no one lives permanently; nothing is there but the church and the cave where holy Moses was. Here the whole passage having been read from the book of Moses, and the oblation made in due order, we communicated; and as I was passing out of the church the priests gave us gifts of blessing from the place; that is, gifts of the fruits grown in the mountain. For although the holy mount of Sinai itself is all rocky, so that it has not a bush on it, yet down near the foot of the mountains – either the central one or those which form the ring – there is a little plot of ground; here the holy monks diligently plant shrubs and lay out orchards and fields; and hard by they place their own cells, so that they may get, as if from the soil of the mountain itself, some fruit which they may seem to have cultivated with their own hands. So, then, after we had communicated, and the holy men had given us these gifts of blessing, and we had come out of the door of the church, I began to ask them to show us the several localities. Thereupon the holy men deigned to show us each place. For they showed us the famous cave where holy Moses was when for the second time he went up to the Mount of God to receive the tables of the laws again after he had broken the first on account of the sin of the people; and the other places also which we desired to see or which they knew better they deigned to show us. But I would have you to know, ladies, venerable sisters, that from the place where we were standing – that is, in the enclosure of the church wall, on the summit of the central mountain – those mountains which we had at first ascended with difficulty were like little hills in comparison with that central one on which we were standing. And yet they were so enormous that I should think I had never seen higher, did not this central one overtop them by so much. Egypt and Palestine and the Red Sea and the Parthenian Sea, which leads to Alexandria, also the boundless territories of the Saracens, we saw below us, hard though it is to believe; all which holy things these holy men pointed out to us.

The Pilgrimage of Etheria

The Death of Moses

And Moses went up from the plains of Moab unto the mountain of Nebo, to the top of Pisgah, that is over against Jericho. And the Lord shewed him all the land of Gilead, unto Dan.

And all Naphtali, and the land of Ephraim, and Manasseh, and all the land of Judah, unto the utmost sea.

And the south and the plain of the valley of Jericho, the city of palm trees, unto Zoar.

And the Lord said unto him, This is the last which I sware unto Abraham, unto Isaac, and unto Jacob, saying, I will give it unto thy seed: I have caused thee to see it with mine eyes, but thou shalt not go over thither.

So Moses the servant of the Lord died there in the land of Moab, according to the word of the Lord.

Deuteronomy, 34

Moses the Mountaineer

For forty years Moses had not been alone. The care and burden of all the people, the weight of their woe, and guilt, and death, had been upon him continually. The multitude had been laid upon him as if he had conceived them; their tears had been his meat, night and day, until he had felt as if God had withdrawn his favour from him, and he had prayed that he might be slain, and not see his wretchedness. And now at last the command came 'Get thee up into this mountain'. The weary hands that had been so long stayed up against the enemies of Israel, might lean again upon the shepherd's staff, and fold themselves for the shepherd's prayer – for the shepherd's slumber. Not strange to his feet, though forty years unknown, the roughness of the bare mountain-path, as he climbed from ledge to ledge of Abarim; not strange to his aged eyes the scattered clusters of the mountain herbage, and the broken shadows of the cliffs, indented far across the silence of uninhabited ravine; scenes such as those among which, with none, as now, beside him but God, he had led his flocks so often; and which he had left, how painfully! taking upon him the appointed power, to make of the fenced city a wilderness and to fill the desert with songs of deliverance. It was not to embitter the last hours of his life that God restored to him, for a day, the beloved solitudes he had lost; and breathed the peace of the perpetual hills around him, and cast the world in which he had laboured and sinned far beneath his feet, in that mist of dying blue; – all sin, all wandering, soon to be forgotten for ever; the Dead Sea – a type of God's anger understood by him, of all men, most clearly, who had seen the earth open her mouth, and the sea his depth, to overwhelm the companies of those who contended with his Master – laid waveless beneath him; and beyond it, the far hills of Judah, and the soft plains and banks of Jordan, purple in the evening light as with the blood of redemption, and fading in their distant fulness into mysteries of promise and of love. There, with his unabated strength, his undimmed glance, lying down upon the utmost rocks, with angels waiting near to contend for the spoils of his spirit, he put off his earthly armour. We do deep reverence to his companion prophet, for whom the chariot of fire came down from heaven; but was his death less noble, whom his Lord Himself buried in the vales of Moab, keeping, in the secrets of the eternal counsels, the knowledge of a sepulchre, from which he was to be called, in the fulness of time, to talk with that Lord, upon Hermon, of the death that He should accomplish at Jerusalem?

John Ruskin, *Modern Painters*

CHAPTER 2

◆

The Mountains of Battle

Throughout history mountain terrain has played a part in determining the outcome of war. This chapter contains accounts of three of the most famous mountain battles: the battle of Thermopylae during the invasion of Greece by the Persian Emperor Xerxes in the fifth century BC; the transit of the Alps by the Carthaginian general Hannibal, invading Italy from Spain in 218 BC; and the eighth-century battle of Roncesvalles in which the Emperor Charlemagne's rearguard was cut off in a Pyrenean pass on the way home from battle against the Muslims of Spain. The death of the Emperor's nephew Roland in this last battle was the topic of one of the most famous Christian epics, the *Chanson de Roland*.

◆ ◆ ◆

The Battle of Thermopylae

King Xerxes, then, lay encamped in that part of Malis which belongs to Trachis, and the Greeks in the midst of the pass: the place where they were is called by most of the Greeks Thermopylae, but by the people of the country and their neighbours Pylae. In these places, then, they lay encamped, Xerxes being master of all that was north of Trachis, and the Greeks of all that lay southward towards this part of the mainland.

The Greeks that awaited the Persians in that place were these: Of the Spartans, three hundred men at arms; a thousand Tegeans and Mantineans, half from each place; from Orchomenus in Arcadia a hundred and twenty, and a thousand from the rest of Arcadia; besides these Arcadians, four hundred from Corinth, two hundred from Phlius, and eighty Myceneans. These were they who had come from Peloponnesus: from Boeotia, seven hundred Thespians and four hundred Thebans.

Besides these the whole power of the Opuntian Locrians and a thousand Phocians had been summoned and came. The Greeks had of their own motion summoned these to their aid, telling them by their messengers that they themselves had come for an advance guard of the rest, that the coming of the remnant of the allies was to be looked for every day, and that the sea was strictly watched by them, being guarded by the Athenians and Aeginetans and all that were enrolled in the fleet; there was nought (they said) for them to fear; for the invader of Hellas was no god, but a mortal man, and there was no mortal, nor ever would be, to whom at birth some admixture of misfortune was not allotted; the greater the man, the greater the misfortune; most surely then he that marched against them, being but mortal, would be disappointed of his hope. Hearing that, the Locrians and Phocians marched to aid the Greeks at Trachis.

All these had their generals, each city its own; but he that was most regarded and was leader of the army was Leonidas of Lacedaemon, who was king at Sparta . . . He now came to Thermopylae, with a picked force of the customary three hundred, and those that had sons; and he brought with him too those Thebans whom I counted among the number, whose general was Leontiades son of Eurymachus . . .

These, the men with Leonidas, were sent before the rest by the Spartans, that by the sight of them the rest of the allies might be moved to arm, and not like others take the Persian part, as might well be if they learnt the Spartans were delaying; and they purposed that later, when they should have kept the feast of the Carnea, which was their present hindrance, they would leave a garrison at Sparta and march out with the whole of their force and with all speed. The rest of the allies had planned to do the same likewise; for an Olympic festival fell due at the same time as these doings; wherefore they sent their advance guard, not supposing that the war at Thermopylae would so speedily come to an issue.

Such had been their intent, but the Greeks at Thermopylae, when the Persian drew near to the entrance of the pass, began to lose heart and debate whether to quit their post or no. The rest of the Peloponnesians were for returning to the Peloponnese and guarding the isthmus; but the Phocians and Locrians were greatly incensed by this counsel, and Leonidas gave his vote for remaining where they were, and sending messages to the cities to demand aid, seeing that he and his were too few to beat off the Median host.

While they thus debated, Xerxes sent a mounted watcher to see how many they were and what they had in hand; for while he was yet in Thessaly, he had heard that some small army was here gathered, and that its leaders were Lacedaemonians, Leonidas a descendant of Heracles among them. The horseman rode up to the camp and viewed and overlooked it, yet not the whole; for it was not possible to see those that were posted within the wall which they had restored and now guarded; but he took note of those that were without, whose arms were piled outside the wall, and it chanced that at that time the Lacedaemonians were posted there. There he saw some of the men at exercise, and others combing their hair. Marvelling at the sight, and taking exact note of their numbers, he rode back unmolested, none pursuing nor at all regarding him; so he returned and told Xerxes all that he had seen.

When Xerxes heard that, he could not understand the truth, namely, that the Lacedaemonians were preparing to slay to the best of their power or to be slain; what they did appeared to him laughable; wherefore he sent for Demaratus the son of Ariston, who was in his camp, and when he came questioned him of all these matters, that he might understand what it was that the Lacedaemonians were about. 'I have told you already,' said Demaratus, 'of these men, when we were setting out for Hellas; but when you heard, you mocked me, albeit I told you of this which I saw plainly would be the outcome; for it is my greatest endeavour, O king, to speak truth in your presence. Now hear me once more: these men are come to fight with us for the passage and for that they are preparing; for it is their custom to dress their hair whensoever they are about to put their lives in jeopardy. Moreover, I tell you, that if you overcome these and what remains behind at Sparta, there is no other nation among men, O king! that will abide and withstand you; now you are face to face with the noblest royalty and city and the most valiant men in Hellas.' Xerxes deemed what was said to be wholly incredible, and further enquired of him how they would fight against his army, being so few. 'O king, use me as a liar, if the event of this be not what I tell you.'

Yet for all that Xerxes would not believe him. For the space of four days the king waited, ever expecting that the Greeks would take to flight; but on the fifth, seeing them not withdrawing and deeming that their remaining there was but shamelessness and folly, he was angered, and sent the Medes and Cissians against them, bidding them take the Greeks alive and bring them into his presence. The Medes bore down upon the Greeks and charged them; many fell, but others attacked in turn; and though they suffered grievous defeat yet they were not driven off. But they made it plain to all and chiefly to the king himself that for all their number of human creatures there were few men among them. This battle lasted all the day.

The Medes being so roughly handled, they were then withdrawn from the fight, and the Persians whom the king called Immortals attacked in their turn, led by Hydarnes. It was thought that they at least would make short and easy work of the Greeks; but when they joined battle they fared neither better nor worse than the Median soldiery, fighting as they were in a narrow space and with shorter spears than the Greeks, where they could make no use of their numbers. But the Lacedaemonians fought memorably. They were skilled warriors against unskilled; and it was among their many feats of arms that they would turn their backs and feign flight; seeing which, the foreigners would pursue after them with shouting and noise; but when the Lacedaemonians were like to be overtaken they turned upon the foreigners, and so rallying overthrew Persians innumerable; wherein some few of the Spartans themselves were slain. So when the Persians, attacking by companies and in every other fashion, could yet gain no inch of the approach, they drew off out of the fight.

During these onsets the king (it is said) thrice sprang up in fear for his army from the throne where he sat to view them. Such was then the fortune of the fight, and on the next day the foreigners had no better luck at the game. They joined battle, supposing that their enemies, being so few, were now disabled by wounds and could no longer withstand them. But the Greeks stood arrayed by battalions and nations, and each of these fought in its turn, save the Phocians, who were posted on the mountains to guard the path. So when the Persians found the Greeks in no way different from what the day before had shown them to be, they drew off from the fight.

The king being at a loss how to deal with the present difficulty, Epialtes son of Eurydemus, a Malian, came to speak with him, thinking so to receive a great reward from Xerxes, and told him of the path leading over the mountain to Thermopylae; whereby he was the undoing of the Greeks who had been left there . . . Xerxes was satisfied with what Epialtes promised to accomplish; much rejoicing thereat, he sent Hydarnes forthwith and Hydarnes' following; and they set forth from the camp about the hour when lamps are lit. Now this path had been discovered by the Malians of the country, who guided the Thessalians thereby into Phocis, at the time when the Phocians sheltered themselves from attack by fencing the pass with a wall; thus early had the Malians shown that the pass could avail nothing.

Now the path runs thuswise. It begins at the river Asopus which flows through the ravine; the mountain there and the path have the same name, Anopaea; this Anopaea crosses the ridge of the mountain and ends at the town of Alpenus, the Locrian town nearest to Malis, where is the rock called Black-buttock and the seats of the Cercopes; and this is its narrowest part.

Of such nature is the path; by this, when they had crossed the Asopus, the Persians marched all night, the Oetean mountains being on their right hand and the Trachinian on their left. At dawn of day they came to the summit of the pass. Now in this part of the mountain-way a thousand Phocians were posted, as I have already shown, to defend their own country and to guard the path; for the lower pass was held by those of whom I have spoken, but the path over the mountains by the Phocians, according to the promise that they had of their own motion given to Leonidas.

Now the mountain-side where the Persians ascended was all covered by oak woods, and the Phocians knew nothing of their coming till they were warned of it, in the still weather, by the much noise of the enemy's tread on the leaves that lay strewn underfoot; whereupon they sprang up and began to arm, and in a moment the foreigners were upon them. These were amazed at the sight of men putting on armour; for they had supposed that no one would withstand them, and now they fell in with an army. Hydarnes feared that the Phocians might be Lacedaemonians, and asked Epialtes of what country they were; being informed of the truth, he arrayed the Persians for battle; and the Phocians, assailed by showers of arrows, and supposing that it was they whom the Persians had meant from the first to attack, fled away up to the top of the mountain and prepared there to perish. Such was their thought; but the Persians with Epialtes and Hydarnes paid no regard to the Phocians, but descended from the mountain with all speed.

The Greeks at Thermopylae were warned first by Megistias the seer; who, having examined the offerings, advised them of the death that awaited them in the morning; and presently came deserters, while it was yet night, with news of the circuit made by the Persians; which was lastly brought also by the watchers running down from the heights when day was now dawning. Thereupon the Greeks held a council, and their opinions were divided, some advising that they should not leave their post and some being contrariwise minded; and presently they parted asunder, these taking their departure and dispersing each to their own cities, and those resolving to remain where they were with Leonidas.

It is said indeed that Leonidas himself sent them away, desiring in his care for them to save their lives, but deeming it unseemly for himself and the Spartans to desert that post which they had first come to defend. But to this opinion I the rather incline, that when Leonidas perceived the allies to be faint of heart and not willing to run all risks with him he bade them go their ways, departure being for himself not honourable; if he remained, he would leave a name of great renown, and the prosperity of Sparta would not be blotted out . . .

Xerxes, having at sunrise offered libations, waited till about the hour of marketing and then made his assault, having been so advised by Epialtes; for the descent from the mountain is more direct and the way is much shorter than the circuit and the ascent. So the foreigners that were with Xerxes attacked; but the Greeks with Leonidas, knowing that they went to their death, advanced now much farther than before into the wider part of the strait. For ere now it was the wall of defence that they had guarded, and all the former days they had withdrawn themselves into the narrow way and fought there; but now they met their enemies outside the narrows, and many of the foreigners were there slain; for their captains came behind the companies with scourges and drove all the men forward with lashes. Many of them were thrust into the sea and there drowned, and more by far were trodden down bodily by each other, none regarding who it was that perished; for inasmuch as the Greeks knew that they must die by the hands of those who came round the mountain, they put forth the very utmost of their strength against the foreigners, in their recklessness and frenzy.

By this time the spears of the most of them were broken, and they were slaying the Persians with their swords. There in that travail fell Leonidas, fighting most gallantly, and with him other famous Spartans, whose names I have learnt for their great worth and desert, and I have learnt besides the names of all the three hundred . . . Two brothers of Xerxes fell there in the battle; and there was a great struggle between the Persians and the Lacedaemonians over Leonidas' body, till the Greeks of their valour dragged it away and four times put their enemies to flight. Nor was there an end of this mellay till the men with Epialtes came up. When the Greeks were aware of their coming, from that moment the face of the battle was changed; for they withdrew themselves back to the narrow part of the way, and passing within the wall they took post, all save the Thebans, upon the hillock that is in the mouth of the pass, where now stands the stone lion in honour of Leonidas. In that place they defended themselves with their swords, as many as yet had such, ay and with fists and teeth; till the foreigners overwhelmed them with missile weapons, some attacking them in front and throwing down a wall of defence, and others standing round them in a ring . . .

All these, and they that died before any had departed at Leonidas' bidding, were buried where they fell, and there is an inscription over them, which is this:

> Four thousand warriors, flower of Pelops' land
> Did here against three hundred myriads stand

This is the inscription common to all; the Spartans have one to themselves:

> Go tell the Spartans, thou that passest by
> That here obedient to their words we lie.

Herodotus, Histories, VII

Hannibal Crosses the Alps

Hannibal, leaving the Druentia, and advancing for the most part through a champaign country, reached the Alps without being molested by the Gauls who inhabited those regions. Then, though report, which is wont to exaggerate uncertain dangers, had already taught them what to expect, still the near view of the lofty mountains, with their snows almost merging in the sky; the shapeless hovels perched on crags; the frost-bitten flocks and beasts of burden; the shaggy, unkempt men; animals and inanimate objects alike stiff with cold, and all more dreadful to look upon than words can tell, renewed their consternation. As their column began to mount the first slopes, mountaineers were discovered posted on the heights above, who, had they lain concealed in hidden valleys, might have sprung out suddenly and attacked them with great rout and slaughter. Hannibal gave the command to halt, and sent forward some Gauls to reconnoitre. When informed by them that there was no getting by that way, he encamped in the most extensive valley to be found in a wilderness of rocks and precipices.

He then employed these same Gauls, whose speech and customs did not differ greatly from those of the mountaineers, to mingle in their councils, and in this way learned that his enemies guarded the pass only by day, and at night dispersed, every man to his own home. As soon as it was light, he advanced up the hills, as though he hoped to rush the defile by an open attack in the daytime. Then having spent the day in feigning a purpose other than his real one, he entrenched a camp on the spot where he had halted. But no sooner did he perceive that the mountaineers had dispersed from the heights and relaxed their vigilance, than, leaving for show more fires than the numbers of those who remained in camp demanded; leaving, too, the baggage and the cavalry and a great part of the infantry, he put himself at the head of some light-armed soldiers – all his bravest men – and, marching swiftly to the head of the defile, occupied those very heights which the enemy had held.

With the ensuing dawn the Carthaginians broke camp and the remainder of their army began to move. The natives, on a signal being given, were already coming in from their fastnesses to occupy their customary post, when they suddenly perceived that some of their enemies were in possession of the heights and threatened them from above, and that others were marching through the pass. Both facts presenting themselves at the same time to their eyes and minds kept them for a moment rooted to the spot. Then, when they saw the helter-skelter in the pass and the column becoming embarrassed by its own confusion, the horses especially being frightened and unmanageable, they thought that whatever they could add themselves to the consternation of the troops would be sufficient to destroy them, and rushed down from the cliffs on either side, over trails and trackless ground alike, with all the ease of habit.

Then indeed the Phoenicians had to contend at one and the same time against their foes and the difficulties of the ground, and the struggle amongst themselves, as each endeavoured to outstrip the rest in escaping from the danger, which was greater than the struggle with the enemy. The horses occasioned the greatest peril to the column. Terrified by the discordant yells, which the woods and ravine redoubled with their echoes, they quaked with fear; and if they happened to be hit or wounded, were so maddened that they made enormous havoc not only of men, but of every sort of baggage. Indeed the crowding in the pass, which was steep and precipitous on both sides, caused many – some of them armed men – to be flung down to a great depth; but when beasts of burden with their packs went hurtling down, it was just like the crash of falling walls.

Dreadful as these sights were, still Hannibal halted for a little while and held back his men, so as not to augment the terror and confusion. Then, when he saw that the column was being broken in two, and there was danger lest he might have got his army over to no avail, if it were stripped of its baggage, he charged down from the higher ground, and routed the enemy by the very impetus of the attack, though he added to the disorder among his own troops. But the flurry thus occasioned quickly subsided, as soon as the roads were cleared by the flight of the mountaineers; and the whole army was presently brought over the pass, not only without molestation but almost in silence. Hannibal then seized a stronghold which was the chief place in that region, together with the outlying hamlets, and with the captured food and flocks supported his troops for three days. And in those three days, being hindered neither by the natives, who had been utterly cowed at the outset, nor very greatly by the nature of the country, he covered a good deal of ground . . .

The elephants could be induced to move but very slowly along the steep and narrow trails; but wherever they went they made the column safe from its enemies, who were unaccustomed to the beasts and afraid of venturing too near them.

On the ninth day they arrived at the summit of the Alps, having come for the most part over trackless wastes and by roundabout routes, owing either to the dishonesty of their guides, or – when they would not trust the guides – to their blindly entering some valley, guessing at the way. For two days they lay encamped on the summit. The soldiers, worn with toil and fighting, were permitted to rest; and a number of baggage animals which had fallen among the rocks made their way to the camp by following the tracks of the army. Exhausted and discouraged as the soldiers were by many hardships, a snow-storm – for the constellation of the Pleiades was now setting – threw them into a great fear. The ground was everywhere covered deep with snow when at dawn they began to march, and as the column moved slowly on, dejection and despair were to be read in every countenance. Then Hannibal, who had gone on before the standards, made the army halt on a certain promontory which commanded an extensive prospect, and pointing out Italy to them, and just under the Alps the plains about the Po, he told them that they were now scaling the ramparts not only of Italy, but of Rome itself; the rest of the way would be level or downhill; and after one, or, at the most, two battles, they would have in their hands and in their power the citadel and capital of Italy.

The column now began to make some progress, and even the enemy had ceased to annoy them, except to make a stealthy raid, as occasion offered. But the way was much more difficult than the ascent had been, as indeed the slope of the Alps on the Italian side is in general more precipitous in proportion as it is shorter. For practically every road was steep, narrow, and treacherous, so that neither could they keep from slipping, nor could those who had been thrown a little off their balance retain their footing, but came down, one on top of the other, and the beasts on top of the men.

Then they came to a much narrower cliff, and with rocks so perpendicular that it was difficult for an unencumbered soldier to manage the descent, though he felt his way and clung with his hands to the bushes and roots that projected here and there. The place had been precipitous before, and a recent landslip had carried it away to the depth of a good thousand feet. There the cavalry came to a halt, as though they had reached the end of the road, and as Hannibal was wondering what it could be that held the column back, word was brought to him that the cliff was impassable. Going then to inspect the place himself, he thought that there was nothing for it but to lead the army round, over trackless and untrodden steeps, however circuitous the detour might be. But that way proved to be insuperable; for above the old untouched snow lay a fresh deposit of moderate depth, through which, as it was soft and not very deep, the men in front found it easy to advance; but when it had been trampled down by the feet of so many men and beasts, the rest had to make their way over the bare ice beneath and the slush of the melting snow. Then came a terrible struggle on the slippery surface, for it afforded them no foothold, while the downward slope made their feet the more quickly slide from under them; so that whether they tried to pull themselves up with their hands, or used their knees, these supports themselves would slip, and down they would come again! Neither were there any stems or roots about, by which a man could pull himself up with foot or hand – only smooth ice and thawing snow, on which they were continually rolling. But the baggage animals, as they went over the snow, would sometimes even cut into the lowest crust, and pitching forward and striking out with their hoofs, as they struggled to rise, would break clean through it, so that numbers of them were caught fast, as if entrapped, in the hard, deep-frozen snow.

At last, when men and beasts had been worn out to no avail, they encamped upon the ridge, after having, with the utmost difficulty, cleared enough ground even for this purpose, so much snow were they obliged to dig out and remove. The soldiers were then set to work to construct a road across the cliff – the only possible way. Since they had to cut through the rock, they felled some huge trees that grew near at hand, and lopping off their branches, made an enormous pile of logs. This they set on fire, as soon as the wind blew fresh enough to make it burn, and pouring vinegar over the glowing rocks, caused them to crumble. After thus heating the crag with fire, they opened a way in it with iron tools, and relieved the steepness of the slope with zigzags of an easy gradient, so that not only the baggage animals but even the elephants could be led down. Four days were consumed at the cliff, and the animals nearly perished of starvation; for the mountain tops are all practically bare, and such grass as does grow is buried under snow. Lower down one comes to valleys and sunny slopes and rivulets, and near them woods, and places that begin to be fitter for man's habitation. There the beasts were turned out to graze, and the men, exhausted with toiling at the road, were allowed to rest. Thence they descended in three days' time into the plain, through a region now that was less forbidding, as was the character of its inhabitants.

Such were the chief features of the march to Italy, which they accomplished five months after leaving New Carthage – as certain authorities state – having crossed the Alps in fifteen days.

Livy, *Histories XXI*

The Massacre at Roncesvalles, 15 August AD 778

The Army had come three days over the ridges of the little hills, each higher than the last, following the great Roman road that led westward to Pampeluna. All the main body had passed long before from its repulse on the Ebro, and this, the rear-guard, was perhaps three miles in length, not more; it was heavily impeded with waggons; some few of the richer men that had fallen sick were carried in litters, and though the way was still hard and good, centuries of usage had weakened it, especially at the base of each ascent, and there were places where it failed altogether, sunk into a marsh or crossing an *arroyo* where the spring freshets of three hundred years had broken the bridge and swept away the talus.

At such places there was always an infinity of trouble – carts held back by hand, horses straining to prevent the rush of the weight behind them, confused noises and arguments and blows. So they went slowly on. They were heavily laden with the spoils of cities, with the loot of the enemies of the Faith, and with that heavy armament which was so ill suited to the South. For very many were covered to the knees with strong leather coats on which great rings of metal interlaced made a complete web, and others had scales of iron overlapping as the scales of a fish overlap. And all the mounted men carried, slung to their saddles beside incongruous bundles of booty, their little steel caps and their great battle-axes, and some of the highest rank were further encumbered with a mighty elephant's tusk curiously carved, which they could wind like a horn to summon their followers.

It was perhaps midday when they came upon a vast open plain sloping gently towards the sun, and here the road they had been following came in at right-angles upon another and a larger road; the main road from Burgos and the south. This was the road that went straight across the Imus Pyrenaeus, the pass into Gaul; it was the road which, with its brother road the Summus Pyrenaeus, four marches to the east, formed the sole gates of the Pyrenees. They halted for the midday meal, but they did not halt for long. It was their business to press forward out of this hard Iberian land. The light cavalry of the Emirs hung all round, white flashes of riding men well out of bow-shot on their little desert horses, with there and there the blazing red cloak of a Sheik or the shining of a steel linked coat among them. The leaders of the Christians knew that by one accident and another since they had ridden out of the gate of Pampeluna the rate of marching had been hindered, and that the main body was now far ahead, over on the French side of the pass. The gap between this rearguard and the bulk of the Emperor's forces was too wide for safety, and, though they had marched under such a sun for so long, they were ordered, in spite of grumbling and some short mutinies, to press straight on.

The plain through which they hurried northward sloped, as I say, slightly to the sun. It was like a glacis, the rampart of which was the interminable line of precipitous white cliffs which marked the crest of the Pyrenees. These cliffs were of limestone; the sun shone on them full, and above them the sky was intensely blue. For miles and miles away to the right they stretched interminably until they were lost in the perspective as one loses a wall of great length standing straight along a level. Just before the army in the few miles between it and the range, a noble great wood of beech and of oaks spread as though it had been poured out in a flood over the sloping landscape. Above these trees again a little grassy col made a notch upon the skyline a little lower than the white mountain cliffs on either side. This col was Roncesvalles; and across the green of it could most clearly be seen climbing up under the sunlight the ribbon of the road.

The villages through which they passed were deserted (for the Basques were almost as much their enemies as the Mohammedans were); they had for food and drink nothing but what they carried; they were exhausted when the last ascent began. It was very soon surmounted; it was but a few hundred feet of easy meadow and the climb was the easier because the troops could here deploy, the column was shortened, and the dust which added so much to their weariness was laid. It was cooler for the height, and the sun, now in full afternoon, was mellower and less dangerous. A chapel which the Basques would use stood on the height before them, and when they reached the easy open saddle, the leaders saw one of those sights whose sudden vision stimulates the legends of history and is part of the glorious adventures attached to the records of armies.

Here was a prodigious cleft running dead north, thousands of feet sunk sheer into the earth, and slowly widening its sides to where, far away at the opening of it in the misty distance, in the V-shaped mouth of the hills, like a calm sea in misty winter, lay the Gascon plains. They were out of the hard Iberian land, they were in sight of home; thick forests clothed the sides of the ravine and the pleasant sound of water in its depths greeted their return to Gaul; the keener-eyed among them descried, or imagined that they descried, upon the very distant landscape, the winding line of the main army that followed Charlemagne. It was but a few miles on to the Castle of St John, the first fortified and secure stronghold of Christendom, which would receive them after the adventure of the raid into the lost land and the dominion of Mahound.

Roland of the Marches, who had with him two companions and a little squad of servants, had ridden rapidly before the rest, partly to grasp in one view the nature of the road upon the downward side, partly – for he was of an affectionate and dreaming kind – to see, the first of all the army he commanded, the fields of kinsmen again and Christian land. They saw him upon his heavy horse against the sky as they climbed the pass behind him. He watched the valley in silence.

In that profound ravine there was no noise at all except the running of the torrent in the forest below. The walls were very steep, so steep that in places the beech-trees had lost their hold and had fallen down the precipitous earth; and perilously along the front of that slope went the road. Roland could see it clearly, first almost horizontal, feeling its way along the safest contour of the precipice; here and there still supported by the huge masonry work of Rome, then plunging steeply in zig-zags to the foot of the gulf, where it was lost beneath the trees. There, on the floor of the defile, perhaps three miles of marching below him, it passed through a narrow place, where steep rocks held it in on either side. No men showed upon the mountains; there was no movement at all. For a moment the commander wondered whether a flanking party ought not to be sent along the ridge to secure the main body from any attempt; in another moment he had seen that the plan would fail. As the valley deepened all communication between the ridge and the road became more difficult until, in but a few hundred yards, it became impracticable altogether, even for a handful of unarmed men. He was determined to risk the road.

He wheeled his horse round upon that little eminence, he and his companions, and stayed there stock still while the long train of men and horses and wheels and the huge *ballistae* and the beasts of burden filed wearily by. He watched in silence without commands of haste or fear, but with an increasing anxiety, the declining of the sun over the plains of Navarre, as the force defiled; then he came on behind them, from which post he could best observe on the falling mountain road the whole of his command.

He had not so ridden a mile when those lonely hills began to have an uneasy and a dreadful life; it was all but evening, yet one could still clearly distinguish the boulders and the bushes upon the higher sweeps of grass and rock, and it seemed that first one bush and then another moved; but there was no glint of steel, there were no cries, there was no sign of that white signal of danger which a scout may catch at almost any range – the face of a man. Nevertheless as the darkness gathered it was certain and more certain that the deep shadows were peopled, and that the forest itself into which the head of the column had now plunged was alive.

It was not yet quite night when suddenly a great boulder leapt from the limestone ridge far, far above the road, bounded down step upon step of the ravine wall, and as it thundered revealed, tiny in the distance of the upper air, a group of wild men whose cries were now answered immediately on every side. The underwood awoke; fierce rushes from above and below broke the line at one point and another and another. The Chivalry in the rear, galloping and pressing through their own men, could do nothing to rescue, and behind them also the clansmen poured in. As the first stars came out above the gorge, a steady carnage had begun . . .

Long before the dawn the inhuman noise of that forest ebbed into silence and was done. The Basques slept by fires undisturbed, and every man of the great Gaulish host, their enemy, was dead. Then for days and days the gold and the steel, the weapons and the horses, the worked timber, and the ivory and the lovely gems – all the arts of Christendom – laboriously found way up tiny mountain paths into the secret places of the Pyrenees.

Hilaire Belloc, *The Eye-Witness*

CHAPTER 3

◆

Saints of the Mountains

Any reader of Gibbon knows that from the earliest ages of the Church many Christians sought holiness by fleeing from the cities into the desert. What is not always realized is that during the centuries of faith 'the desert' was as likely to mean a mountain fastness as a cave amid sand-dunes. St Basil was one of the earliest saints to withdraw (temporarily) to the mountains, and writing to a friend he described his mountain retreat in enthusiastic tones. The great St Benedict began his career as a mountain hermit, and St Bruno founded the Grande Chartreuse which has ever since been a place of mountain pilgrimage. The climax of the life of St Francis of Assisi, the imprinting of the stigmata of Christ's passion, took place while he was in a hermitage on the mount of La Verna, to which he withdrew in 1213.

◆ ◆ ◆

St Basil's Description of his Retreat

It is a lofty mountain overshadowed with a deep wood, irrigated on the north by cold and transparent streams. At its foot is spread a low plain, enriched perpetually with the streams from the mountains. The wood, a virgin forest of trees of various kinds and foliage which grows around it, almost serves as a rampart; so that even the Isle of Calypso, which Homer evidently admired as a paragon of loveliness, is nothing in comparison with this . . . My hut is built on another point, which uplifts a lofty pinnacle on the summit, so that the plain is outspread before the gaze, and from the height I can catch a glimpse of the river flowing around, which to my fancy affords no less delight than the view of the Strymone as you look from Amphipolis . . . The Iris, on the other hand, flowing with a swifter course than any river I know, for a short space billows along the adjacent rock, and then, plunging over it, rolls into a deep whirlpool, affording a most delightful view to me and to every spectator, and abundantly supplying the needs of the inhabitants, for it nurtures an incredible number of fishes in its eddies. Why need I tell you the sweet exhalations from the earth or the breezes of the river? Other persons might admire the multitude of the flowers, or the lyric birds, but I have no time to attend to them. But my highest eulogy of the spot is, that, prolific as it is of all kinds of fruits from its happy situation, it bears for me the sweetest of all fruits, tranquillity.

St Basil, Letter to St Gregory Nazianzen

Saint Benedict at Subiaco

Saint Benedict or Bennet was a native of Norcia, formerly an episcopal see in Umbria, and was descended from a family of note, and born about the year 480 . . . When he was fit for higher studies, he was sent by his parents to Rome, and there placed in the public schools. He, who till that time, knew not what vice was, and trembled at the shadow of sin, was not a little shocked at the licentiousness which he observed in the conduct of some of the Roman youth with whom he was obliged to converse; and he was no sooner come into the world but he resolved to bid an eternal farewell to it, not to be entangled in its snares. He therefore left the city privately, and made the best of his way towards the deserts. His nurse, Cyrilla, who loved him tenderly, followed him thirty miles from Rome, where he found means to get rid of her, and pursued his journey alone to the desert mountains of Subiaco, near forty miles from Rome. It is a barren, hideous chain of rocks, with a river and lake in the valley. Near this place the Saint met a monk of a neighbouring monastery, called Romanus, who gave him the monastic habit, with suitable instructions, and conducted him to a deep narrow cave in the midst of these mountains, almost inaccessible to men. In this cavern, now called the Holy Grotto, the young hermit kept his abode; and Romanus, who kept his secret, brought him hither, from time to time, bread and the like slender provisions, which he retrenched from his own meals, and let them down to the holy recluse with a line, hanging a bell to the cord to give him notice . . .

In 497, a certain pious priest in that country, whilst he was preparing a dinner for himself on Easter Sunday, heard a voice which said 'You are preparing for yourself a banquet, while my servant Bennet, at Subiaco, is distressed with hunger.' The priest immediately set out in quest of the hermit, and with much difficulty found him out . . . The Priest invited the saint to eat, saying it was Easter Day, on which it is not reasonable to fast; though St Bennet answered him, that he knew not it was the day of so great a solemnity . . .

After their repast, the priest returned home. Soon after, certain shepherds discovered the Saint near his cave, but at first took him for a wild beast; for he was clad with the skins of beasts, and they imagined no human creature could live among those rocks. When they found him to be a servant of

God, they respected him exceedingly, and many of them were moved by his heavenly discourse to embrace with fervour a course of contemplation . . .

Butler's *Lives of the Saints*

The Foundation of the Grande Chartreuse

St Bruno and six companions arrived at Grenoble about mid-summer 1084, and cast themselves at the feet of [the bishop] St Hugh, begging of him some place in his diocese where they might serve God, remote from worldly affairs, and without being burdensome to men. The holy prelate, understanding their errand, rejoiced exceedingly, and received them with open arms, not doubting but these seven strangers were represented to him in a vision he had the night before in his sleep; wherein he thought he saw God himself building a church in the desert of his diocese, called the Chartreuse, and seven stars rising from the ground, and forming a circle, which went before him to that place, as it were, to show him the way to the church. He embraced them very lovingly, thinking he could never sufficiently commend their generous resolution; and assigned them that desert of Chartreuse for their retreat, promising his utmost assistance to establish them there; but to the end they might be armed against the difficulties they would meet with, lest they should enter upon so great an undertaking without having well considered it; he, at the same time, represented to them the dismal situation of that solitude, beset with very high craggy rocks, almost all the year covered with snow and thick fogs, which rendered them not habitable. St Hugh having kept them some days in his palace, conducted them to this place, and made over to them all the right he had in that forest; and, some time after, Siguin, Abbot of Chaise-Dieu, in Auvergne, who was joint lord of the same. Bruno and his companions immediately built an oratory there, and very small cells, at a little distance one from the other, like the ancient Lauras of Palestine. Such was the original of the order of the Carthusians, which took its name from this desert of Chartreuse . . .

St Bruno retired to this wilderness in June 1084, as one of his epitaphs and Sigebert of Gembloux, a contemporary writer, expressly mention. St Hugh by a charter dated in the month following forbade any woman to go into their lands, or any person to fish, hunt, or drive cattle that way. They first built a church on a summit, and cells near it, in which they lived two together in each cell, soon after single, meeting in church at matins and vespers; other hours, prime, tierce, sext, none and compline they recited in their cells. They never took two refections in a day, except on the greatest festivals, on which they were together in a refectory. On other days they were in their cells as hermits. Pulse was given to them in a certain measure on days when it was allowed them.

It is hard to represent the wonderful life of these holy anchorites in their desert. Peter the Venerable, abbot of Cluny fifty years after St Bruno, writes of them: 'Their dress is meaner and poorer than that of other monks; so short and scanty, and so rough, that the very sight affrights one. They wear coarse hair shirts next their skin, fast almost perpetually; eat only bran bread; never touch flesh, either sick or well; never buy fish, but eat it if given them as an alms; eat eggs and cheese on Sundays and Thursdays; on Tuesdays and Saturdays their fare is pulse or herbs boiled; on Mondays, Wednesdays and Fridays they take nothing but bread and water; and they have only one meal a day, except within the octaves of Christmas, Easter, Whitsuntide, Epiphany and some other festivals. Their constant occupation is praying, reading, and manual labour, which consists chiefly in transcribing books.'

Butler's *Lives of the Saints*

Saint Francis on La Verna

Saint Francis, being forty and three years of age, in the year 1224, being inspired of God, set out from the Vale of Spoleto for to go into Romagna with Brother Leo his companion; and as they went, they passed by the foot of the Castle of Montefeltro; in the which Castle there was at that time a great company of gentle folk, and much feasting, by reason of the knighting of one of the same Counts of Montefeltro. And Saint Francis, hearing of the festivities that were holden there, and how that many gentle folk of divers countries were there gathered together, spake unto Brother Leo: 'Let us go up unto this feast, for with the help of God we may win some good fruit of souls.' Among the other gentle folk from that country, that were of that knightly company, was a great and wealthy gentleman of Tuscany, by name Orlando da Chiusi, of Casentino; who by reason of the marvellous things that he had heard of the sanctity and the miracles of Saint Francis, bore him great devotion, and felt an exceeding strong desire to see him and to hear him preach. Coming to the castle, Saint Francis entered in, and came to the courtyard where all that great company of gentle folk was gathered together, and in fervour of spirit stood up upon a parapet, and began to preach . . .

Orlando, touched in the heart by God through the marvellous preaching of Saint Francis, set it in his heart to confer and to have speech with Saint Francis, after the sermon, touching the state of his soul. Therefore, when the preaching was done, he drew Saint Francis aside, and said unto him: 'Oh father, I would confer with thee touching the salvation of my soul.' Replied Saint Francis: 'It pleaseth me right well; but go this morning and do honour to thy friends, who have called thee to the feast, and dine with them; and after thou hast dined, we will speak together as much as thou wilt.' So Orlando gat him to the dinner: and after that he had dined, he returned to Saint Francis, and conferred with him, and set forth unto him fully the state of his soul.

And at the end of this, Orlando said to Saint Francis: 'I have in Tuscany a mountain, most proper for devotion, the which is called the Mount of Alvernia, and is very lonely and right well fitted for whoso may wish to do penance in a place remote from men, or whoso may desire to live a solitary life; if it should please thee, right willingly would I give it to thee and thy companions for the salvation of my soul.' Saint Francis hearing this liberal offer of the thing that he so much desired, rejoiced with exceeding great joy; and praising and giving thanks first to God, and then to Orlando, he spake thus: 'Orlando, when you have returned to your house, I will send unto you certain of my companions and you shall show them that mountain; and if it shall seem to them well fitted for prayer and penitence, I accept your loving offer even now.' And this said, Saint Francis departed: and when his journey was done, returned to Saint Mary of the Angels: and likewise Orlando, when the festivities of that knightly company were over, returned to his castle, which was called, Chiusi, the which was but a mile distant from Alvernia.

Whenas Saint Francis had returned to Saint Mary of the Angels, he sent two of his companions to the said Orlando; who, when they were come to him, were received of him with exceeding great joy and charity. And desiring to show them the Mount of Alvernia, he sent with them full fifty men-at-arms to defend them from the wild beasts of the wood, and thus accompanied these brothers climbed up the mountain and searched diligently; and at last they came to a part of the mountain that was well fitted for devotion and contemplation; for in that part there was some level ground; and this place they chose out for them and for Saint Francis to dwell therein; and with the help of the men-at-arms that bore them company, they made a little cell of branches of trees: and so they accepted in the name of God, and took possession of the Mount of Alvernia and of the dwelling-place of the brothers on the mountain, and departed, and returned to Saint Francis.

And when they were come unto him they told him how and in what manner they had taken a place on the Mount of Alvernia, most fitted for prayer and meditation. Hearing these tidings, Saint Francis was right glad, and praising and giving thanks to God he spake to those brothers with joyful countenance, and said: 'My son, our forty days' fast of St Michael the Archangel draweth near: I firmly believe that it is the will of God that we keep this fast on the Mount of Alvernia, which by divine decree hath been made ready for us, to the end that to the honour and glory of God and of His Mother, the glorious Virgin Mary, and of the holy Angels, we may, through penance, merit at the hands of Christ the consolation of consecrating this blessed mountain.' . . .

In the morning, his companions, being aware that through the fatigues of the night, which he had passed without sleep, Saint Francis was much weakened in body and could but ill go on his way afoot, went to a poor peasant of those parts, and begged him, for the love of God, to lend his ass for Brother Francis, their Father, that could not go afoot. Hearing them make mention of Brother Francis, he asked them: 'Are ye of the brethren of that brother of Assisi, of whom so much good is spoken?' The brothers answered: 'Yes,' and that in very sooth it was for him that they asked for the sumpter beast. Then the good man, with great diligence and devotion, made ready the ass, and brought it to Saint Francis, and with great reverence let mount him thereon, and they went on their way; and he with them, behind his ass . . .

And when that they were come about half way up the mountain, as the heat was very great and the ascent was weary, the peasant became very thirsty, in such sort that he began to cry aloud behind Saint Francis, saying: 'Woe is me, for I die of thirst: if I find not something to drink, I shall choke outright.' Wherefore Saint Francis got down off the ass and fell on his knees in prayer; and remained so long kneeling with his hands lifted up to heaven, until he knew by revelation that God had heard his prayer. Then said Saint Francis to the peasant: 'Run quickly to that rock, and there shalt thou find the living water, which Jesu Christ in this hour, of His mercy, hath made to come forth from out that rock.' So he ran to the place that Saint Francis had shown him, and found a fair spring that had been brought out of the hard rock by virtue of the prayer of Saint Francis: and he drank his fill thereof and was comforted. And it doth well appear that this spring was brought out by God in miraculous fashion at the prayers of Saint Francis, seeing that neither before nor after was there ever seen in that place a spring of water, nor any living water near to that place for a great space around.

This done, Saint Francis with his companions and the peasant gave thanks unto God for the miracle shown forth to them, and then went they on their way. And as they drew near to the foot of the rock of Alvernia itself, it pleased Saint Francis to rest a little under the oak that was by the way, and is there to this day; and as he stood under it, Saint Francis began to take note of the situation of the place and of the country round. And as he was thus gazing, lo! there came a great multitude of birds from divers parts, the which, with singing and flapping of their wings, all showed joy and gladness exceeding great, and came about Saint Francis in such fashion that some settled on his head, some on his shoulders, and some on his arms, some in his lap, and some round his feet. When his companions and the peasant marvelled, beholding this, Saint Francis, all joyful in spirit, spake thus unto them: 'I believe, brothers most dear, that it is pleasing unto our Lord Jesu Christ that we should dwell in this lonely mountain, seeing that our little sisters and brothers the birds show such joy at our coming.' And said these words, they arose, and went on their way and came at last to the place that his companions had first chosen . . .

A few days thereafter, as Saint Francis was standing hard by [his] cell, pondering on the form of the mountain, and marvelling at the huge clefts and openings in the mighty rocks, he set himself to pray: and then it was revealed to him of God that those marvellous clefts had been miraculously made in the hour of the Passion of Christ when, as saith the Evangelist, the rocks were rent asunder. And it was the will of God that this should in especial manner be made manifest upon that Mount of Alvernia, for that there the Passion of our Lord Jesu Christ should be renewed in his soul through love and pity, and in his body through the imprinting of the most holy Stigmata . . .

There came the day of the most Holy Cross: and early in the morning before dawn, Saint Francis fell on his knees in prayer in front of the entrance to his cell, and turning his face towards the East, prayed in this manner: 'Oh my Lord Jesu Christ, I pray thee grant me two graces, before I die: the first, that in my life-time I may feel in my soul and in my body, so far as may be, the pain that Thou, sweet Lord, didst bear in the hour of Thy most bitter passion; the second is, that I may feel in my heart, as far as may be, that exceeding love, wherewith Thou, O Son of God, wast kindled to willingly endure such agony for us sinners.' And as he thus continued a long time in prayer, he came to know that God would hear him and that as far as possible for the mere creature, so far would it be granted him to feel the things aforesaid. Having this promise, Saint Francis began with exceeding great devotion to contemplate the passion of Christ and His infinite love: and the fervour of devotion so grew in him that he was altogether transformed into Jesu through love and pity. And as he was thuswise set on fire in this contemplation, on that same morn he saw descend from heaven a Seraph with six wings resplendent and aflame, and as with swift flight the Seraph drew nigh unto Saint Francis, so that he could discern him, he clearly saw that he bore in him the image of a man crucified: and his wings were in such guise displayed, that two wings were spread above his head, two were spread out to fly, and the other twain covered all his body. Seeing this, Saint Francis was sore adread, and was filled at once with joy and grief and marvel. He felt exceeding joy at the gracious look of Christ, who appeared to him so lovingly, and gazed on him so graciously: but on the other hand, seeing him crucified upon the cross, he felt immeasurable grief for pity's sake. Therewith, he marvelled much at so amazing and unwonted a vision, knowing full well that the weakness of the Passion agreeth not with the immortality of the seraphic spirit. And as he thus marvelled, it was revealed by Him that appeared to him: that by divine providence this vision had been shown in such form, to the end that he might understand that not by the martyrdom of the body, but by the enkindling of his mind, must he needs be wholly transformed into the express image of Christ Crucified, in that wondrous apparition. Then the whole Mount of Alvernia appeared as though it burned with bright-shining flames, that lit up all the mountains and valleys round as though it had been the sun upon the earth; whereby the shepherds, that were keeping watch in those parts, seeing the mountain aflame and so great a light around, had exceeding great fear, according as they afterwards told unto the brothers, declaring that this flame rested upon the Mount of Alvernia for the space of an hour and more. In like manner, at the bright shining of this light, which through the windows lit up the hostels of the country round, certain muleteers that were going into Romagna, arose, believing that the day had dawned, and saddled and laded their beasts: and going on their way, they saw the said light die out and the material sun arise . . .

Then this marvellous vision vanishing away, after long space and secret converse, left in the heart of Saint Francis an exceeding ardour and flame of love divine: and in his flesh a marvellous image and copy of the passion of Christ. For straightway in the hands and feet of Saint Francis began to appear the marks of the nails, in such wise as he had seen them in the body of Jesu Christ, the Crucified, the which had shown Himself to him in the likeness of a seraph: and thus his hands and feet appeared to be pierced through the middle with nails, and the heads of them were in the palms of his hands and the soles of his feet outside the flesh, and their points came out on the back of his hands and of his feet, so that they seemed bent back and rivetted in such fashion that under the bend and rivetting, which all stood out above the flesh, might easily be put a finger of the hand, as in a ring: and the heads of the nails were round and black. Likewise in the right side appeared an image of a wound make by a lance, unhealed, and red and bleeding, the which afterwards ofttimes dropped blood from the sacred breast of Saint Francis, and stained with blood his tunic and his hose. Wherefore his companions, before they knew it of his own lips, perceiving nevertheless that he uncovered not his hands and feet, and that he could not put the soles of his feet to the ground; and afterwards finding his tunic and his hose all stained with blood, what time they washed them, knew of a surety that in his hands and feet and likewise in his side he bore the express image and similitude of our Lord Jesu Christ Crucified.

The Little Flowers of St Francis

CHAPTER 4

◆

The Medieval Mountaineer

The greater part of medieval literature consists of philosophical and theological texts. Whenever a theologian has to comment on a Biblical text about mountains, he will turn to allegorical interpretation (the mountains are the virtues, or the angels, or the devils, or what you will); and in the writings of the philosophers golden mountains are more likely to appear than real ones. But there were medieval travellers who found their way into the mountains for non-religious purposes, of whom the most famous was the explorer Marco Polo passing through Afghanistan and the Pamirs on his way to China. The poet Petrarch is often claimed as the first genuine mountaineer, on the basis of the letter printed below. It is hard to take the letter completely at face value, but there is no good reason to treat it, as some scholars do, as being simply yet another allegory. But if Petrarch's letter can still be defended as the story of a genuine ascent, the same cannot be said of the account of Mount Ararat in the travels of Sir John Mandeville.

◆ ◆ ◆

On the Road to Cathay

Badakhshan or Balashan is a country whose inhabitants worship Mahomet and have a language of their own. It is a large kingdom, twelve days' journey in length, ruled by hereditary kings of a lineage descended from King Alexander and the daughter of Darius, the Great King of Persia. In honour of Alexander the Great, all its kings still bear the title Zulkarnein, the Saracen equivalent of our name Alexander.

In this country originate the precious stones called balass rubies, of great beauty and value. They are dug out of rocks among the mountains by tunnelling to great depths, as is done by miners working a vein of silver. They are found in one particular mountain called Sighinan. And I would have you know that they are mined only for the king and by his order; no one else could go to the mountain and dig for these gems without incurring instant death, and it is forbidden under pain of death and forfeiture to export them out of the kingdom. The king sends them by his own men to other kings and princes and great lords, to some as tribute, to others as a token of amity; and some he barters for gold and silver. This he does so that these balass rubies may retain their present rarity and value. If he let other men mine them and export them throughout the world, there would be so many of them on the market that the price would fall and they would cease to be so precious. That is why he has imposed such a heavy penalty on anyone exporting them without authority.

And it is a fact that in this same country, in another mountain, are found the stones from which is made lapis lazuli, of the finest quality in the world. These stones originate among the mountains as a vein like the veins of other minerals. There are also mountains here in which are found veins yielding silver, copper, and lead in great abundance . . .

The kingdom has many narrow passes and natural fortresses, so that the inhabitants are not afraid of any invader breaking in to molest them. Their cities and towns are built on mountain tops or sites of great natural strength. It is a characteristic of these mountains that they are of immense height, so that for a man to climb from the bottom to the top is a full day's journey, from dawn till dusk. On the top are wide plateaux, with a lush growth of grass and trees and copious springs of the purest water, which pour down over the crags like rivers into the valley below. In these streams are found trout and other choice fish. On the mountain tops the air is so pure and so salubrious that if a man living in the cities and houses built in the adjoining valleys falls sick of a fever, whether tertian, quartan, or hectic, he has only to go up into the mountains, and a few days rest will banish the malady and restore him to health. Messer Marco Polo vouches for this from his own experience. Two or three of the mountains consist largely of sulphur, and springs of sulphurous water issue from them.

The people here are good archers and keen huntsmen and most of them wear costumes of skin, because they are very short of cloth. The ladies of the nobility and gentry wear trousers, such as I will describe to you. There are some ladies who in one pair of trousers or breeches put anything up to a hundred ells of cotton cloth, folded in pleats. This is to give the impression that they have plump hips, because their menfolk delight in plumpness . . .

When the traveller leaves Badakhshan, he goes twelve days' journey east-north-east up a river valley belonging to the brother of the lord of Badakhshan, where there are towns and homesteads in plenty, peopled by a warlike race who worship Mahomet. After these twelve days he reaches a country called Wakhan of no great size, for it is three days' journey across every way. The people, who worship Mahomet and speak a language of their own, are doughty warriors. They have no ruler except one whom they call *nona*, that is to say in our language 'count', and are subject to the lord of Badakhshan. They have wild beasts in plenty and game of all sorts for the chase.

When the traveller leaves this place, he goes three days' journey towards the north-east, through mountains all the time, climbing so high that this is said to be the highest place in the world. And when he is in this high place, he finds a plain between two mountains, with a lake from which flows a very fine river. Here is the best pasturage in the world; for a lean beast grows fat here in ten days. Wild game of every sort abounds. There are great quantities of wild sheep of huge size. Their horns grow to as much as six palms in length and are never less than three or four. From these horns the shepherds make big bowls from which they feed, and also fences to keep in their flocks. There are also innumerable wolves, which devour many of the wild rams. The horns and bones of the sheep are found in such numbers that men build cairns of them beside the tracks to serve as landmarks to travellers in the snowy season.

This plain, whose name is Pamir, extends fully twelve days' journey. In all these twelve days there is no habitation or shelter, but travellers must take their provisions with them. No birds fly here because of the height and the cold. And I assure you that, because of this great cold, fire is not so bright here nor of the same colour as elsewhere, and food does not cook well.

Now let us pursue our course towards the north-east and east. At the end of this twelve days' journey, the traveller must ride fully forty days more east-north-east, always over mountains and along hillsides and gorges, traversing many rivers and many deserts. And in all this journey he finds no habitation or shelter, but must carry his stock of provisions. This country is called Belor. The inhabitants live very high up in the mountains. They are idolaters and utter savages, living entirely by the chase and dressed in the skins of beasts. They are out and out bad.

Marco Polo, *The Travels*

An Ascent in Provence

To Fr Denis da Borgo San Sepolcro, 26 April 1335

I have this day ascended the highest mountain in this district, which is very deservedly called Le Ventoux, for the sake of seeing the remarkable altitude of the place. I have cherished this project for many years. You know that from my boyhood, whilst fate has been disposing of the affairs of men, I have been passing my time here. This mountain, which is visible from a great distance, was always before my eyes, but it was long before I could find any one to accompany me, till I opened the matter to my only younger brother, whom you know; and as he was delighted at my proposal, so I was pleased to have a friend and a brother for my companion. On the appointed day we left home, and we got to Malaucène in the evening. This place is at the foot of the mountain towards the north. We stayed there one day, and this morning we started, with some servants, on our ascent, which we did not complete without much difficulty, for the mountain is extremely steep, and an almost inaccessible mass of rock . . .

The day was long, the air balmy, we were supported by the vigour of our minds, and such bodily strength and activity as we possess, so that the nature of the place was the only obstacle. We met with an old shepherd in one of the dells of the mountain, who did all he could to dissuade us from our attempt, telling us that, some fifty years before, he had been invited to go to the summit by the ardour of youth, that he had got nothing by it but discouragement and fatigue, and that his body as well as his cloak were torn by the rocks and brambles; he added that he never heard of any similar enterprise being undertaken either before or since. Whilst he was vociferating all this, our desire to proceed (for thus it is with the incredulous minds of young men) increased with the objections he made. When the old man perceived that all his remarks were vain, he accompanied us a little way amongst the rocks, and pointed out a small path, giving us at the same time a vast deal of good advice, and making repeated signs to us after we had gone. We threw off such of our garments as might have embarrassed us, and began the ascent with great vigour and gaiety.

But, as usually happens, fatigue very soon follows great efforts. We soon sat down upon a rock, whence we again started at a more moderate pace, I more especially lessened my mountaineering enthusiasm, and whilst my brother was seeking for short cuts over the steepest parts of the mountain, I more warily kept below, and when he pointed out the path to me, I answered that I hoped to find an easier access, and that I willingly went round in order to advance on more level ground. But whilst I was alleging this excuse for my laziness, the others got far above me, and I was wandering in the gullies of the mountain, where my path was far from being easier, so that the way was lengthened, and my useless labour became more and more irksome. As it was too late to repent of my error, I determined to go straight up, and I at last rejoined my brother, whom I had lost from sight, and who had been quietly resting on a rock, after much toil and anxiety, so that we again started together. The same thing, however, happened again and again in a few hours, and I began to find that human ingenuity was not a match for the nature of things, and that it was impossible to gain heights by moving downwards.

Passing, however, with the readiness of thought from corporeal things, I could not help apostrophising myself in the following words: 'The very thing which has happened to thee in the ascent of this mountain, happens to thee and to many of those who seek to arrive at final beatitude, though it is less evident, because the motives of the body are palpable and open, those of the mind are invisible and concealed. The life of the blest is indeed set on a high place, straight is the path which leads to it, many are the hills which intervene, and the pilgrim must advance with great strides from virtue to virtue.

What, then, retains thee? Nothing, indeed, but the apparent ease and advantage of that path which lies through earthly and low pleasures, wherein when thou hast gone astray, thou must either mount straight to the summit under all the weight of thy misspent toil, or thou must lie thee down in the trenched valleys of thy sins to be haunted by the shadows and darkness of death, and to pass an eternal night in perpetual torture.' This reflection seemed to reanimate my sinking vigour, and enabled me to complete my ascent. I only wish that I may accomplish that journey of the soul, for which I daily and nightly sigh, as well as I have done this day's journey of the feet, after having overcome so many difficulties. And I do not know whether that pilgrimage, which is performed by an active and immortal soul, in the twinkling of an eye, without any local motion, be not easier than that which is carried on in a body worn out by the attacks of death and decay, and laden with the weight of heavy members.

The highest peak of all is called 'Le petit-fils', by a sort of antiphrasis, for it seems rather to be the father of all the mountains in the neighbourhood. There is a little plot upon the summit, where we were all very glad to sit down. Since, father, thou hast read of all the perils of our ascent, vouchsafe to listen to the rest, and to the remaining occurrences of this one day of my life. At first I was so affected by the unaccustomed spirit of the air, and by the free prospect, that I stood as one stupefied. I look back; clouds were beneath my feet. I began to understand Athos and Olympus, since I found that what I had heard and read of them was true of a mountain of far less celebrity. I turn my eyes to that Italian region to which my soul most inclines, and the great rugged Alps (through which, we are told, that the greatest enemy of Rome made his way with vinegar) seemed quite close to me, though they really were at a great distance. I confess that I sighed for that Italian air, more sensible to the soul than to the eyes, and an intense longing came upon me to behold my friends and my country once more. Then a new reflection arose in my mind, I passed from place to time. I recollected that on this day ten years had elapsed since I terminated my youthful studies in Bologna, and, O immortal God, O immutable Wisdom, how many changes has that interval witnessed . . . Whilst I was rejoicing in my heart, father, at my advancement in years, I wept over my imperfections, I mourned the common mutability of human actions, I forgot the place I was in and the reason of my coming thither till, deferring my meditations to a fitter opportunity, I looked about to discern that which I came to see. The frontier of France and the Pyrenees of Spain were not to be descried (though nothing, that I know of, intervened) by reason of the impotence of mortal sight. But I could very clearly see the mountains about Lyons on the right, and on the left the Bay of Marseilles, which is distant some days' journey. The Rhône flowed beneath our eyes. But whilst I was admiring so many individual objects of the earth, and that my soul rose to lofty contemplations, by the example of the body, it occurred to me that I would look into the book of Augustine's *Confessions*, which I owe to your kindness, and which I generally carry about with me, as it is a volume of small dimensions, though of great sweetness. I open it at a venture, meaning to read whatever might present itself – for what could have presented itself that was not pious and devout? The volume opened at the tenth book. My brother was expecting to hear the words of Augustine from my lips, and he can testify that in the first place I lighted upon, it was thus written: 'There are men who go to admire the high places of mountains, the great waves of the sea, the wide currents of rivers, the circuit of the ocean, and the orbits of the stars – and who neglect themselves.' I confess that I was amazed; I begged my brother, who was anxious to hear more, not to interrupt me, and I shut the book half angry with myself, that I, who was even now admiring terrestrial things, ought already to have learnt from the philosophers that nothing is truly great except the soul. I was sufficiently satisfied with what I had seen upon the mountain, and I turned my eyes back unto myself, so that from that hour till we came to the bottom, no one heard me speak. The words I had read busied me deeply, for I could scarcely imagine that they had occurred fortuitously, or that they were addressed to any one but myself. Thou mayest imagine how often on that day I looked back to the summit of the mountain, which seemed but a cubit high in comparison with the height of human contemplation, were it not too often merged in the corruptions of the earth. At every step I thought, if it cost so much sweat and toil to bring the body a little nearer to heaven, great indeed must be the cross, the dungeon and the sting which should terrify the soul as it draws nigh unto God, and crush the turgid height of insolence and the fate of man . . .

In these undisguised reflections, I felt not the stones upon the path, and I regained the rustic cottage which I had left before the dawn, at an advanced hour of the night; the constant moon afforded sweet attendance to us as we talked: and now, whilst the servants are busy preparing supper, I have stolen aside to write you these lines on the spur of the moment, lest with change of scene and the variety of impressions the thoughts I have penned should have deserted me. Thou seest, most beloved father, that there is nothing in me which I desire to conceal from your eyes, since I not only disclose to you my own life, but even my individual reflections. Father, I crave your prayers, that whatever in me is vague and unstable may be strengthened, and that the thoughts I waste abroad on many things, may be turned to that one thing, which is true, good, and secure. Farewell.

Petrarch, *Letters*

Tall Stories from the Caucasus

Men go from Trebizond toward Armenia the great unto a city that is clept Erzerum; that was wont to be a good city and plentiful, but the Turks have greatly wasted it. Thereabout growth no wine nor fruit but little or else none. In this land is the earth more high than in any other, and that maketh great cold. And there be many good waters and good wells that come under earth from the flume of Paradise that is clept Euphrates, that is a journey beside that city. And that river cometh towards India under earth and resorteth unto the land of Altasar.

And so pass men by this Armenia, and enter the sea of Persia. From that city of Erzerum go men to an hill that is clept Sabissocolle; and there beside is another hill that men clepen Ararat, where Noah's ship rested, and it is upon that mountain and men may see it afar in clear weather. And that mountain is well a seven mile high. And some say that they have seen and touched the ship and put their finger in the place where the fiend went out, when that Noah said Benedicite. But they that say such words say their will. For a man may not go up the mountain for great plenty of snow that is always on that mountain neither summer nor winter, so that no man may go up there, nor never man did since the time of Noah save a monk that, by the grace of God, brought one of the planks down, that it is in the minster at the foot of the mountain.

And beside is the city of Dayne that Noah founded, and fast by is the city of Any in which were wont to be a thousand churches. But upon that mountain to go up this monk had great desire and so upon a day he went up and when he was upward the third part of the mountain he was so weary that he might no further and so he rested him and fell asleep. And when he woke he found himself at the foot of the mountain. And then he prayed devoutly to God that he would vouchsafe to suffer him go up. And an angel came to him and said that he should go up. And so he did, and since that time never none; wherefore men should not believe such words.

The Travels of Sir John Mandeville

CHAPTER 5

◆

Altitudes of Renaissance and Baroque

The year 1492, the year of Columbus' arrival in America, was an important one in the history of mountaineering. In that year Charles VII of France passed through Dauphiny, and was much impressed by the appearance of Mont Aiguille, a rocky peak near Grenoble that was then called Mont Inaccessible. This mountain is only some seven thousand feet in height, but it is a genuine rock climb, and is still considered difficult. Charles VII ordered his Chamberlain, Dompjulian de Beaupré, to make an ascent of the mountain. A letter describing his ascent is printed below.

Despite this promising start, the sixteenth and seventeenth centuries were not great ages of mountaineering and produced few notable mountain lovers. Leonardo da Vinci ascended Mount Monboso, which may or may not have been Monte Rosa; his brief account, not printed here, does not give enough information to enable us to decide which mountain he climbed or how far he got up it. Theologians commenting on mountain passages in the Bible continued to read them in an allegorical sense. The Spanish mystic St John of the Cross saw the whole spiritual life as being an Ascent of Mount Carmel, and carried the art of mountain allegory to new heights. The extracts below from his *Spiritual Canticle* (a mystical treatise in the form of a commentary on one of his own poems, based on the *Song of Songs*) show that to a devoted allegorist a mountain could mean almost anything except a mountain.

Those who comb great literature for mountain references find the works of Shakespeare a great disappointment. The problem was a serious one for Ruskin, who was passionately committed to the defence of the thesis that intimacy with mountains was a *sine qua non* for the production of great art and literature. He did the best he could with Shakespeare in the passage printed below.

The account of the crossing of the Simplon by the diarist Evelyn is typical of the disgust of the average post-Renaissance tourist forced to cross the Alps on the way to or from the congenial plains of Italy.

◆ ◆ ◆

The Ascent of the Inaccessible

Monsieur the President [of the Parliament of Grenoble]

I send you my hearty greetings. When I left the King he charged me to cause an attempt to be made to see whether it was possible to climb the mountain which was said to be inaccessible; which mountain I, by subtle means and engines, have found the means of climbing, thanks be to God; and now I have been here three days; and more than ten companions are with me – both Church men and other respectable people, and also one of the King's ladder-men; and I do not mean to leave here until I have received your answer, in order that, if you wish to send a few people to see us here, you may be able to do so; though I warn you that you will find few men who, when they see us up above, and see all the passage that I have caused to be made, will dare to come here; for it is the most horrible and frightful passage that I or any of my company have ever seen. I inform you of this in order that, having made sure of it at your pleasure, you may be so good as to write to the King by my lackey, the bearer of this; and I assure you that you will be causing him great pleasure, and me also, and you may be sure that if I can do anything for you, I will do so according to the pleasure of our master, so that he may give you that which you most desire.

Written the 28th day of June, on Eguille-Fort, called Mount Inaccessible; for the people of the country call it Leguille; and in order that I might not forget it, I have had the mountain named in the name of the Father, the Son, and the Holy Ghost, of Saint Charlemagne, for love of the name of the King; and I have had mass said upon it, and have caused three crosses to be set up. To describe the mountain to you – it is about a French league in circumference, a quarter of a league in length, and a cross-bow shot in width, and is covered with a beautiful meadow; and we have found a beautiful herd of chamois, which will never be able to get away, and some little ones of this year with them, one of which was killed, in spite of our intentions when we entered, for until the King gives other orders I do not intend to have any of them taken. You have to ascend half a league by ladder, and a league by other ways, and it is the most beautiful place that I have ever visited.

Wholly yours,
Dompjulien

Francis Gribble, *The Early Mountaineers*

On the Slopes of Mount Carmel

The Song of the Bride

> Whither hast thou hidden thyself, And hast left me, O Beloved
> to my sighing?
> Thou didst flee like the hart, having wounded me: I went out
> after thee, calling, and thou wert gone.
> Shepherds, ye that go, Yonder, through the sheepcotes, to the
> hill,
> If perchance ye see him that I most love, Tell ye him that I
> languish, suffer and die.
> Seeking my loves, I will go o'er yonder mountains and banks;
> I will neither pluck the flowers nor fear the wild beasts; I
> will pass by the mighty and cross the frontiers.
> O woods and thickets, Planted by the hand of the Beloved!
> O meadow of verdure, enamelled with flowers. Say if he has
> passed by you . . .

From the Commentary:

The soul says here: Seeking my loves

> *I will go o'er yonder mountains and banks;*

By the mountains, which are lofty, she here means the virtues; first, by reason
of their loftiness; second, because of the difficulty and toil which are experienced in climbing them; and o'er these mountains she says that she will
go, by practising the contemplative life. By the banks, which are low, she
means mortifications, penances and spiritual exercises; and o'er these she says
also that she will go, by practising in them the active life, together with the
contemplative life, whereof she has spoken, for in order to see God surely,
and to acquire the virtues, there is need of both. This, then, is as much as
to say: Seeking my Beloved, I will ever put into practice the lofty virtues and
abase myself in lowly mortifications and exercises of humility . . .

Song of the Spouse

> My Beloved, the mountains, The solitary, wooded valleys,
> The strange islands, the sonorous rivers, The whisper of the
> amorous breezes,
> The tranquil night, At the time of rising of the dawn,
> The silent music, the sounding solitude, The supper that
> recreates and enkindles love . . .

Reply of the Bride

> Let us rejoice, Beloved. And let us go to see ourselves in
> thy beauty.
> To the mountain and the hill where flows the pure water; Let
> us enter farther into the thicket.

From the Commentary:

All that is expounded here is in God in an eminent and infinite manner, or, to express it better, each of these grandeurs which are spoken of is God, and they are all of them God; for inasmuch as in this case the soul is united with God, it feels that all things are God, even as Saint John felt when he said *Quod factum est, in ipso vita erat*. That is to say: That which was made in Him was life. It is not to be understood that, in that which the soul is here said to feel, it is, as it were, seeing things in the light, or creatures in God, but that in that possession the soul feels that all things are God to it. Neither is it to be understood that, because the soul has such lofty feelings concerning God in that which we are saying, it sees God essentially and clearly, for this is no more than a powerful and abundant communication, and a glimpse of that which He is in Himself, wherein the soul feels this goodness concerning the things which we shall expound in these lines, as follows:

My beloved, the mountains,

The mountains have height, they are abundant, extensive and beautiful, graceful, flowery and fragrant. These mountains my Beloved is to me.

The solitary, wooded valleys,

The solitary valleys are quiet, pleasant, cool, shady, abounding in fresh water; and with the variety of their groves and the sweet song of the birds they greatly recreate and delight the senses, in their solitude and silence giving refreshment and rest. These valleys my Beloved is to me . . .

Now that the perfect union of love is made between the soul and God, the soul desires to employ and exercise herself in the properties which pertain to love, and thus it is she who speaks in this stanza with the Spouse, praying him for three things which are proper to love. First she desires to receive the joy and sweetness of love, and for this she prays him when she says: 'Let us rejoice, Beloved.' The second desire is that she may become like to the Beloved, and for this she prays Him when she says: 'Let us go to see ourselves in Thy beauty.' And the third desire is to delve into the things and secrets of the same Beloved, and to know them, and for this she prays Him when she says: 'Let us enter farther into the thicket.' . . .

To the mountain and the hill

This means to the morning and essential knowledge of God, which is knowledge in the Divine Word, Who, because of His height, is here understood by the mountain; as Isaias says, calling men to a knowledge of the Son of God, and saying: 'Come, let us go up to the mountain of the Lord.' Again 'The mountain of the house of the Lord shall be prepared.' And to the hill – that is, to the evening knowledge of God, which is the wisdom of God in his creatures and works and wondrous ordinances, which is here signified by the hill, since this wisdom is lower than that of the morning; but the soul prays for both morning and evening wisdom when she says: 'To the mountain and the hill.'

When the soul, then, says: 'Let us go to the mountain to see ourselves in Thy beauty' she means: Transform me in the beauty of Divine Wisdom, and make me like to It, which Wisdom, as we said, is the Word, the Son of God. And when she says: 'to the hill': she is praying God to inform her in the beauty of this other and lesser wisdom, which is in His creatures and mysterious works, which also is beauty of the Son of God wherein the soul desires to see herself enlightened.

The soul cannot see herself in the beauty of God save by being transformed in the Wisdom of God, wherein she sees herself to possess that which is above and that which is below. To this mountain and hill the Bride desired to come when she said: 'I will go to the mountain of myrrh and to the hill of frankincense' – meaning by the mountain of myrrh the clear vision of God and by the hill of frankincense the knowledge of Him in the creatures, for the myrrh on the mountains is of a higher order than the frankincense on the hill.

Saint John of the Cross, *Spiritual Canticle*

Shakespeare and Mountains

In such slight allusions as [Shakespeare] makes to mountain scenery itself, it is very curious to observe the accurate limitation of his sympathies to such things as he had known in his youth; and his entire preference of human interest, and of courtly and kingly dignities, to the nobleness of the hills. This is most marked in *Cymbeline*, where the term mountaineer is, as with Dante, always one of reproach, and the noble birth of Arviragus and Guiderius is shown by their holding their mountain cave as

> A cell of ignorance; travelling abed;
> A prison for a debtor;

and themselves, educated among hills, as in all things contemptible.

> We are beastly; subtle as the fox, for prey;
> Like warlike as the wolf, for what we eat;
> Our valour is to chase what flies; our cage
> We make our choir, as doth the prisoned bird.

A few phrases occur here and there which might justify the supposition that he had seen high mountains, but never implying awe or admiration. Thus Demetrius:

> These things seem small and indistinguishable
> Like far off mountains, turned into clouds.

'Taurus snow' and the 'frosty Caucasus' are used merely as types of purity or cold; and though the avalanche is once spoken of as an image of power, it is with instantly following depreciation.

> Rush on his host, as doth the melted snow
> Upon the valleys, whose low vassal seat
> The Alps does spit, and void his rheum upon.

There was only one thing belonging to hills that Shakespere seemed to feel as noble – the pine tree, and that because he had seen it in Warwickshire, clumps of pine occasionally rising on little sandstone mounds, as at the place of execution of Piers Gaveston, above the lowland woods. He touches on this tree fondly again and again:

> As rough
> Their royal blood enchafed, as the rud'st wind
> That by his top doth take the mountain pine
> And make him stoop to the vale.

> The strong based promontory
> Have I made shake, and by the spurs plucked up
> The pine and cedar.

Where note his observances of the peculiar horizontal roots of the pine, spurred as it is by them like the claw of a bird, and partly propped, as the aiguilles by those rock promontories at their bases which I have always called their spurs, this observance of the pine's strength and animal-like grasp being the chief reason for his choosing it, above other trees, for Ariel's prison. Again:

> You may as well forbid the mountain pines
> To wag their high tops, and to make no noise
> When they are fretted with the gusts of heaven.

And yet again:

But when, from under this terrestrial ball,
He fires the proud tops of the eastern pines.

We may judge, by the impression which this single feature of hill scenery seems to have made on Shakespere's mind, because he had seen it in his youth, how his whole temper would have been changed if he had lived in a more sublime country, and how essential it was to his power of contemplation of mankind that he should be removed from the sterner influences of nature. For the rest, so far as Shakespere's work has imperfections of any kind – the trivialness of many of his adopted plots, for instance, and the comparative rarity with which he admits the ideal of an enthusiastic virtue arising out of principle; virtue being with him, for the most part, founded simply on the affections joined with inherent purity in his women, or on mere manly pride and honour in his men; – in a word, whatever difference, involving inferiority, there exists between him and Dante, in his conceptions of the relation between this world and the next, we may partly trace, as we did the difference between Bacon and Pascal, to the less noble character of the scenes around him in his youth; and admit that, though it was necessary for his special work that he should be put, as it were, on a level with his race, on those plains of Stratford, we should see in this a proof, instead of a negation, of the mountain power over human intellect. For breadth and perfectness of condescending sight, the Shakesperian mind stands alone; but in *ascending* sight it is limited. The breadth of grasp was innate; the stoop and slightness of it were given by the circumstances of scene: and the difference between those careless masques of heathen gods, or unbelieved, though mightily conceived visions of fairy, witch, or risen spirit, and the earnest faith of Dante's vision of Paradise, is the true measure of the difference in influence between the willowy banks of Avon, and the purple hills of Arno.

John Ruskin, *Modern Painters*

Evelyn Crossing the Simplon

The first day then we got as far as *Castellanza*, by which runs a spacious river into *Lago Maggiore*: Here at dinner were two or three *Jesuites* who were very pragmatical & inquisitive, whom we declin'd conversation with as decently as we could: so we pursu'd our journey through a most fruitfull plaine, but the weather wet & uncomfortable: At night we lay at *Sesto* & next morning (leaving our Coach) Imbarked in a boate to waft us over the *Lago* (being one of the largest in Europe) & whence we could perfectly see the touring *Alps* & amongst them *Il Gran San Bernardo* esteemed the highest mountaine in Europe, appearing some miles above the Clouds: Through this vast Water passes the River *Ticinus* which discharges itself into the Po, by which means *Helvetia* transports her Merchandizes into *Italy*, which we now begin to leave behind us: Having now sail'd about 2 leagues we were hal'd on shore at *Arona*, a strong Towne belonging to the Dutchy of *Milan*, where being examined by the Governor, & paying a small duty, we were dismiss'd. Opposite to this Fort is *Angiera*, another small Towne; the passage very pleasant, with the horrid prospect of the *Alps*, covered with Pine trees, & Firrs & above them Snow: The next we pass'd was the pretty Iland *Isabella*, that lies about the middle of the Lake, & has a faire house built on a Mount, indeede the whole Iland is a Mount, ascended by severall *Terraces* & walks all set about with Oranges & Citron trees, the reflection from the Water rendring the place very warme, at least during the Summer & Autumn: The next we saw was *Isola*, & left on our right hand the Ile of St Jovanni, & so sailing by another small Towne (built also upon an Iland) we ariv'd at night to *Marguzzo* an obscure village at the end of the Lake, & very foote of the Alpes, which now rise as it were suddainly, after some hundred of miles of the most even Country in the World, & where there is hardly a stone to be found, as if nature had here swept up the rubbish of the Earth in the Alpes, to forme & cleare the Plaines of *Lumbardy*, which hitherto we had pass'd since our coming from *Venice*:

In this wretched place I lay on a bed stuff'd with leaves, which made such a Crackling, & did so prick my skin through the tick, that I could not sleepe: The next morning I was furnish'd with an Asse (for we could not get horses) but without stirrops, but we had ropes tied with a loope to put our feete in, that supplied other trappings, & thus with my gallant steede, bridld with my Turkish present, we pass'd thro a reasonable pleasant, but very narrow Vally, 'til we came to *Duomo*, where we rested, & having shew'd the *Spanish* pass, we brought from the Ambassador; the Governor would presse another on us: though onely that his Secretary might get a Croune: Here we exchang'd our *Asses* for *Mules* sure footed on the hills & precipices, as accustom'd to passe them, & with a Guide, which now we hired, we were brought that night, through very steepe, craggy & dangerous passages, to a Village cal'd *Vedra*, being the last of the King of *Spaines* Dominion in the Dutchy of *Milan*, a very infamous wretched lodging:

Next morning we mount againe through strange, horrid & firefull Craggs & tracts abounding in Pine trees, & only inhabited with Beares, Wolves & *Wild Goates*, nor could we any where see above a pistol shoote before us, the horizon being terminated with rocks, & mountaines, whose tops cover'd with Snow, seem'd to touch the Skies, & in many places pierced the Clowdes. Some of these vast mountaines were but one intire stone, 'twixt whose clefts now & then precipitated greate Cataracts of Mealted Snow, and other Waters, which made a tirrible roaring, Echoing from the rocks & Cavities, & these Waters in some places, breaking in the fall, wett us as if we had pas'd through a mist, so as we could neither see nor heare one another, but trusting to our honest Mules, jog on our Way: The narrow bridges in some places, made onely by felling huge Fir-trees & laying them athwart from mountaine to mountaine, over Cataracts of stupendous depth, are very dangerous & so are the passages & edges made by cutting away the maine rock: others in steps, & in some places we passe betweene mountaines that have ben broken & falln upon one another, which is very tirrible, & one had neede of a sure foote, & steady head to climb some of these precipices, harbours for the Beares, & Woulves, who sometimes have assaulted Travellers: In these straits we frequently alighted, freezing in the Snow, & anon frying by the rever-beration of the Sun against the Cliffs as we descend lower, where we meete now & then a few miserable Cottages, built so upon the declining of the rocks, as one would expect their sliding down: Amongst these inhabite a goodly sort of People having monstrous Gullets or Wenns of flesse growing to their throats, some of which I have seene as big as an hundred pound bag of silver hanking under their Chinns; among the Women especially, & that so ponderous, as that to Ease them, they many of them were a linnen cloth, bound about their head & coming under the chin to support it . . . Their drinking so much snow water is thought to be the Cause of it, the men using more wine, are not so strumous as the Women: but the very truth is, they are a race of people, & many greate Water-drinkers here have not those prodigious tumors: It runs as we say in the bloud, & is a vice in the race, & renders them so ougly, shrivel'd & deform'd, by drawing the skin of the face downe, that nothing can be more fritefull; to which add a strange puffing habit, furrs, & barbarous Language, being a misture of corrupt high *German, French* & Italian: The people are of gigantic Stature, extreamly fierce & rude, yet very honest & trustie: This night, through unaccessible heights, we came in prospect of *Mons Sempronius*, now *Mount Sampion*, which has on its summit a few hutts, & a Chapell: Approaching this Captaine Wrays Water Spaniel (a huge filthy Curr, that had follow'd him out of England), hunted an heard of Goates down the rocks, into a river made by the dissolutions of the Snow: Ariv'd at our cold harbour (though the house had in every roome a Stove), supping with Cheeze and Milke & wretched wine to bed we go in Cupbords, & so high from the floore, that we climb'd them by a Ladder, & as we lay on feathers, so are cover'd with them, that is, between two tickes stuff'd with feathers, & all little enough to keepe one warme: The Ceilings of the roomes are strangely low for those tall people. The house was now in September, halfe cover'd with Snow, nor is there ever a tree or bush growing in many miles: from this unhospitable place then we hasted away early next morning, but as we were getting on our Mules, comes a huge young fellow, demanding mony for a Goate, Cap: Wrays Dog (he affirm'd) had kild the other day: expostulating the matter, & impatient of staying in the Cold, we set spurrs & endeavor'd to ride away, when a multitude of People, being by this time gotten together about us (it being Sonday morning & attending for the Priest to say Masse) stop our Mules, beate us off our saddles & immediately disarming us of our Carbines, drew us into one of the roomes of our Lodging, & set a guard upon us. Thus we continu'd Prisoners til Masse was ended, & then came there halfe a Score grimm Swisse, & taking upon them to be Magistrates, sate downe on the Table, and condemn'd us to pay the fellow a pistol for his Goate, & ten more for attempting to ride away: Threatening that if we did not do it speedily, they would send us to another Prison, & keep us to a day of publique Justice, where, as they perhaps would have exaggerated the Crime, for they pretended we span'd our Carabines & would have shot some of them (as indeede the Captaine was about to do) we might have had our heads cut off, for amongst these barbarous people, a very small misdemeanor dos often meete that animadversion: This we were afterwards told; & though the proceeding appeerd highly unjust, upon Consultation among ourselves, we thought it safer to rid our selves out of their hands, & the trouble we were brought in, than to expostulate it among such brutes, & therefore we patiently lay'd downe the mony & with fierce Countenances had our Mules & armes deliverd us, and glad to scape as we did: This was cold entertainment, but our journey after was colder, the rest of the Way having (tis sai'd) ben cover'd with Snow since the Creation; for that never man remember'd it to be without; & because by the frequent Snowing, the tracks are continualy fill'd up, we passe by severall tall Masts, set up, to guide Those who travell, so as for many miles they stand in ken of one another, like to our Beacons: In some places of divided Mountaines, the Snow quite fills up a Cleft, whilst the bottome being thaw'd leaves it as it were a frozen Arch of Snow, & that so hard, as to beare the greatest weight, for as it snows often so it perpetualy freezes, & of this I was so sensible, as it flaw'd the very skin of my face: Beginning now to descend a little, Cap: Wrays horse, that was our Sumpter (& carried all our bagage) plunging thro a bank of loose Snow, slid down a firefull precipice, more than thrice the height of St Paules, which so incens'd the Cholerique Cavalier his Master, that he was sending a brace of bullets into the poore beast, least the Swisse, that was our Guide, should recover him & run away with his burden: But just as his hand was lifting up his Carbine, we gave such a Shout & pelted the horse so with Snow balls, as with all his might plunging thro the snow he fell from another steepe place into another bottome neere a path we were to passe: It was yet a good while 'ere we got to him, but at last we recovered the place, & easing him of his Charge, hal'd him out of the Snow, where he had ben certainely frozen in, if we had not prevented it before night: It was (as we judg'd) almost two miles that he had slid and fall'n, and yet without any other harme, than the benumming of his limbs for the present, which with lusty rubbing & chafing he began to move, & after a little walking perform'd his journey well enough: All this

Way (affrited with the dissaster of the Captaines horse) we trudg'd on foote, driving our Mules before uys: & sometimes we fell, & sometimes slid thro this ocean of featherd raine, which after October is impassible: Towards night we came into a larger way, thro vast woods of Pines which cloth the middle parts of these rocks: here they were burning some to make *Pitch* & *Rosin*, piling the knotty branches, as we do to make Char-Coale, & reserving that which mealts from them, which harden into Pitch &c: & here we passd severall Cascads of dissolv'd Snow, that had made Channels of formidable depth in the Crevices of the Mountaines, & with such a firfull roaring, as for 7 long miles we could plainely heare it: It is from these Sourses, that the swift & famous *Rhodanus*, & the *Rhyne* which passe thro all France & Germanie, derive their originals.

Late at night then we got to a Towne call'd *Briga*, which is build at the foote of the *Alpes* in the *Valtoline*: every doore almost had nailed on the outside, & next the Streete, a Beares, Wolfes or foxes head & divers of them all Three, which was a Salvage kind of sight: but as the Alps are full of these beasts, the People often kill them:

The next morning we return'd our Guide, & tooke fresh Mules & another to conduct us to the Lake of *Geneva*, pasing through as pleasant a country, as that which before we had travel'd was melancholy & troublesome . . .

John Evelyn, *Diary*, May 1646

CHAPTER 6

◆

Philosophers and Volcanoes

Throughout recorded history, volcanoes have been a special focus for human curiosity. In the ancient world the philosopher Empedocles was rumoured to have died in the crater of Etna, but whether he had climbed to the summit for scientific investigation, or out of lunatic vainglory, was already in doubt in antiquity; indeed it was questioned whether he had been there at all. The legend continued to fascinate in the nineteenth century, as will be seen in a later chapter.

The Roman naturalist Pliny the Elder died in the eruption of Vesuvius in AD 79, and his death was recorded by his nephew Pliny the Younger in a letter to Tacitus printed below. In later centuries many distinguished visitors risked the ascent to the summit of the volcano. John Evelyn's account of his trip is printed in this chapter, and the visits of some of his Victorian successors will be found in Chapter Eighteen.

◆   ◆   ◆

The Death of Empedocles

As to his death different accounts are given. Heraclides, after telling the story of a woman in a trance, how that Empedocles became famous because he had sent away the dead woman alive, goes on to say that he was offering a sacrifice close to the field of Peisianax. Some of his friends had been invited to the sacrifice, including Pausanias. Then, after the feast, the remainder of the company dispersed and retired to rest, some under the trees in the adjoining field, others wherever they chose, while Empedocles himself remained on the spot where he had reclined at table. At daybreak all got up, and he was the only one missing. A search was made, and they questioned the servants, who said they did not know where he was. Thereupon someone said that in the middle of the night he heard an exceedingly loud voice calling Empedocles. Then he got up and beheld a light in the heavens and a glitter of lamps, but nothing else. His bearers were amazed at what had occurred, and Pausanias came down and sent people to search for him.

But later he bade them take no further trouble, for things beyond expectation had happened to him, and it was their duty to sacrifice to him since he was now a god.

Hermippus tells us that Empedocles cured Panthea, a woman of Agrigentum, who had been given up by the physicians, and this was why he was offering sacrifice, and that those invited were about eighty in number. Hippobotus, again, asserts that, when he got up, he set out on his way to Etna; then, when he had reached it, he plunged into the fiery craters and disappeared, his intention being to confirm the report that he had become a god. Afterwards the truth was known, because one of his slippers was thrown up in the flames; it had been his custom to wear slippers of bronze. To this story Pausanias is made (by Heraclides) to take exception.

Diodorus of Ephesus, when writing of Anaximander, declares that Empedocles emulated him, displaying theatrical arrogance and wearing stately robes. We are told that the people of Selinus suffered from pestilence owing to the noisome smells from the river hard by, so that the citizens themselves perished and their women died in childbirth, that Empedocles conceived the plan of bringing two neighbouring rivers to the place at his own expense, and that by this admixture he sweetened the waters. When in this way the pestilence had been stayed and the Selinuntines were feasting on the river bank, Empedocles appeared; and the company rose up and worshipped and prayed to him as to a god. It was then to confirm this belief of theirs that he leapt into the fire. These stories are contradicted by Timaeus, who expressly says that he left Sicily for Peloponnesus and never returned at all; and this is the reason Timaeus gives for the fact that the manner of his death is unknown. He replies to Heraclides, whom he mentions by name, in his fourteenth book. Peisianax, he says, was a citizen of Syracuse, and possessed no land at Agrigentum. Further, if such a story had been in circulation, Pausanias would have set up a monument to his friend, as to a god, in the form of a statue or shrine, for he was a wealthy man. 'How came he,' adds Timaeus, 'to leap into the craters, which he had never once mentioned though they were not far off? He must then have died in Peloponnesus. It is not at all surprising that his tomb is not found; the same is true of many other men.' After urging some such arguments Timaeus goes on to say, 'But Heraclides is everywhere such a collector of absurdities, telling us, for instance, that a man dropped down to earth from the moon.' . . .

There is an epigram of my own on him in my *Pammetros* in a satirical vein, as follows:

Thou, Empedocles, didst cleanse thy body with nimble flame, fire didst thou drink from everlasting bowls. I will not say that of thine own will thou didst hurl thyself into the stream of Etna; thou didst fall in against thy will when thou wouldst fain not have been found out.

Diogenes Laertius, *Lives of the Philosophers*

Vesuvius in Eruption, AD 79

Pliny the Younger to Tacitus

Your request that I would send you an account of my uncle's death, in order to transmit a more exact relation of it to posterity, deserves my acknowledgements: for if this accident shall be celebrated by your pen, the glory of it I am well assured, will be rendered for ever illustrious. And notwithstanding he perished by a misfortune, which, as it involved at the same time a most beautiful country in ruins, and destroyed so many populous cities, seems to promise him an everlasting remembrance; notwithstanding he has himself composed many and lasting works; yet I am persuaded the mentioning of him in your immortal writings will greatly contribute to render his name immortal . . .

He was at that time with the fleet under his command at Misenum. On the 24th of August, about one in the afternoon, my mother desired him to observe a cloud of very unusual size and shape. He had just taken a turn in the sun, and, after bathing himself in cold water, and making a light luncheon, gone back to his books: he immediately arose and went out upon a rising ground from whence he might get a better sight of this very uncommon appearance. A cloud, from which mountain was uncertain, at this distance (but it was found afterwards to come from Mount Vesuvius), was ascending, the appearance of which I cannot give you a more exact description of than by likening it to that of a pine tree, for it shot up to a great height in the form of a very tall trunk, which spread itself out at the top into a sort of branches; occasioned, I imagine, either by a sudden gust of air that impelled it, the force of which decreased as it advanced upwards, or the cloud itself being pressed back again by its own weight, expanded in the manner I have mentioned; it appeared sometimes bright and sometimes dark and spotted, according as it was either more or less impregnated with earth and cinders. This phenomenon seemed to a man of such learning and research as my uncle extraordinary and worth further looking into.

He ordered a light vessel to be got ready and gave me leave, if I liked, to accompany him. I said I had rather go on with my work; and it so happened he had himself given me something to write out. As he was coming out of the house he received a note from Rectina, the wife of Bassus, who was in the utmost alarm at the imminent danger which threatened her; for her villa lying at the foot of Mount Vesuvius, there was no way of escape but by sea; she earnestly entreated him therefore to come to her assistance. He accordingly changed his first intention, and what he had begun from a philosophical, he now carried out in a noble and generous spirit.

He ordered the galleys to put to sea and went himself on board one with an intention of assisting not only Rectina, but the several other towns which lay thickly strewn along that beautiful coast. Hastening then to the place from whence others fled with the utmost terror, he steered his course direct to the point of danger, and with so much calmness and presence of mind as to be able to make and dictate his observations upon the motion and all the phenomena of that dreadful scene.

He was now so close to the mountain that the cinders, which grew thicker and hotter the nearer he approached, fell into the ships, together with pumice-stones and black pieces of burning rock: they were in danger too not only of being aground by the sudden retreat of the sea, but also from the vast fragments which rolled down from the mountain, and obstructed all the shore. Here he stopped to consider whether he should turn back again; to which the pilot advising him, 'Fortune,' said he, 'favours the brave; steer to where Pomponianus is.' Pomponianus was then at Stabiae, separated by a bay, which the sea, after several insensible windings, forms with the shore. He had already sent his baggage on board; for though he was not at that time in actual danger, yet being within sight of it, and indeed extremely near, if it should in the least increase, he was determined to put to sea as soon as the wind, which was blowing dead in-shore, should go down. It was favourable, however, for carrying my uncle to Pomponianus, whom he found in the greatest consternation: he embraced him tenderly, encouraging and urging him to keep up his spirits, and, the more effectually to soothe his fears by seeming unconcerned himself, ordered a bath to be got ready, and then, after having bathed, sat down to supper with great cheerfulness, or at least (what is just as heroic) with every appearance of it.

Meanwhile broad flames shone out in several places from Mount Vesuvius, which the darkness of the night contributed to render still brighter and clearer. But my uncle, in order to soothe the apprehension of his friend, assured him it was only the burning of the villages, which the country people had abandoned to the flames: after this he retired to rest, and it is most certain he was so little disquieted as to fall into a sound sleep: for his breathing, which, on account of his corpulence, was rather heavy and sonorous, was heard by the attendants outside. The court which led to his apartment being now almost filled with stones and ashes, if he had continued there any time longer, it would have been impossible for him to have made his way out. So he was awoke and got up, and went to Pomponianus and the rest of his company, who were feeling too anxious to think of going to bed.

They consulted together whether it would be most prudent to trust to the houses, which now rocked from side to side with frequent and violent concussions as though shaken from their very foundations; or fly to the open fields, where the calcined stones and cinders, though light indeed, yet fell in large showers, and threatened destruction. In this choice of dangers they resolved for the fields: a resolution which, while the rest of the company were hurried into by their fears, my uncle embraced upon cool and deliberate consultation.

They went out then, having pillows tied upon their heads with napkins; and this was their whole defence against the storm of stones that fell round them. It was now day everywhere else, but *there* a deeper darkness prevailed than in the thickest night; which however was in some degree alleviated by torches and other lights of various kinds. They thought proper to go farther down upon the shore to see if they might safely put out to sea, but found the waves still running extremely high and boisterous. There my uncle, laying himself down upon a sail-cloth, which was spread for him, called twice for some cold water, which he drank, when immediately the flames, preceded by a strong whiff of sulphur, dispersed the rest of the company and obliged him to rise. He raised himself up with the assistance of two of his servants, and instantly fell down dead; suffocated, as I conjecture, by some gross and noxious vapour, having always had a weak throat, which was often inflamed.

As soon as it was light again, which was not till the third day after this melancholy accident, his body was found entire and without any marks of violence upon it, in the dress in which he fell, and looking more like a man asleep than dead.

Pliny the Younger, *Letters*

Evelyn on Vesuvius

The next day being Saturday we went 4 miles out of Towne on Mules to see that famous Vulcano or burning mountaine of Vesuvius; here we pass a faire Fountaine cal'd Labulla, which continualy boyles, supposed to proceede from Vesuvius; & thence over a river and bridg . . . Being now approching the [hill] as we were able with our Mules, we alighted, crawling up the rest of the proclivity, with extraordinary difficulty, now with our feete & hands, not without many untoward slipps, which did much bruise us on the various colourd Cinders with which the whole Mountaine is cover'd, some like pitch, others full of perfect brimstone, other metalique interspers'd with innumerable Pumices (of all which I made a collection) we at last gain'd the summit, which I take to be one of the highest terraces in Europ (for 'tis of an excessive altitude) turning our faces towards Naples, it presents us one of the goodliest prospects in the World; & truely, I do not thinke there is a greater & more noble; all the Baiae, Cuma, Elysian fields, Capra, Ischia, Prochita, Misenum, Puteoli, that goodly & gentile Citty, with a vast portion of the Tyrrhan Sea offering themselves to your view at once, & at so sweete & agreable a distance, as nothing can be more greate & delightfull. The mountaine consists of a double top; the one pointed very sharp, and commonly appearing above any clowds; the other blunt; here as we approch'd we met many large and gaping clefts and chasm's, out of which issu'd such sulphurous blasts & Smoake, that we durst not stand long neere them: having gaind the very brim of the top, I layd my selfe on my belly to looke over & into that most frightfull & terrible Vorago, a stupendious pit (if any there be in the whole Earth) of neere three miles in Circuit, and halfe a mile in depth, by a perpendicular hollow cliffe, like that from the highest part of Dover-Castle, with now & then a craggy prominency jetting out: The area at the bottom is plaine, like a curiously even'd floore, which seemes to be made by the winds circling the ashes by its eddy blasts: in the middle & center is a rising or hill shaped like a greate browne loafe, appearing to consist of a sulphurous matter, continualy vomiting a foggy exhalation, & ejecting huge stones with an impetuous noise & roaring, like the report of many musquets discharging: This horrid Barathrum engaged our contemplation for some whole houres both for the strangeness of the spectacle, and for the mention which the old histories make of it, as one of the most stupendious curiosities in nature, & which made the learned & inquisitive Pliny adventure his life, to detect the causes & to loose it in too desperat an approch: It is likewise famous for the Stratagemm of the rebell Spartacus, who did so much mischiefe to the state, by his lurking & protection amongst these horrid Caverns, when it was more accessible, & less dangerous than now it is: But especialy, notorious it is, for the last conflagration when in Ann: 1630 it burst out beyond what it had ever don since the memory of any history, spewing out huge stones & fiery pumices in such quantity, as not onely inviron'd the whole mountaine, but totaly buried, & overwhelme'd divers Townes, people & inhabitants, scattering the ashes more than an hundred miles distance, & utterly devasting all those goodly Vineyards, where formerly grew the most incomparable Greco; when bursting through the bowels of the Earth it absorb'd the very Sea and with its whirling Waters drew in divers Gallys & other Vessells to their destruction; as is faithfully recorded: Some there are who maintaine it the very Mouth of hell it selfe, others of Purgatory, certainely it must be acknowledged one of the most horrid spectacles in the World: We descen'd with infinite more ease, than we climbd up; namely, through a deep Vallie of pure ashes (at the laste eruption a flowing river of mealted & burning brimestone) and so we came at last to our Mules, which with our Veturino, attended us neere the foote of the Mountaine.

John Evelyn, *Diary*, February 1645

CHAPTER 7

◆

Mountains in the Age of Reason

According to the received wisdom, it was in the eighteenth century that high mountains changed, in the perception of mankind, from being hideous terrors to be avoided if possible to being magnets that attracted fascinated votaries. The credit for the change is often given to Jean Jacques Rousseau, partly on the basis of a passage from his *Confessions* printed below. Readers of previous chapters will know that the contrast between old hatred and new love for the mountains is somewhat overdrawn. Few, in any age, have expressed so eloquently the mixture of delight and horror caused by the first acquaintance with precipitous mountains as the literary critic John Dennis, who crossed the Alps in 1688. In this chapter we see the reaction to the Alps of Berkeley, Gray, and Hume, in each of whom love and hatred were mixed, in various proportions. Gray, describing the English Lake District, is clearly writing at a time when one already has to apologize if one does not climb Skiddaw, given an opportunity. Windham was the first British traveller seriously to explore the glaciers below Mont Blanc. The chapter closes with Johnson's magisterial expression of the reaction of the eighteenth-century city-lover brought face to face with the mountains.

◆ ◆ ◆

Nature's Extravagancies

Letter from Turin, 25 October 1688

Octob.21. We entred into *Savoy* in the Morning, and past over Mount *Aiguebelette*. The ascent was the more easie, because it wound about the Mountain. But as soon as we had conquer'd one half of it, the unusual heighth in which we found our selves, the impending Rock that hung over us, the dreadful Depth of the Precipice, and the Torrent that roar'd at the bottom, gave us such a view as was altogether new and amazing. On the other side of that Torrent, was a Mountain that equall'd ours, about the distance of thirty Yards from us. Its craggy Clifts, which we half discern'd, thro the misty gloom of the Clouds that surrounded them, sometimes gave us a horrid Prospect. And sometimes its face appear'd Smooth and Beautiful as the most even and fruitful Vallies. So different from themselves were the different parts of it: In the very same place Nature was seen Severe and Wanton. In the mean time we walk'd upon the very brink, in a litteral sense, of Destruction; one Stumble, and both Life and Carcass had been at once destroy'd. The sense of all this produc'd different motions in me, *viz.* a delightful Horrour, a terrible Joy, and at the same time, that I was infinitely pleas'd, I trembled.

From thence we went thro a pleasant Valley bounded with Mountains, whose high but yet verdant Tops seem'd at once to forbid and incite Men. After we had march'd for a League thro the Plain, we arriv'd at the place which they call *La Cave*; where the late Duke of *Savoy* in the Year Seventy, struck out a Passage thro a rocky Mountain that had always before been impassible: Performing that by the force of Gun-powder, which Thunderbolts or Earthquakes could scarce have effected. This Passage is a quarter of an English Mile, made with incredible labour, and the expence of four Millions of Livers . . .

At *Chambery* we din'd, the Capital Town of *Savoy*. In our way from thence to *Montmelian*, Nature seem'd quite to have changed her Face. There craggy Rocks look'd horrid to the Eye, and Hills appear'd on every side of so stupendous an heighth, that the Company was divided at a distance, whether they should believe them to be sunny Clouds, or the Snowy tops of Mountains. Here appear'd a Hill with its top quite hid in black Clouds, and beyond that Hill, & above those Clouds some higher Mountain show'd its hoary Head. With this strange entertainment by the way, we came that Night to *Montmelian*.

On the 22. We set forward in the morning. The Mountains appear'd to grow still more Lofty. We din'd that day at *Aiguebelle*. In the Afternoon we proceeded on our way, sometimes thro the Plain, and sometimes on the side of the *Alps;* with which we were hemm'd in on all sides. We then began that day to have the additional diversion, of a Torrent, that ran sometimes with fury beneath us, and of the noise of the Cascades, or the down fall of Waters, which sometimes came tumbling a main from the Precipices. We lay that night at *La Chambre*.

On the 23. The morning was very cold, which made us have dismal apprehensions of Mount *Cenis*, since we felt its influence so severely at so great a distance. We arriv'd by Noon at St. *Michel*. In the Afternoon we continued our Journey mostly upon the sides of the Mountains, which were sometimes all cover'd with Pines, and sometimes cultivated, ev'n in places where one would swear the thing were impossible, for they were only not perpendicular. We lay that night at *Modane*.

Oct. 24. *Modane* is within a dozen Miles of Mount *Cenis*, and therefore the next morning we felt the Cold more severely. We went to Dinner at *Laneburgh*, situate at the foot of Mount *Cenis*.

As soon as we had din'd, we sent our Horses about, and getting up upon Mules began to ascend the Mountain. I could not forbear looking back now and then to contemplate the Town and the Vale beneath me. When I was arriv'd within a hundred Yards of the Top, I could still discern *Laneburgh* at the Bottom, distant Three tedious Miles from me. What an amazing distance? Think what an impression a place must make upon you, which you should see as far under you as 'tis from your House to *Hampstead*. And here I wish I had force to do right to this renown'd Passage of the *Alpes*. 'Tis an easie thing to describe *Rome* or *Naples* to you, because you have seen something your self that holds at least some resemblance with them; but impossible to set a Mountain before your eyes, that is inaccessible almost to the sight, and wearies the very Eye to climb it. For when I tell you that we were arriv'd within a hundred yards of the Top: I mean only the Plain, thro which we afterwards pass'd, but there is another vast Mountain still upon that. If these Hills were first made with the World, as has been a long time thought, and Nature design'd them only as a Mound to inclose her Garden *Italy*: Then we may well say of her what some affirm of great Wits, that her careless, irregular and boldest Strokes are most admirable. For the *Alpes* are works which she seems to have design'd, and executed too in Fury. Yet she moves us less, where she studies to please us more. I am delighted, 'tis true, at the prospect of Hills and Valleys, of flowry Meads, and murmuring Streams, yet it is a delight that is consistent with Reason, a delight that creates or improves Meditation. But transporting Pleasures follow'd the sight of the *Alpes*, and what unusual transports think you were those, that were mingled with horrours, and sometimes almost with despair? But if these Mountains were not a Creation, but form'd by universal Destruction, when the Arch with a mightly flaw dissolv'd and fell into the vast Abyss (which surely is the best opinion) then are these Ruines of the old World the greatest wonders of the New. For they are not only vast, but horrid, hideous, ghastly Ruins. After we had gallop'd a League over the Plain, and came at last to descend, to descend thro the very Bowels as it were of the Mountains, for we seem'd to be enclosed on all sides: What an astonishing Prospect was there? Ruins upon Ruins in monstrous Heaps, and Heaven and Earth confounded. The uncouth Rocks that were above us, Rocks that were void of all form, but what they had receiv'd from Ruine; the frightful view of the Precipices, and the foaming Waters that threw themselves headlong down them, made all such a Consort up for the Eye, as that sort of Musick does for the Ear, in which Horrour can be joyn'd with Harmony. I am afraid you will think that I have said too much. Yet if you had but seen what I have done, you would surely think that I have said too little. However Hyperboles might easily here be forgiven. The *Alpes* appear to be Nature's extravagancies, and who should blush to be guilty of Extravagancies, in words that make mention of her's?

John Dennis, *Miscellanies in Verse and Prose*

Berkeley's Winter Crossings of the Alps

To Prior, Turin, 6 January 1714

Dear Tom,

At Lyons, where I was about eight days, it was left to my choice whether I would go from thence to Toulon, and there embark for Genoa, or else pass through Savoy, cross the Alps, and so through Italy. I chose the latter route . . .

The first day we made from Lyons to Chambery, the capital of Savoy, which is reckoned sixty miles. The Lionnois and Dauphiné were very well, but Savoy was a perpetual chain of rocks and mountains, almost impassible for ice and snow. And yet I rode post through it, and came off with only four falls; from which I received no other damage than the breaking my sword, my watch, and my snuff-box.

On New Year's Day we passed Mount Cenis, one of the most difficult and formidable parts of the Alps which is ever passed over by mortal men. We were carried in open chairs by men used to scale these rocks and precipices, which in this season are more slippery and dangerous than at other times, and at the best are high, craggy, and steep enough to cause the heart of the most valiant man to melt within him. My life often depended on a single step. No one will think that I exaggerate, who considers what it is to pass the Alps on New Year's Day. But I shall leave particulars to be described by the fire-side . . .

To Percival, Turin, 24 November 1716

. . . I never thought I should pass Mount Cenis a second time in winter. But we have now passed in a worse condition than it was when I saw it before. It blew and snowed bitterly all the time. The snow almost blinded us and reached above the waists of the men who carried us. They let me fall six or seven times, and thrice on the brinks of horrid precipices, the snow having covered the path so that it was impossible to avoid making false steps. The porters assured us they never in their lives had passed the mountain in such an ill wind and weather. However, blessed be God, we arrived safe at Turin two nights ago, and design to set out from hence towards Milan tomorrow.

I forgot to tell you that we saw two avalanches of snow (as the men called them) on the mountain, I mean huge quantities of snow fallen from the side and top of rocks, sufficient to have overwhelmed a regiment of men. They told us of fourteen men, and about fifty mules that were some time since destroyed by an accident of that kind. I must not omit another adventure in Dauphiné. A huge dark coloured Alpine wolf ran across an open plain when our chaise was passing, when he came near us he turned about and made a stand with a very fierce and daring look, I instantly drew my sword and Mr Ashe fired his pistol. I did the same too, upon which the beast very calmly retired, looking back ever and anon. We were much mortified that he did not attack us and give us the opportunity of killing him.

George Berkeley, Collected Works, Volume VIII

Rousseau Entertains Himself

I like to walk at my leisure, and halt when I please. The wandering life is what I like. To journey on foot, unhurried, in fine weather and in fine country, and to have something pleasant to look forward to at my goal, that is of all ways of life the one that suits me best. It is already clear what I mean by fine country. Never does a plain, however beautiful it may be, seem so in my eyes. I need torrents, rocks, firs, dark woods, mountains, steep roads to climb or descend, abysses beside me to make me afraid. I had these pleasures, and I relished them to the full, as I came near to Chambéry. At a place called Chailles, not far from a precipitous mountain wall called the Pas de L'Échelle, there runs boiling through hideous gulfs below the high road – which is cut into the rock – a little river which would appear to have spent thousands of centuries excavating its bed. The road has been edged with a parapet to prevent accidents, and so I was able to gaze into the depths and make myself as giddy as I pleased. For the amusing thing about my taste for precipitous places is that they make my head spin; and I am very fond of this giddy feeling so long as I am in safety. Supporting myself firmly on the parapet, I craned forward and stayed there for hours on end, glancing every now and then at the foam and the blue water, whose roaring came to me amidst the screams of the ravens and birds of prey which flew from rock to rock and from bush to bush, a hundred fathoms below me. At those spots where the slope was fairly smooth, and the bushes thin enough to allow of stones bouncing through, I collected some of the biggest I could carry from a little way off and piled them up on the parapet. Then I threw them down, one after another, and enjoyed watching them roll, rebound, and shiver into a thousand pieces before they reached the bottom of the abyss.

Nearer to Chambéry I saw a similar sight, though from an opposite angle. The road passes the foot of the finest waterfall I have seen in all my life. The mountain is so sheer that the water springs away and falls in an arc wide enough for a man to walk between the falls and the rock-face, sometimes without getting damp. But unless one is careful one can easily make a mistake, as I did. For, because of the immense height, the water breaks and falls in a spray; and if one goes a little too near without at first noticing that one is getting wet, one is soaked in a moment.

Jean-Jacques Rousseau, *Confessions*

Mountains Pregnant with Religion and Poetry

To Richard West, Turin, 16 November 1739

After eight days journey through Greenland, we arrived at Turin . . . The palace here in town is the very quintessence of gilding and looking-glass; inlaid floors, carved pannels, and painting, wherever they could stick a brush. I own I have not, as yet, any where met with those grand and simple works of Art, that are to amaze one, and whose sight one is to be the better for: But those of Nature have astonished me beyond expression. In our little journey up to the Grande Chartreuse I do not remember to have gone ten paces without an exclamation, that there was no restraining: Not a precipice, not a torrent, not a cliff, but is pregnant with religion and poetry. There are certain scenes that would awe an atheist into belief, without the help of other argument. One need not have a very fantastic imagination to see spirits there at noon-day: You have Death perpetually before your eyes, only so far removed, as to compose the mind without frighting it. I am well persuaded St Bruno was a man of no common genius, to choose such a situation for his retirement; and perhaps should have been a disciple of his, had I been born in his time. You may believe Abelard and Heloïse were not forgot upon this occasion: If I do not mistake, I saw you too every now and then at a distance among the trees . . . You seemed to call to me from the other side of the precipice, but the noise of the river below was so great, that I really could not distinguish what you said; it seemed to have a cadence like verse. In your next you will be so good as to let me know what it was. The week we have since passed among the Alps, has not equalled the single day upon that mountain, because the weather was rather too far advanced, and the weather a little foggy. However, it did not want its beauties; the savage rudeness of the view is inconceivable without seeing it: I reckoned in one day, thirteen cascades, the last of which was, I dare say, one hundred feet in height . . . The creatures that inhabit them are, in all respects, below humanity; and most of them, especially women, have the tumidum guttur, which they call goscia. Mont Cenis, I confess, carries the permission mountains have of being frightful rather too far; and its horrors were accompanied with too much danger to give one time to reflect upon their beauties.

Thomas Gray, Correspondence

The Glaciers of Savoy

We set out about Noon, the 22nd of June, and crossed the *Arve* over a wooden Bridge. Most Maps place the *Glacieres* on the same side with *Chamoigny*, but this is a Mistake. We were quickly at the Foot of the Mountain, and began to ascend by a very steep Path through a Wood of Firs and Larche Trees. We made many Halts to refresh ourselves, and take breath, but we kept on at a good Rate. After we had passed the Wood, we came to a kind of Meadow, full of large Stones, and Pieces of Rocks, that were broke off, and fallen down from the Mountain; the Ascent was so steep that we were obliged sometimes to cling to them with our Hands, and make use of Sticks, with sharp Irons at the End, to support ourselves. Our Road lay slantways, and we had several Places to cross where the *Avalanches* of Snow were fallen, and had made terrible Havock; there was nothing to be seen but Trees torn up by the Roots, and large Stones, which seemed to lie without any Support; every step we set, the Ground gave way, the Snow which was mixed with it made us slip, and had it not been for Staffs, and our Hands, we must many times have gone down the Precipice. We had an uninterrupted View quite to the Bottom of the Mountain, and the Steepness of the Descent, join'd to the Height where we were, made a View terrible enough to make most People's Heads turn. In short, after climbing with great Labour for four Hours and three Quarters, we got to the Top of the Mountain, from whence we had the Pleasure of beholding Objects of an extraordinary Nature. We were on the Top of a Mountain, which, as well as we could judge, was at least twice as high as Mount *Saleve*, from thence we had a full View of the *Glacieres*. I own to you that I am extremely at a Loss how to give a right Idea of it, as I know no one thing which I have ever seen that has the least Resemblance to it.

The Description which Travellers give of the Seas of *Greenland* seems to come the nearest to it. You must imagine your Lake put in Agitation by a strong Wind, and frozen all at once, perhaps even that would not produce the same Appearance.

The *Glacieres* consist of three large Valleys, that form a kind of Y, the Tail reached into the *Val d'Aoste*, and the two Horns into the Valley of *Chamoigny*, the Place where we ascended was between them, from whence we saw plainly the Valley, which forms one of these Horns.

I had unluckily left at *Chamoigny* a pocket Compass, which I had carried with me, so that I could not well tell the Bearings as to its Situation; but

I believe it to be pretty nearly from North to South. These Valleys, although at the top of a high Mountain, are surrounded with other Mountains; the Tops of which, being naked and craggy rocks, shoot up immensely high; something resembling old Gothic Buildings or Ruines, nothing grows upon them, they are all the Year round covered with Snow; and our Guides assured us, that neither the *Chamois* nor any Birds, ever went so high as the Top of them.

Those who search after Crystal, go in the Month of *August* to the Foot of these Rocks, and strike against them with Pick-Axes; if they hear them resound as if they were hollow, they work there, and opening the Rock, they find Caverns full of Crystalisations. We should have been very glad to have gone there, but the Season was not enough advanced, the Snow not being yet sufficiently melted. As far as our Eye-sight could reach, we saw nothing but this Valley; the Height of the Rocks, which surrounded it, made it impossible for the Eye to judge exactly how wide it was; but I imagine it must be near three Quarters of a League. Our Curiosity did not stop here, we were resolved to go down upon the Ice; we had about four hundred Yards to go down, the Descent was excessively steep, and all of a dry crumbling Earth, mixt with Gravel, and little loose Stones, which afforded us no firm footing; so that we went down partly falling, and partly sliding on our Hands and Knees. At length we got upon the Ice, where our difficulty ceased, for that was extremely rough, and afforded us good footing; we found in it an infinite number of Cracks, some we could step over, others were several Feet wide. These Cracks were so deep, that we could not even see to the Bottom; those who go in search of Crystal are often lost in them, but their Bodies are generally found again after some Days, perfectly well preserved. All our Guides assured us, that these Cracks change continually, and that the whole *Glaciere* has a kind of Motion. In going up the Mountain we often heard something like a Clap of Thunder, which, as we were informed by our Guides, was caused by fresh Cracks then making; but as there were none made while we were upon the Ice, we could not determine whether it was that, or *Avalanches* of Snows, or perhaps Rocks falling; though since Travellers observe, that in *Greenland* the Ice cracks with a Noise that resembles Thunder, it might very well be what our Guides told us. As in all Countries of Ignorance People are extremely superstitious, they told us many strange Stories of Witches, etc., who came to play their Pranks upon the *Glacieres*, and dance to the Sound of Instruments. We should have been surprised if we had not been entertained in these Parts, with some such idle Legends. The *Bouquetins* [ibex] go in Herds often to the number of fifteen or sixteen upon the Ice, we saw one of them; there were some *Chamois* which we shot at but at too great Distance to do any Execution.

There is Water continually issuing out of the *Glacieres*, which the People look on as so very wholesome, that they say it may be drank of in any Quantities without Danger, even when one is hot with Exercise.

The Sun shone very hot, and the Reverberation of the Ice and circumjacent Rocks, caused a great deal of thaw'd Water to lie in all the Cavities of the Ice; but I fancy it freezes there constantly as soon as Night comes on.

Our Guides assured us, that, in the time of their Fathers, the *Glaciere* was but small, and that there was even a Passage thro' these Valleys, by which they could go into the *Val d'Aoste* in six hours; But that the *Glaciere* was so much increased, that the Passage was then quite stopped up, and that it went on increasing every Year.

We found on the Edge of the *Glaciere* several Pieces of Ice, which we took at first for Rocks, being as big as a House; these were Pieces quite separate from the *Glaciere*. It is difficult to conceive how they came to be formed there.

Having remained about half an Hour upon the *Glaciere*, and having drunk there in Ceremony Admiral Vernon's Health, and Success to the *British* Arms, we climb'd to the Summit, from whence we came, with incredible Difficulty, the Earth giving way at every step we set. From thence, after having rested ourselves a few Minutes, we began to descend and arrived at *Chamouny* just about Sun-set, to the great astonishment of all the People of the Place, and even of our Guides, who owned to us they thought we should not have gone through with our Undertaking.

William Windham, *An Account of the Glacieres of Savoy*, 1744

Barbarism and Beauty

To John Home of Ninewells, Knittefeldt in Stiria, 28th April 1748

This is about 120 Miles from Vienna. The first 40 is a fine well cultivated Plain: After which we enter the Mountains; and as we are told, we have three hundred Miles more of them, before we reach the Plains of Lombardy. The way of travelling thro' a mountainous Country is generally very agreeable. We are oblig'd to trace the Course of the Rivers; and are always in a pretty Valley surrounded by high Hills, and have a constant and very quick Succession of wild agreeable Prospects every quarter of a Mile. Thro Stiria nothing can be more curious than the Scenes. In the Vallies, which are fertile and finely cultivated, there is at present a full Bloom of Spring: The Hills, to a certain Height, are cover'd with Firs & Larch-Trees: the Tops are all shining with snow. You may see a Tree white with Blossom; & fifty Fathom farther up, the Ground white with Snow. These Hills, as you may imagine, give a great Command of Water to the Vallies, which the industrious

Inhabitants distribute into every Field & render the whole very fertile. There are many Iron Mines in the Country; & the Vallies are upon that Account extremely populous. But as much as the Country is agreeable in its Wildness; as much are the Inhabitants savage & deform'd & monstrous in their Appearance. Very many of them have ugly swelld Throats: Idiots, & Deaf People swarm in every Village; & the general Aspect of the People is the most shocking I ever saw. One wou'd think, that as this was the great Road, thro which all the barbarous Nations made their Irruptions into the Roman Empire, they always left here the Refuse of their Armies before they entered into the Enemies Country; and that from thence the present Inhabitants are descended. Their Dress is scarce European as their Figure is scarce human. There happen'd, however a thing to day, which surpriz'd us all. The Empress Queen, regarding this Country as a little barbarous, has sent some Missionaries of Jesuites to instruct them. They had Sermons to day in the Street under our Windows, attended with Psalms: And believe me, nothing cou'd be more harmonious, better tun'd, or more agreeable than the Voices of these Savages, and the Chorus of a French Opera does not sing in better Time . . .

Trent 8th of May
We are still amongst Mountains, & follow the Tract of Rivers in order to find our Way: But the Aspect of the People is wonderfully chang'd on entering the Tirol. The Inhabitants are there as remarkably beautiful as the Stirians are ugly. An Air of Humanity, & Spirit & Health & Plenty is seen in every Face: Yet their Country is wilder than Stiria. The Hills higher, & the Vallies narrower & more barren. They are both Germans subject to the House of Austria; so that it wou'd puzzle a Naturalist or Politician to find the Reason of so great and remarkable a Difference. We trac'd up the Drave to its Source (That River, you know, falls into the Danube & into the Black Sea:) It ended in a small Rivulet, & that in a Ditch, & that in a little Bog. On the Top of the Hill, (tho there was there a well cultivated Plain) there was no more Appearance of Spring than at Christmas. In about half a mile after we had seen the Drave extinguish, we observ'd a little Strype of Water to move: This was the beginning of the Adige, & the rivers then run into the Adriatic. We were now turning towards the South part of the Hill; and descended with great Rapidity. Our little Brook in three or four Miles became a considerable River, and every hours travelling show'd us a new Aspect of Spring. So that in one day, we past thro' all the Gradations of that Beautiful Season, as we descended lower into the Vallies, from its first faint Dawn till its full Bloom & Glory.

David Hume, *Letters*

Gray in Borrowdale, 1769

October 3.   Wind at S.E.; a heavenly day. Rose at 7, and walked out under the conduct of my landlord to Borrodale. The grass was covered with a hoar frost, which soon melted, and exhaled in a thin blueish smoke. Crossed the meadows obliquely, catching a diversity of views among the hills over the lake and islands, and changing prospect at every ten paces; left *Cockshut* and *Castlehill* (which we formerly mounted) behind me, and drew near the foot of *Walla-crag*, whose bare and rocky brow, cut perpendicularly down above 400 feet, as I guess, awefully overlooks the way; our path here tends to the left, and the ground gently rising, and covered with a glade of scattering trees and bushes on the very margin of the water, opens both ways the most delicious view, that my eyes ever beheld. Behind you are the magnificent heights of *Walla-crag*; opposite lie the thick hanging woods of Lord Egremont, and *Newland* valley, with green and smiling fields embosomed in the dark cliffs; to the left the jaws of *Borrodale*, with the turbulent chaos of mountain behind mountain, rolled in confusion; beneath you, and stretching far away to the right, the shining purity of the *Lake*, just ruffled by the breeze, enough to shew it is alive, reflecting rocks, woods, fields, and inverted tops of mountains, with the white buildings of *Keswick*, *Crosthwait* church, and *Skiddaw* for a back ground at a distance . . .

The crags, named *Lodor-banks*, now begin to impend terribly over your way; and more terribly, when you hear, that three years since an immense mass of rock tumbled at once from the brow, and barred all access to the dale (for this is the only road) till they could work their way through it. Luckily no one was passing at the time of this fall; but down the side of the mountain, and far into the lake lie dispersed the huge fragments of this ruin in all shapes and in all directions. Something farther we turned aside into a coppice, ascending a little in front of *Lodor* water-fall, the height appears to be about 200 feet, the quantity of water not great, though (these three days excepted) it had rained daily in the hills for near two months before: but then the stream was nobly broken, leaping from rock to rock, and foaming with fury. On one side a towering crag, that spired up to equal, if not to overtop, the neighbouring cliffs (this lay all in shade and darkness) on the other hand a rounder broader projecting hill shagged with wood and illumined by the sun, which glanced sideways on the upper part of the cataract. The force of the water wearing a deep channel in the ground hurries away to join the lake. We descended again, and passed the stream over a rude bridge. Soon after we came under *Gowder* crag, a hill more formidable to the eye and to the apprehension than that of *Lodor*; the rocks a-top, deep-cloven perpendicularly by the rains, hanging loose and nodding forwards, seem just starting from their base in shivers; the whole way down, and the road on both sides is strewed with piles of the fragments strangely thrown across each other, and of a dreadful bulk. The place reminds one of those passes in the Alps, where the guides tell you to move on with speed, and say nothing, lest the agitation of the air should loosen the snows above, and bring down a mass, that would overwhelm a caravan . . .

Met a civil young farmer overseeing his reapers (for it is oat-harvest here) who conducted us to a neat white house in the village of Grange, which is built on a rising ground in the midst of a valley. Round it the mountains form an awful amphitheatre, and through it obliquely runs the Derwent clear as glass, and shewing under its bridge every trout that passes. Beside the village rises a round eminence of rock, covered entirely with old trees, and over that more proudly towers Castle-crag, invested also with wood on its sides, and bearing on its naked top some traces of a fort said to be Roman. By the side of this hill, which almost blocks up the way, the valley turns to the left and contracts its dimensions, till there is hardly any road but the rocky bed of the river. The wood of the mountains increases and their summits grow loftier to the eye, and of more fantastic forms: among them appear *Eagles's Cliff, Dove's Nest, Whitedale-pike, &C* celebrated names in the annals of Keswick. The dale opens about four miles higher till you come to *Sea Whaite* (where lies the way mounting the hills to the right, that leads to the *Wadd-mines*) all farther access is here barred to prying mortals, only there is a little path winding over the Fells, and for some weeks in the year passable to the Dale's-men; but the mountains know well, that these innocent people will not reveal the mysteries of their ancient kingdom, the reign of Chaos and Old Night. Only I learned, that this dreadful road, dividing again, leads one branch to *Ravenglas*, and the other to *Hawkshead*.

For me I went no farther than the farmer's (better than 4 m: from Keswick) at *Grange*: his mother and he brought us butter, that Siserah would have jumped at, though not in a lordly dish, bowls of milk, thin oaten cakes, and ale; and we had carried a cold tongue thither with us. Our farmer was himself the man, that last year plundered the eagle's eirie: all the dale are up in arms on such an occasion, for they lose abundance of lambs yearly, not to mention hares, partridge, grouse &c. He was let down from the cliff in ropes to the shelf of rock, on which the nest was built, the people above shouting and hollowing to fright the old birds, which flew screaming round, but did not dare to attack him. He brought off the eaglet (for there is rarely more than one) and an addle egg. The nest was roundish and more than a yard over, made of twigs twisted together . . .

Walked leisurely home the way we came, but saw a new landscape: the features indeed were the same in part, but many new ones were disclosed by the midday sun, and the tints were entirely changed. Take notice this was the best or perhaps the only day for going up Skiddaw, but I thought it better employed: it was perfectly serene, and hot as Midsummer.

Thomas Gray, *Journal in the Lakes*

Johnson in the Highlands

The journey of this day was long, not that the distance was great, but that the way was difficult. We were now in the bosom of the Highlands, with full leisure to contemplate the appearance and properties of mountainous regions, such as have been, in many countries, the last shelters of national distress, and are every where the scenes of adventures, stratagems, surprises and escapes.

Mountainous countries are not passed but with difficulty, not merely from the labour of climbing; for to climb is not always necessary: but because that which is not mountain is commonly bog, through which the way must be picked with caution. Where there are hills, there is much rain, and the torrents pouring down into the intermediate spaces, seldom find so ready an outlet, as not to stagnate, till they have broken the texture of the ground.

Of the hills, which our journey offered to the view on either side, we did not take the height, nor did we see any that astonished us with their loftiness. Towards the summit of one, there was a white spot, which I should have called a naked rock, but the guides, who had better eyes, and were acquainted with the phaenomena of the country, declared it to be snow. It had already lasted to the end of August, and was likely to maintain its contest with the sun, till it should be reinforced by winter.

The height of mountains philosophically considered is properly computed from the surface of the next sea; but as it affects the eye or imagination of the passenger, as it makes either a spectacle or an obstruction, it must be reckoned from the place where the rise begins to make a considerable angle with the plain. In extensive continents the land may, by gradual elevation, attain great height without any other appearance than that of a plane gently inclined, and if a hill placed upon such raised ground be described, as having its altitude equal to the whole space above the sea, the representation will be fallacious.

These mountains may be properly enough measured from the inland base; for it is not much above the sea. As we advanced at evening towards the western coast, I did not observe the declivity to be greater than is necessary for the discharge of the inland waters.

We passed many rivers and rivulets, which commonly ran with a clear shallow stream over a hard pebbly bottom. These channels, which seem so much wider than the water that they convey would naturally require, are formed by the violence of wintry floods, produced by the accumulation of innumerable streams that fall in rainy weather from the hills, and bursting away with resistless impetuosity, make themselves a passage proportionate to their mass.

Such capricious and temporary waters cannot be expected to produce many fish. The rapidity of the wintry deluge sweeps them away, and the scantiness of the summer stream would hardly sustain them above the ground. This is the reason why in fording the northern rivers, no fishes are seen, as in England, wandering in the waters.

Of the hills many may be called with Homer's Ida *abundant in springs*, but few can deserve the epithet which he bestows on Pelion by *waving their leaves*. They exhibit very little variety; being almost wholly covered with dark heath, and even that seems to be checked in its growth. What is not heath is nakedness, a little diversified by now and then a stream rushing down the steep. An eye accustomed to flowery pastures and waving harvests is astonished and repelled by this wide extent of hopeless sterility. The appearance is that of matter incapable of form or usefulness, dismissed by nature from her care and disinherited of her favours, left in its original elemental state, or quickened only with one sullen power of useless vegetation.

It will very readily occur, that this uniformity of barrenness can afford very little amusement to the traveller; that it is easy to sit at home and conceive rocks and heath, and waterfalls; and that these journeys are useless labours, which neither impregnate the imagination, nor enlarge the understanding. It is true that of far the greater part of things, we must content ourselves with such knowledge as description may exhibit, or analogy supply; but it is true likewise, that these ideas are always incomplete, and that at least, till we have compared them with realities, we do not know them to be just. As we see more, we become possessed of more certainties, and consequently gain more principles of reasoning, and found a wider basis of analogy.

Regions mountainous and wild, thinly inhabited, and little cultivated, make a great part of the earth, and he that has never seen them, must live unacquainted with much of the face of nature, and with one of the great scenes of human existence.

As the day advanced towards noon, we entered a narrow valley not very flowery, but sufficiently verdant. Our guides told us, that the horses could not travel all day without rest or meat, and intreated us to stop here, because no grass would be found in any other place. The request was reasonable and the argument cogent. We therefore willingly dismounted and diverted ourselves as the place gave us opportunity.

I sat down on a bank, such as a writer of Romance might have delighted to feign. I had indeed no trees to whisper over my head, but a clear rivulet streamed at my feet. The day was calm, the air soft, and all was rudeness, silence and solitude. Before me, and on either side, were high hills, which by hindering the eye from ranging, forced the mind to find entertainment for itself. Whether I spent the hour well I know not; for here I first conceived the thought of this narration.

We were in this place at ease and by choice, and had no evils to suffer or to fear; yet the imaginations excited by the view of an unknown and untravelled wilderness are not such as arise in the artificial solitude of parks and gardens, a flattering notion of self-sufficiency, a placid indulgence of voluntary delusions, a secure expansion of the fancy, or a cool concentration of the mental powers. The phantoms which haunt a desert are want, and misery, and danger; the evils of dereliction rush upon the thoughts; man is made unwillingly acquainted with his own weakness, and meditation shows him only how little he can sustain, and how little he can perform. There were no traces of inhabitants, except perhaps a rude pile of clods called a summer hut, in which a herdsman had rested in the favourable seasons. Whoever had been in the place where I then sat, unprovided with provisions and ignorant of the country, might, at least before the roads were made, have wandered among the rocks, till he had perished with hardship, before he could have found either food or shelter. Yet what are these hillocks to the ridges of Taurus, or these spots of wildness to the deserts of America?

Samuel Johnson, *A Journey to the Western Islands of Scotland*

Boswell on the Same Road

We passed through Glensheal, with prodigious mountains on each side. We saw where the battle was fought in the year 1719. Dr Johnson owned he was now in a scene of as wild nature as he could see; but he corrected me sometimes in my inaccurate observations. 'There (said I) is a mountain like a cone'. *Johnson*. 'No, sir. It would be called so in a book; and when a man comes to look at it, he sees it is not so. It is indeed pointed at the top; but one side of it is larger than the other'. – Another mountain I called immense. – *Johnson*. 'No; it is no more than a considerable protuberance.'

James Boswell, *Journal of a Tour to the Hebrides*

CHAPTER 8

◆

The Ascent of Mont Blanc

Mont Blanc, the highest mountain in the Alps, was also the first of its major peaks to be climbed. The first ascent was made in 1786 by Michel Gabriel Paccard, a physician, and Jacques Balmat, a peasant crystal collector. The account printed below was dictated by Balmat to Alexandre Dumas; it is very self-serving, giving Balmat the major credit for the ascent. Modern scholars have shown beyond doubt that in fact Paccard and Balmat played equal parts in leading the ascent. But though it should be read with caution as a historical narrative, the Balmat-Dumas account remains a marvellous story.

◆ ◆ ◆

Balmat's Dream Come True

In those days I really was something worth looking at. I had a famous calf and a stomach like cast-iron, and could walk three days consecutively without eating, a fact I found useful to me when lost on the Buet. I munched a little snow – nothing more. Every now and then I cast a sidelong look at Mont Blanc and said to myself, 'My fine fellow, whatever you may say or whatever you may do, I shall get to the top of you some day. You will not escape me!' Night and day this thought kept running in my brain. By day I used to climb the Brévent, whence Mont Blanc can be seen to such advantage. I passed hours there searching with eagerness to discover a route. 'Bah!' said I, 'if there is no way up the mountain I must make one, for up I must go.' At night everything was changed. No sooner were my eyes closed than I found myself 'en route' and went along as gaily as if there had been a royal road to the summit. 'Upon my word,' I would say to myself in my dream, 'I was a fool to think Mont Blanc was a difficulty.' Then little by little the way would get narrower, but still there was a good footpath like the one up the Flégère. I would keep on and come at last to where there was no road at all, and then, stumbling on in unknown regions, the ground would move and swallow me up to the knees. 'Never mind,' I would say, and go struggling on – how stupid one is in a dream! – I should get out at last, but have to go on all fours as the way became steeper and steeper and everything worse and worse.

I would plant my feet on pieces of rock and feel them shake like loose teeth, and the sweat would fall from me in great drops. I felt stifled and as if I had nightmare. Never mind, keep going. I was like a lizard on a wall. I saw the earth sinking away beneath me. It was all the same, I only looked at the sky. All I cared for was to reach the top; but my legs, my grand legs, failed me, and I could no longer bend them. I would catch at the stones with my nails and feel that I was going to fall, and then would say to myself, 'Jacques Balmat, my friend, if you don't catch hold of that branch your time has come.' I shall always remember that accursed branch; one night I touched it with the tips of my fingers, and drawing up my legs as if I were rowing, clutched it, saying, 'Now I have you! now all will go well.' At that moment I was awakened by a vigorous box on the ear by my wife, and, would you believe it, I had caught hold of her ear and was tugging at it as if it were indiarubber.

After that awakening I felt that the time for action was come, and I determined on leaving my bed to set to work in earnest. I began by pulling on my gaiters. 'Where are you going?' said my wife. 'To look for crystals,' I replied, 'and don't be uneasy if I don't come back to-night; if I am not home by nine o'clock I shall be sleeping somewhere on the mountains.' I did not want her to know my intentions. I took a stout alpenstock tipped with iron, double the length and thickness of an ordinary one, filled my gourd with brandy, put some bread in my pocket, and set off.

I had already made several attempts to climb the mountain by the Mer de Glace and had always been stopped by the Mont Maudit. I would some-times try by the Aiguille de Gouter, but thence to the Dome there was a kind of arête about a quarter of a league long and one or two feet wide and more than 1800 feet in depth. 'No, thank you, not that way,' I said. I there-fore determined this time to change the route, and went by the Montagne de la Côte. At the end of three hours I reached the Glacier des Bossons. No great difficulty there. Four hours after that I arrived at the Grands Mulets. 'Well,' I thought, 'now I deserve some breakfast,' and I took a bit of bread and a sup from my gourd. That was good!

At this time there was no level ground at the Grands Mulets, and you may fancy it was not over comfortable. I was getting uneasy as to finding a place higher up to pass the night and was alarmed at seeing none, so determined to go further and trust to Providence. At the end of two hours and a half I found a capital place, hard and dry, where the rocks came through the snow and gave me a place of about six or seven feet to lie on, not to sleep however, but to sit upon and wait for daylight, with rather more comfort than lying on the snow. It was now about seven o'clock in the evening, so I broke off my second piece of bread, drank another drop of Cognac, and settled myself on the rock where I should have to pass the night. It did not take long to make my bed. About nine o'clock the mist began to rise like a thick smoke from the valley, and in half an hour it reached and enveloped me; but I was still cheered by the light of the last rays of the setting sun, which had scarcely left the highest summit of Mont Blanc. I followed them with my eyes as long as I could, but at last they disappeared and the day was done. My face was turned towards Chamonix. At my left lay a huge plain of snow which reached up to the Dome du Gouter. At my right, and only a few paces distant, was a precipice of about 800 feet. I did not dare to sleep for fear of rolling down this abyss in a dream. I seated myself on my knapsack and began to knock my hands and feet together to keep them warm. Soon the moon rose, pale and surrounded by clouds which nearly hid her till eleven o'clock. I saw at the same time a hateful cloud come rolling down from the Aiguille du Gouter, which no sooner reached me than it lashed my face with snow.

I covered my face with a handkerchief and said, 'All right, go on; don't mind me.' I heard the falling avalanches rolling and grumbling like thunder. The glaciers cracked, and at every crack it seemed to me as if the mountain moved. I felt neither hungry nor thirsty, but had a violent aching in my head which began at the top and reached to the eyebrows. All this time the fog was as thick as ever. My breath was frozen and my handkerchief and my clothes were soaked with snow, and soon I felt as if I were stark naked. I moved my hands and feet faster, and began to sing to drive away the thoughts that were seething in my brain. My voice seemed to die away in the snow, no echo replied; everything was dead in this ice-bound world and the sound of my own voice almost terrified me. I became silent and afraid. At two o'clock the heavens grew white towards the east, and with the dawn my courage revived. The sun was fighting with the clouds which covered Mont Blanc, and I hoped every moment that he would disperse them, but about four o'clock they grew thicker. The sun was blotted out, and I began to fear that my enterprise must be abandoned for that day. In order to make some progress, even if the ascent should prove impossible, I began to explore the neighbourhood of my rock and spent the whole day on the glacier looking for the best routes. As evening approached, and with it the mist, I descended as far as the Bec à l'Oiseau, where night overtook me. This night was passed more agreeably than the last. I was not on the ice, and was able to sleep a little; but I awoke quite benumbed, and as soon as daylight appeared I crept down to the valley, having promised my wife that I would not be away more than three days. My clothes did not thaw till I reached the village of La Côte. I had hardly gone a hundred steps past it, when I met François Paccard, Joseph Carrier, and Jean Michel Tournier, three guides; they had their knapsacks and alpenstocks with them and wore their climbing clothes. I asked where they were going, and they said in search of kids which had strayed from the children who had been watching them. As these animals are of little value, I felt that the men were trying to deceive, and at once surmised that they were about to attempt the journey which I had just failed to achieve. M. de Saussure had promised a reward to the first man who should gain the summit. Paccard putting one or two questions to me, such as where one could sleep on the Bec à l'Oiseau, my surmise was confirmed. I replied that snow lay everywhere and that a good sleeping place was not possible. I saw that he exchanged signs with the others, which I pretended not to notice. They turned aside and consulted together, and ended by proposing that I should join them and that we should all ascend the mountain together.

I agreed, but said that I must first go home, as I had promised, so as not to break faith with my wife. I went and told her not to be uneasy at another absence. I changed my stockings and gaiters, took some provisions and started at eleven o'clock the same night without taking any rest. At one o'clock I found my comrades at the Bec à l'Oiseau, about four leagues below the place where I had slept. They were sleeping like marmots. I awoke them, and all four began the march upward. That day we crossed the glacier of Taconnay and reached the Grands Mulets, where two days previously I had passed such a dreadful night. We turned to the right, and at three o'clock were on the Dome du Gouter. One of us (Paccard) had begun to be out of breath after the Grands Mulets, and now lay down on one of our coats. On reaching the top of the Dome we saw something black moving on the Aiguille du Gouter, and could not tell whether it was a man or a chamois. We cried out and some one replied. Then after a minute we kept silent, and then words came, 'Hallo, you fellows, stop a bit, we want to climb with you.' We waited for them, which enabled Paccard to reach us, having recovered his powers. At the end of half an hour the others joined us. They were Pierre Balmat and Marie Couttet, who had made a bet that they would be on the Dome du Gouter before my companions. They lost their wager. Meantime I had been using the time to explore, and had gone on nearly a quarter of a league, almost sitting astride on the top of the arête which joins the Dome du Gouter to the top of Mont Blanc. It seemed a path fit only for a rope-dancer, but I did not care, and I believe I should have reached the top if the Pointe Rouge had not barred the way. As it was impossible, however, to get past that, I returned to the spot where I had left my companions; but found nothing but my knapsack. Convinced that they could not get up Mont Blanc that day, they had gone down to the valley, no doubt saying 'Balmat is very active and will soon overtake us'. Finding myself alone, I hesitated for a moment between the desires of following them and the longing to attempt the ascent by myself. I was vexed at their departure, but felt that this time I might be successful, so determined to try. I shouldered my knapsack and started. It was now four o'clock. I crossed the Grand Plateau and came to the Brenva glacier, from which I could see Courmayeur and the Valley of Aosta in Piedmont. Clouds being on the top of Mont Blanc, I did not attempt to climb up, less from the fear of getting lost, than from the certainty that the others, unless they could see me, would never believe that I had reached the summit. I profited by the little daylight still left to seek some place of shelter, but after an hour's search found nothing, and remembering my recent experience, determined to return. I began my descent and reached the Grand Plateau. As I had not then learnt, as I have since done, the use of a veil to preserve my eyes, they became so fatigued by the constant glare of the snow that I could distinguish nothing, but seemed to see patches of blood around me. I sat down to rest, shut my eyes, and let my head fall between my hands. After half an hour my sight was restored, but night was setting in, and as there was no time to be lost I got up and set off. I had not gone many steps when my baton showed that there was no ice below me. I had come to the edge of the great crevasse in which three men had died and out of which Marie Couttet had been pulled up. 'Ah!' I said, 'is that you?' We had, in fact, crossed it in the morning on an ice bridge covered with snow. I searched for it, but as the night became darker could not find it. My sight became worse, the aching in my head returned, I felt no desire for food or drink and was miserably sick and ill.

Obliged to remain near the crevasse till daylight, I put my knapsack on the snow, covered my face with my handkerchief and prepared as best I could to pass another dreadful night. As I was now about two thousand feet higher the cold was more piercing. A fall of fine snow froze me, irresistible drowsiness came over me and thoughts of death passed through my mind. These were evil signs, and I knew that if I had the bad luck to close my eyes they might never re-open. From my perch I could see, ten thousand feet below me, the lights of Chamonix, where my late comrades would be sitting by their firesides or lying snugly in bed, and said to myself, 'Very likely not one of them has a thought to spare for me! Perhaps one may say, while he is poking his fire, or drawing his bedclothes over his ears, "That fool Jacques is very likely knocking his feet together up there!"' I felt no lack of courage, only of strength. No man is made of iron, and I felt far from cheerful. During the short intervals between the crash of avalanches I heard distinctly the barking of a dog at Courmayeur, though it was more than a league and a half to that village from the spot where I was lying. The noise served to distract my thoughts, for it was the only earthly sound that reached me. About midnight the barking ceased, and nothing remained but the deadly silence of the grave. The noise of the glaciers and avalanches could reassure no human being, they could only frighten him. At two o'clock appeared on the horizon that same white line I had formerly observed, and the sun followed as before. Mont Blanc had his nightcap on, and when such is the case he is in a bad temper and no one dare approach him. I knew his disposition and was sufficiently despondent, and began my descent into the valley. I was despondent, but not disheartened by these two vain attempts, but felt quite certain I should be more fortunate a third time. Five hours more and I was back in the village. It was eight o'clock. All was right at home; my wife gave me something to eat, but I was more sleepy than hungry. She wanted me to lie down in the bedroom, but I was afraid of being tormented by the flies, so I went into the barn, stretched myself upon the hay and slept without waking for twenty-four hours.

Three weeks passed without any favourable change in the weather taking place, and without in the least lessening my desire to try again. Dr Paccard, a relative of the guide I have spoken about, desired this time to accompany me, and we agreed to set out on the first fine day. At last, on the eighth of August, 1786, the weather seemed sufficiently settled to venture. I went to Paccard and said, 'Well, Doctor, are you determined? Are you afraid of the cold or the snow or the precipices? Speak out like a man.' 'With you I fear nothing,' was his reply. 'Well then, the time has come to climb the molehill.' The Doctor said that he was quite ready, but just as he shut the door of his house I think his heart failed him a little, for he could not get the key out of the lock and kept turning it first one way and then the other. 'I say, Balmat,' he said, 'if we did the right thing we should take two guides.' 'No,' I replied, 'either you and I go together, or you go with the others. I want to be first, not second.' He thought for a moment, drew out the key, put it in his pocket, and with his head bent down followed me mechanically. In about a minute he gave himself a shake and said, 'Well, I must trust to you Balmat.' 'Forward,' said I, 'and let us trust to Providence.' He tried, but could not sing in tune, which annoyed him. I took him by the arm, and said, 'This project must be known to ourselves only.' We were obliged, however, to take a third person into our confidence. This was the shopkeeper from whom we bought some syrup to mix with the water we should carry. Brandy and wine would have been too strong for such an expedition. As the woman was suspicious we told her everything, and asked her to look out next day on the Dome du Gouter side about nine o'clock in the morning, as we hoped to be there then. We made all our arrangements, took leave of our wives, and set off about five o'clock in the evening, one taking the right and the other the left side of the Arve, so that we might not attract attention. We met again at the village of La Côte. The same evening we slept on the top of La Côte, between the glaciers of Bossons and Taconnay. I carried a rug and used it to muffle the Doctor up like a baby. Thanks to this precaution he passed a tolerable night. As for me, I slept soundly until half-past one. At two the white line appeared, and soon the sun rose without a cloud, brilliant and beautiful, a promise of a glorious day! I awoke the Doctor and we began our day's march. At the end of a quarter of an hour we were struggling with the glacier of Taconnay, a sea full of great crevasses whose depth could not be measured by the eye. The snow bridges gave way under our feet. The Doctor's first steps were halting and uncertain, but the sight of my alertness gave him confidence, and we went on safe and sound. Then began the ascent to the Grands Mulets, which was soon left behind. I showed the doctor where I had passed the first night. He made an expressive grimace, and kept silent for ten minutes; then, stopping suddenly, said, 'Balmat, do you really think we shall get to the top of Mont Blanc today?' I saw how his thoughts were drifting, and laughingly answered him, but gave no promise. Ascending for about two hours we came to the Plateau, where the wind became more and more boisterous, and arrived at last at the projecting rock known as Les Petits Mulets, when a gust of wind carried off the Doctor's hat. I turned round on hearing his cry, and saw the felt hat careering down the mountain towards Courmayeur. With his arms stretched out he looked after it. 'We must go into mourning for it,' I said; 'you will never see it again for it has gone to Piedmont, and good luck be with it!' It seemed as if my little joke had given offence to the wind, for my mouth had scarcely closed when a more violent gust obliged us to lie down on our stomachs to prevent our following the hat. For ten minutes, rise we could not. The wind lashed the mountain sides and passed whistling over our heads, driving great balls of snow almost as big as houses before it. The Doctor was dismayed, but I only thought of the shopwoman we had told to look out for us about this time on the Dome du Gouter. At the first respite I rose, but the Doctor could only follow on all fours; we then came to a point from which we could see the village. Taking out my glass, there, twelve thousand feet below, was our gossiping friend and fifty others snatching a glass from hand to hand to look at us. Considerations of self-respect induced the Doctor to stand up, and that moment we saw that we were recognized, he by his big coat, and I by my ordinary clothes. They made signs to us by waving their hats. I replied by waving mine, but, alas the Doctor's had already taken leave. Having used up all his strength in getting on his feet, neither the encouragement from below, nor my own earnest entreaties could induce him to continue the ascent. My eloquence exhausted, I told him to keep moving so as not to get benumbed. He listened, without seeming to understand, and replied, 'All right'. I saw that he was suffering from the cold, while I also was nearly frozen. Leaving him the bottle, I went on alone, saying that I should very soon come back to find him. He answered 'Yes! yes!' and telling him again to be sure not to stand still, I went off. I had hardly gone thirty paces when, on turning round, I saw him actually sitting down on the snow, with his back turned to the wind as some precaution. From that time onward the route presented no very great difficulty, but as I rose higher the air became much less easy to breathe, and I had to stop almost every ten steps and wheeze like one with consumption. I felt as if my lungs had gone and my chest was quite empty. I folded my handkerchief over my mouth, which made me a little more comfortable as I breathed through it. The cold got worse and worse, and to go a quarter of a league took an hour. I kept walking upward, with my head bent down, but finding that I was on a peak which was new to me, I lifted my head and saw that at last I had reached the summit of Mont Blanc!

I looked round, trembling for fear that there might yet be further some new unattainable aiguille. But no! no! I had no longer any strength to go higher; the muscles of my legs seemed only held together by my trousers. But behold I was at the end of my journey; I was on a spot where no living being had ever been before, no eagle nor even a chamois! I had come alone with no help but my own will and my own strength. Everything around belonged to me! I was the monarch of Mont Blanc! I was the statue on this unique pedestal! Ah, then I turned towards Chamonix and waved my hat on the end of my stick. I could see through my glass the response. My subjects in the valley perceived. The whole village was gathered together in the market place.

When my first moments of exultation were over, my thoughts turned to my poor Doctor, and I went towards him as quickly as I could, calling out his name and getting greatly alarmed at hearing no reply. In a quarter of an hour, I saw him far off rolled up like a ball, but he was quite immovable and made no reply to the shouts which he must certainly have heard. I found him doubled up with his head between his knees, just like a cat when she makes herself into a muff. Tapping him on the shoulder, he raised his head, and I told him that I had been on the top of Mont Blanc. Even this did not interest him; he only asked, 'Where can I lie down and go to sleep?' I told him he had started to go to the top of the mountain and there he would have to go. I lifted him up from the ground, took him by the shoulder and forced him forward several steps. He seemed quite torpid and to care neither whether he went up or down. However, his blood seemed to circulate a little more freely after my efforts, and he asked if there were more gloves like those on my hands, which were of hareskin and made especially for this excursion, without fingers. At that moment I would not have parted with both of them even to my brother, but I gave him one. Shortly after six o'clock we were on the summit and, though the sun shone brilliantly, we saw stars shining in the deep blue sky.

Beneath was nothing but gaunt peaks, ice, rocks, and snow. The great chain which crosses the Dauphiné and stretches as far as the Tyrol was spread out before us, its four hundred glaciers shining in the sunlight. Could there be space for any green ground on the earth? The lakes of Geneva and Neuchâtel were specks of blue on the horizon. To the left lay the mountains of my dear country all fleecy with snow, and rising from meadows of the richest green. To the right was all Piedmont, and Lombardy as far as Genoa, and Italy was opposite.

Paccard could see nothing, but I felt no fatigue and scarcely noticed the difficulty of breathing which had an hour before so oppressed me. We stayed thirty-three minutes, until seven o'clock in the evening, and as there would only be two hours and a half more daylight, I began to descend, taking Paccard in my arms, and waving my hat as one last signal to those in the valley. There was no track to guide us, and the wind was so piercingly cold that the snow remained frozen, and we could only see the little round holes which the iron points of our alpenstocks had made. Paccard was like a child, no energy or will. I guided him along the good places, and pushed, or carried him, along the bad. Night came on, and when we had crossed the crevasse at the foot of the Grand Plateau we were in the dark. Paccard stopped every few minutes, saying he could go no further, and I had to make him, not by persuasion only, but by brute force. At eleven o'clock we left the ice and set foot on solid ground, having lost all the sun's reflected light for more than an hour. Then I allowed Paccard to stop, and was just going to wrap a rug around him when I saw that he could not move his hands. I asked him about them, and he replied that they were useless and with no feeling in them whatever. I took off his gloves and found his hands were dead white, and my own hands also from which I had taken the glove was quite numb. I said, 'Well, we have three frost-bitten hands between us.' He did not mind, but only wanted to lie down and sleep. He told me, however, to rub them with snow, and that was easily done. I began by rubbing his hands and finished by rubbing my own. Soon sensation returned, but accompanied by pains as sharp as if every vein had been pricked by needles. I rolled my baby up in his rug and put him to bed under the shelter of a rock; we ate and drank a little, pressed as close to one another as possible, and fell fast asleep.

In the morning at six o'clock I was awakened by Paccard. 'It is funny Balmat,' he said, 'I can hear the birds singing but can see no daylight. Perhaps because I cannot open my eyes,' and yet they were glaring like those of a horned owl. I replied that he was under a delusion and that he ought to see very well. Then he asked for a little snow, and melting it in the hollow of his hand with a little brandy, rubbed his eyelids with it. This done he saw no better, but his eyes watered profusely. 'Very well,' he said, 'having gone blind, how shall I be able to get down?' 'You must hold on to the strap of my knapsack,' I said, 'and walk behind me', and in this way we descended to the village of La Côte. There I had to leave the Doctor, as I feared my wife would be uneasy, and he managed to get home by feeling his way with his stick. I returned home, and then saw what I looked like. I was quite unrecognisable. My eyes were red, my face black, and my lips blue. Every time I laughed or yawned the blood spouted out from my lips and cheeks, and in addition I was half blind.

Four days afterwards I set out for Geneva to inform M. de Saussure that I had succeeded in scaling Mont Blanc. He had already heard the news from some Englishmen. He came at once to Chamonix and tried the ascent with me, but the weather only allowed us to get as far as the Montagne de la Côte, and it was not till the following year that he carried out his great project.

Jacques Balmat, in Dumas, *Impressions de voyage Suisse*

CHAPTER 9

◆

Wordsworth and Coleridge

All the Romantic poets sought inspiration from the mountains. Wordsworth in *The Prelude* uses recollections of an ascent of Snowdon and of a crossing of the Alps to embody sublime intimations of imagination and intellect. A more lighthearted reaction to the beauty of the mountains is expressed in two of his occasional Lakeland pieces. Coleridge, like Wordsworth, drew from the mountains messages of semi-pantheistic grandeur, but his well-known 'Hymn before Sunrise' is less successful as an evocation of mountain scenery than his long unpublished diary of Lakeland climbing, which is reproduced here. In the last extract of this chapter, we see, through Southey's eyes, the mature Wordsworth celebrating the defeat of Napoleon at a bonfire on Skiddaw, in company with James Boswell's son and a seventy-seven year old Irish peer.

◆ ◆ ◆

Wordsworth on Snowdon

In one of those excursions (may they ne'er
Fade from remembrance!) through the Northern tracts
Of Cambria ranging with a youthful friend,
I left Bethgelert's huts at couching-time,
And westward took my way, to see the sun
Rise from the top of Snowdon. To the door
Of a rude cottage at the mountain's base
We came, and roused the shepherd who attends
The adventurous stranger's steps, a trusty guide;
Then, cheered by short refreshment, sallied forth.

It was a close, warm, breezeless summer night
Wan, dull, and glaring, with a dripping fog,
Low-hung and thick that covered all the sky;
But, undiscouraged, we began to climb
The mountain-side. The mist soon girt us round,
And, after ordinary travellers' talk

With our conductor, pensively we sank
Each into commerce with his private thoughts:
Thus did we breast the ascent, and by myself
Was nothing either seen or heard that checked
Those musings or diverted, save that once
The shepherd's lurcher, who, among the crags,
Had to his joy unearthed a hedgehog, teased
His coiled-up prey with barkings turbulent.
This small adventure, for even such it seemed
In that wild place and at the dead of night,
Being over and forgotten, on we wound,
In silence as before. With forehead bent
Earthward, as if in opposition set
Against an enemy, I panted up
With eager pace, and no less eager thoughts.
Thus might we wear a midnight hour away,
Ascending at loose distance each from each,
And I, as chanced, the foremost of the band;
When at my feet the ground appeared to brighten,
And with a step or two seemed brighter still;
Nor was time given to ask or learn the cause,
For instantly a light upon the turf
Fell like a flash, and lo! as I looked up,
The Moon hung naked in a firmament
Of azure without cloud, and at my feet
Rested a silent sea of hoary mist.
A hundred hills their dusky backs upheaved
All over this still ocean; and beyond,
Far, far beyond, the solid vapours stretched,
In headlands, tongues, and promontory shapes,
Into the main Atlantic, that appeared
To dwindle, and give up his majesty,
Usurped upon far as the sight could reach.
Not so the ethereal vault; encroachment none
Was there, nor loss; only the inferior stars
Had disappeared, or shed a fainter light
In the clear presence of the full-orbed Moon,
Who, from her sovereign elevation, gazed
Upon the billowy ocean, as it lay
All meek and silent, save that through a rift –
Not distant from the shore whereon we stood,
A fixed, abysmal, gloomy, breathing-place –
Mounted the roar of waters, torrents, streams

Innumerable, roaring with one voice!
Heard over earth and sea, and, in that hour,
For so it seemed, felt by the starry heavens.

When into air had partially dissolved
That vision, given to spirits of the night
And three chance human wanderers, in calm thought
Reflected, it appeared to me the type
Of a majestic intellect, its acts
And its possessions, what it has and craves,
What in itself it is, and would become.
There I beheld the emblem of a mind
That feeds upon infinity, that broods
Over the dark abyss, intent to hear
Its voices issuing forth to silent light
In one continuous stream; a mind sustained
By recognitions of transcendent power,
In sense conducting to ideal form,
In soul of more than mortal privilege.
One function, above all, of such a mind
Had Nature shadowed there, by putting forth
'Mid circumstances awful and sublime,
That mutual domination which she loves
To exert upon the face of outward things,
So moulded, joined, abstracted, so endowed
With interchangeable supremacy,
That men, least sensitive, see, hear, perceive,
And cannot choose but feel. The power, which all
Acknowledge when thus moved, which Nature thus
To bodily sense exhibits, is the express
Resemblance of that glorious faculty
That higher minds bear with them as their own.
This is the very spirit in which they deal
With the whole compass of the universe:
They from their native selves can send abroad
Kindred mutations; for themselves create
A like existence; and, whene'er it dawns
Created for them, catch it, or are caught
By its inevitable mastery,
Like angels stopped upon the wing by sound
Of harmony from Heaven's remotest spheres.

Wordsworth, *The Prelude*, Book XIV

The Crossing of the Alps

                              That day we first
Beheld the summit of Mont Blanc, and grieved
To have a soulless image on the eye
Which had usurped upon a living thought
That never more could be. The wondrous Vale
Of Chamouny did, on the following dawn,
With its dumb cataracts and streams of ice,
A motionless array of mighty waves,
Five rivers broad and vast, make rich amends,
And reconciled us to realities;
There small birds warble from the leafy trees,
The eagle soareth in the element,
There doth the reaper bind the yellow sheaf,
The maiden spread the haycock in the sun,
While Winter like a tamèd lion walks,
Descending from the mountain to make sport
Among the cottages by beds of flowers.

Whate'er in this wide circuit we beheld,
Or heard, was fitted to our unripe state
Of intellect and heart. By simple strains
Of feeling, the pure breath of real life,
We were not left untouched. With such a book
Before our eyes, we could not choose but read
A frequent lesson of sound tenderness,
The universal reason of mankind,
The truth of young and old. Nor, side by side
Pacing, two brother pilgrims, or alone
Each with his humour, could he fail to abound
(Craft this which hath been hinted at before)
In dreams and fictions pensively composed:
Dejection taken up for pleasure's sake
And gilded sympathies, the willow wreath,
Even among those solitudes sublime,
And sober posies of funereal flowers,
Culled from the gardens of the lady Sorrow
Did sweeten many a meditative hour.

Yet still in me, mingling with these delights,
Was something of stern mood, an under-thirst
Of vigour, never utterly asleep.

Far different dejection once was mine
A deep and genuine sadness then I felt;
The circumstances here I will relate
Even as they were. Upturning with a Band
Of Travellers, from the Valais we had clomb
Along the road that leads to Italy;
A length of hours, making of these our Guides,
Did we advance, and having reached an Inn
Among the mountains, we together ate
Our noon's repast, from which the Travellers rose,
Leaving us at the Board. Ere long we followed,
Descending by the beaten road that led
Right to a rivulet's edge, and there broke off.
The only track now visible was one
Upon the further side, right opposite,
And up a lofty Mountain. This we took
After a little scruple, and short pause,
And climbed with eagerness, though not, at length,
Without surprise and some anxiety
On finding that we did not overtake
Our Comrades gone before. By fortunate chance,
While every moment now encreased our doubt,
A peasant met us, and from him we learned
That to the place which had perplexed us first
We must descend, and there should find the road
Which in the stony channel of the Stream
Lay a few steps, and then along its Banks:
And further, that thenceforward all our course
Was downwards, with the current of the Stream.
Hard of belief, we questioned him again,
And all the answers which the Man returned
To our inquiries, in their sense and substance,
Translated by the feeling which we had,
Ended in this, *that we had crossed the Alps.*

Imagination! lifting up itself
Before the eye and progress of my Song
Like an unfathered vapour; here that Power,
In all the might of its endowments, came
Athwart me; I was lost as in a cloud,
Halted, without a struggle to break through.
And now recovering, to my Soul I say
'I recognise thy glory.' In such strength

Of usurpation, in such visitings
Of awful promise, when the light of sense
Goes out in flashes that have shown to us
The invisible world, doth Greatness make abode,
There harbours whether we be young or old.
Our destiny, our nature, and our home,
Is with infinitude and only there;
With hope it is, hope that can never die,
Effort, and expectation, and desire,
And something evermore about to be.
The mind beneath such banners militant
Thinks not of spoils or trophies, nor of aught
That may attest its prowess, blest in thoughts
That are their own perfection and reward,
Strong in itself, and in the access of joy
Which hides it like the overflowing Nile.

The dull and heavy slackening that ensued
Upon those tidings by the peasant given
Was soon dislodged; downwards we hurried fast,
And entered with the road which we had missed
Into a narrow chasm. The brook and road
Were fellow-travellers in this gloomy Pass,
And with them did we journey several hours
At a slow step. The immeasurable height
Of woods decaying, never to be decayed,
The stationary blasts of water-falls,
And every where along the hollow rent
Winds thwarting winds, bewildered and forlorn,
The torrents shooting from the clear blue sky,
The rocks that muttered close upon our ears,
Black drizzling crags that spake by the way-side
As if a voice were in them, the sick sight
And giddy prospect of the raving stream,
The unfettered clouds and region of the heavens,
Tumult and peace, the darkness and the light
Were all like workings of one mind, the features
Of the same face, blossoms upon one tree,
Characters of the great Apocalypse,
The types and symbols of Eternity
Of first and last, and midst, and without end.

Wordsworth, *The Prelude*, Book VI

Coleridge's Descent from Broad Crag

6 August 1802

There is one sort of Gambling, to which I am much addicted; and that not of the least criminal kind for a Man who has Children and a Concern. It is this. When I find it convenient to descend from a Mountain, I am too confident and too indolent to look round about and winde about 'till I find a track or other symptom of safety; but I wander on, and where it is first *possible* to descend, there I go, relying upon fortune for how far down this possibility will continue. So it was yesterday afternoon. I passed down from Broad-Crag, skirted the Precipices, and found myself cut off from a most sublime Crag-Summit, that seemed to rival Sca' Fell Man in height, and to outdo it in fierceness. A Ridge of Hill lay low down, and divided this Crag (called Doe-Crag) and Broad-Crag – even as the hyphen divides the word broad and crag. I determined to go thither; the first place I came to, that was not direct Rock, I slipped down, and went on for a while with tolerable ease – but now I came (it was midway down) to a smooth perpendicular Rock about 7 feet high – this was nothing – I put my hands on the Ledge, and dropped down. In a few yards came just such another. I *dropped* that too. And yet another, seemed not higher – I would not stand for a trifle, so I dropped that too – but the stretching of the muscle of my hands and arms, and the jolt of the Fall on my Feet, put my whole Limbs in a *Tremble*, and I paused, and looking down, saw that I had a little else to encounter but a succession of these little Precipices – it was in truth a Path that in a very hard Rain is, no doubt, the channel of a most splendid Waterfall. So I began to suspect that I ought not to go on; but then unfortunately tho' I could with ease drop down a smooth Rock of 7 feet high, I could not *climb* it, so go on I must; and on I went. The next 3 drops were not half a Foot, at least not a foot, more than my own height, but every Drop increased the Palsy of my Limbs. I shook all over, Heaven knows without the least influence of Fear. And now I had only two more to drop down – to return was impossible – but of these two the first was tremendous, it was twice my own height, and the Ledge at the bottom was exceedingly narrow, that if I drop down upon it I must of necessity have fallen backwards and of course kill myself. My limbs were all in a tremble. I lay upon my Back to rest myself, and was beginning according to my Custom to laugh at myself for a Madman, when the sight of the Crags above me on each side, and the impetuous Clouds just over them, posting so luridly and so rapidly to northward, overawed me. I lay in a state of almost prophetic Trance and Delight and blessed God aloud for the powers of Reasons and the Will, which remaining no Danger can overpower us! O God, I exclaimed aloud, how calm, how blessed am I now. I know not how to proceed, how to return, but I am calm and fearless and confident. If this Reality were a Dream, if

I were asleep, what agonies had I suffered! what screams! When the Reason
and the Will are away, what remain to us but Darkness and Dimness and
a bewildering Shame, and Pain that is utterly Lord over us, or fantastic
Pleasure that draws the Soul along swimming through the air in many
shapes, even as a Flight of Starlings in a Wind. – I arose, and looking down
saw at the bottom a heap of Stones which had fallen abroad and rendered
the narrow Ledge on which they had been piled doubly dangerous. At the
bottom of the third Rock that I dropt from, I met a dead Sheep quite rotten.
This heap of stones, I guessed, and have since found that I guessed aright,
had been piled up by the Shepherd to enable him to climb up and free the
poor Creature whom he had observed to be crag-fast, but seeing nothing but
rock over rock, he had desisted and gone for help and in the mean time the
poor Creature had fallen down and killed itself. As I was looking at these
I glanced my eye to my left, and observed that the Rock was rent from top
to bottom. I measured the breadth of the Rent, and found that there was
no danger of my being *wedged* in, so I put my knap-sack round to my side,
and slipped down as between two walls, without any danger or difficulty.
The next Drop brought me down on the Ridge called the How. I hunted
out my Besom Stick, which I had flung before me when I first came to the
Rocks, and wisely gave over all thought of ascending Doe-Crag, for now the
Clouds were again coming in most tumultously. So I began to descend,
when I felt an odd sensation across my whole Breast – not pain nor
itching – and putting my hand on it I found it all bumpy – and on looking
saw the whole of my Breast from my Neck – to my Navel, exactly all that
my Kamell-hair Breast-shield covers, filled with great red heat-bumps, so
thick that no hair could lie between them. They still remain but are evidently less and I have no doubt will wholly disappear in a few Days. It was
however a startling proof to me of the violent exertions which I had made.
I descended this low Hill which was all hollow beneath me – and was like
the rough green Quilt of a Bed of Waters. At length two streams burst out
and took their way down, one on one side a high Ground upon this Ridge,
the other on the other. I took that to my right (having on my left this high
ground, and the other Stream, and beyond that Doe-Crag, on the other side
of which is Esk Halse, where the head-spring of the Esk rises, and running
down the Hill and in upon the Vale looks and actually deceived me, as a
great Turnpike Road – in which, as in many other respects the Head of
Eskdale much resembles Langdale) and soon the Channel sank all at once,
at least 40 yards, and formed a magnificent Waterfall – and close under this
a succession of Waterfalls 7 in number, the third of which is nearly as high
as the first. When I had almost reached the bottom of the Hill, I stood so
as to command the whole 8 Waterfalls, with the great triangle-crag looking
in above them, and on the one side of them the enormous and more than
perpendicular Precipices and *Bull's-Brows*, of Sca' Fell! And now the

Thunder Storm was coming on, again and again! Just at the bottom of the Hill I saw on before me in the Vale, lying just above the River on the side of a Hill, one, two, three, four Objects; I could not distinguish whether Peat-hovels, or hovel-shaped Stones. I thought in my mind, that 3 of them would turn out to be stones – but that the fourth was certainly a Hovel. I went on toward them, crossing and recrossing the Becks and the River and found that they were all huge Stones – the one nearest the Beck which I had determined to be really a Hovel, retained its likeness when I was close beside. In size it is nearly equal to the famous Bowder Stone, but in every other respect greatly superior to it – it has a complete Roof, and that perfectly *thatched* with weeds, and Heath, and Mountain-Ash Bushes. I now was obliged to ascend again, as the River ran greatly to the Left, and the Vale was nothing more than the Channel of the River, all the rest of the interspace between the Mountains was a tossing up and down of Hills of all sizes – and the place at which I am now writing is called Te-as, and spelt Toes – as the Toes of Sca'Fell. It is not possible that any name can be more descriptive of the Head of Eskdale. I ascended close under Sca' Fell and came to a little Village of Sheep-folds – there were 5 together – and the redding Stuff, and the Shears, and an old Pot, was in the passage of the first of them. Here I found an imperfect Shelter from a Thunder-Shower accompanied with such Echoes! O God! What thoughts were mine! O how I wished for Health and Strength that I might wander about for a Month together, in the stormiest month of the year, among these Places, so lonely and savage and full of sounds!

Samuel Taylor Coleridge, *Lake Journal*

'To Joanna'

Amid the smoke of cities did you pass
The time of early youth; and there you learned,
From years of quiet industry, to love
The living Beings by your own fire-side,
With such a strong devotion, that your heart
Is slow to meet the sympathies of them
Who look upon the hills with tenderness,
And make dear friendship with the streams and groves.
Yet we, who are transgressors in this kind,
Dwelling retired in our simplicity
Among the woods and fields, we love you well,
Joanna! and I guess, since you have been
So distant from us now for two long years,
That you will gladly listen to discourse

However trivial, if you thence be taught
That they, with whom you once were happy, talk
Familiarly of you and of old times.

While I was seated, now some ten days past
Beneath those lofty firs, that overtop
Their ancient neighbour, the old steeple-tower
The Vicar from his gloomy house hard by
Came forth to greet me; and when he had asked,
'How fares Joanna, that wild-hearted Maid!
And when will she return to us?' he paused;
And, after short exchange of village news,
He with grave looks demanded for what cause,
Reviving obsolete idolatry,
I, like a Runic Priest, in characters
Of formidable size had chiselled out
Some uncouth name upon the native rock,
Above the Rotha, by the forest-side.
– Now, by those dear immunities of heart,
Engendered between malice and true love,
I was not loth to be so catechised,
And this was my reply:- 'As it befell,
One summer morning we had walked abroad,
At break of day, Joanna and myself.
– 'Twas that delightful season when the broom,
Full-flowered, and visible on every steep,
Along the copses runs in veins of gold.
Our pathway led us on to Rotha's banks;
And, when we came in front of that tall rock
That eastward looks, I there stopped short – and stood
Tracing the lofty barrier with my eye
From base to summit; such delight I found
To note in shrub and tree, in stone and flower,
That intermixture of delicious hues,
Along so vast a surface, all at once,
In one impression, by connecting force
Of their own beauty, imaged in the heart.
– When I had gazed perhaps two minutes' space
Joanna, looking in my eyes, beheld
That ravishment of mine, and laughed aloud.
The Rock, like something starting from a sleep,
Took up the Lady's voice, and laughed again;
That ancient Woman seated on Helm-crag

Was ready with her cavern; Hammar-scar,
And the tall Steep of Silver-how, sent forth
A noise of laughter; southern Loughrigg heard,
And Fairfield answered with a mountain tone;
Helvellyn far into the clear blue sky
Carried the Lady's voice, – old Skiddaw blew
His speaking-trumpet; – back out of the clouds
Of Glaramara southward came the voice;
And Kirkstone tossed it from his misty head.
– Now whether (said I to our cordial Friend
Who in the hey-day of astonishment
Smiled in my face) this were in simple truth
A work accomplished by the brotherhood
Of ancient mountains, or my ear was touched
With dreams and visionary impulses
To me alone imparted, sure I am
That there was a loud uproar in the hills.
And, while we both were listening, to my side
The fair Joanna drew, as if she wished
To shelter from some object of her fear.
– And hence, long afterwards, when eighteen moons
Were wasted, as I chanced to walk along
Beneath this rock, at sunrise, on a calm
And silent morning, I sat down, and there,
In memory of affections old and true,
I chiselled out in those rude characters
Joanna's name deep in the living stone:-
And I, and all who dwell by my fireside,
Have called the lovely rock, JOANNA'S ROCK.

William Wordsworth, *Poems on the Naming of Places*

'To — on her first ascent to the Summit of Helvellyn'

Inmate of a mountain-dwelling,
Thou hast clomb aloft, and gazed
From the watch-towers of Helvellyn;
Awed, delighted, and amazed!

Potent was the spell that bound thee
Not unwilling to obey;
For blue Ether's arms, flung round thee
Stilled the pantings of dismay.

Lo! The dwindled woods and meadows;
What a vast abyss is there!
Lo! the clouds, the solemn shadows,
And the glistenings – heavenly fair!

And a record of commotion
Which a thousand ridges yield;
Ridge, and gulf, and distant ocean
Gleaming like a silver shield!

Maiden! now take flight; – inherit
Alps or Andes – they are thine!
With the morning's roseate Spirit
Sweep their length of snowy line;

Or survey their bright dominions
In the gorgeous colours drest
Flung from off the purple pinions,
Evening spreads throughout the west!

Thine are all the choral fountains
Warbling in each starry vault
Of the untrodden lunar mountains;
Listen to their songs! or halt.

To Niphates' top invited
Whither spiteful Satan steered;
Or descend where the ark alighted,
When the green earth re-appeared;

For the power of hills is on thee,
As was witnessed through thine eye
Then, when old Helvellyn won thee
To confess their majesty!

William Wordsworth, *Poems of the Imagination*

The Bonfire on Skiddaw

To Dr H.H. Southey, for his birthday, 23 August 1815

Monday, the 21st of August, was not a more remarkable day in your life than
it was in that of my neighbour Skiddaw, who is a much older personage. The

weather served for our bonfire, and never, I believe, was such an assemblage upon such a spot. To my utter astonishment, Lord Sunderlin rode up, and Lady S., who has endeavoured to dissuade *me* from going, as a thing too dangerous, joined the walking party. Wordsworth, with his wife, sister, and eldest boy, came over on purpose. James Boswell arrived that morning at the Sunderlins. [My wife] Edith, the Senhora, Edith May, and Herbert were my convoy, with our three maid-servants, some of our neighbours, some adventurous Lakers, and Messrs. Rag, Tag, and Bobtail, made up the rest of the assembly. We roasted beef and boiled plum-puddings there; sung 'God save the King' round the most furious body of flaming tar-barrels that I ever saw; drank a huge wooden bowl of punch; fired cannon at every health with three times three, and rolled large blazing balls of tow and turpentine down the steep side of the mountain. The effect was grand beyond imagination. We formed a huge circle round the most intense light, and behind us was an immeasurable arch of the most intense darkness, for our bonfire fairly put out the moon.

The only mishap which occurred will make a famous anecdote in the life of a great poet, if James Boswell, after the example of his father, keepeth a diary of the sayings of remarkable men. When we were craving for punch, a cry went forth that the kettle had been knocked over, with all the boiling water! Colonel Barker, as Boswell named the Senhora, from her having had the command on this occasion, immediately instituted a strict inquiry to discover the culprit, from a suspicion that it might have been done in mischief, water, as you know, being a commodity not easily replaced on the summit of Skiddaw. The persons about the fire declared it was one of the gentlemen – they did not know his name; but he had a red cloak on; they pointed him out in the circle. The red cloak (a maroon one of Edith's) identified him; Wordsworth had got hold of it, and was equipped like a Spanish Don – by no means the worst figure in the company. He had committed this fatal *faux pas*, and thought to slink off undiscovered. But as soon as, in my inquiries concerning the punch, I learnt his guilt from the Senhora, I went round to all our party, and communicated the discovery, and getting them about him, I punished him by singing a parody, which they all joined in: ' 'Twas *you* that kicked the kettle down! 'twas you, Sir, you!'

The consequences were, that we took all the cold water upon the summit to supply our loss. Our myrmidons and Messrs. Rag and Co. had, therefore, none for their grog; they necessarily drank the rum pure; and you, who are physician to the Middlesex Hospital, are doubtless acquainted with the manner in which alcohol acts upon the nervous system. All our torches were lit at once by this mad company and our way down the hill was marked by a track of fire, from flambeaux dropping the pitch, tarred ropes, & c. One fellow was so drunk that his companions placed him upon a horse, with his face to the tail, to bring him down, themselves being just sober enough to guide and hold him on. Down, however, we all got safely by midnight; and nobody, from the old Lord of seventy-seven to my son Herbert, is the worse for the toil of the day, though we were eight hours from the time we set out till we reached home.

Robert Southey, *Selected Letters*

CHAPTER 10

◆

Post-War Romantics

The reopening of the Alps to British tourists after the defeat of Napoleon in 1815 had considerable significance for mountain literature. The Swiss tour of Percy and Mary Shelley, recorded below in Mary's journal, bore fruit both in *Frankenstein* and in the best of the Romantic odes to Mont Blanc. Lord Byron's Swiss poems were familiar to every Victorian visitor to the country; his more recently published journals evoke the countryside for a modern reader in a manner that is even more lively. Devastated, in 1816, by his wife's severance of relations, he regarded his sister Augusta as his only stable support; and it was for her that he wrote the journal of his travels between Geneva, Chamonix, and the Bernese Oberland in company with his college friend John Hobhouse. John Keats found material for verse, both grave and comic, during a vigorous ascent of Ben Nevis.

◆ ◆ ◆

With Shelley in Chamonix

21 July 1816

At Bonneville the Alps commence, one of which clothed in forest rises almost immediately from the opposite bank of the Arve. From Bonneville to Cluses the road conducts thro a spacious & fertile plain surrounded on all sides by mountains; covered, like those of Mellerie, with forests of intermingled pine & chesnut. At Cluses the route turns suddenly to the right following the Arve along the chasm which it seems to have followed among the perpendicular mountains. The scene assumes here also a more savage & colossal character. The valley becomes narrow affording no more space than is sufficient for the river and the road. The pines descend to the banks, imitating with their regular spires the pyramidal crags which lift themselves far above the regions of forest. The scene, at the distance of half a mile from Cluses differs from that of Matlock in little else than the immensity of its proportions & in its untameable, inaccessible solitude. We now saw many goats browsing on the rocks – Near Maglans, within a league of each other we saw two waterfalls.

They were no more than mountain rivulets, but the height from which they fell, at least 200 feet, made them assume a character inconsistent with the smallness of their stream. The first fell in two parts; – & struck first on an enormous rock resembling precisely some colossal Egyptian statue of a female deity. It struck the head of the visionary Image & gracefully dividing then fell in folds of foam, more like cloud than water, imitating a veil of the most exquisite woof: – It united then, concealing the lower part of the statue, & hiding itself in a winding of its channel burst into a deeper fall, & crossed our route in its path towards the Arve. The other water fall was more continuous, & larger. The violence with which it fell, made it look rather like some shape which an exhalation had assumed – than like water – for it fell beyond the mountain, which appeared dark behind it as it might have appeared behind an evanescent cloud. – The character of the scenery continued the same until we arrived at St Martin. Clouds had overspread the evening & hid the summit of Mont Blanc – its base was visible from the Balcony of the Inn.

Chamounix, July 22 Monday

We leave St Martin on mules at seven o'clock – the road for a league lay through a plain at the end of which we were taken to see the Cascade – the water here falls 250 feet dashing & casting a spray which formed a mist around it – when we approached near to it the rain of the spray reached us and our clothes were wetted with the quick falling but minute particles of water. This cataract fell into the Arve which dashed against its banks like a wild animal who is furious in constraint. As we continued our route to Cervaux the mountains encreased in height & beauty – the summits of the highest were hid in Clouds but they sometimes peeped out into the blue sky higher one would think than the safety of God would permit since it is well known that the tower of Babel did not nearly equal them in immensity – Our route also lay by les chutes d'Arve which is neither so high or grand as the cataract among the mountains but there is something so divine in all this scenery that you love & admire it even where its features are less magnificent than usual.

From Cervaux we continued on a mountainous & rocky path & passed a pine bridge over the Arve – this is one of the loveliest scenes in the world – the white & foamy river broke proudly through the rocks that opposed its progress – Immense pines covered the bases of the Mountains that closed around it & a rock covered with woods & seemingly detached from the rest stood at the End & closed the ravine.

As we mounted still higher this appeared the most beautiful part of our journey – the river foamed far below & the rocks & glaciers towered above – the mighty pines filled the vale & sometimes obstructed our view. We then entered the valley of Chamounix which was much wider than that we had just left & gave room for cultivated fields & cottages – the mountains assumed a more formidable appearance & the Glaciers approached nearer to the road – La Glace de Buisson has the appearance at a distance of a foaming cataract – & on a rear approach the ice seems to have taken the form of pyramids & stactalites – In one village they offered us for sale a poor squirrel which they had caught three days before – We bought it but no sooner had I got it in my hand than he bit my finger & forced me to let it go – we caught it however again & Shelley carried it some time – it appeared at length resigned to its fate when we put it on a railing where it paused an instant wondering where it was & then scampered up its native trees.

As we went along we heard a sound like the rolling of distant thunder & beheld an avalanche rush down the ravine of the rock – it stopped midway but in its course forced a torrent from its bed which now fell to the base of the mountain.

We had passed the torrent here in the morning – the torrents had torn away the road and it was with difficulty we crossed – Clare went on her mule – S. walked & I was carried.

Fatigued to death we arrived at seven oclock at Chamounix.

At the in at servreaux among other laws of the same nature there was an edict of the king of Sardinia's prohibiting his subjects from holding private assemblies on pain of a fine of 12 francs & in default of payment imprisonment – Here also we saw some stones picked up in the mountains & made some purchases.

Tuesday 23rd Chamounix

In the morning after breakfast we mount our mules to see the source of the arveron – when we had gone about three parts of the way we descended & continued our route on foot over loose stones many of which were of an enormous size – We came to the source which lies like a stage surrounded on the three sides by mountains & glaciers – we sat on a rock which formed the fourth – gazing on the scene before us – an immense Glacier was on our left which continually rolled stones to its foot – it is very dangerous to go directly under this – Our Guide told us a story of two Hollanders who went without any guide into a cavern of the Glacier & fired a pistol there which drew down a large piece on them – we see several Avalanches – some very small others of great magnitude which roared and smoked overwhelming every thing as it passed along & precipitating great pieces of ice into the valley below – This Glacier is encreasing every day a foot closing up the valley – We drink some water of the arveron & return – After dinner think it will rain & Shelley goes alone to the Glacier of Boison – I stay at home – read several tales of Voltaire – in the evening I copy S's letter to Peacock.

Mary Shelley, *Geneva Journal*

'Mont Blanc. Lines written in the Vale of Chamouni'

I

The everlasting universe of things
Flows through the mind, and rolls its rapid waves,
Now dark – now glittering – now reflecting gloom –
Now lending splendour, where from secret springs
The source of human thought its tribute brings
Of waters, – with a sound but half its own,
Such as a feeble brook will oft assume
In the wild woods, among the mountains lone,
Where waterfalls around it leap for ever,
Where woods and winds contend, and a vast river
Over its rocks ceaselessly bursts and raves.

II

Thus thou, Ravine of Arve – dark, deep Ravine –
Thou many-coloured, many-voiced vale,
Over whose pines, and crags, and caverns sail
Fast cloud-shadows and sunbeams: awful scene,
Where Power in likeness of the Arve comes down
From the ice-gulfs that gird his secret throne,
Bursting through these dark mountains like the flame
Of lightning through the tempest; – thou dost lie,
Thy giant brood of pines around thee clinging,
Children of elder time, in whose devotion
The chainless winds still come and ever came
To drink their odours, and their mighty singing
To hear – an old and solemn harmony;
Thine earthly rainbows stretched across the sweep
Of the aethereal waterfall, whose veil
Robes some unsculptured image; the strange sleep
Which when the voices of the desert fail
Wraps all in its own deep eternity; –
Thy caverns echoing to the Arve's commotion,
A loud, lone sound no other sound can tame;
Thou are pervaded with that ceaseless motion,
Thou art the path of that unresting sound –
Dizzy ravine! and when I gaze on thee
I seem as in a trance sublime and strange
To muse on my own separate fantasy,
My own, my human mind, which passively
Now renders and receives fast influencings,

Holding an unremitting interchange
With the clear universe of things around;
One legion of wild thoughts, whose wandering wings
Now float above thy darkness, and now rest
Where that or thou art no unbidden guest,
In the still cave of the witch Poesy,
Seeking among the shadows that pass by
Ghosts of all things that are, some shade of thee,
Some phantom, some faint image; till the breast
From which they fled recalls them, thou art there!

III

Some say that gleams of a remoter world
Visit the soul in sleep, – that death is slumber,
And that its shapes the busy thoughts outnumber
Of those who wake and live! – I look on high;
Has some unknown omnipotence unfurled
The veil of fire and death? Or do I lie
In dream, and does the mightier world of sleep
Spread far around and inaccessibly
Its circles? For the very spirit fails,
Driven like a homeless cloud from steep to steep
That vanishes among the viewless gales!
Far, far above, piercing the infinite sky,
Mont Blanc appears, – still, snowy and serene –
Its subject mountains their unearthly forms
Pile around it, ice and rock; broad vales between
Of frozen floods, unfathomable deeps
Blue as the overhanging heaven, that spread
And wind among the accumulated steeps;
A desert peopled by the storms alone,
Save when the eagle brings some hunter's bone,
And the wolf tracks her there – how hideously
Its shapes are heaped around! rude, bare, and high
Ghastly, and scarred, and riven. – Is this the scene
Where the old Earthquake-daemon taught her young
Ruin? Were these their toys? Or did a sea
Of fire envelop once this silent snow?
None can reply – all seems eternal now.
The wilderness has a mysterious tongue
Which teaches awful doubt, or faith so mild,
So solemn, so serene, that man may be,
But for such faith, with nature reconciled;

Thou hast a voice, great Mountain, to repeal
Large codes of fraud and woe; not understood
By all, but which the wise, and great, and good
Interpret, or make felt, or deeply feel.

IV

The fields, the lakes, the forests, and the streams,
Ocean, and all the living things that dwell
Within the daedal earth; lightning, and rain,
Earthquake, and fiery flood, and hurricane,
The torpor of the year when feeble dreams
Visit the hidden buds, or dreamless sleep
Holds every future leaf and flower; – the bound
With which from that detested trance they leap;
The works and ways of man, their death and birth,
And that of him and all that his may be;
All things that move and breathe with toil and sound
Are born and die; revolve, subside, and swell.
Power dwells apart in its tranquillity,
Remote, serene, and inaccessible:
And *this*, the naked countenance of earth,
On which I gaze, even these primaeval mountains
Teach the adverting mind. The glaciers creep
Like snakes that watch their prey, from their far fountains,
Slow rolling on; there, many a precipice,
Frost and the Sun in scorn of mortal power
Have piled: dome, pyramid and pinnacle,
A city of death, distinct with many a tower
And wall impregnable of beaming ice.
Yet not a city, but a flood of ruin
Is there, that from the boundaries of the sky
Rolls its perpetual stream; vast pines are strewing
Its destined path, or in the mangled soil
Branchless and shattered stand; the rocks, drawn down
From yon remotest waste, have overthrown
The limits of the dead and living world,
Never to be reclaimed. The dwelling-place
Of insects, beasts, and birds, becomes its spoil;
Their food and their retreat for ever gone,
So much of life and joy is lost. The race
Of man flies far in dread; his work and dwelling
Vanish, like smoke before the tempest's stream,
And their place is not known. Below, vast caves

Shine in the rushing torrents' restless gleam,
Which from those secret chasms in tumult welling
Meet in the vale, and one majestic River,
The breath and blood of distant lands, for ever
Rolls its loud waters to the ocean-waves,
Breathes its swift vapours to the circling air.

V

Mont Blanc yet gleams on high: the power is there,
The still and solemn power of many sights,
And many sounds, and much of life and death.
In the calm darkness of the moonless nights,
In the lone glare of day, the snows descend
Upon that Mountain; none beholds them there,
Nor when the flakes burn in the sinking sun,
Or the star-beams dart through them: – Winds contend
Silently there, and heap the snow with breath,
Rapid and strong, but silently! Its home
The voiceless lightning in these solitudes
Keeps innocently, and like vapour broods
Over the snow. The secret Strength of things
Which governs thought, and to the infinite dome
Of heaven is as a law, inhabits thee!
And what were thou, and earth, and stars, and sea,
If to the human mind's imaginings
Silence and solitude were vacancy?

Percy Bysshe Shelley

The Monster on the Montanvert

I spent the following day roaming through the valley. I stood beside the sources of the Arveiron, which take their rise in a glacier, that with slow pace is advancing down from the summit of the hills to barricade the valley. The abrupt sides of vast mountains were before me; the icy wall of the glacier overhung me; a few scattered pines were scattered around; and the solemn silence of this glorious presence-chamber of imperial nature was broken only by the brawling waves or the fall of some vast fragment, the thunder sound of the avalanche, or the cracking, reverberated along the mountains, of the accumulated ice, which, through the silent working of immutable laws, was ever and anon rent and torn, as if it had been but a plaything in their hands. These sublime and magnificent scenes afforded me the greatest consolation that I was capable of receiving. They elevated me from all littleness of feeling, and although they did not remove my grief, they subdued and tranquillized it. In some degree, also, they diverted my mind from the thoughts over which it had brooded for the last month. I retired to rest at night; my slumbers, as it were, waited on and ministered to by the assemblance of grand shapes which I had contemplated during the day. They congregated round me; the unstained snowy mountain-top, the glittering pinnacle, the pine woods, and ragged bare ravine, the eagle, soaring amidst the clouds – they all gathered round me and bade me be at peace.

Where had they fled when the next morning I awoke? All of soul-inspiriting fled with sleep, and dark melancholy clouded every thought. The rain was pouring in torrents, and thick mists hid the summits of the mountains, so that I even saw not the faces of those mighty friends. Still I would penetrate their misty veil and seek them in their cloudy retreats. What were rain and storm to me? My mule was brought to the door, and I resolved to ascend to the summit of Montanvert. I remembered the effect that the view of the tremendous and ever-moving glacier had produced upon my mind when I first saw it. It had then filled me with a sublime ecstasy that gave wings to the soul and allowed it to soar from the obscure world to light and joy. The sight of the awful and majestic in nature had indeed always the effect of solemnizing my mind and causing me to forget the passing cares of life. I determined to go without a guide, for I was well acquainted with the path, and the presence of another would destroy the solitary grandeur of the scene.

The ascent is precipitous, but the path is cut into continual and short windings, which enable you to surmount the perpendicularity of the mountain. It is a scene terrifically desolate. In a thousand spots the traces of the winter avalanche may be perceived, where trees lie broken and strewed upon the ground, some entirely destroyed, others bent, leaning upon the jutting rocks of the mountain or transversely upon other trees. The path, as you ascend higher, is intersected by ravines of snow, down which· stones continually roll from above; one of them is particularly dangerous, as the slightest sound, such as even speaking in a loud voice, produces a concussion of air sufficient to draw destruction upon the head of the speaker. The pines are not tall or luxuriant, but they are sombre and add an air of severity to the scene. I looked on the valley beneath; vast mists were rising from the rivers which ran through it and curling in thick wreaths around the opposite mountains, whose summits were hid in the uniform clouds, while rain poured from the dark sky and added to the melancholy impression I received from the objects around me. Alas! Why does man boast of sensibilities superior to those apparent in the brute; it only renders them more necessary beings. If our impulses were confined to hunger, thirst, and desire, we might be nearly free; but now we are moved by every wind that blows and a chance word or scene that that word may convey to us.

We rest; a dream has power to poison sleep.
    We rise; one wand'ring thought pollutes the day.
We feel, conceive, or reason; laugh or weep,
    Embrace fond woe, or cast our cares away;
It is the same: for, be it joy or sorrow,
    The path of its departure still is free.
Man's yesterday may ne'er be like his morrow;
    Nought may endure but mutability!

It was nearly noon when I arrived at the top of the ascent. For some time I sat upon the rock that overlooks the sea of ice. A mist covered both that and the surrounding mountains. Presently a breeze dissipated the cloud, and I descended upon the glacier. The surface is very uneven, rising like the waves of a troubled sea, descending low, and interspersed by rifts that sink deep. The field of ice is almost a league in width, but I spent nearly two hours in crossing it. The opposite mountain is a bare perpendicular rock. From the side where I now stood Montanvert was exactly opposite, at the distance of a league; and above it rose Mont Blanc, in awful majesty. I remained in a recess of the rock, gazing on this wonderful and stupendous scene. The sea, or rather the vast river of ice, wound among its dependent mountains, whose aerial summits hung over its recesses. Their icy and glittering peaks shone in the sunlight over the clouds. My heart, which was before sorrowful, now swelled with something like joy; I exclaimed – 'Wandering spirits, if indeed ye wander, and do not rest in your narrow beds, allow me this faint happiness, or take me, as your companion, away from the joys of life.'

As I said this I suddenly beheld the figure of a man, at some distance, advancing towards me with superhuman speed. He bounded over the crevices in the ice, among which I had walked with caution; his stature, also as he approached, seemed to exceed that of man. I was troubled; a mist came over my eyes, and I felt a faintness seize me; but I was quickly restored by the cold gale of the mountains. I perceived, as the shape came nearer (sight tremendous and abhorred!) that it was the wretch whom I had created. I trembled with rage and horror, resolving to wait his approach and then close with him in mortal combat.

Mary Shelley, *Frankenstein*

A Journal for Augusta

Yesterday September 17th 1816 I set out (with H[obhouse]) on an excursion of some days to the Mountains. – I shall keep a short journal of each day's progress for my Sister Augusta –

Septr. 17th.

Rose at 5. – left Diodati about seven – in one of the country carriages – (A Charaban) – our servants on horseback – weather very fine – the Lake calm and clear – Mont Blanc – and the Aiguille of Argentière both very distinct – the borders of the Lake beautiful – reached Lausanne before Sunset – stopped & slept at Ouchy. H. went to dine with a Mr Okeden – I remained with our Caravansera (though invited to the house of H's friend – too lazy or tired – or something else to go) and wrote a letter to Augusta – Went to bed at nine – sheets damp – swore and stripped them off & flung them – Heaven knows where – wrapt myself up in the blankets – and slept like a Child of a month's existence – till 5 o clock of . . .

Septr. 18th.

Called by Berger (my Courier who acts as Valet for a day or two – the learned Fletcher being left in charge of Chattels at Diodati) got up – H. walked on before – a mile from Lausanne – the road overflowed by the lake – got on horseback & and rode – till within a mile of Vevey – the Colt young but went very well – overtook H. & resumed the carriage which is an open one – stopped at Vevey two hours (the second time I have visited it) walked to the Church – view from the Churchyard superb . . .

Walked down to the Lake side – servants – Carriage – saddle – horses – all set off and left us plantés la by some mistake – and we walked on after them towards Clarens – H. ran on before and overtook them at last – arrived the second time (1st time was by water) at Clarens beautiful Clarens! – went to Chillon through Scenery worthy of I know not whom – went over the Castle of Chillon again – on our return met an English party in a carriage – a lady in it fast asleep! – fast asleep in the most anti-narcotic spot in the world – excellent – I remember at Chamouni – in the very eyes of Mont Blanc – hearing another woman – English also – exclaim to her party – 'Did you ever see anything more *rural*' – as if it was Highgate or Hampstead – or Brompton – or Hayes. '*Rural*' quotha! – Rocks – pines – torrents – Glaciers – Clouds – and Summits of eternal snow far above them – and '*Rural*!' I did not know the thus exclaiming fair one – but she was a – very good kind of a woman . . .

Septr. 19th.

Rose at 5 – ordered the carriage round. – Crossed the mountains to Montbovon on horseback – and on Mules – and by dint of scrambling on foot also, – the whole route beautiful as a *Dream* and now to me almost as indistinct, – I am so tired – for though healthy I have not the strength I possessed but a few years ago. At Mont Davant we breakfasted – afterwards on a steep ascent – dismounted – tumbled down & cut a finger open – the baggage also got loose and fell down a ravine, till stopped by a large tree – swore – recovered baggage – horse tired & dropping – mounted Mule – at the approach of the summit of Dent Jamant – dismounted again with H. & all the party. – Arrived at a lake in the very nipple of the bosom of the Mountain. – left our quadrupeds with a Shepherd – & ascended further – came to see snow in patches – upon which my forehead's perspiration fell like rain making the same dints as in a sieve – the chill of the wind & the snow turned me giddy – but I scrambled on & upwards. H. went to the highest *pinnacle* – I did not – but paused within a few yards (at an opening of the Cliff) – in coming down the Guide tumbled three times – I fell a laughing and tumbled too – the descent luckily soft though steep & slippery – H. also fell – but nobody hurt. The whole of the Mountain superb – the shepherd on a very steep & high cliff playing upon his *pipe* – very different from Arcadia – (where I saw the pastors with a long Musquet instead of a Crook – and pistols in their Girdles) – our Swiss Shepherd's pipe was sweet – & his time agreeable – saw a cow strayed – told they often break their necks on & over the crags – descended to Montbovon – pretty scraggy village with a wild river – and a wooden bridge – H. went to fish – caught one – our carriage not come – our horses – mules &c. knocked up – ourselves fatigued – (but so much the better – I shall sleep). The view from the highest point of today's journey comprized on one side the greatest part of Lake Leman – on the other – the valleys & mountains of the Canton Fribourg – and an immense plain with the Lakes of Neufchatel & Morat – and all which the borders of these and of the Lakes of Geneva inherit – we had both sides of the Jura before us in one point of view, with Alps in plenty. – In passing a ravine – the Guide recommended strenuously a quickening of pace – as the stones fall with great rapidity & occasional damage – the advice is excellent – but like most good advice impracticable – the road being so rough in this precise point – that neither mules nor mankind – nor horses – can make any violent progress. – Passed without any fractures or menaces thereof. – The music of the Cow's bells (for their wealth like the Patriarchs is cattle) in the pastures (which reach to a height far above any mountains in Britain) and the Shepherds' shouting to us from crag to crag & playing on their reeds where the steeps appeared almost inaccessible, with the surrounding scenery – realized all that I have ever heard or imagined of a pastoral existence – much more so than Greece or Asia Minor – for there we are a little too much of the sabre & musquet order – and if there is a Crook in one hand, you are sure to see a gun in the other – but this was pure and unmixed – solitary – savage and patriarchal – the effect I cannot describe – as we went they played the 'Ranz des Vaches' and other airs by way of farewell. I have lately repeopled my mind with Nature.

Septr. 20th.

Up at 6 – off at 8 – the whole of this day's journey at an average of between from two thousand seven hundred to three thousand feet above the level of the Sea. This valley the longest – narrowest – & considered one of the finest of the Alps – little traversed by travellers – saw the Bridge of La Roche – the bed of the river very low & deep between immense rocks & rapid as anger – a man & mule said to have tumbled over without damage – (the mule was lucky at any rate – unless I knew the *man* I should be loth to pronounce *him* fortunate). The people looked free & happy and *rich* (which last implies neither of the former) the cows superb – a Bull nearly leapt into the Charaban – 'agreeable companion in a postchaise' – Goats & Sheep very thriving – a mountain with enormous Glaciers to the right – the Kletsgeberg – further on – the Hockthorn – nice names – so soft – Hockthorn I believe very lofty & craggy – patched with snow only – no Glaciers on it – but some good epaulettes of clouds. – Past the boundaries – out of Vaud – & into Bern Canton – French exchanged for a bad German – the district famous for Cheese – liberty – property & no taxes. H. went to fish – caught none – strolled to river – saw a boy [and] a kid – kid followed him like a dog – kid could not get over a fence & bleated piteously – tried myself to help kid – but nearly overset both self & kid into the river. Arrived here about six in the evening – nine o clock – going to bed – H. in next room – knocked his head against the door – and exclaimed of course against doors – not tired today but hope to sleep nevertheless – women gabbling below – read a French translation of Schiller – Good Night – Dearest Augusta.

Septr. 21st.
Off early – the valley of Simmenthal as before – entrance to the plain of Thoun very narrow – high rocks – wooded to the top – river – new mountains – with fine Glaciers – Lake of Thoun – extensive plain with a girdle of Alps – walked down to the Chateau de Schadau – view along the lake – crossed the river in a boat rowed by women – *women* [went?] right for the first time in my recollection. – Thoun a pretty town – the whole day's journey Alpine & proud.

Septr. 22d.
Left Thoun in a boat which carried us the length of the Lake in three hours – the lake small – but the banks fine – rocks down to the water's edge. – Landed at Neuhause – passed Interlachen – entered upon a range of scenes beyond all description – or previous conception. – Passed a rock – inscription – 2 brothers – one murdered the other – just the place fit for it. After a variety of windings came to an enormous rock – Girl with fruit – very pretty – blue eyes – good teeth – very fair – long but good features – reminded me of F[ann]y. Bought some of her pears – and patted her upon the cheek – the expression of her face very mild – but good – and not at all coquettish. – Arrived at the foot of the Mountain (the Yung-frau – i.e. the

Maiden) Glaciers – torrents – one of these torrents *nine hundred feet* in height of visible descent – lodge at the Curate's – set out to see the Valley – heard an Avalanche fall – like thunder – saw Glacier – enormous – Storm came on – thunder – lightning – hail – all in perfection – and beautiful – I was on horseback – Guide wanted to carry my cane – I was going to give it to him when I recollected that it was a Swordstick and I thought that the lightning might be attracted towards him – kept it myself – a good deal encumbered with it & my cloak – as it was too heavy for a whip – and the horse was stupid – & stood still every other peal. Got in – not very wet – the Cloak being staunch – H. wet through – H. took refuge in cottage – sent man – umbrella & cloak (from the Curate's when I arrived) after him. – Swiss Curate's house – very good indeed – much better than most English Vicarages – it is immediately opposite the torrent I spoke of – the torrent is in shape curving over the rock – like the *tail* of a white horse streaming in the wind – such as it might be conceived would be that of the '*pale* horse' on which *Death* is mounted in the Apocalypse. – It is neither mist nor water but a something between both. – its immense height (nine hundred feet) gives it a wave – a curve – a spreading here – a condensation there – wonderful – & indescribable. – I think upon the whole – that this day has been better than any of this present excursion.

Septr. 23d.

Before ascending the mountain – went to the torrent (7 in the morning) again – the Sun upon it forming a *rainbow* of the lower part of all colours – but principally purple and gold – the bow moving as you move – I never saw anything like this – it is only in the Sunshine. – Ascended the Wengren Mountain. – at noon reached a valley near the summit – left the horses – took off my coat & went to the summit – 7000 feet (English feet) above the level of the *sea* – and about 5000 above the valley we left in the morning – on one side our view comprized the *Yung frau* with all her glaciers – then the *Dent d'Argent* – shining like truth – the the *Little Giant* (the Kleiner Eigher) & the great Giant (the Grosse Eigher) and last not least – the Wetterhorn. – The height of the Yung frau is 13000 feet above the sea – and 11000 above the valley – she is the highest of this range, – heard the Avalanches falling every five minutes nearly – as if God was pelting the Devil down from Heaven with snow balls – from where we stood on the *Wengren* Alp – we had all these in view on one side – on the other the clouds rose from the opposite valley curling up perpendicular precipices – like the form of the Ocean of Hell during a Springtide – it was white & sulphery – immeasurably deep in appearance – the side we ascended was (of course) not of so precipitous a nature – but on arriving at the summit we looked down the other side upon a boiling sea of cloud – dashing against the crags on which we stood (these crags on one side quite perpendicular);

staid a quarter of an hour – began to descend – quite clear from cloud on that side of the mountain – in passing the masses of snow – I made a snowball & pelted H. with it – got down to our horses again – eat something – remounted – heard the Avalanches still – came to a morass – H. dismounted – H. got well over – I tried to pass my horse over – the horse sunk up to the chin – & of course he & I were in the mud together – bemired all over – but not hurt – laughed and rode on – Arrived at the Grindenwald – dined – mounted again & rode to the higher Glacier – twilight – but distinct – very fine Glacier – like a *frozen hurricane* – Starlight – beautiful – but a devil of a path – never mind – got safe in – a little lightning – but the whole of the day as fine in point of weather – as the day on which Paradise was made. – Passed *whole woods of withered pines – all withered* – trunks stripped & barkless – branches lifeless – done by a single winter – their appearance reminded me of me & my family.

Septr. 24th

Set out at seven – up at five – passed the black Glacier – the Mountain Wetterhorn on the right – crossed the Scheideck mountain – came to the Rose Glacier – said to be the largest & finest in Switzerland. *I* think the Bossons Glacier at Chamouni – as fine – H.does not – came to the Reichenback waterfall – two hundred feet high – halted to rest the horses – arrived in the valley of Oberhasli – rain came on – drenched a little – only 4 hours rain however in 8 days – came to Lake of Brientz – then to town of Brientz – changed – H. hurt his head against door. In the evening four Swiss Peasant Girls of Oberhasli came & sang the airs of their country – two of the voices beautiful – the tunes also – they sing too that *Tyrolese air* & song which you love – Augusta – because I love it – & I love because you love it – they are still singing – Dearest – you do not know how I should have liked this – were you with me – the airs are so wild & original at the same time of great sweetness. – The singing is over – but below stairs I hear the notes of a Fiddle which bode no good to my nights rest. – The Lord help us! – I shall go down & see the dancing.

Lord Byron, *Alpine Journal*

Keats on Ben Nevis

To Thomas Keats, Findlay, 3 August 1818

Ah mio ben

My dear Tom,

We have made but poor progress Lately, chiefly from bad weather for my throat is in a fair way of getting quite well, so I have had nothing of consequence to tell you till yesterday when we went up Ben Nevis, the highest Mountain in Great Britain – On that account I will never ascend another in this empire – Skiddaw is no thing to it either in height or in difficulty. It is above 4300 feet from the Sea level and Fortwilliam stands at the head of a Salt water lake, consequently we took it completely from that level. I am heartily glad it is done – it is almost like a fly crawling up a wainscot – Imagine the task of mounting 10 Saint Pauls without the convenience of Stair cases. We set out about five in the morning with a Guide in the Tartan and Cap and soon arrived at the foot of the first ascent which we immediately began upon – after much fag and tug and a rest and a glass of whiskey apiece we gained the top of the first rise and saw then a tremendous chap above us which the guide said was still far from the top – After the first Rise our way lay along a heath valley in which there was a Loch – after about a Mile in this valley we began upon the next ascent more formidable by far than the last and kept mounting with short intervals of rest until we got above all vegetation, among nothing but loose Stones which lasted us to the very top – the Guide said we had three Miles of a stony ascent – we gained the first tolerable level after the valley to the height of what in the Valley we had thought the top and saw still above us another huge crag which still the Guide said was not the top – to that we made with an obstinate fag and having gained it there came on a Mist, so that from that part to the very top we walked in a Mist. The whole immense head of the Mountain is composed of large loose stones – thousands of acres – Before we had got half way up we passed large patches of snow and near the top there is a chasm some hundred feet deep completely glutted with it – talking of chasms they are the finest wonder of the whole – they appear great rents in the very heart of the mountain though they are not, being at the side of it, but other huge crags arising round it give the appearance to Nevis of a shattered heart or Core in itself – These Chasms are 1500 feet in depth and are the most tremendous places I have ever seen – they turn one giddy if you choose to give way to it – We tumbled in large stones and set the echoes at work in fine style. Sometimes these chasms are tolerably clear, sometimes there is a misty cloud which seems to steam up and sometimes they are entirely smothered with clouds.

After a little time the Mist cleared away but still there were large Clouds about attracted by old Ben to a certain distance so as to form as it appeared large dome curtains which kept sailing about, opening and shutting at intervals here and there and everywhere; so that although we did not see one vast wide extent of prospect all round we saw something perhaps finer – these cloud-veils opening with a dissolving motion and showing us the mountainous region beneath as through a loop hole – these Mouldy loop holes ever varying and discovering fresh prospect east, west, north and south – Then it was misty again and again it was fair – then puff came a cold breeze of wind and bared a craggy chap we had not yet seen though in close neighbourhood – Every now and then we had over head blue Sky clear and the sun pretty warm. I do not know whether I can give you an Idea of the prospect from a large Mountain top – you are on a stony plain which of course makes you forget you are on any but low ground – the horison or rather edges of this plain being above 4000 feet above the Sea hide all the Country immediately beneath you, so that the next objects you see all round next to the edges of the flat top are the Summits of Mountains of some distance off – as you move about on all sides you see more or less of the near neighbour country according as the Mountain you stand upon is in different parts steep or rounded – but the most new thing of all is the sudden leap of the eye from the extremity of what appears a plain into so vast a distance. On one part of the top there is a handsome pile of stones done pointedly by some soldiers of artillery, I climbed onto them and so got a little higher than old Ben himself. It was not so cold as I expected – yet cold enough for a glass of Whiskey now and then – There is not a more fickle thing than the top of a Mountain – what would a Lady give to change her head-dress as often and with as little trouble! – There are a good many red deer upon Ben Nevis we did not see one – the dog we had with us kept a very sharp look out and really languished for a bit of a worry – I have said nothing yet of our getting on among the loose stones large and small sometimes on two sometimes on three sometimes four legs – sometimes two and stick, sometimes three and stick, then four again, then two, then a jump, so that we kept on ringing changes on foot, hand, stick, jump boggle, stumble, foot, hand, foot, (very gingerly) stick again, and then again a game at all fours. After all there was one Mrs Cameron of 50 years of age and the fattest woman in all inverness shire who got up this Mountain some few years ago – true she had her servants – but then she had her self – She ought to have hired Sysiphus – 'Up the high hill he heaves a huge round – Mrs Cameron' 'Tis said a little conversation took place between the mountain and the Lady – After taking a glass of Wiskey as she was tolerably seated at ease she thus began –

> Mrs C.
> Upon my Life Sir Nevis I am pique'd
> That I have so far panted tugg'd and reek'd
> To do an honour to your old bald pate
> And now am sitting on you just to bate
> Without your paying me one compliment.
> Alas, 'tis so with all, when our intent
> Is plain, and in the eye of all Making
> We fair ones show a preference, too blind
> You Gentlemen immediately turn tail –

O let me then my hapless fate bewail!
Ungrateful Baldpate have I not disdaind
The pleasant Valleys – have I not madbraind
Deserted all my Pickles and preserves
My china closet too – with wretched Nerves
To boot – say wretched ingrate have I not
Left my soft cushion chair and caudle pot.
'Tis true I had no corns – no! thank the fates
My Shoemaker was always Mr Bates.
And if not Mr Bates why I'm not old!
Still dumb ungrateful Nevis – still so cold! . . .

But what surprises me above all is how this Lady got down again. I felt
it horribly. 'Twas the most vile descent – shook me all to pieces. Over leaf
you will find a Sonnet I wrote on the top of Ben Nevis. We have just entered
Inverness. I have three letters from you and one from Fanny – and one from
Dilke. I would set about crossing this all over for you but I will first write
to Fanny and Mrs Wilie then I will begin another to you and not before
because I think it better you should have this as soon as possible – my Sore
throat is not quite well and I intend stopping here a few days.

Read me a Lesson muse, and speak it loud
    Upon the top of Nevis blind in Mist!
I look into the Chasms and a Shroud
    Vaprous doth hide them; just so much I wist
Mankind doth know of Hell: I look o'erhead
    And there is sullen Mist; even so much
Mankind can tell of Heaven: Mist is spread
    Before the Earth beneath me – even such
Even so vague is Man's sight of himself.
    Here are the craggy Stones beneath my feet;
Thus much I know, that a poor witless elf
    I tread on them; that all my eye doth meet
Is mist and Crag – not only on this height
But in the World of thought and mental might –

Good bye till tomorrow

Your most affectionate Brother
John

John Keats, *Letters*

CHAPTER 11

◆

Science Comes to the Mountains

Many of the earliest mountaineers were, or professed to be, drawn to the mountains more by scientific curiosity than by love of adventure for its own sake. One whose scientific credentials are beyond question was Charles Darwin, who undertook a crossing of the Andes in 1835 from Santiago in Chile to the Republic of Mendoza, now part of Argentina. John Ruskin, not normally thought of either as a mountaineer or a scientist, displays considerable geological knowledge in his *Modern Painters*, and undertook some modest observations with a view to determining the movements of glaciers. John Tyndall, who later became President of the Royal Society, was one of the most courageous of Victorian mountaineers: his attempt to determine the winter temperature, and the boiling point of water, on the summit of Mont Blanc nearly cost one of his guides dearly, as described below.

◆ ◆ ◆

The Passage of the Cordillera

March 18. We set out for the Portillo pass. Leaving Santiago we crossed the wide burnt-up plain on which that city stands, and in the afternoon arrived at the Maypu, one of the principal rivers in Chile. The valley, at the point where it enters the first Cordillera, is bounded on each side by lofty barren mountains; and although not broad, it is very fertile. Numerous cottages were surrounded by vines, and by orchards of apple, nectarine and peach trees – their boughs breaking with the weight of the beautiful ripe fruit. In the evening we passed the custom house, where our luggage was examined. The frontier of Chile is better guarded by the Cordillera, than by the waters of the sea. There are very few valleys which lead to the central ranges, and the mountains are quite impassable in other parts by beasts of burden. The custom-house officers were very civil, which was perhaps partly owing to the passport which the President of the Republic had given me; but I must express my admiration at the natural politeness of almost every Chileno. In this instance, the contrast with the same class of men in most other countries was strongly marked . . .

My companions were Mariano Gonzales, who had formerly accompanied me in Chile, and an 'arriero', with his ten mules and a 'madrina'. The madrina (or godmother) is a most important personage: she is an old steady mare, with a little bell round her neck; and wherever she goes, the mules, like good children, follow her. The affection of these animals for their madrinas saves infinite trouble. If several large troops are turned into one field to graze, in the morning the muleteers have only to lead the madrinas a little apart, and tinkle their bells; and although there may be two or three hundred together, each mule immediately knows the bell of its own madrina, and comes to her. It is nearly impossible to lose an old mule; for if detained for several hours by force she will, by the power of smell, like a dog, track out her companions, or rather the madrina, for, according to the muleteer, she is the chief object of affection. The feeling, however, is not of an individual nature; for I believe I am right in saying that any animal with a bell will serve as a madrina. In a troop each animal carries on a level road, a cargo weighing 416 pounds (more than 29 stone), but in a mountainous country 100 pounds less; yet with what delicate slim limbs, without any proportional bulk of muscle, these animals support so great a burden! The mule always appears to me a most surprising animal. That a hybrid should possess more reason, memory, obstinacy, social affection, powers of muscular endurance, and length of life, than either of its parents, seems to indicate that art has here outdone nature . . .

March 19. We rode during this day to the last, and therefore most elevated house in the valley. The number of inhabitants became scanty; but wherever water could be brought on the land, it was very fertile . . .

The rivers which flow in these valleys ought rather to be called mountain-torrents. Their inclination is very great, and their water the colour of mud. The roar which the Maypu made, as it rushed over the great rounded fragments, was like that of the sea. Amidst the din of rushing waters, the noise from the stones, as they rattled one over another, was most distinctly audible even from a distance. This rattling noise, night and day, may be heard along the whole course of the torrent. The sound spoke eloquently to the geologist; the thousands and thousands of stones which, striking against each other, made the one dull uniform sound, were all hurrying in one direction. It was like thinking on time, where the minute that now glides past is irrecoverable. So was it with these stones; the ocean is their eternity, and each note of that wild music told of one more step towards their destiny . . .

20th. – As we ascended the valley the vegetation, with the exception of a few pretty alpine flowers, became exceedingly scanty; and of quadrupeds, birds, or insects, scarcely one could be seen. The lofty mountains, their summits marked with a few patches of snow, stood well separated from each other; the valleys being filled up with an immense thickness of stratified alluvium. The features in the scenery of the Andes which struck me most, as contrasted with the other mountain chains with which I am acquainted, were, – the flat fringes sometimes expanding into narrow plains on each side of the valleys, – the bright colours, chiefly red and purple, of the utterly bare and precipitous hills of porphyry, – the grand and continuous wall-like dikes, – the plainly-divided strata which, where nearly vertical, formed the picturesque and wild central pinnacles, but where less inclined, composed the great massive mountains on the outskirts of the range, – and lastly, the smooth conical piles of fine and brightly coloured detritus, which sloped up at a high angle from the base of the mountains, sometimes to a height of more than 2000 feet . . .

As the evening drew to a close, we reached a singular basin-like plain, called the Valle del Yeso. It was covered by a little dry pasture, and we had the pleasant sight of a herd of cattle amidst the surrounding rocky deserts. The valley takes its name of Yeso from a great bed, I should think at least 2000 feet thick, of white, and in some parts quite pure, gypsum. We slept with a party of men, who were employed in loading mules with this substance, which is used in the manufacture of wine. We set out early in the morning (21st) and continued to follow the course of the river, which had become very small, till we arrived at the foot of the ridge, that separates the waters flowing into the Pacific and Atlantic Oceans. The road, which as yet had been good with a steady but very gradual ascent, now changed into a steep zig-zag track up the great range, dividing the republics of Chile and Mendoza . . .

About noon we began the tedious ascent of the Peuquenes ridge, and then for the first time experienced some little difficulty in our respiration. The mules would halt every fifty yards, and after resting for a few seconds the poor willing animals started of their own accord again. The short breathing from the rarefied atmosphere is called by the Chilenos 'puna'; and they have most ridiculous notions concerning its origin. Some say 'all the waters here have puna'; others that 'where there is snow there is puna'; – and this no doubt is true. The only sensation I experienced was a slight tightness across the head and chest, like that felt on leaving a warm room and running quickly in frosty weather. There was some imagination even in this; for upon finding fossil shells on the highest ridge, I entirely forgot the puna in my delight. Certainly the exertion of walking was extremely great, and the respiration became deep and laborious: I am told that in the Potosi (about 13,000 feet above the sea) strangers do not become thoroughly accustomed to the atmosphere for an entire year. The inhabitants all recommend onions for the puna; as this vegetable has sometimes been given in Europe for pectoral complaints, it may possibly be of real service: – for my part I found nothing so good as the fossil shells!

When about halfway up we met a large party with seventy loaded mules. It was interesting to hear the wild cries of the muleteers, and to watch the long descending string of the animals; they appeared so diminutive, there being nothing but the bleak mountains with which they could be compared. When near the summit, the end, as generally happens, was impetuous and extremely cold. On each side of the ridge we had to pass over broad bands of perpetual snow, which were now soon to be covered by a fresh layer. When we reached the crest and looked backwards, a glorious view was presented. The atmosphere resplendently clear; the sky an intense blue; the profound valleys; the wild broken forms; the heaps of ruins, piled up during the lapse of ages; the bright-coloured rocks, contrasted with the quiet mountains of snows; all these together produced a scene no one could have imagined. Neither plant nor bird, excepting a few condors wheeling around the higher pinnacles, distracted my attention from the inanimate mass. I felt glad that I was alone: it was like watching a thunderstorm, or hearing in full orchestra a chorus of the Messiah.

On several patches of the snow I found the Protococcus nivalis, or red snow, so well known from the accounts of Arctic navigators. My attention was called to it, by observing the footsteps of the mules stained a pale red, as if their hoofs had been slightly bloody. I at first thought that it was owing to dust blown from the surrounding mountains of red porphyry; for from the magnifying power of the crystals of snow, the groups of these microscopical plants appeared like coarse particles. The snow was coloured only where it had thawed very rapidly, or had been accidentally crushed. A little rubbed on paper gave it a faint rose tinge mingled with a little brick-red. I afterwards scraped some off the paper and found that it consisted of groups of little spheres in colourless cases, each the thousandth part of an inch in diameter . . .

Having crossed the Peuquenes, we descended into a mountainous country, intermediate between the two main ranges, and then took up our quarters for the night. We were now in the republic of Mendoza. The elevation was probably not under 11,000 feet, and the vegetation in consequence exceedingly scanty. The root of a small scrubby plant served as fuel, but it made a miserable fire, and the wind was piercingly cold. Being quite tired with my day's work, I made up my bed as quickly as I could, and went to sleep . . .

At the place where we slept water necessarily boiled, from the diminished pressure of the atmosphere, at a lower temperature than it does in a less lofty country. Hence the potatoes, after remaining for some hours in the boiling water, were nearly as hard as ever. The pot we left on the fire all night, and next morning it was boiled again, but yet the potatoes were not cooked. I found out this, by overhearing my two companions discussing the cause;

they had come to the simple conclusion 'that the cursed pot (which was a new one) did not choose to boil potatoes.'

March 22nd. – After eating our potato-less breakfast, we travelled across the intermediate tract to the foot of the Portillo range . . . We had a fine view of a mass of mountains called Tupungato, the whole clothed with unbroken snow, in the midst of which there was a blue patch, no doubt a glacier; – a circumstance of rare occurrence in these mountains. Now commenced a heavy and long climb, similar to that up the Peuquenes. Bold conical hills of red granite rose on each hand; in the valleys there were several broad fields of perpetual snow. These frozen masses, during the process of thawing, had in some parts been converted into pinnacles or columns, which, as they were high and close together, made it difficult for the cargo mules to pass. On one of these columns of ice, a frozen horse was sticking as on a pedestal, but with its hind legs straight up in the air. The animal, I suppose, must have fallen with its head downward into a hole, when the snow was continuous, and afterwards the surrounding parts must have been removed by the thaw.

When nearly on the crest of the Portillo, we were enveloped in a falling cloud of minute frozen spicula. This was very unfortunate, as it continued the whole day, and quite intercepted our view. The pass takes its name of Portillo, from a narrow cleft or doorway on the highest ridge, through which the road passes. From this point, on a clear day, those vast plains which uninterruptedly extend to the Atlantic Ocean, can be seen. We descended to the upper limit of vegetation, and found good quarters for the night under the shelter of some large fragments of rock. We met here some passengers, who made anxious inquiries about the state of the road. Shortly after it was dark the clouds suddenly cleared away, and the effect was quite magical. The great mountains, bright with the full moon, seemed impending over us on all sides, as over a deep crevice: one morning, very early, I witnessed the same striking effect. As soon as the clouds were dispersed it froze severely; but as there was no wind, we slept very comfortably.

The increased brilliancy of the moon and stars at this elevation, owing to the perfect transparency of the atmosphere, was very remarkable. Travellers having observed the difficulty of judging heights and distances amidst lofty mountains, have generally attributed it to the absence of objects of comparison. It appears to me, that it is fully as much owing to the transparency of the air confounding objects at different distances, and likewise partly to the novelty of an unusual degree of fatigue arising from a little exertion – habit being thus opposed to the evidence of the senses. I am sure that this extreme clearness of the air gives a peculiar character to the landscape, all objects appearing to be brought nearly into one plane, as in a drawing or panorama. The transparency is, I presume, owing to the equable and high state of atmospheric dryness. This dryness was shown by the manner in which woodwork shrank (as I soon found by the trouble my geological hammer gave me); by articles of food, such as bread and sugar, becoming extremely hard; and by the preservation of the skin and parts of the flesh of the beasts, which had perished on the road. To the same cause we must attribute the singular facility with which electricity is excited. My flannel-waistcoat, when rubbed in the dark, appeared as if it had been washed with phosphorus; – every hair on a dog's back crackled; – even the linen sheets, and leathern straps of the saddle, when handled, emitted sparks.

March 23rd. – The descent on the eastern side of the Cordillera, is much shorter or steeper than on the Pacific side; in other words, the mountains rise more abruptly from the plains than from the alpine country of Chile. A level and brilliantly white sea of clouds was stretched out beneath our feet, shutting out the view of the equally level Pampas. We soon entered the band of clouds, and did not again emerge from it that day. About noon, finding pasture for the animals and bushes for firewood at Los Arenales, we stopped for the night. This was near the uppermost limit of bushes, and the elevation, I suppose, was between seven and eight thousand feet.

I was much struck with the marked difference between the vegetation of these eastern valleys and those on the Chilian side: yet the climate, as well as the kind of soil, is nearly the same, and the difference of longitude very trifling. The same remark holds good with the quadrupeds, and in a lesser degree with the birds and insects. I may instance the mice, of which I obtained thirteen species on the shores of the Atlantic, and five on the Pacific, and not one of them is identical. We must except all those species, which habitually or occasionally frequent elevated mountains; and certain birds, which range as far south as the Strait of Magellan. This fact is in perfect accordance with the geological history of the Andes; for these mountains have existed as a great barrier, since the present races of animals have appeared; and therefore, unless we suppose the same species to have been created in two different places, we ought not to expect any closer similarity between the organic beings on the opposite sides of the Andes, than on opposite shores of the ocean. In both cases, we must leave out of the question those kinds which have been able to cross the barrier, whether of solid rock or salt water.

March 24th. – Early in the morning I climbed up a mountain on one side of the valley, and enjoyed a far extended view over the Pampas. This was a spectacle to which I had always looked forward with interest, but I was disappointed: at the first glance it much resembled a distant view of the ocean, but in the northern parts many irregularities were soon distinguishable. The most striking feature consisted in the rivers, which, facing the rising sun, glittered like silver threads, till lost in the immensity of the distance. At midday we descended the valley, and reached a hovel, where an officer and three soldiers were posted to examine passports . . . At sunset we pulled up in the first snug corner and there bivouacked.

Charles Darwin, *The Voyage of the Beagle*

The Motion of the Glaciers

Close beside the path by which travellers ascend the Montanvert from the valley of Chamouni, on the right hand, where it first begins to rise among the pines, there descends a small stream from the foot of the granite peak known to the guides as the Aiguille Charmoz. It is concealed from the traveller by a thicket of alder, and its murmur is hardly heard, for it is one of the weakest streams of the valley. But it is a constant stream; fed by a permanent though small glacier, and continuing to flow even to the close of the summer, when more copious torrents, depending only on the melting of the lower snows, have left their beds 'stony channels in the sun'.

I suppose that my readers must be generally aware that glaciers are masses of ice in slow motion, at the rate of from ten to twenty inches a day, and that the stones which are caught between them and the rocks over which they pass, or which are embedded in the ice and dragged along by it over those rocks, are of course subjected to a crushing and grinding power altogether unparalleled by any other force in constant action. The dust to which these stones are reduced by the friction is carried down by the streams which flow from the melting glacier, so that the water which in the morning may be pure, owing what little strength it has chiefly to the rock springs, is in the afternoon not only increased in volume, but whitened with dissolved dust of granite, in proportion to the heat of the preceding hours of the day, and to the power and size of the glacier which feeds it.

The long drought which took place in the autumn of the year 1854, sealing every source of waters except these perpetual ones, left the torrent of which I am speaking, and such others, in a state peculiarly favourable to observances of their least action on the mountains from which they descend. They were entirely limited to their own ice fountains, and the quantity of powdered rock which they brought down was, of course, at its minimum, being nearly unmingled with any earth derived from the dissolution of softer soil, or vegetable mould, by rains.

At three in the afternoon, on a warm day in September, when the torrent had reached its average maximum strength for the day, I filled an ordinary Bordeaux wine flask with the water where it was least turbid. From this quart of water I obtained twenty-four grains of sand and sediment, more or less fine. I cannot estimate the quantity of water in the stream; but the runlet of it at which I filled the flask was giving about two hundred bottles a minute, or rather more, carrying down therefore about three-quarters of a pound of powdered granite every minute. This would be forty-five pounds an hour; but allowing for the inferior power of the stream in the cooler periods of the day, and taking into consideration, on the other side, its increased power in rain, we may, I think, estimate its average hour's work at twenty-eight or thirty pounds, or a hundredweight every four hours. By this insignificant runlet, therefore, some four inches wide and four inches deep, rather more than two tons of the substance of the Mont Blanc are displaced, and carried down a certain distance every week; and as it is only for three or four months that the flow of the stream is checked by frost, we may certainly allow eighty tons for the mass which it annually moves.

It is not worth while to enter into any calculation of the relation borne by this runlet to the great torrents which descend from the chain of Mont Blanc into the valley of Chamouni. To call it the thousandth part of the glacier waters, would give a ludicrous under-estimate of their total power; but even so calling it, we should find for result that eighty thousand tons of mountain must be yearly transformed into drifted sand, and carried down a certain distance. How much greater than this is the actual quantity so transformed I cannot tell; but take this quantity as certain, and consider that this represents merely the results of the labour of the constant summer streams, utterly irrespective of all sudden falls of stone and of masses of mountain (a single thunderbolt will sometimes leave a scar on the flank of a soft rock, looking like a trench for a railroad); and we shall then begin to apprehend something of the operation of the great laws of changes, which are the conditions of all material existence, however apparently enduring. The hills, which, as compared with living beings, seem 'everlasting' are, in truth, as perishing as they: its veins of flowing fountain weary the mountain heart, as the crimson pulse does ours; the natural force of the iron crag is abated in its appointed time, like the strength of the sinews in a human old age; and it is but the lapse of the longer years of decay which, in the sight of its Creator, distinguishes the mountain range from the moth and the worm.

John Ruskin, *Modern Painters*

How Many Degrees below Freezing?

Climbing zigzag, we soon reached the summit of the Mur, and immediately afterwards found ourselves in the midst of cold drifting clouds, which obscured everything. They dissolved for a moment and revealed to us the sunny valley of Chamouni; but they soon swept down again and completely enveloped us. Upon the Calotte, or last slope, I felt no trace of the exhaustion which I had experienced last year, but enjoyed free lungs and a quiet heart. The clouds now whirled wildly round us, and the fine snow, which was caught by the wind and spit bitterly against us, cut off all visible communication between us and the lower world. As we approached the summit the air thickened more and more, and the cold, resulting from the withdrawal of the sunbeams, became intense. We reached the top, however, in good condition, and found the new snow piled up into a sharp *arête*, and the summit of a form quite different from that of the *Dos d'un Ane*, which it had presented the previous year. Leaving Balmat to make a hole for the thermometer, I collected a number of batons, drove them into the snow, and, drawing my plaid round them, formed a kind of extempore tent to shelter my boiling-water apparatus. The covering was tightly held, but the snow was as fine and dry as dust, and penetrated everywhere: my lamp could not be secured from it, and half a box of matches was consumed in the effort to ignite it. At length it did flame up, and carried on a sputtering combustion. The cold of the snow-filled boiler condensing the vapour from the lamp gradually produced a drop, which, when heavy enough to detach itself from the vessel, fell upon the flame and put it out. It required much patience and the expenditure of many matches to relight it. Meanwhile the absence of muscular action caused the cold to affect our men severely. My beard and whiskers were a mass of clotted ice. The batons were coated with ice, and even the stem of my thermometer, the bulb of which was in hot water, was covered by a frozen enamel. The clouds whirled, and the little snow granules hit spitefully against the skin wherever it was exposed. The temperature of the air was 20° Fahrenheit below the freezing point. I was too intent upon my work to heed the cold much, but I was numbed; one of my fingers had lost sensation, and my right heel was in pain: still I had no thought of forsaking my observation until Mr Wills came to me and said that we must return speedily, for Balmat's hands were *gelées*. I did not comprehend the full significance of the word; but, looking at the porters, they presented such an aspect of suffering that I feared to detain them longer. They looked like worn old men, their hair and clothing white with snow, and their faces blue, withered, and anxious-looking. The hole being ready, I asked Balmat for the magnet to arrange the index of the thermometer: his hands seemed powerless. I struck my tent, deposited the instrument, and as I watched the covering of it up, some of the party, among whom were Mr Wills and Balmat, commenced the descent.

I followed them speedily. Midway down the Calotte I saw Balmat, who was about a hundred yards in advance of me, suddenly pause and thrust his hands into the snow, and commence rubbing them vigorously. The suddenness of the act surprised me, but I had no idea at the time of its real significance: I soon came up to him; he seemed frightened, and continued to beat and rub his hands, plunging them, at quick intervals, into the snow.

Still I thought the thing would speedily pass away, for I had too much faith in the man's experience to suppose that he would permit himself to be seriously injured. But it did not pass as I hoped it would, and the terrible possibility of his losing his hands presented itself to me. He at length became exhausted by his own efforts, staggered like a drunken man, and fell upon the snow. Mr Wills and myself took each a hand, and continued the process of beating and rubbing. I feared that we should injure him by our blows, but he continued to exclaim 'N'ayez pas peur, frappez toujours, frappez fortement!' We did so until Mr Wills became exhausted and a porter had to take his place. Meanwhile Balmat pinched and bit his fingers at intervals, to test their condition; but there was no sensation. He was evidently hopeless himself; and seeing him thus, produced an effect upon me that I had not experienced since my boyhood – my heart swelled, and I could have wept like a child. The idea that I should be in some measure the cause of his losing his hands was horrible to me; schemes for his support rushed through my mind with the usual swiftness of such speculations, but no scheme could restore to him his lost hands. At length returning sensation in one hand announced itself by excruciating pain. 'Je souffre!' he exclaimed at intervals – words which, from a man of his iron endurance, had a more than ordinary significance. But pain was better than death, and, under the circumstances, a sign of improvement. We resumed our descent, while he continued to rub his hands with snow and brandy, thrusting them at every few paces into the mass through which we marched. At Chamouni he had skilful medical advice, by adhering to which he escaped with the loss of six of his nails – his hands were saved.

John Tyndall, *The Glaciers of the Alps*

CHAPTER 12

◆

The Heyday of the Alps

In the later years of the eighteenth and early years of the nineteenth century many people followed Paccard and Balmat to the summit of Mont Blanc. One of the more interesting climbers was Henriette d'Angeville, the first great female mountaineer, who ascended the mountain in 1838. But it was in the middle years of the century that the other major Alpine peaks were climbed. The foundation of the Alpine Club in 1857 provided a forum for the exchange of plans and experience, and its publication *Peaks, Passes and Glaciers* went through many editions as the bible of several generations of Alpinists. From the plethora of accounts of first ascents during this period I have chosen Tyndall's account of his conquest of the Weisshorn.

◆ ◆ ◆

The Fiancée of Mont Blanc

The Grands Mulets
Sept 3

Our porters are leaving us here: I am giving them a present of ten francs and entrusting them with a short letter addressed to Jeanette, which contains news of the three parties who are here.

M. Stoppen is using the same opportunity of sending down a note to his wife; he had already written from Pierre à l'Echelle. The pigeon is eating well and drinking well, and seems full of life. M. Eisenkramer and his dog are lying beside each other, overcome by an irresistible desire for sleep. M. Stoppen feels no fatigue, and is eating an excellent dinner. For my part, I am not a bit sleepy, and am enjoying a chicken with a couple of glasses of lemonade and a few prunes.

After dinner I have come back to the panorama of the Alps of which I am trying to make a sketch. My sketching is interrupted by the appearance of a small mouse which creates quite a stir among those who are enjoying the hospitality of the Grands Mulets. All the ledges of rock are filled by groups of men, some of them resting, others cooking. Some are asleep on points of rock with a great drop below, others are starting a fire. I am above these groups sitting just below a rock on which a small table has been set up. I am sitting on a pile of rugs, my feet in a cosy fur and a glorious scene to look at . . .

We have finished sketching, chattering and supping, daylight is fading. We are preparing for the night and the fires are beginning to burn bright. The thermometer has sunk to only four degrees above zero in this warm niche of ours under the rocks. The other two parties are singing national airs round a huge fire which must be visible from the valley. My request for the evening hymn is answered by something much more mundane.

My ordinary feminine garb is now exchanged for that of *la fiancée de Mont Blanc*. The lamps are being hoisted on the alpenstocks, the beds are being got ready . . . The moon has just caught the Dome du Gouter in her beams. The glaciers framed by the sharp black spire of the rocky chain of the Grands Mulets and the Mont Maudit are still in shadow. The distant range of Les Aravis is vague and misty, that of the Brévent has its peaks in full moonlight, with the shadow of the Mont Blanc Aiguilles outlined below them and the snowy summit of the Buet rising above, a picture full of poetry to contemplate as I lie on my couch and which I am trying to put into words while I am still under the actual impression it makes upon me as I look at it. If only I were a poet, what a hymn would pour forth from my lyre!

We are to start an hour before daybreak tomorrow and there is every promise of a grand day.

I am calm in my mind and I have a presentiment we shall get up.

Sept 4

I have had some rest, but no sleep; in the night I heard three avalanches fall from the Mont Maudit. At half-past one our three parties began getting ready and exactly at two o'clock we all started off in the opposite order to that of yesterday, so that each can take its turn at making the track. Just before starting I had some beef-tea and a dozen prunes.

Two stout fellows had gone up some way the day before to find the best route and tread out a track; they were D. Couttet and J. Mugnier. We followed this track across the slope below the Dome du Gouter, then up the slope leading to the petit plateau which is long and steep. We reached the petit plateau at a quarter to four and the grand plateau at a quarter to six. There we had a marvellous view which included the broken pyramidal ice-cliffs of the Dome du Gouter. The thermometer indicated nine degrees below zero when we started after breakfast. I drank a cup of lemonade, but I ate nothing. Legs, lungs and morale all right so far.

Going up the slopes above the Grand Plateau my back felt tired and I was sleepy. I found I could not take more than 84 steps without stopping; then it came down to 68, then 65 – 100 once by an exceptional effort. My pulse was hard to find, and I counted 136 beats. The Mur de la Côte was reached at 9.30, and there I began to suffer atrociously and unexpectedly. I had to struggle against two enemies of equal violence – suffocating palpitations of the heart when I walked, and a lethargic drowsiness whenever I stopped. It was not the sort of drowsiness that comes to one every evening, but an overwhelming sense of sleepiness which began in my eyes and passed through all my limbs. The efforts of will that I had to make to get rid of this torpor are more than I can tell you. I was obliged to wind up my will power as far as it would go, and in this way I obtained a nervous paroxysm of strength which lasted a few minutes and enabled me to stagger on for from seven to ten paces; then my heart beat again as though it would burst my chest, and when the suffocation came I threw myself on the ground, overcome by the stupefying drowsiness of which I have spoken to you.

I was in this state of agony for four hours without thinking, for one instant, of giving up my enterprise. That will show you how deeply the idea was rooted in my mind. For there the remedy was: I had only to turn back and go down again to be completely cured. At one moment I thought that my carnal body was going to be the victim of the despotic wishes of my higher self. Then I said to my guides: 'If I die before getting to the top, drag my body up and leave it there; my family will reward you for carrying out my last wishes.' God helping me, I managed to drag myself along to the end without assistance, and the very moment my foot was planted on the summit, I recovered, as it were, by a miracle. A life-giving air poured into my lungs, the drowsiness disappeared, the vigour returned to my limbs; and it was in the full possession of my physical and moral faculties that I was able to admire the magnificent panorama which unrolled itself before my wondering eyes.

Henriette d'Angeville, in *Annals of Mont Blanc*

Suggestions for Alpine Travellers

Mode of Travelling in the High Alps

This subject requires a few words of allusion to the difficulties and dangers incident to travelling in a region where, excepting steep faces of rock, the surface is covered with snow or ice. These may at once be divided into two classes, – the real and the imaginary. Where a ridge or slope of rock or ice is such that it could be traversed without difficulty if it lay but a few feet above the level of a garden, the substitution on either side of a precipice some thousands of feet in depth, or of a glacier crevasse, makes no real difference in the work to be executed, but may act intensely on the imagination of the traveller. The only means for removing this source of danger is habit; those who cannot accustom themselves to look unmoved down vertical precipices, and, in cases of real difficulty, to fix their attention exclusively upon the ledge or jutting crag to which they must cling with foot or hand, should forego the attempt to take part in expeditions where they will not only expose themselves to danger, but may be the cause of equal danger to others.

The real dangers of the high Alps may, under ordinary circumstances, be reduced to three. First, the yielding of the snow bridges that cover glacier crevasses; second, the risk of slipping upon steep slopes of hard ice; third, the fall of ice or rocks from above.

From the first, which is also the most frequent source of danger, absolute security is obtained by a simple precaution, now generally known, yet unfortunately often neglected. The reader of this volume can scarcely fail to remark that, in the course of the expeditions here recounted, repeated accidents occurred, and that many of the best and most experienced Alpine travellers have narrowly escaped with their lives, under circumstances in which no danger whatever would have been encountered if the party had been properly tied together with rope. Sometimes that indispensable article is forgotten; more often the use of it is neglected in positions where no immediate necessity for it is apparent. A strange notion seems to prevail with some travellers, and occasionally among the guides, that the constant use of the rope is a sign of timidity and over caution. But in the upper region, where the ice is covered with snow or nevé, it is absolutely the only security against a risk which the most experienced cannot detect beforehand; and so far from causing delay, it enables a party to advance more rapidly and with less trouble when they are dispensed from the inconvenience of sounding with the alpenstock in doubtful positions. It is true that this latter precaution should not be omitted in places that are manifestly unsafe, but, at the best, it merely detects a particular danger without giving that confidence which the rope alone can afford. It may be hoped that before long the rope will be considered as essential a part of an Alpine traveller's equipment as reins are in a horse's harness. A man who should undertake to drive a cab without reins from Charing Cross to London Bridge, would scarcely be looked upon as an example for spirit, even if he sat alone; but if he were to induce a party of friends to travel in the same vehicle, he would justly be accused of wantonly risking the lives of others.

It is sometimes thought that for complete security, in case of the yielding of a snow bridge, the party tied together should be not less than three in number; in order that two may be available to draw out of a crevasse the one who may have fallen. But if the simple precaution of keeping eight or ten paces apart be observed by two travellers who are tied together, there is not the slightest risk incurred. The whole mass of snow covering a crevasse does not give way together, and a moderate amount of assistance from the rope will always enable the traveller to extricate himself. A good cragsman may go alone up and down the steepest pinnacles of rock; but, however strong may be the inducements to solitary wanderings amidst the grand scenery of the High Alps, the man who travels without a companion in the snow region can scarcely be thought more reasonable than the supposed cab-driver alluded to in the last paragraphs.

Against the risk of slipping upon steep slopes, the rope is usually a protection as effectual as it is in the first case. There may be positions in which the footing of each traveller is so precarious, that if tied together a slip on the part of any one of them would probably cause the destruction of all. Such positions are, however, very rare, if indeed they anywhere occur. There are few descents steeper than that of the ice-wall of the Strahleck, yet Desor recounts a case in which three travellers, all slipping at the same time, were upheld, and saved from falling into the *bergschrund* by a rope sustained on the arm of a single guide who came last in the descent.

For surmounting steep ice slopes the axe is the proper instrument, but there is some difference of opinion as to the most available form and dimensions to be given to it. In considerable expeditions it is well to be provided with two axes, both to save time, by enabling two to work together, and to provide for the accident of one being lost or broken. In cases where there is not much work to be done in cutting steps, a moderately heavy geological hammer, of which one side is made in the form of a short pick, is sometimes a serviceable weapon.

The general experience of Alpine travellers is not favourable to *crampons*, but many have found advantage in screws armed with a projecting double-pointed head, which are sold at the Pavillon on the Mont Anvert. Screws of the same kind, but made of better steel, and arranged in a convenient way for driving them into the soles and heels of boots, are sold in London by Lund in Fleet Street.

In the lower part of a glacier, a traveller is sometimes arrested by a short, steep bank of ice, when unprovided with any convenient means of cutting steps. In such a case, and especially when armed with steel points in the heels of his boots, he will sometimes find it easier and safer to mount backwards, propping himself with his alpenstock, and biting into the ice with his heels.

To experienced travellers, no caution as to alpenstocks is needed, but to others it may be well to say, that those commonly sold in Switzerland are never to be relied upon. There is scarcely one of them that is not liable to break, if suddenly exposed to a severe strain. A stout ash pole, well seasoned, and shod with a point of tough, hardened steel, three inches long, instead of the soft iron commonly used, will not only serve all the ordinary purposes, but will help to cut steps in a steep descent where it is difficult to use the axe with effect.

The danger of ice and fragments of rock falling on travellers in high mountains, may, to a great extent, be avoided by a judicious choice of route.

Experience and observation enable a traveller to recognize at once the positions in which ice is detached from a higher level and falls abruptly over a precipice, or steep slope of rock. In certain situations this is a matter of hourly occurrence, especially in warm weather, and as the falling ice never keeps together in a single mass, but breaks into blocks of various sizes, up to three or four hundred weight, positive risk is incurred by passing in the track of their descent. The guides are usually alive to this sort of danger, and very careful to avoid it, unless in the case of absolute necessity; it is considerably diminished when the exposed place is passed early in the morning, before the sun has reached the upper plateau from which the ice is detached, or late in the evening, after his rays have been withdrawn.

The least avoidable, but also the most unusual, source of danger in Alpine excursions, arises from the fall of rocks, which may strike the traveller in their descent, or else detach themselves while he is in the act of climbing over them. The first accident is more frequent during, or immediately after, bad weather, and need scarcely count among the ordinary perils of Alpine travels; the second is almost peculiar to limestone rocks, which, especially in the dolomite region of the eastern Alps, often have their outer surface broken into loose and treacherous blocks, that yield to the pressure of hand or foot. Close attention, aided by some experience, will direct the traveller to test the stability of each projecting crag, so as to avoid unnecessary risk.

Besides the ordinary risks of Alpine adventure, which, by reasonable caution, may be brought within as narrow limits as those of other active pursuits, there are the special risks that are sometimes encountered during the continuance, or immediately on the cessation, of bad weather. These are sometimes serious, and should not be made light of by those who care either for their own safety, or that of their companions. Bearings carefully taken with the compass, and attention to land-marks, will generally enable a party to retrace their steps, even when these have been effaced by falling snow, and in case of decided bad weather, there is no other rational alternative. Newly-fallen snow, lying upon the steep frozen slopes of the nevé, presents a serious danger to those who attempt to traverse it . . .

In the matter of clothing and diet the tastes of Alpine travellers naturally vary; but perhaps twenty years' experience of the advantages of a Scotch plaid by one who has made it an invariable companion, may entitle him to recommend it. Whether for protection in case of an unexpected bivouac, for sleeping in suspicious quarters, or on hay of doubtful dryness, for shelter against the keen wind, while perched on a peak or the ridge of a high pass, or against rain and snow, this most portable of garments is equally serviceable. For excursions where some days must be spent in chalets, and no supplies but milk and cheese can be counted on, rice is the most portable and convenient provision. One pound is more than enough for a man's daily diet when well cooked with milk, and with this he is independent of all

other supplies. To some persons tea will provide the only luxury that need
be desired in addition. A few raisins are a very grateful *bonne bouche* during
a long and steep ascent; but the best preservative against thirst is to keep
in the mouth a quartz pebble, an article which the bounty of nature supplies
abundantly in most parts of the Alps.

John Ball, in *Peaks, Passes and Glaciers*

The First Ascent of the Weisshorn

I took the diligence to Visp, and engaged a porter immediately to Randa.
I had sent Benen thither, on reaching the Bel Alp, to seek out a resting place
whence the Weisshorn might be assailed. On my arrival I learned that he
had made the necessary reconnaissance, and entertained hopes of our being
able to gain the top.

This noble mountain had been tried on various occasions and from
different sides by brave and competent men, but had never been scaled; and
from the entries in the travellers' books I might infer that formidable
obstacles stood in the way of a successful ascent. The peak of the mountain
is not visible at Randa, being far withdrawn behind the Alps. Beyond the
Biezbach its ramparts consist of a craggy slope crowned above by three tiers
of rocky strata. In front of the hotel is a mountain slope with pines clinging
to its ledges, while stretching across the couloir of the Biezbach the divided
ramparts are connected by battlements of ice. A quantity of debris which
has been carried down the couloir spreads out in the shape of a fan at the
bottom; near the edge of this debris stands a group of dingy houses, and
close alongside them our pathway up the mountain runs.

Previous to quitting Randa I had two pair of rugs sewed together so as to
form two sacks. These and other coverlets intended for my men, together
with our wine and provisions, were sent on in advance of us. At 1 p.m. on
the 18th of August, we, that is Benen, Wenger and myself, quitted the hotel
and were soon zigzagging among the pines of the opposite mountain.
Wenger had been the guide of my friend F. and had shown himself so active
and handy on the Strahleck, that I commissioned Benen to engage him.
During the previous night I had been very unwell, but I hoped that the
strength left me, if properly applied, and drained to the uttermost, would
still enable me to keep up with my companions. As I climbed the slope I
suffered from intense thirst, and we once halted beside a fillet of clear spring
water to have a draught. It seemed powerless to quench the drought which
beset me. We reached a chalet; milking time was at hand, at our request
a smart young Senner caught up a pail, and soon returned with it full of
delicious milk. It was poured into a small tub. With my two hands I seized
the two ends of a diameter of this vessel, gave it the necessary inclination,

and stooping down, with a concentration of purpose which I had rarely before exerted, I drew the milk into me. Thrice I returned to the attack before that insatiate thirst gave way. The effect was astonishing. The liquid appeared to lubricate every atom of my body, and its fragrance to permeate my brain. I felt a growth of strength at once commence within me; all anxiety as to physical power with reference to the work in hand soon vanished, and before retiring to rest I was able to say to Benen, 'Go where thou wilt tomorrow, and I will follow thee.'

Two hours' additional climbing brought us to our bivouac. A ledge of rock jutted out from the mountain side, and formed an overhanging roof. On removing the stones from beneath it, a space of comparatively dry clay was laid bare. This was to be my bed, and to soften it Wenger considerably stirred it up with his axe. The position was excellent, for lying upon my left side I commanded the whole range of Monte Rosa, from the Mischabel to the Breithorn. We were on the edge of an amphitheatre. Beyond the Schallenbach was the stately Mettelhorn. A row of eminent peaks swept round to the right, linked by lofty ridges of cliffs, thus forming the circus in which the Schallenberg glacier originated. They were, however, only a spur cast out from the vaster Weisshorn, the cone of which was not visible from our dormitory. I wished to examine it, and in company with Benen skirted the mountain for half-an-hour, until the whole colossal pyramid stood facing us. When I first looked at it my hope sank, but both of us gathered confidence from a more lengthened gaze. The mountain is a pyramid with three faces, the intersections of which form three sharp edges or *arêtes*. The end of the western *arête* was nearest to us, and on it our attention was principally fixed. A couloir led up to it filled with snow, which Benen, after having examined it with the telescope, pronounced 'furchtbar steil'. This slope was cut across by a bergschrund, which we also carefully examined, and finally, Benen decided on the route to be pursued next morning. A chastened hope was predominant in both our breasts as we returned to our shelter . . .

The sun is going, but not yet gone; while up the arch of the opposite heavens, the moon, within one day of being full, is hastening to our aid. She finally appears exactly behind the peak of the Rympfischhorn: the cone of the mountain being projected for a time as a triangle on the disc. Only for a moment, however; for the queenly orb sails aloft, clears the mountain, and bears splendidly away through the tinted sky. The motion was quite visible, and resembled that of a vast balloon. As the day approached its end the scene assumed the most sublime aspect. All the lower portions of the mountains were deeply shaded, while the loftiest peaks, ranged upon a semicircle, were fully exposed to the sinking sun. They seemed pyramids of solid fire, while here and there long stretches of crimson light drawn over the higher snowfields linked the glorified summits together. An intensely illuminated geranium flower seems to swim in its own colour which apparently surrounds the petals like a layer, and defeats by its lustre any attempt of the eye to seize upon the sharp outlines of the leaves. A similar effect was here observed upon the mountains; the glory did not seem to come from them alone, but seemed also effluent from the air around them. This gave them a certain buoyancy which suggested entire detachment from the earth. They swam in splendour, which intoxicated the soul, and I will not now repeat in my moments of soberness the extravagant analogies which then ran through my brain. As the evening advanced, the eastern heavens low down assumed a deep purple hue, above which, and blending with it by infinitesimal gradations, was a belt of red, and over this again zones of orange and violet. I walked round the corner of the mountain at sunset, and found the western sky glowing with a more transparent crimson than that which overspread the east. The crown of the Weisshorn was embedded in this magnificent light. After sunset the purple of the east changed to a deep neutral tint, and against the faded red which spread above it, the sun-forsaken mountains laid their cold and ghastly heads. The ruddy colour vanished more and more; the stars lengthened in lustre, until finally the moon and they held undisputed possession of the blue grey sky.

I lay with my face turned towards the moon until it became so chilled that I was forced to protect it by a light handkerchief. The power of blinding the eyes is ascribed to the moonbeams, but the real mischief is that produced by radiation from the eyes into clear space, and the inflammation consequent upon the chill. As the cold increased I was fain to squeeze myself more and more underneath my ledge, so as to lessen the space of sky against which my body could radiate. Nothing could be more solemn than the night. Up from the valley came the low thunder of the Vispbach. Over the Dom flashed in succession the stars of Orion, until finally the entire constellation hung aloft. Higher up in heaven was the moon, and her rays as they fell upon the snowfields and pyramids were sent back in silvery lustre by some, while others remained dull. These, as the orb sailed round, came duly in for their share of the glory. The Twins caught it at length and retained it long, shining with a pure spiritual radiance while the moon continued to ride above the hills.

I looked at my watch at 12 o'clock; and a second time at 2 a.m. The moon was just then touching the crest of the Schallenberg, and we were threatened with the withdrawal of her light. This soon occurred. We rose at 2½ a.m., consumed our coffee, and had to wait idly for the dawn. A faint illumination at length overspread the west, and with this promise of the coming day we quitted our bivouac at 3½ a.m. No cloud was to be seen; as far as the weather was concerned we were sure to have fair play. We rounded the shingly shoulder of the mountain to the edge of a snow field, but before entering upon it I disburthened myself of my strong shooting jacket, and left it on the mountain side. The sunbeams and my own exertion would, I knew, keep me only too warm during the day. We crossed the snow, cut our way through a piece of entangled glacier, reached the bergschrund and passed it without a rope. We ascended the frozen snow of the couloir by steps, but soon diverged from it to the rocks at our right, and scaled them to the end of the eastern *arête* of the mountain.

Here a saddle of snow separates us from the next higher rocks. With our staff-spikes at one side of the saddle, we pass by steps cut upon the other. The snow is firmly congealed. We reach the rocks, which we find hewn into fantastic turrets and obelisks, while the loose chips of this colossal sculpture are strewn confusedly upon the ridge. Amid the chips we cautiously pick our way, winding round the towers or scaling them amain. From the very first the work is heavy, the bending, twisting, reaching, and drawing up, calling upon all the muscles of the frame. After two hours of this work we halt, and looking back we observe two moving objects on the glacier below us. At first we take them to be chamois, but they are instantly pronounced men, and the telescope at once confirms this. The leader carries an axe, and his companion a knapsack and alpenstock. They are following our traces, losing them apparently now and then, and waiting to recover them. Our expedition had put Randa in a state of excitement, and some of its best climbers had come to Benen and urged him to take them with him. But this he did not deem necessary, and now here were two of them determined to try the thing on their own account; and perhaps to dispute with us the honour of the enterprise. On this point, however, our uneasiness was small.

Resuming our gymnastics, the rocky staircase led us to the flat summit of a tower, where we found ourselves cut off from a similar tower by a deep gap bitten into the mountain. Retreat appeared inevitable, but it is wonderful how many ways out of difficulty open to a man who diligently seeks them. The rope is here our refuge. Benen coils it round his waist, scrapes along the surface of the rock, fixes himself on a ledge, where he can lend me a helping hand. I follow him, Wenger follows me, and in a few minutes all three of us stand in the middle of the gap. By a kind of screw motion we twist ourselves round the opposite tower, and reach the *arête* behind it. Work of this kind, however, is not to be performed by the day, and with a view of sparing our strength, we quit the *arête* and endeavour to get along the southern slope of the pyramid. The mountain is here scarred by longitudinal depressions which stretch a long way down it. These are now filled with clear hard ice, produced by the melting and refreezing of the snow. The cutting of steps across these couloirs proves to be so tedious and fatiguing that I urge Benen to abandon it and try the *arête* once more. By a stout tug we regain the ridge and work along it as before. Here and there from the northern side the snow has folded itself over the crags, and along it we sometimes work upward. The *arête* for a time has become gradually narrower, and the precipices on each side more sheer. We reach the end of one of the subdivisions of the ridge, and find ourselves separated from the next rocks by a gap about twenty yards across. The *arête* here has narrowed to a mere wall, which, however, as rock would present no serious difficulty. But upon the wall of rock is placed a second wall of snow, which dwindles to a knife edge at the top. It is white and pure, of very fine grain, and a little moist. How to pass this snow catenary I knew not, for I had no idea of a human foot trusting itself upon so frail a support. Benen's practical sagacity was, however, greater than mine. He tried the snow by squeezing it with his foot, and to my astonishment commenced to cross. Even after the pressure of his feet the space he had to stand on did not exceed a hand-breadth. I followed him, exactly as a boy walking along a horizontal pole, with toes turned outwards. Right and left the precipices were appalling; but the sense of power on such occasions is exceedingly sweet. We reached the opposite rock, and here a smile rippled over Benen's countenance as he turned towards me. He knew that he had done a daring thing, though not a presumptuous one. 'Had the snow', he said, 'been less perfect, I should not have thought of attempting it, but I knew after I had set my foot upon the ridge that we might pass without fear.'

It is quite surprising what a number of things the simple observation made by Faraday, in 1846, enables us to explain. Benen's instinctive act is justified by theory. The snow was fine in grain, pure and moist. When pressed, the attachments of its granules were innumerable, and their perfect cleanness enabled them to freeze together with a maximum energy. It was this freezing together of the particles at innumerable points which gave the mass its sustaining power. Take two fragments of ordinary table ice and bring them carefully together, you will find that they instantly freeze, and by laying hold of either of them gently, you can drag the other after it through the water. Imagine such points of attachment distributed without number through a mass of snow. The substance becomes thereby a semi-solid instead of a mass of powder. My guide, however, unaided by any theory, did a thing from which I, though backed by all the theories in the world, should have shrunk in dismay.

After this we found the rocks on the ridge so shaken to pieces that it required the greatest caution to avoid bringing them down upon us. With all our care, however, we sometimes dislodged vast masses which leaped upon the slope adjacent, loosened others by their shock, these again others, until finally a whole flight of them would escape, setting the mountain in a roar as they whizzed and thundered along its side to the snowfields 4000 feet below us. The day is hot, the work hard, and our bodies are drained of their liquids as by a Turkish bath. The perspiration trickles down our faces, and drops profusely from the projecting points. To make good our loss we halt at intervals where the melted snow forms a liquid vein, and quench our thirst. We possess, moreover, a bottle of champagne, which, poured sparingly into our goblets on a little snow, furnished Wenger and myself with many a refreshing draught. Benen fears his eyes, and will not touch champagne. The less, however, we rest the better, for after every pause I find a certain unwillingness to renew the toil. The muscles have become set, and some minutes are necessary to render them again elastic. But the discipline is first-rate for both mind and body. There is scarcely a position possible to a human being which, at one time or another during the day, I was not forced to assume. The fingers, wrist, and forearm, were my main reliance, and as a mechanical instrument the human hand appeared to me this day in a light which it never assumed before. It is a miracle of constructive art.

We were often during the day the victims of illusions regarding the distance which we had to climb. For the most part the summit was hidden from us, but on reaching the eminences it came frequently into view. After three hours spent on the *arête*, about five hours that is, subsequent to starting, the summit was clearly in view; we looked at it over a minor summit, which gave it illusive proximity. 'You have now good hopes,' I remarked, turning to Benen. 'Not only good hopes,' he replied, 'but I do not allow myself to entertain the idea of failure.' Well, six hours passed on the *arête*, each of which put in its inexorable claim to the due amount of mechanical work; the lowering and the raising of three human bodies through definite spaces, and at the end of this time we found ourselves apparently no nearer to the summit than when Benen's hopes cropped out in confidence. I looked anxiously at my guide as he fixed his weary eyes upon the distant peak. There was no confidence in the expression of his countenance; still I do not believe that either of us entertained for a moment the thought of giving in. Wenger complained of his lungs, and Benen counselled him several times to stop and let him and me continue the ascent; but this the Oberland man refused to do. At the commencement of a day's work I often find myself anxious, if not timid; but this feeling vanishes when I become warm and interested. When the work is very hard we become callous and sometimes stupefied by the incessant knocking about. This was my case at present, and I kept watch lest my indifference should become carelessness. I supposed repeatedly a case where a sudden effort might be required of me, and felt all through that I had a fair residue of strength to fall back upon. I tested this conclusion sometimes by a spurt; flinging myself suddenly from rock to rock, and thus proved my condition by experiment instead of relying on opinion. An eminence in the ridge which cut off the view of the summit was now the object of our exertions. We reached it; but how hopelessly distant did the summit appear! Benen laid his face upon his axe for a moment; a kind of sickly despair was in his eyes as he turned to me, remarking 'Lieber Herr, die Spitze ist noch sehr weit oben'.

Lest the desire to gratify me should urge him beyond the bounds of prudence, I said to Benen that he must not persist on my account, if he ceased to feel confidence in his own powers; that I should cheerfully return with him the moment he thought it no longer safe to proceed. He replied that though weary he felt quite sure of himself, and asked for some food. He had it, and a gulp of wine, which mightily refreshed him. Looking at the mountain with a firmer eye, he exclaimed, 'Herr! wir müssen ihn haben,' and his voice, as he spoke, rung like steel within my heart . . .

Another eminence now fronted us, behind which, how far we knew not, the summit lay. We scaled this height, and above us, but clearly within reach, a silvery pyramid projected itself against the blue sky. I was assured ten times by my companions that it was the highest point before I ventured to stake my faith upon the assertion. I feared that it also might take rank with the illusions which had so often beset our ascent, and shrunk from the consequent moral shock. Towards the point, however, we steadily worked. A large prism of granite, or granitic gneiss, terminated the *arête*, and from it a knife edge of pure white snow ran up a little point. We passed along the edge, reached that point, and instantly swept with our eyes the whole range of the horizon. The crown of the Weisshorn was underneath our feet.

The long pent feelings of my two guides found vent in a wild and reiterated cheer. Benen shook his arms in the air and shouted as a Valaisian, while Wenger chimed in with the shriller yell of the Oberland. We looked along the *arête*, and far below perched on one of its crags, could discern the two Randa men. Again and again the roar of triumph was sent down to them. They had accomplished but a small portion of the ridge, and soon after our success they wended their way homewards. They came, willing enough no doubt, to publish our failure had we failed; but we found out afterwards that they had been equally strenuous in announcing our success; they had seen us, they affirmed, like three flies upon the summit of the mountain . . .

Benen wished to leave some outward and visible sign of our success on the summit. He deplored having no flag; but as a substitute it was proposed that he should knock the head off his axe, use the handle as a flagstaff, and surmount it by a red pocket-handkerchief. This was done, and for some time subsequently the extempore banner was seen flapping in the wind. To his extreme delight, it was shown to Benen himself three days afterwards by my friend Mr Galton from the Riffel Hotel . . .

Over the peaks and through the valleys the sunbeams poured, unimpeded save by the mountains themselves, which in some cases drew their shadows in straight bars of darkness through the illuminated air. I had never before witnessed a scene which affected me like this. Benen once volunteered some information regarding its details, but I was unable to hear him. An influence seemed to proceed from it direct to the soul; the delight and exultation experienced were not those of Reason or Knowledge, but of

BEING: I was part of it and it of me, and in the transcendent glory of Nature I entirely forgot myself as man. Suppose the sea waves exalted to nearly a thousand times their normal height, crest them with foam, and fancy yourself upon the most commanding crest, with the sunlight from a deep blue heaven illuminating such a scene, and you will have some idea of the form under which the Alps present themselves from the summit of the Weisshorn. East, west, north, and south, rose those 'billows of a granite sea', back to the distant heaven, which they hacked into an indented shore. I opened my note-book to make a few observations, but I soon relinquished the attempt. There was something incongruous, if not profane, in allowing the scientific faculty to interfere where silent worship was the 'reasonable service'.

John Tyndall, *Mountaineering in 1861*

CHAPTER 13

◆

The Mountain Backcloth

Mountains were an important feature in the sensibility of many Victorians who were by no means mountaineers. Just before the accession of Queen Victoria, Newman wrote ecstatically of the mountain scenery of Sicily. Bagehot was enchanted by the Alpine snow. For Ruskin, mountains were the beginning and end of all natural scenery.

Many Victorians learned their first love of the mountains from their university tutors, who would take them during the summer vacation into mountainous regions for a 'reading party', a mixture of seminar and holiday. Many writers have left prose descriptions of such reading parties, but the best description of all is Clough's account in his novel in verse *The Bothie of Tober-na-vuolich*. The extract here printed describes the Scottish mountain excursions of the pupils on the reading party, which eventually culminates in the hero Philip Hewson's falling in love with a crofter's daughter and emigrating with her to New Zealand.

◆ ◆ ◆

A Garden of Eden in Sicily

To Harriet Newman, 25 April 1883

. . . We set off between 5 and 6, and had 12 miles to go to breakfast, at Taormini. As we approached it, the country got more and more striking. – (Syracuse, April 27). The two last miles we diverged from the road up a steep path and soon came to the ancient stone ascent leading to Taurominium. I never saw anything more enchanting than this spot – It realized all one had read of in books of the perfection of scenery – a deep valley – brawling streams – beautiful trees – but description is nothing – the sea was heard in the distance. But when after breakfast, with the advantage of a bright day we mounted to the theatre, and saw the view thence, what shall I say then? why that I never before knew that nature could be so beautiful, and that to have seen the view thence was a nearer approach to seeing Eden, than anything I had conceived possible. O happy I, it was worth coming all the way, to endure the loneliness and sadness of my progress and the weariness of the voyage to see it. I felt for the first time in my life with my eyes open that I must be better and more religious, if I lived there. Never before have I brought home to my mind the reality of foreign scenery. I mean that I have gazed on mountains and vegetation, and felt it was not English, yet could not believe it was not a dream – but now I see what real beautiful scenery is – long slopes which seem as if they never would end, cultivated to the top – or overhung there with jutting rocks – bold precipitous crags standing, because they choose to stand, independently – range after range of heights, so that you wonder the series does not proceed for ever. The theatre is situated in a hollow hill and the scene forms a screen – through it you see magnificent steeps, falling down and down – and above all, Etna towers – at the bottom you see the sea, and the coast circling into a bay and then jutting out into a point, where formerly stood Naxos, the first Greek settlement. This superb view, the most wonderful I can ever hope to see, is but one of at least ½ a dozen which surpass all other views in the world *in beauty*. On the back of the Theatre, you have a wonderful view of Calabria and the Messina side of Sicily – and going out of Taurominium down the hill you have a very novel and striking effect. The slants centre almost in a point, so that you seem descending into a pit – they were clad with the bright green of corn when it looks brightest – yet so distant and broken with olives and terraces on which the soil lay that it had nothing formal in it . . . I went off to Giarra – a *large town for Sicily* 12 miles off Taormini – and off the high road to Palermo which I had hitherto travelled. Here first I went thro' the beds of river, which no description gives an idea of. The country receded and appeared more brown from seeing the interstices of the vines – Etna was magnificent beyond description – the scene around was sombre with clouds, when suddenly as the sun descended upon the cone, its rays shot between the clouds and the snow, lighting upon the latter, and disposing the former about it in vertical curtains – on one side the ascent to the top half showed itself like a Jacob's ladder (it had hitherto been hidden) – I no longer wonder at the poets placing the abode of the Highest upon Mount Olympus.

John Henry Newman, *Letters*

The Economist in the Alps

On Wednesday morning we proceeded to Thun. It was our plan to get on to Lauterbrunnen or Interlacken at the least. But we were so taken with the sight of the lake of Thun, and the Muen, a bold and lofty promontory jutting out into the middle of it, with the glaciers behind it and setting off its sombre colour, that we stayed there, and strolled up to the summer house to see the sunset. I have seen many finer as far as clouds are concerned, but I never before watched the pink tint gradually fading from the 'Alpine snow'. It by degrees crept up the mountains as the sun descended till just before it descended the summits only partook of it. According to an old national custom in Switzerland still, I believe, preserved in retired valleys, this moment was seized to blow the Alpine horn which was re-echoed from hill to hill, and whenever the sound was heard, the shepherds fell on their knees to render thanks to God for the day's light and their preservation. A similar custom of choosing sunset for a public act of adoration is very prevalent in the East.

Walter Bagehot, *Travel Journal*

The Mountain Glory

To myself, mountains are the beginning and the end of all natural scenery; in them, and in the forms of inferior landscape that lead to them, my affections are wholly bound up; and though I can look with happy admiration at the lowland flowers, and woods, and open skies, the happiness is tranquil and cold, like that of examining detached flowers in a conservatory, or reading a pleasant book; and if the scenery be resolutely level, insisting upon the declaration of its own flatness in all the detail of it, as in Holland, or Lincolnshire, or Central Lombardy, it appears to me like a prison, and I cannot long endure it. But the slightest rise and fall in the road, – a mossy bank at the side of a crag of chalk, with brambles at its brow, overhanging it, – a ripple over three or four stones in the stream by the bridge – above all, a wild bit of ferny ground under a fir or two, looking as if, possibly, one might see a hill if one got to the other side of the trees, will instantly give me intense delight, because the shadow, or the hope, of the hills, is in them.

And thus, although there are few districts of Northern Europe, however apparently dull or tame, in which I cannot find pleasure, though the whole of Northern France (except Champagne), dull as it seems to most travellers, is to me a perpetual Paradise; and, putting Lincolnshire, Leicestershire, and one or two such other perfectly flat districts aside, there is not an English county which I should not find entertainment in exploring the cross-roads of, foot by foot; yet all my best enjoyment would be owing to the imagination of the hills, colouring, with their far-away memories, every lowland stone and herb. The pleasant French coteau, green in the sunshine, delights me, either by what real mountain character it has in itself (for in extent and succession of promontory the flanks of the French valleys have quite the sublimity of true mountain distances) or by its broken ground and rugged steps among the vines, and rise of the leafage above, against the blue sky, as it might rise at Vevey or Como. There is not a wave of the Seine but is associated in my mind with the first raises of the sandstones and forest pines of Fontainebleau; and with the hope of the Alps, as one leaves Paris with the horses' heads to the southwest, the morning sun flashing on the bright waves at Charenton. If there be *no* hope or association of this kind, and if I cannot deceive myself into fancying that perhaps at the next rise of the road there may be seen the film of a blue hill in the gleam of sky at the horizon, the landscape, however beautiful, produces in me even a kind of sickness and pain; and the whole view from Richmond Hill or Windsor Terrace, – nay, the gardens of Alcinous with their perpetual summer, – or of the Hesperides (if they were flat, and not close to Atlas), golden apples and all, – I would give away in an instant, for one mossy granite stone a foot broad, and two leaves of lady-fern.

John Ruskin, *Modern Painters*

A Reading Party in Scotland: The Pupils Disperse and Return

But the Tutor enquired, the grave man, nick-named Adam,
Where do you mean to go, and whom do you mean to visit?
And he was answered by Hope, the Viscount, His Honour, of Ilay,
Kitcat, a Trinity coach, has a party at Drumnadrochet,
Up on the side of Loch Ness, in the beautiful valley of Urquhart;
Mainwaring says they will lodge us, and feed us, and give us a lift too:
Only they talk ere long to remove to Glenmorison. Then at
Castleton, high in Braemar, strange home, with his earliest party,
Harrison, fresh from the schools, has James and Jones and Lauder.
Thirdly, a Cambridge man I know Smith, a senior wrangler,
With a mathematical score hangs-out at Inverary . . .
So in the golden morning they parted and went to the westward.
And in the cottage with Airlie and Hobbes remained the Tutor;
Reading nine hours a day with the Tutor Hobbes and Airlie;
One between bathing and breakfast, and six before it was dinner,
(Breakfast at eight, at four, after bathing again, the dinner)
Finally, two after walking and tea, from nine to eleven.
Airlie and Adam at evening their quiet stroll together
Took on the terrace-road, with the western hills before them;
Hobbes, only rarely a third, now and then in the cottage remaining,
E'en after dinner, eupeptic, would rush yet again to his reading;
Other times, stung by the oestrum of some swift working conception,
Ranged, tearing-on in his fury, an Io-cow, through the mountains
Heedless of scenery, heedless of bogs and of perspiration,
On the high peaks, unwitting, the hares and ptarmigan starting.
And the three weeks past, the three weeks three days over,
Neither letter had come, nor casual tidings any,
And the pupils grumbled, the Tutor became uneasy,

And in the golden weather they wondered, and watched to the westward.
   There is a stream, I name not its name, lest inquisitive tourist
Hunt it, and make it a lion, and get it at last into guide-books,
Springing far off from a loch unexplored in the folds of great
      mountains,
Falling two miles through rowan and stunted alder, enveloped
Then for four more in a forest of pine, where broad and ample
Spreads, to convey it, the glen with heathery slopes on both sides:
Broad and fair the stream, with occasional falls and narrows;
But, where the glen of its course approaches the vale of the river,
Met and blocked by a huge interposing mass of granite,
Scarce by a channel deep-cut, raging up, and raging onward,
Forces its flood through a passage so narrow a lady would step it.
There, across the great rocky wharves, a wooden bridge goes,
Carrying a path to the forest; below, three hundred yard, say,
Lower in level some twenty-five feet, through flats of shingle,
Stepping-stones and a cart-track cross in the open valley.
   But in the interval here the boiling, pent-up water
Frees itself by a final descent, attaining a bason,
Ten feet wide and eighteen long, with whiteness and fury
Occupied partly, but mostly pellucid, pure, a mirror;
Beautiful there for the colour derived from green rocks under;
Beautiful, most of all, where beads of foam uprising
Mingle their clouds of white with the delicate hue of the stillness.
Cliff over cliff for its sides, with rowan and pendent birch boughs,
Here it lies, unthought of above at the bridge and pathway,
Still more enclosed from below by wood and rocky projection.
You are shut in, left alone with yourself and perfection of water,
Hid on all sides, left alone with yourself and the goddess of bathing.
   Here, the pride of the plunger, you stride the fall and clear it;
Here, the delight of the bather, you roll in beaded sparklings,
Here into pure green depth drop down from lofty ledges.
   Hither, a month agone, they had come, and discovered it; hither
(Long a design, but long unaccountably left unaccomplished,)
Leaving the well-known bridge and pathway above to the forest,
Turning below from the track of the carts over stone and shingle,
Piercing a wood, and skirting a narrow and natural causeway
Under the rocky wall that hedges the bed of the streamlet,
Rounded a craggy point, and saw on a sudden before them
Slabs of rock, and a tiny beach, and perfection of water,
Picture-like beauty, seclusion sublime, and the goddess of bathing.
There they bathed, of course, and Arthur, the Glory of headers,
Leapt from the ledges with Hope, he twenty feet, he thirty;

There, overbold, great Hobbes from a ten-foot height descended,
Prone, as a quadruped, prone with hands and feet protending;
There in the sparkling champagne, ecstatic, they shrieked and shouted.
'Hobbes's gutter' the Piper entitles the spot, profanely,
Hope, 'the Glory' would have, after Arthur, the Glory of headers:
But, for before they departed, in shy and fugitive reflex,
Here in the eddies and there did the splendour of Jupiter glimmer
Adam adjudged it the name of Hesperus, star of the evening.
    Hither, to Hesperus, now, the star of evening above them,
Come in their lonelier walk the pupils twain and the Tutor;
Turned from the track of the carts, and passing the stone and shingle,
Piercing the wood, and skirting the stream by the natural causeway,
Rounded the craggy point, and now at their ease looked up; and
Lo, on the rocky ledge, regardant, the Glory of headers,
Lo, on the beach, expecting the plunge, not cigarless, the Piper. –
    And they looked, and wondered, incredulous, looking yet once more.
Yes, it was he, on the ledge, bare-limbed, an Apollo, down-gazing,
Eyeing one moment the beauty, the life, ere he flung himself in it,
Eyeing through eddying greenwaters the green-tinting floor underneath
      them,
Eyeing the bead on the surface, the bead, like a cloud, rising to it,
Drinking-in, deep in his soul, the beautiful hue and the clearness,
Arthur, the shapely, the brave, the unboasting, the Glory of headers;
Yes, and with fragrant weed, by his knapsack, spectator and critic,
Seated on slab by the margin, the Piper, the Cloud-compeller.
    Yes, they were come; were restored to the party, its grace and its gladness,
Yes, were here, as of old; the light-giving orb of the household,
Arthur, the shapely, the tranquil, the strength-and-contentment-diffusing,
In the pure presence of whom none could quarrel long, nor be pettish,
And, the gay fountain of mirth, their dearly beloved of Pipers.
Yes, they were come, were here: but Hewson and Hope – where they then?
Are they behind, travel-sore, or ahead, going straight, by the pathway?
And from his seat and cigar spoke the Piper, the Cloud-compeller.
Hope with the uncle abideth for shooting. Ah me, were I with him!
Ah, good boy that I am to have stuck to my word and my reading!
Good, good boy to be here, far away, who might be at Balloch!
Only one day to have stayed who might have been welcome for seven,
Seven whole days in castle and forest, gay in the mazy
Moving, imbibing the rosy, and pointing a gun at the horny!
    And the Tutor impatient, expectant, interrupted,
Hope with the uncle, and Hewson – with him? or where have you left him?
    And from his seat and cigar spoke the Piper, the Cloud-compeller.
Hope with the uncle, and Hewson – Why, Hewson we left in Rannoch,

By the lochside and the pines, in a farmer's house, – reflecting –
Helping to shear, and dry clothes, and bring in peat from the peat-stack.
    And the Tutor's countenance fell, perplexed, dumbfoundered
Stood he, slow and with pain disengaging jest from earnest.
    He is not far from home, said Arthur from the water,
He will be with us tomorrow at latest, or the next day.
    And he was even more reassured by the Piper's rejoinder.
Can he have come by the mail, and have got to the cottage before us?
    So to the cottage they went, and Philip was not at the cottage;
But by the mail was a letter from Hope, who himself was to follow.
    Two whole days and nights succeeding brought not Philip,
Two whole days and nights exhausted not question and story.
    For it was told, the Piper narrating, corrected of Arthur,
Often by word corrected, more often by smile and motion,
How they had been to Iona, to Staffa, to Skye, to Culloden,
Seen Loch Awe, Loch Tay, Loch Fyne, Loch Ness, Loch Arkaig,
Been up Ben-nevis, Ben-more, Ben-cruachan, Ben-muick-dhui;
How they had walked and eaten, and drunken, and slept in kitchens,
Slept upon floors of kitchens, and tasted the real Glen-livat,
Walked up perpendicular hills, and also down them,
Hither and thither had been, and this and that had witnessed,
Left not a thing to be done, and had not a copper remaining.
    For it was told withal, he telling and he correcting,
How in the race they had run, and beaten the gillies of Rannoch,
How in forbidden glens, in Mar and midmost Athol,
Philip insisting hotly, and Arthur and Hope compliant,
They had defied the keepers; the Piper alone protesting,
Liking the fun, it was plain, in his heart, but tender of game-law;
Yes, too, in Mealy glen, the heart of Lochiel's fair forest,
Where Scotch firs are darkest and amplest, and intermingle
Grandly with rowan and ash – in Mar you have no ashes,
There the pine is alone, or relieved by the birch and the alder –
How in Mealy glen, while stags were starting before, they
Made the watcher believe they were guests from Achnacarry.
    And there was told moreover, he telling, the other correcting,
Often by word, more often by mute significant motion,
Much of the Cambridge coach and his pupils at Inverary,
Huge barbarian pupils, Expanded in Infinite Series,
Firing off signal guns (great scandal) from window to window,
(For they were lodging perforce in distant and numerous houses,)
Signals, when, one retiring, another should go to the Tutor:-
Much too of Kitcat, of course, and the party at Drumnadrochet,
Mainwaring, Foley and Fraser, their idleness horrid and dog-cart;

Drumnadrochet was *seedy*, Glenmorison *adequate*, but at
     Castleton, high in Braemar, were the *clippingest* places for bathing,
One by the bridge in the village, indecent, *the Town-Hall* christened,
Where had Lauder howbeit been bathing, and Harrison also,
Harrison even, the Tutor; another like Hesperus here, and
Up the water of Eye, half-a-dozen at least, all *stunners*.
   And it was told, the Piper narrating and Arthur correcting,
Colouring he, dilating, magniloquent, glorying in picture,
He to a matter-of-fact still softening, paring, abating,
He to the great might-have-been upsoaring, sublime and ideal,
He to the merest it-was restricting, diminishing, dwarfing,
River to streamlet reducing, and fall to slope subduing,
So it was told, the Piper narrating, corrected of Arthur,
How under Linn of Dee, where over rocks, between rocks
Freed from prison the river comes, pouring, rolling, rushing,
Then at a sudden descent goes sliding, gliding, unbroken,
Falling, sliding, gliding, in narrow space collected,
Save for a ripple at last, a sheeted descent unbroken, –
How to the element offering their bodies, downshooting the fall, they
Mingled themselves with the flood and the force of imperious water.
   And it was told too, Arthur narrating, the Piper correcting,
How, as one comes to the level, the weight of the downward impulse
Carries the head under water, delightful, unspeakable; how the
Piper, here ducked and blinded, got stray, and borne off by the
     current,
Wounded his lily-white thighs, below at the craggy corner.
   And it was told, the Piper resuming, corrected of Athur
More by word than motion, change ominous, noted of Adam,
How at the floating-bridge of Laggan, one morning at sunrise,
Came, in default of the ferryman, out of her bed a brave lassie;
And as Philip and she together were turning the handles,
Winding the chain by which the boat works over water,
Hands intermingled with hands, and at last, as they stept from the
     boatie,
Turning about, they saw lips also mingle with lips; but
That was flatly denied and loudly exclaimed at by Arthur:
How at the General's hut, the Inn by the Foyers Fall, where
Over the loch looks at you the summit of Mealfourvonie,
How here too he was hunted at morning and found in the kitchen
Watching the porridge being made, and asking the lassie that made them,
What was the Gaelic for *girl*, and what was the Gaelic for *pretty*;
How in confusion he shouldered his knapsack, yet blushingly stammered,
Waving a hand to the lassie, that blushingly bent o'er the porridge,

Something outlandish – *Slan*-something, *Slan leat*, he believed, *Caleg
    Looach*,
That was the Gaelic it seemed for 'I bid you good-bye, bonnie lassie';
Arthur admitted it true, not of Philip, but of the Piper.

Arthur Hugh Clough, The Bothie of Tober-na-Vuolich

CHAPTER 14

◆

Monasteries in the Clouds

The successors of the saints who founded hermitages in the mountains continued to dwell in mountain monasteries in the nineteenth century – as they do to this day. The mountain monasteries made a strong impression on Victorian visitors, whether favourable (as in Dickens), ambiguous (as in Arnold and Ruskin), or downright hostile (as in Lear).

◆ ◆ ◆

Travellers at the Great St Bernard

In the autumn of the year, Darkness and Night were creeping up to the highest ridges of the Alps.

It was vintage time in the valleys on the Swiss side of the Pass of the Great Saint Bernard, and along the banks of the Lake of Geneva. The air there was charged with the scent of gathered grapes. Baskets, troughs, and tubs of grapes, stood in the dim village door-ways, stopped the steep and narrow village streets, and had been carrying all day along the roads and lanes. Grapes, split and crushed under foot, lay about everywhere. The child carried in a sling by the laden peasant woman toiling home, was quieted with picked-up grapes; the idiot sunning his big goitre under the eaves of the wooden chalet by the way to the waterfall, sat munching grapes; the breath of the cows and goats was redolent of leaves and stalks of grapes; the company in every little cabaret were eating, drinking, talking grapes. A pity that no ripe touch of this generous abundance could be given to the thin, hard, stony wine, which after all was made from the grapes!

The air had been warm and transparent through the whole of the bright day. Shining metal spires and church-roofs, distant and rarely seen, had sparkled in the view; and the snowy mountain-tops had been so clear that unaccustomed eyes, cancelling the intervening country, and slighting their rugged height for something fabulous, would have measured them as within a few hours' easy reach. Mountain-peaks of great celebrity in the valleys, whence no trace of their existence was visible sometimes for months together, had been since morning plain and near, in the blue sky. And now, when it was dark below, though they seemed solemnly to recede, like spectres who were going to vanish, as the red dye of the sunset faded out of them and left them coldly white, they were yet distinctly defined in their loneliness, above the mists and shadows.

Seen from these solitudes, and from the pass of the Great Saint Bernard, which was one of them, the ascending Night came up the mountain like a rising water. When it at last rose to the walls of the convent of the Great Saint Bernard, it was as if that weather-beaten structure were another Ark, and floated on the shadowy waves.

Darkness, outstripping some visitors on mules, had risen thus to the rough convent walls, when those travellers were yet climbing the mountain. As the heat of the glowing day, when they had stopped to drink at the streams of melted ice and snow, was changed to the searching cold of the frosty rarefied night air at a great height, so the fresh beauty of the lower journey had yielded to barrenness and desolation. A craggy track, up which the mules in single file scrambled and turned from block to block, as though they were ascending the broken staircase of a gigantic ruin, was their way now. No trees were to be seen, nor any vegetable growth, save a poor brown scrubby moss, freezing in the chinks of rock. Blackened skeleton arms of wood by the wayside pointed upward to the convent, as if the ghosts of former travellers overwhelmed by the snow haunted the scenes of their distress. Icicle-hung caves and cellars built for refuges from sudden storms, were like so many whispers of the perils of the place; never-resting wreaths and mazes of the mist wandered about, hunted by a moaning wind; and snow, the besetting danger of the mountain, against which all its defences were taken, drifted sharply down.

The file of mules, jaded by their day's work, turned and wound slowly up the steep ascents; the foremost led by a guide on foot, in his broad-brimmed hat and round jacket, carrying a mountain staff or two upon his shoulder, with whom another guide conversed. There was no speaking among the string of riders. The sharp cold, the fatigue of the journey, and a new sensation of a catching in the breath, partly as if they had just emerged from very clear crisp water, and partly as if they had been sobbing, kept them silent.

At length, a light in the summit of the rocky staircase gleamed through the snow and mist. The guides called to the mules, the mules pricked up their drooping heads, the travellers' tongues were loosened, and in a sudden burst of slipping, climbing, jingling, clinking and talking, they arrived at the convent door.

Other mules had arrived not long before, some with peasant riders and some with goods, and had trodden the snow about the door into a pool of mud. Riding-saddles and bridles, pack-saddles and strings of bells, mules and men, lanterns, torches, sacks, provender, barrels, cheeses, kegs of honey and butter, straw bundles and packages of many shapes, were crowded confusedly together in this thawed quagmire, and about the steps. Up here in the clouds, everything was seen through cloud and seemed dissolving into cloud. The breath of the men was cloud, the breath of the mules was cloud, the lights were encircled by cloud, speakers close at hand were not seen for cloud, though their voices and all other sounds were surprisingly clear. Of the cloudy line of mules hastily tied to rings in the wall, one would bite another, or kick another, and then the whole mist would be disturbed: with men diving into it, and cries of men and beasts coming out of it, and no bystander discerning what was wrong. In the midst of this, the great stable of the convent, occupying the basement storey, and entered by the basement door, outside which all the disorder was, poured forth its contribution of cloud, as if the whole rugged edifice were filled with nothing else, and would collapse as soon as it had emptied itself, leaving the snow to fall upon the bare mountain summit.

While all this noise and hurry were rife among the living travellers, there, too, silently assembled in a grated house, half-a-dozen paces removed, with the same cloud enfolding them, and the same snow flakes drifting in upon them, were the dead travellers found upon the mountain. The mother, storm-belated many winters ago, still standing in the corner with her baby at her breast; the man who had frozen with his arm raised to his mouth in fear or hunger, still pressing it with his dry lips after years and years. An awful company, mysteriously come together! A wild destiny for that mother to have foreseen. 'Surrounded by so many and such companions upon whom I never looked, and never shall look, I and my child will dwell together inseparable, on the Great Saint Bernard, outlasting generations who will come to see us, and will never know our name, or one word of our story but the end.'

The living travellers thought little or nothing of the dead just then. They thought much more of alighting at the convent door, and warming themselves at the convent fire. Disengaged from the turmoil, which was already calming down as the crowd of mules began to be bestowed in the stable, they hurried shivering up the steps and into the building. There was a smell within, coming up from the floor, of tethered beasts, like the smell of a menagerie of wild animals. There were strong arched galleries within, huge stone piers, great staircases, and thick walls pierced with small sunken windows – fortifications against the mountain storms, as if they had been human enemies. There were gloomy vaulted sleeping-rooms within, intensely cold, but clean and hospitably prepared for guests. Finally, there was a parlour for guests to sit in and sup in, where a table was already laid, and where a blazing fire shone red and high. In this room, after having had their quarters for the night allotted to them by two young Fathers, the travellers presently drew round the hearth.

Charles Dickens, *Little Dorrit*

Stanzas from the Grande Chartreuse

Through Alpine meadows soft-suffused
With rain, where thick the crocus blows,
Past the dark forges long disused,
The mule-track from Saint Laurent goes.
The bridge is cross'd, and slow we ride
Through forest, up the mountain-side.

The autumnal evening darkens round,
The wind is up, and drives the rain;
While hark! far down, with strangled sound
Doth the Dead Guier's stream complain,
Where that wet smoke, among the woods,
Over his boiling cauldron broods.

Swift rush the spectral vapours white
Past limestone scars with ragged pines,
Showing – then blotting from our sight! –
Halt – through the cloud-drift something shines!
High in the valley, wet and drear,
The huts of Courrerie appear.

Strike leftward! cries our guide; and higher
Mounts up the stony forest-way.
At last the encircling trees retire;
Look! through the showery twilight grey
What pointed roofs are these advance? –
A palace of the kings of France?

Approach, for what we seek is here!
Alight, and sparely sup, and wait
For rest in this outbuilding near;
Then cross the sward and reach that gate.
Knock; pass the wicket! Thou art come
To the Carthusians' world-famed home.

The silent courts, where night and day
Into their stone-carved basins cold
The splashing icy fountains play –
The humid corridors behold!
Where, ghostlike in the deepening night
Cowl'd forms brush by in gleaming white.

The chapel, where no organ's peal
Invests the stern and naked prayer
With penitential cries they kneel
And wrestle; rising then, with bare
And white uplifted faces stand,
Passing the Host from hand to hand;

Each takes, and then his visage wan
Is buried in his cowl once more.
The cells! – the suffering Son of Man
Upon the wall – the knee-worn floor –
And where they sleep, that wooden bed,
Which shall their coffin be, when dead!

The library, where tract and tome
Not to feed priestly pride are there,
To hymn the conquering march of Rome,
Nor yet to amuse, as ours are!
They paint of souls the inner strife
Their drops of blood, their death in life.

The garden, overgrown – yet mild,
See, fragrant herbs are flowering there!
Strong children of the Alpine wild
Whose culture is the brethren's care
Of human tasks their only one,
And cheerful works beneath the sun.

Those halls, too, destined to contain
Each its own pilgrim-host of old,
From England, Germany, or Spain –
All are before me! I behold
The House, the Brotherhood austere!
– And what am I, that I am here?

For rigorous teachers seized my youth
And purged its faith, and trimm'd its fire
Show'd me the high, white star of Truth,
There bade me gaze, and there aspire.
Even now their whispers pierce the gloom:
What dost thou in this living tomb?

Forgive me, masters of the mind!
At whose behest I long ago
So much unlearnt, so much resign'd –
I come not here to be your foe!
I seek those anchorites, not in ruth,
To curse and to deny your truth;

Not as their friend, or child, I speak!
But, as on some far northern strand,
Thinking of his own Gods, a Greek
In pity and mournful awe might stand
Before some fallen Runic stone –
For both were faiths, and both are gone.

Wandering between two worlds, one dead,
The other powerless to be born,
With nowhere yet to rest my head,
Like these, on earth I wait forlorn.
Their faith, my tears, the world deride –
I come to shed them at their side.

Oh, hide me in your gloom profound,
Ye solemn seats of holy pain!
Take me, cowl'd forms, and fence me round,
Till I possess my soul again;
Till free my thoughts before me roll,
Not chafed by hourly false control!

For the world cries your faith is now
But a dead time's exploded dream;
My melancholy, sciolists say,
Is a pass'd mode, an outworn theme –
As if the world had ever had
A faith, or sciolists been sad!

Ah, if it *be* pass'd, take away,
At least, the restlessness, the pain;
Be man henceforth no more a prey
To these out-dated stings again!
The nobleness of grief is gone –
Ah, leave us not the fret alone!

But – if you cannot give us ease –
Last of the race of them who grieve
Here leave us to die out with these
Last of the people who believe!
Silent, while years engrave the brow;
Silent – the best are silent now.

Achilles ponders in his tent,
The kings of modern thought are dumb;
Silent they are, though not content,
And wait to see the future come.
They have the grief men had of yore
But they contend and cry no more.

Our fathers water'd with their tears
This sea of time whereon we sail,
Their voices were in all men's ears
Who pass'd within their puissant hail.
Still the same ocean round us raves,
But we stand mute, and watch the waves.

For what avail'd it, all the noise
And outcry of the former men?
Say, have their sons achieved more joys,
Say, is life lighter now than then?
The sufferers died, they left their pain –
The pangs which tortured them remain.

What helps it now, that Byron bore,
With haughty scorn which mock'd the smart,
Through Europe to the Aetolian shore
The pageant of his bleeding heart?
That thousands counted every groan
And Europe made his woe her own?

What boots it, Shelley! that the breeze
Carried thy lovely wail away,
Musical through Italian trees
Which fringe thy soft blue Spezzian bay?
Inheritors of thy distress
Have restless hearts one throb the less?

Or are we easier, to have read,
O Obermann! the sad, stern page,
Which tells us how thou hidd'st thy head
From the fierce tempest of thine age
In the loan brakes of Fontainebleau,
Or chalets near the Alpine snow?

Ye slumber in your silent grave! –
The world, which for an idle day
Grace to your mood of sadness gave,
Long since hath flung her weeds away.
The eternal trifler breaks your spell;
But we – we learnt your lore too well!

Years hence, perhaps, may dawn an age,
More fortunate, alas! than we,
Which without hardness will be sage
And gay without frivolity.
Sons of the world, oh speed those years;
But, while we wait, allow our tears!

Allow them! We admire with awe
The exulting thunder of your race;
You give the universe your law,
You triumph over time and space!
Your pride of life, your tireless powers,
We laud them, but they are not ours.

We are like children rear'd in shade
Beneath some old-world abbey wall,
Forgotten in a forest-glade,
And secret from the eyes of all.
Deep, deep the greenwood round them waves
Their abbey, and its close of graves.

But, where the road runs near the stream,
Oft through the trees they catch a glance
Of passing troops in the sun's beam –
Pennon, and plume, and flashing lance!
Forth to the world these soldiers fare,
To life, to cities, and to war!

And through the wood, another way,
Faint bugle-notes from far are borne,
Where hunters gather, staghounds bay,
Round some fair forest-lodge at morn.
Gay dames are there, in sylvan green;
Laughter and cries – those notes between!

The banners flashing through the trees
Make their blood dance and chain their eyes.
That bugle-music on the breeze
Arrests them with a charm'd surprise.
Banner by turns and bugle woo:
Ye shy recluses, follow too!

O children, what do ye reply? –
'Action and pleasure, will ye roam
Through these secluded dells to cry
And call us? – But too late ye come!
Too late for us your call ye blow
Whose bent was taken long ago.

'Long since we pace this shadow'd nave;
We watch those yellow tapers shine,
Emblems of hope over the grave,
In the high altar's depth divine;
The organ carries to our ear
Its accents of another sphere.

'Fenced early in this cloistral round
Of reverie, of shade, of prayer,
How should we grow in other ground?
How can we flower in foreign air?
 – Pass, banners, pass, and bugles, cease;
And leave our desert to its peace!'

Matthew Arnold, 'Stanzas from the Grande Chartreuse'

Ruskin's Rebuke to the Hermits

'Mont Blanc Revisited'
(Written at Nyon in 1845)

O Mount beloved, mine eyes again
Behold the twilight's sanguine stain

Along the peaks expire.
O Mount beloved, thy frontier waste
I seek with a religious haste
   And reverent desire.

They meet me, 'midst thy shadows cold; –
Such thoughts as holy men of old
   Amid the desert found; –
Such gladness, as in Him they felt
Who with them through the darkness dwelt,
   And compassed all around.

Ah, happy, if His will were so,
To give me manna here for snow,
   And by the torrent side
To lead me as he leads His flocks
Of wild deer through the lonely rocks
   In peace unterrified;

Since, from the things that trustful rest,
The partridge on her purple nest
   The marmot in his den,
God wins a worship more resigned,
A purer praise than He can find,
   Upon the lips of men.

Alas for man! who hath no sense
Of gratefulness nor confidence,
   But still regrets and raves,
Till all God's love can scarcely win
One soul from taking pride in sin,
   And pleasure over graves.

Yet teach me God, a milder thought,
Lest I, of all Thy blood has bought,
   Least honourable be;
And this, that leads me to condemn
Be rather want of love for them
   Than jealousy for Thee.

These verses, above noticed, with one following sonnet, as the last rhymes
I attempted in any seriousness, were nevertheless themselves extremely
earnest, and express, with more boldness and simplicity than I feel able to

use now with my readers, the real temper in which I began the best work of my life. My mother at once found fault with the words 'sanguine stain', as painful, and untrue of the rose-colour in snow at sunset; but they had their meaning to myself, – the too common Evangelical phrase, 'washed in the blood of Christ', being, it seemed to me, if true at all, true of the earth and her purest snow, as well as of her purest creatures; and the claim of being able to find among the rock-shadows thoughts such as hermits of old found in the desert, whether it seem immodest or not, was wholly true. Whatever might be my common faults or weaknesses, they were rebuked among the hills; and the only days I can look back to as, according to the powers given me, rightly or wisely in entireness spent, have been in sight of Mont Blanc, Monte Rosa, or the Jungfrau.

When I was most strongly under this influence I tried to trace – and I think have traced rightly, so far as I was then able, – in the last chapter of *Modern Painters*, the power of mountains in solemnizing the thoughts and purifying the hearts of the greatest nations of antiquity and the greatest teachers of Christian faith. But I did not then dwell on what I had only felt, but not ascertained, the destruction of all sensibility of this high order in the populations of modern Europe, first by the fine luxury of the fifteenth century, and then by the coarse lusts of the eighteenth and early nineteenth: destruction so total that religious men themselves became incapable of education by any natural beauty or nobleness; and though still useful to others by their ministrations and charities, in the corruption of cities, were themselves lost – or even degraded, if they ever went up into the mountain to preach, or into the wilderness to pray.

There is no word, in the fragment of diary recording our brief visit to the Grande Chartreuse, of anything we saw or heard there that made impression upon any of us. Yet a word was said, of significance enough to alter the courses of religious thought in me, afterwards, for ever.

I had been totally disappointed with the Monastery itself, with the pass of approach to it, with the mountains round it, and with the monk who showed us through it. The building was meanly designed and confusedly grouped; the road up to it nothing like so terrific as most roads in the Alps up to anywhere; the mountains round were simplest commonplace of Savoy cliff, with no peaks, no glaciers, no cascades nor even any slopes of pine in extent of majesty. And the monk who showed us through the corridors had no cowl worth the wearing, no beard worth the wagging, no expression but of superciliousness without sagacity, and an ungraciously dull manner, showing that he was much tired of the place, more of himself, and altogether of my father and me.

Having followed him for a time about the passages of the scattered building, in which there was nothing to show, – not a picture, not a statue, not a bit of old glass, or well-wrought vestment or jewellery; nor any architectural feature in the least ingenious or lovely, we came to a pause at last in what I suppose was a type of a modern Carthusian's cell wherein, leaning on the window sill, I said something, in the style of *Modern Painters*, about the effect of the scene outside upon religious minds. Where-upon, with a curl of his lip 'We do not come here,' said the monk, 'to look at the mountains.' Under which rebuke I bent my head silently, thinking however all the same, 'What then, by all that's stupid, do you come here for at all?'

Which, from that hour to this, I have not conceived; nor after giving my best attention to the last elaborate account of Carthusian faith, 'La Grande Chartreuse, par un Chartreux, Grenoble, 5, Rue Brocherie 1884' am I the least wiser. I am informed by that author that his fraternity are *Eremite* beyond all other manner of men, – that they delight in solitude, and in that amiable disposition pass lives of an angelic tenor, meditating on the charms of the next world, and the vanities of this one.

I sympathise with them in their love of quiet – to the uttermost; but do not hold that liking to be the least pious or amiable in myself, nor under-stand why it seems so to them; or why their founder, St Bruno, – a man of the brightest faculties in teaching, and exhorting, and directing; also, by favour of fortune, made a teacher and governor in the exact centre of European thought and order, the royal city of Rheims, – should think it right to leave all that charge, throw down his robe of rule, his crozier of protection, and come away to enjoy meditation on the next world by himself.

And why meditation among the Alps? He and his disciples might as easily have avoided the rest of mankind by shutting themselves into a penitentiary on a plain, or in whatever kind country they chanced to be born in, without danger to themselves of being buried by avalanches, or trouble to their venerating visitors in coming so far up hill.

Least of all I understand how they could pass their days of meditation without getting interested in plants and stones, whether they would or no; nor how they could go on writing books in scarlet and gold, – (for they were great scribes, and had a beautiful library,) – persisting for centuries in the same patterns, and never trying to draw a bird or a leaf rightly – until the days when books were illuminated no more for religion, but for luxury and the amusement of sickly fancy . . .

While [my] convictions prevented me from being ever led into acceptance of Catholic teaching by my reverence for the Catholic art of the great ages, – and the less, because the Catholic art of these small ages can say but little for itself – I grew also daily more sure that the peace of God rested on all the dutiful and kindly hearts of the laborious poor; and that the only constant form of pure religion was in useful work, faithful love, and stintless charity.

In which pure religion neither St Bruno himself nor any of his true disciples failed: and I perceive it finally notable of them, that, poor by resolute choice of a life of hardship, without any sentimental or fallacious glorifying of 'Holy poverty' as if God had never promised full garners for a blessing; and always choosing men of high intellectual power for the heads of their community, they have had more directly wholesome influence on the outer world than any other order of monks so narrow in number, and restricted in habitation. For while the Franciscan and Cistercian monks became everywhere a constant element in European society, the Carthusians, in their active sincerity, remained, in groups of not more than from twelve to twenty monks in any single monastery, the tenants of a few wild valleys of the north-western Alps; the subsequent overflowing of their brotherhood into the Certosas of the Lombard plains being mere waste and wreck of them; and the great Certosa of Pavia one of the worst shames of Italy, associated with the accursed reign of Galeazzo Visconti. But in their strength, from the foundation of the order, at the close of the eleventh century, to the beginning of the fourteenth, they reared in their mountain fastnesses, and sent out to minister to the world, a succession of men of immense mental grasp, and serenely authoritative innocence; among whom our own Hugo of Lincoln, in his relations with Henry II and Coeur de Lion, is to my mind the most beautiful sacerdotal figure known to me in history. The great Pontiffs have a power which in its strength can scarcely be used without cruelty, nor in its scope without error; the great Saints are always in some degree incredible or unintelligible; but Hugo's power is in his own personal courage and justice only; and his sanctity as clear, frank, and playful as the waves of his own Chartreuse well.

John Ruskin, *Praeterita*

Gloomy Blackclad Men

To Emily Tennyson, Corfu, 9 October 1856

What a place – what a strange place is that Mount Athos! – Apart from the very valuable set of drawings I have brought back, my tour there has been one of the most singular bits of my whole life. Excepting at those Monasteries in Thibet of which Messrs. Huc & Gabet tell us, there is nothing in the world like the Athos peninsular: For the St Bernard & St Gothard monasteries are placed there for a good purpose & do much to benefit others: while at Mt. Athos, many many thousand monks live on through a long long life of mere formal blank. God's word maimed & turned upside down: – God's will laughed at & falsified: nature wounded and trampled on: – that half of our species which it is the natural & best feeling of mankind to love & esteem most – ignored & forbidden: – this is what I saw at Athos: – & if what I saw be Xtianity, then the sooner it be rooted out, the better for humanity. A Turk with 5 wives, a Jew working hard for little old clo'babies – these I believe to be far nearer what Jesus Christ intended man to become than those foolish & miserable monks, what tho' they have the name of Christ written on every garment & every wall & tho they repeat endless parrotprayers daily & nightly.

Do you know the history of Athos – the ancient Acte? – a long mountain narrow peninsular ridge standing up in the sea – joined at one end to the main land by a very narrow isthmus wh: once Xerxes chopped through, & its southern end rising into a pyramid 6700 feet high, strictly the Mount Athos of geography. This peak alone is bare – all the rest of the ridge is a dense world of Ilex, beech, oak & pine. From Constantine & Justinian, who gave up the whole of Acte to Christian hermits, – to the Byzantine Emperors who added to convents already built, & founded others, and down to Sultans as far as our own day – every ruling power in the East has confirmed this territory to the monks as theirs, on proviso of paying £1500 per ann. to the Porte. So the whole strange place has gradually grown into one large nest of monkery – there being as I saw 20 large monasteries, & perhaps 5 or 600 small-hermitages or chapel-cottages holding 1–2 more of the fish and watermelon eating, prayermuttering old creatures who vegetate there, or at best, carve little wooden crosses, of which I have bought you one to put on some little table on a future day.

I will not weary you by accounts of the mode of government of the monasteries – for I dare say I shall publish my doings some day or other; nor much shall I relate of Kariéss the capital of the monks: – nor how my servant was ill and nearly died: & how I was afterwards very ill: – nor many other matters. But I can tell you that I never saw any more striking scenes than those forest screens & terrible crags, all lonely lonely lonely: paths thro' them leading to hermitages where these dead men abide, – or to the immense monasteries where many hundred of these living corpses chant prayers nightly & daily: the blue sea dash dash against the hard iron rocks below – & the oak fringed or chestnut covered height above, with always the great peak of Athos towering over all things, & beyond all the island edged horizon of wide ocean.

The Monasteries – the large ones, are like great castles – fortified with walls & towers: within are courtyards holding churches, clocks & refectories: – the smaller hermitages often stand in gardens, & are gay without though filthy and mournful within. These, which often are clustered so as to seem like villages, – are perhaps the saddest of all – for you think there must be some child – or a dog – or other life than those gloomy blackclad men: – but no – Tomcats & mules are the only beasts allowed on the holy mountain: & crowing cocks the only birds. I solemnly declare such a perversion of right & nature is enough to madden a wise man – & many of these men are more than half foolish: they murmur & mutter & mop & mow. The greater part are utterly ignorant – & only those who manage the affairs of the convents are at all intelligent. Someday perhaps I shall be able to shew you the views I made of these very strange dwellings. – And so I will say no more of gloomy & terrible Athos.

Edward Lear, *Selected Letters*

CHAPTER 15

◆

The Matterhorn

Long after all the other major Alpine peaks had been climbed, the Matterhorn retained a fearsome reputation for inaccessibility. Two men alone believed it was climbable, and persisted in their attempts to reach the summit: the Englishman Edward Whymper, and the Italian, Jean-Antoine Carrel. The extracts in this chapter describe the final attempts on the summit by these two mountaineers, within a few days of each other. Whymper's account of his ascent from Zermatt is taken from his book *Scrambles in the Alps* which remains the greatest classic of mountaineering; the account of the Italian attempt is taken from the letters between the two Italian politicians who had hired Carrel to prepare the way to the summit for them from the Italian side. A little known poem by Thomas Hardy commemorates, thirty-two years later, the glory and the tragedy of the conquest of the Matterhorn.

◆ ◆ ◆

Triumph and Tragedy

On the 7th of July 1865, I crossed the Valcournera pass, in company with Christian Almer and Franz Biener, *en route* for Breuil. My thoughts were fixed on the Matterhorn, and my guides knew that I wished them to accompany me. They had an aversion to the mountain, and repeatedly expressed their belief that it was useless to try to ascend it. '*Anything* but Matterhorn, dear sir!' said Almer; '*anything* but Matterhorn.' He did not speak of difficulty, nor was he shirking *work*. He offered to go *anywhere*; but he entreated that the Matterhorn should be abandoned. Both men spoke fairly enough. They did not think that an ascent could be made; and for their own credit, as well as for my sake, they did not wish to undertake a business which, in their opinion, would only lead to loss of time and money.

I sent them on to Breuil, and walked down to Val Tournanche to look for Jean-Antoine Carrel. He was not there. The villagers said that he, and three others, had started on the 6th to try the Matterhorn by the old way, on their own account. They will have no luck, I thought, for the clouds were low down on the mountains; and I walked up to Breuil, fully expecting to meet them.

Nor was I disappointed. About half way up I saw a group of men clustered around a chalet upon the other side of the torrent, and, crossing over, found that the party had returned. Jean-Antoine and Caesar were there, C.E. Gorret, and J-J. Maquignaz. They had had no success. The weather, they said, had been horrible, and they had scarcely reached the Glacier du Lion.

I explained the situation to Carrel, and proposed that we, with Caesar and another man, should cross the Théodule by moonlight on the 9th, and that upon the 10th we should pitch the tent as high as possible upon the east face. He was unwilling to abandon the old route, and urged me to try it again. I promised to do so, provided the new route failed. This satisfied him, and he agreed to my proposal. I then went up to Breuil, and discharged Almer and Biener – with much regret, for no two men ever served me more faithfully or more willingly. On the next day they crossed to Zermatt.

The 8th was occupied with preparations. The weather was stormy; and black, rainy vapours obscured the mountains. Towards evening a young man came from Val Tournanche, and reported that an Englishman was lying there, extremely ill; and on the morning of Sunday the 9th I went down the valley to look after the sick man. On my way I passed a foreign gentleman, with a mule and several porters laden with baggage. Amongst these men were Jean-Antoine and Caesar, carrying some barometers. 'Hullo!' I said, 'what are you doing?' They explained that the foreigner had arrived just as they were setting out, and that they were assisting his porters. 'Very well; go on to Breuil, and await me there; we start at midnight as agreed.' Jean-Antoine then said that he should not be able to serve me after Tuesday the 11th, as he was engaged to travel 'with a family of distinction' in the Valley of Aosta. 'And Caesar?' 'And Caesar also.' 'Why did you not say this before?' 'Because,' said he, 'it was not settled. The engagement is of long standing, but the *day* was not fixed. When I got back to Val Tournanche on Friday night, after leaving you, I found a letter naming the day.' I could not object to the answer; still the prospect of being left guideless was provoking. They went up, and I down, the valley.

The sick man declared that he was better, though the exertion of saying as much tumbled him over on to the floor in a fainting fit. He was badly in want of medicine, and I tramped down to Chatillon to get it. It was late before I returned to Val Tournanche, for the weather was tempestuous, and rain fell in torrents. A figure passed me under the church-porch. '*Qui vive?*' 'Jean-Antoine.' 'I thought you were at Breuil.' 'No, sir: when the storms came on I knew we should not start tonight, and so came down to sleep here.' 'Ha, Carrel!' I said; 'this is a great bore. If tomorrow is not fine we shall not be able to do anything together. I have sent away my guides, relying on you; and now you are going to leave me to travel with a party of ladies. That work is not fit for *you* (he smiled, I supposed at the implied compliment); can't you send someone else instead?' 'No, Monsieur. I am sorry but my word is pledged. I should like to accompany you; but I can't break my engagement.' By this time we had arrived at the inn door. 'Well, it is no fault of yours. Come presently with Caesar, and have some wine.' They came, and we sat up till midnight, recounting our old adventures, in the inn of Val Tournanche.

The weather continued bad upon the 10th, and I returned to Breuil. The two Carrels were again hovering about the above-mentioned chalet, and I bade them adieu. In the evening the sick man crawled up, a good deal better; but his was the only arrival. The Monday crowd did not cross the Théodule, on account of the continued storms. The inn was lonely. I went to bed early, and was awoke the next morning by the invalid inquiring if I had 'heard the news'. 'No; what news?' 'Why,' said he, 'a large party of guides went off this morning to try the Matterhorn, taking with them a mule laden with provisions.'

I went to the door, and with a telescope saw the party upon the lower slopes of the mountain. Favre, the landlord, stood by. 'What is all this about?' I inquired, 'Who is the leader of this party?' 'Carrel.' 'What! Jean-Antoine?' 'Yes; Jean-Antoine.' 'Is Caesar there too?' 'Yes, he is there.' Then I saw in a moment that I had been bamboozled and humbugged; and learned, bit by bit, that the affair had been arranged long beforehand. The start on the 6th had been for a preliminary reconnaissance; the mule, that I passed, was conveying stores for the attack; the 'family of distinction' was Signor F. Giordano, who had just despatched the party to facilitate the way to the summit, and who, when the facilitation was completed, was to be taken to the top along with Signor Sella!

I was greatly mortified. My plans were upset; the Italians had clearly stolen a march upon me, and I saw that the astute Favre chuckled over my discomfiture, because the route by the eastern face, if successful, would not benefit his inn. What was to be done? I retired to my room, and soothed by tobacco, re-studied my plans, to see if it was not possible to outmanoeuvre the Italians. 'They have taken a mule's load of provisions. That is *one* point in my favour, for they will take two or three days to get through the food, and until that is done, no work will be accomplished. How is the weather?' I went to the window. The mountain was smothered up in mist. Another point in my favour. 'They are to facilitate the way. Well, if they do that to any purpose, it will be a long job.' Altogether, I reckoned that they could not possibly ascend the mountain and come back to Breuil in less than seven days. I got cooler, for it was evident that the wily ones might be outwitted after all. There was time enough to go to Zermatt, to try the eastern face, and, should it prove impracticable, to come back to Breuil before the men returned; and then, it seemed to me, as the mountain was not padlocked, one might start at the same time as the Messieurs, and yet get to the top before them.

The first thing to do was to go to Zermatt. Easier said than done. The seven men upon the mountain included the ablest mountaineers in the valley, and none of the ordinary muleteer-guides were at Breuil. Two men, at least, were wanted for my baggage, but not a soul could be found. I ran about, and sent in all directions, but not a single porter could be obtained. One was with Carrel; another was ill; another was at Chatillon, and so forth. This, however, did not much trouble me, for it was evident that so long as the weather stopped traffic over the Théodule, it would hinder the men equally upon the Matterhorn; and I knew that directly it improved company would certainly arrive.

About mid-day on Tuesday the 11th a large party hove in sight from Zermatt, preceded by a nimble young Englishman, and one of old Peter Taugwalder's sons. I went at once to this gentleman to learn if he could dispense with Taugwalder. He said that he could not, as they were going to recross to Zermatt on the morrow, but that the young man should assist in transporting my baggage, as he had nothing to carry. We naturally got into conversation. I told my story, and learned that the young Englishman was Lord Francis Douglas, whose recent exploit – the ascent of the Gabelhorn – had excited my admiration. He brought good news. Old Peter had lately been beyond the Hörnli, and had reported that he thought an ascent of the Matterhorn was possible upon that side. Almer had left Zermatt, and could not be recovered, so I determined to seek for old Peter. Lord Francis Douglas expressed a warm desire to ascend the mountain, and before long it was determined that he should take part in the expedition.

Favre could no longer hinder our departure, and lent us one of his men. We crossed the Col Théodule on Wednesday morning, the 12th of July, rounded the foot of the Ober Theodulgletscher, traversed the Furggengletscher, and deposited tent, blanket, ropes, and other matters in the little chapel at the Lac Noir. All four were heavily laden for we brought across the whole of my stores from Breuil. Of rope alone there was about 600 feet. There were three kinds. First, 200 feet of Mr Buckingham's Manilla rope; second, 150 feet of a stouter, and possibly stronger rope than the first; and third, more than 200 feet of a lighter and weaker rope than the first, of a kind that I used formerly (stout sashline).

We descended to Zermatt, sought and engaged old Peter, and gave him permission to choose another guide. When we returned to the Monte Rosa Hotel, whom should we see sitting upon the wall in front but my old *guide chef*, Michel Croz. I supposed that he had come with Mr B – but I learned that that gentleman had arrived in ill-health at Chamonix, and had returned to England. Croz, thus left free, had been immediately engaged by the Rev. Charles Hudson, and they had come to Zermatt with the same object as ourselves – namely, to attempt the ascent of the Matterhorn!

Lord Francis Douglas and I dined at the Monte Rosa Hotel and had just finished when Mr Hudson and a friend entered the *salle à manger*. They had returned from inspecting the mountain, and some idlers in the room demanded their intentions. We heard a confirmation of Croz's statement, and learned that Mr Hudson intended to set out on the morrow at the same hour as ourselves. We left the room to consult, and agreed it was undesirable that two independent parties should be on the mountain at the same time with the same object. Mr Hudson was therefore invited to join us, and he accepted our proposal. Before admitting his friend – Mr Hadow – I took the precaution to inquire what he had done in the Alps, and, as well as I remember, Mr Hudson's reply was 'Mr Hadow has done Mont Blanc in less time than most men.' He then mentioned several other excursions that were unknown to me, and added, in answer to a further question. 'I consider he is a sufficiently good man to go with us.' Mr Hadow was admitted, and we then went into the matter of guides. Hudson thought that Croz and old Peter would be sufficient. The question was referred to the men themselves, and they made no objection.

We started from Zermatt on the 13th of July 1865, at half-past 5, on a brilliant and perfectly cloudless morning. We were eight in number – Croz, old Peter and his two sons, Lord F. Douglas, Hadow, Hudson, and I. To ensure steady motion, one tourist and one native walked together. The youngest Taugwalder fell to my share, and the lad marched well, proud to be on the expedition, and happy to shew his powers. The wine-bags also fell to my lot to carry, and throughout the day, after each drink, I replenished them secretly with water, so that at the next halt they were found fuller than before! This was considered a good omen, and little short of miraculous.

On the first day we did not intend to ascend to any great height, and we mounted, accordingly, very leisurely; picked up the things which were left in the chapel at the Schwarzsee at 8.20, and proceeded thence along the ridge connecting the Hörnli with the Matterhorn. At half-past 11 we arrived at the base of the actual peak; then quitted the ridge, and clambered to the left round some ledges, on to the eastern face. We were now fairly upon the mountain, and were astonished to find that places which from the Riffel, or even from the Furggengletscher, looked entirely impracticable, were so easy that we could *run about*.

Before twelve o'clock we had found a good position for the tent, at a height of 11,000 feet. Croz and young Peter went on to see what was above, in order to save time on the following morning. They cut across the heads of the snow-slopes which descended towards the Furggengletscher, and disappeared round a corner; but shortly afterwards we saw them high up on the face, moving quickly. We others made a solid platform for the tent in a well-protected spot, and then watched eagerly for the return of the men. The stone which they upset told us that they were very high, and we supposed that the way must be easy. At length, just before 3 p.m., we saw them coming down, evidently much excited. 'What are they saying, Peter?' 'Gentlemen, they say it is no good.' But when they came near we heard a different story. 'Nothing but what was good; not a difficulty, not a single difficulty! We could have gone to the summit and returned to-day easily!'

We passed the remaining hours of daylight – some basking in the sunshine, some sketching or collecting; and when the sun went down, giving, as it departed, a glorious promise for the morrow, we returned to the tent to arrange for the night. Hudson made tea, I coffee, and we then retired, each to his blanket bag; the Taugwalders, Lord Francis Douglas, and myself, occupying the tent, the others remaining, by preference, outside. Long after dusk the cliffs above echoed with our laughter, and with the songs of the guides, for we were happy that night in camp, and feared no evil.

We assembled together outside the tent before dawn on the morning of the 14th, and started directly it was light enough to move. Young Peter came on with us as a guide, and his brother returned to Zermatt. We followed the route which had been taken on the previous day, and in a few minutes turned the rib which had intercepted the view of the eastern face from our tent platform. The whole of this great slope was now revealed, rising for 3000 feet like a huge natural staircase. Some parts were more, and others were less, easy; but we were not once brought to a halt by any serious impediment, for when an obstruction was met in front it could always be turned to the right or to the left. For the greater part of the way there was, indeed, no occasion for the rope, and sometimes Hudson led, sometimes myself. At 6.20 we had attained a height of 12,800 feet, and halted for half an hour; we then continued the ascent until 9.55, when we stopped for fifty minutes at a height of 14,000 feet. Twice we struck the N.E. ridge and followed it for some little distance – to no advantage, for it was usually more rotten and steep, and always more difficult than the face. Still, we kept near to it, lest stones perchance might fall.

We had now arrived at the foot of that part which, from the Riffelberg or from Zermatt, seems perpendicular or overhanging, and could not longer continue upon the eastern side. For a little distance we ascended by snow upon the arête – that is, the crest of the ridge – descending towards Zermatt, and then, by common consent, turned over to the right or to the northern side. Before doing so we made a change in the order of ascent. Croz went first, I followed, Hudson came third; Hadow and old Peter were last. 'Now' said Croz, as he led off, 'now for something altogether different.' The work became difficult and required caution. In some places there was little to hold, and it was desirable that those should be in front who were least likely to slip. The general slope of the mountain at this part was *less* than 40 degrees, and snow had accumulated in, and had filled up, the interstices of the rock face, leaving only occasional fragments projecting here and there.

These were at times covered with a thin film of ice, produced from the melting and refreezing of the snow. It was a place over which any fair mountaineer might pass in safety, and Mr Hudson ascended this part, and, so far as I know, the entire mountain, without having the slightest assistance rendered to him upon any occasion. Sometimes, after I had taken a hand from Croz, or received a pull, I turned to offer the same to Hudson; but he invariably declined, saying it was not necessary. Mr Hadow, however, was not accustomed to this kind of work, and required continual assistance. It is only fair to say that the difficulty which he found at this part arose simply and entirely from want of experience.

The solitary difficult part was of no great extent. We bore away over it at first, nearly horizontally, for a distance of about 400 feet; then ascended directly towards the summit for about 60 feet; and then doubled back to the ridge which descends towards Zermatt. A long stride round a rather awkward corner brought us to snow once more. The last doubt vanished! The Matterhorn was ours! Nothing but 200 feet of easy snow remained to be surmounted! . . .

You must now carry your thoughts back to the seven Italians who started from Breuil on the 11th of July. Four days had passed since their departure, and we were tormented with anxiety lest they should arrive on the top before us. All the way up we had talked of them, and many false alarms of 'men on the summit' had been raised. The higher we rose, the more intense became the excitement. What if we should be beaten at the last moment? The slope eased off, at length we could be detached, and Croz and I, dashing away, ran a neck-and-neck race, which ended in a dead heat. At 1.40 p.m. the world was at our feet, and the Matterhorn was conquered. Hurrah! Not a footstep could be seen.

It was not yet certain that we had not been beaten. The summit of the Matterhorn was formed of a rudely level ridge, about 350 feet long, and the Italians might have been at its farther extremity. I hastened to the southern end, scanning the snow right and left eagerly. Hurrah! again; it was untrodden. 'Where were the men?' I peered over the cliff, half doubting, half expectant, and saw them immediately – mere dots on the ridge, at an immense distance below. Up went my arms and my hat. 'Croz! Croz!! come here!' 'Were are they Monsieur?' 'There, don't you see them, down there?' 'Ah! the *coquins*, they are low down.' 'Croz, we must make those fellows hear us.' We yelled until we were hoarse. The Italians seemed to regard us – we could not be certain. 'Croz, we *must* make them hear us; they *shall* hear us!' I seized a block of rock and hurled it down, and called upon my companion, in the name of friendship, to do the same. We drove our sticks in, and prised away the cracks, and soon a torrent of stones poured down the cliffs. There are no mistake about it this time. The Italians turned and fled . . .

The others had arrived, so we went back to the northern end of the ridge. Croz now took the tent-pole, and planted it in the highest snow. 'Yes,' we said, 'there is the flag-staff, but where is the flag?' 'Here it is,' he answered, pulling off his blouse and fixing it to the stick. It made a poor flag, and there was no wind to float it out, yet it was seen all around. They saw it at Zermatt – at the Riffel – in the Val Tournanche. At Breuil, the watchers cried, 'Victory is ours!' They raised 'bravos' for Carrel, and 'vivas' for Italy and hastened to put themselves *en fete*. On the morrow they were undeceived. 'All was changed; the explorers returned sad – cast down – disheartened – confounded – gloomy.' 'It is true,' said the men. 'We saw them ourselves – they hurled stones at us! The old traditions *are* true, – there are spirits on the top of the Matterhorn!'

We returned to the southern end of the ridge to build a cairn, and then paid homage to the view. The day was one of those superlatively calm and clear ones which usually precede bad weather. The atmosphere was perfectly still, and free from all clouds or vapours. Mountains fifty – nay a hundred – miles off, looked sharp and near. All their details – ridge and crag, snow and glacier – stood out with faultless definition. Pleasant thoughts of happy days in bygone years came up unbidden, as we recognised the old, familiar forms. All were revealed – not one of the principal peaks of the Alps was hidden. I see them clearly now – the great inner circles of giants, backed by the ranges, chains and *massifs*. First came the Dent Blanche, hoary and grand; the Gabelhorn and pointed Rothorn; and then the peerless Weisshorn; the towering Mischabelhörner, flanked by the Allalinhorn, Strahlhorn, and Rimpfischhorn; then Monte Rosa – with its many Spitzes – the Lyskamm and the Breithorn. Behind were the Bernese Oberland, governed by the Finsteraarhorn; the Simplon and St Gothard groups; the Disgrazia and the Ortler. Towards the south we looked down to Chivasso on the plain of Piedmont, and far beyond. The Viso – one hundred miles away – seemed close upon us; the Maritime Alps – one hundred and thirty miles distant – were free from haze. Then came my first love – the Pelvoux; the Ecrins and the Meije; the clusters of the Graians; and lastly, in the west, glowing in full sunlight, rose the monarch of all – Mont Blanc. Ten thousand feet beneath us were the green fields of Zermatt, dotted with chalets, from which blue smoke rose lazily. Eight thousand feet below, on the other side, were the pastures of Breuil. There were forests black and gloomy, and meadows bright and lively; bounding waterfalls and tranquil lakes; fertile lands and savage wastes; sunny plains and frigid *plateaux*. There were the most rugged forms, and the most graceful outlines – bold, perpendicular cliffs, and gentle undulating slopes; rocky mountains and snowy mountains, sombre and solemn, or glittering and white with walls – turrets – pinnacles – pyramids – domes – cones – and spires! There was every combination that the world can give, and every contrast that the heart could desire.

We remained on the summit for one hour –

'One crowded hour of glorious life.'

It passed away too quickly, and we began to prepare for the descent.

Hudson and I again consulted as to the best and safest arrangement of the party. We agreed that it would be best for Croz to go first, and Hadow second; Hudson, who was almost equal to a born mountaineer in sureness of foot, wished to be third; Lord Francis Douglas was placed next, and old Peter, the strongest of the remainder, after him. I suggested to Hudson that we should attach a rope to the rocks on our arrival at the difficult bit, and hold it as we descended, as an additional protection. He approved the idea, but it was not definitely settled that it should be done. The party was being arranged in the above order whilst I was sketching the summit, and they had finished, and were waiting for me to be tied in line, when some one remembered that our names had not been left in a bottle. They requested me to write them down, and moved off while it was being done.

A few minutes afterwards I tied myself to young Peter, ran down after the others, and caught them just as they were commencing the descent of the difficult part. Great care was being taken. Only one man was moving at a time; when he was firmly planted the next advanced and so on. They had not, however, attached the additional rope to rocks, and nothing was said about it. The suggestion was not made for my own sake, and I am not sure that it even occurred to me again. For some little distance we two followed the others, detached from them, and should have continued so had not Lord Francis Douglas asked me, about 3 p.m., to tie on to old Peter, as he feared, he said, that Taugwalder would not be able to hold his ground if a slip occurred.

A few minutes later, a sharp-eyed lad ran into the Monte Rosa hotel, to Seiler, saying that he had seen an avalanche fall from the summit of the Matterhorn on to the Matterhorngletscher. The boy was reproved for telling idle stories; he was right, nevertheless, and this was what he saw.

Michel Croz had laid aside his axe, and in order to give Mr Hadow greater security, was absolutely taking hold of his legs, and putting his feet, one by one, into their proper positions. So far as I know, no one was actually descending. I cannot speak with certainty, because the two leading men were partially hidden from my sight by an intervening mass of rock, but it is my belief, from the movements of their shoulders, that Croz, having done as I have said, was in the act of turning round, to go down a step or two himself; at this moment Mr Hadow slipped, fell against him, and knocked him over. I heard one startled exclamation from Croz, then saw him and

Mr Hadow flying downwards; in another moment Hudson was dragged from his steps, and Lord Francis Douglas immediately after him. All this was the work of a moment. Immediately we heard Croz's exclamation, old Peter and I planted ourselves as firmly as the rocks would permit: the rope was taut between us, and the jerk came on us both as on one man. We held: but the rope broke midway between Taugwalder and Lord Francis Douglas. For a few seconds we saw our unfortunate companions sliding downwards on their backs, and spreading out their hands, endeavouring to save themselves. They passed from our sight uninjured, disappeared one by one, and fell from precipice to precipice onto the Matterhorngletscher below, a distance of nearly 4,000 feet in height. From the moment the rope broke it was impossible to help them.

So perished our comrades! For the space of half-an-hour we remained on the spot without moving a single step. The two men, paralysed by terror, cried like infants, and trembled in such a manner as to threaten us with the fate of the others. Old Peter rent the air with exclamations of 'Chamonix! Oh, what will Chamonix say?' He meant, Who would believe that Croz could fall? The young man did nothing but scream or sob, 'We are lost! We are lost!' Fixed between the two I could neither move up nor down. I begged young Peter to descend, but he dared not. Unless he did, we could not advance. Old Peter became alive to the danger, and swelled the cry 'We are lost! we are lost!' The father's fear was natural – he trembled for his son; the young man's fear was cowardly – he thought of self alone. At last old Peter summoned up courage and changed his position to a rock to which he could fix the rope; the young man then descended, and we all stood together. Immediately we did so, I asked for the rope which had given way, and found, to my surprise – indeed, to my horror – that it was the weakest of the three ropes. It was not brought, and should not have been employed, for the purpose for which it was used. It was old rope, and compared with the others, was feeble. It was intended as a reserve, in case we had to leave much rope behind, attached to rocks. I saw at once that a serious question was involved, and made him give me the end. It had broken in mid-air, and did not appear to have sustained previous injury.

For more than two hours afterwards I thought almost every moment that the next would be my last; for the Taugwalders, utterly unnerved, were not only incapable of giving assistance, but were in such a state that a slip might have been expected from them at any moment. After a time, we were able to do that which should have been done at first, and fixed rope to firm rocks, in addition to being tied together. These ropes were cut from time to time, and were left behind. Even with their assistance the men were afraid to proceed, and several times old Peter turned with ashy face and faltering limbs, and said, with terrible emphasis, 'I *cannot*!'

About 6 p.m. we arrived at the snow upon the ridge descending towards Zermatt, and all peril was over. We frequently looked, but in vain, for traces of our unfortunate companions; we bent over the ridge and cried to them, but no sound returned. Convinced at last that they were neither within sight nor hearing, we ceased from our useless efforts; and, too cast down for speech, silently, gathered up our things, and the little effects of those who were lost, preparatory to continuing the descent. When lo! a mighty arch appeared, rising above the Lyskamm, high into the sky. Pale, colourless, and noiseless, but perfectly sharp and defined, except where it was lost in the clouds, this unearthly apparition seemed like a vision from another world; and, almost appalled, we watched with amazement the gradual development of two vast crosses, one on either side. If the Taugwalders had not been the first to perceive it, I should have doubted my senses. They thought it had some connection with the accident, and I, after a while, that it might bear some relation to ourselves. But our movements had no effect upon it. The spectral forms remained motionless. It was a fearful and wonderful sight; unique in my experience, and impressive beyond description, coming at such a moment.

I was ready to leave and waiting for the others. They had recovered their appetites, and the use of their tongues. They spoke in patois, which I did not understand. At length the son said in French 'Monsieur.' 'Yes.' 'We are poor men; we have lost our Herr; we shall not get paid; we can ill afford this.' 'Stop!' I said, interrupting him, 'that is nonsense; I shall pay you, of course, just as if your Herr were here.' They talked together in their patois for a short time, and then the son spoke again. 'We don't wish you to pay us. We wish you to write in the hotel-book at Zermatt, and to your journals, that we have not been paid.' 'What nonsense are you talking? I don't understand you. What do you mean?' He proceeded – 'Why, next year there will be many travellers at Zermatt, and we shall get more *voyageurs*.'

Who would answer such a proposition? I made them no reply in words, but they knew very well the indignation that I felt. They filled the cup of bitterness to overflowing, and I tore down the cliff, madly and recklessly, in a way that caused them, more than once, to inquire if I wished to kill them. Night fell; and for an hour the descent was continued in the darkness. At half-past 9 a resting-place was found, and upon a wretched slab, barely large enough to hold the three, we passed six miserable hours. At daybreak the descent was resumed and from the Hörnli ridge we ran down to the chalets of Buhl, and on to Zermatt. Seiler met me at his door, and followed in silence to my room. 'What is the matter?' 'The Taugwalders and I have returned.' He did not need more, and burst into tears; but lost no time in useless lamentations and set to work to arouse the village. Ere long a score of men had started to ascend the Hohlicht heights, above Kalbermatt and

Z'mutt, which commanded the plateau of the Matterhorngletscher. They returned after six hours, and reported that they had seen the bodies lying motionless on the snow. This was on Saturday; and they proposed that we should leave on Sunday evening, so as to arrive upon the plateau at daybreak on Monday. Unwilling to lose the slightest chance, the Rev. J. M'Cormick and I resolved to start . . .

We started at 2 a.m. on Sunday the 16th and followed the route that we had taken on the previous Thursday as far as the Hörnli. Thence we went down to the right of the ridge, and within sight of the corner in which we knew my companions must be. As we saw one weather-beaten man after another raise the telescope, turn deadly pale, and pass it on without a word to the next, we knew that all hope was gone. We approached. They had fallen below as they had fallen above – Croz a little in advance, Hadow near him, and Hudson some distance behind; but of Lord Francis Douglas we could see nothing. We left them where they fell; buried in snow at the base of the grandest cliff of the most majestic mountain of the Alps.

Edward Whymper, *Scrambles in the Alps*

The Italian Angle

To Quintino Sella, Turin, 7 July, 1865

DEAR QUINTINO, – I am starting off, heavily armed, for the destination you wot of. I sent off the day before yesterday the first tent, 300 metres of rope, and some iron hoops and rings, besides various kinds of provisions for ourselves, a spirit-lamp for heating water, tea, etc. All these things together weigh about 100 kilos. I have also sent Carrel 200 fcs, in order that he may meet these articles at Châtillon and transport them to Valtournanche and Breuil at once. I shall be up there myself to-morrow evening, to superintend the work.

I am taking with me a second tent, three barometers, your own among them, and the *Annuaire du Bureau des Longitudes*. As soon as I reach the scene of operations I will write to you again.

You need only trouble about your own personal requirements, viz., your headgear, a few rugs, etc., and – some good cigars; if possible, also a little good wine and a few shekels, because I have only been able to bring about 3000 fcs. with me.

Let us then, set out to attack this Devil's mountain, and let us see that we succeed, if only Whymper has not been beforehand with us.

BREUIL HOTEL, AT THE FOOT OF THE THEODUL
July 11th, evening

DEAR QUINTINO, – It is high time for me to send you news from here. I reached Valtournanche on Saturday at midday. There I found Carrel, who had just returned from a reconnoitring expedition on the Matterhorn, which had proved a failure, owing to bad weather.

Whymper had arrived two or three days before; as usual, he wished to make the ascent, and had engaged Carrel, who, not having yet had my letters, had agreed, but for a few days only. Fortunately, the weather turned bad. Whymper was unable to make his fresh attempt, and Carrel left him and came with me, together with five other picked men who are the best guides in the valley. We immediately sent off our advance guard, with Carrel at its head. In order not to excite remark we took the rope and other materials to Avouil, a hamlet which is very remote and close to the Matterhorn, and this is to be our lower base. Of our six men, four are to work up above, and two will act continuously as porters, a task which is at least as difficult as the other.

I have taken up my quarters at Breuil for the time being. The weather, the god whom we fear and on whom all will depend, has been hitherto very changeable and rather bad. As lately as yesterday morning it was snowing on the Matterhorn, but yesterday evening it cleared. In the night (10th-11th) the men started with the tents, and I hope that by this time they will have reached a great height; but the weather is turning misty again, and the Matterhorn is still covered; I hope the mists will soon disperse. Weather permitting, I hope in three or four days to know how I stand. Carrel told me not to come up yet, until he should send me word; naturally he wishes personally to make sure of the last bits. As seen from here, they do not seem to me to be absolutely inaccessible, but before saying that one must try them; and it is also necessary to ascertain whether we can bivouac at a point much higher than Whymper's highest. As soon as I have any good news I will send a message to St Vincent, the nearest telegraph office, with a telegram containing a few words; and do you then come at once. Meanwhile, on receipt of the present, please send me a few lines in reply, with some advice, because I am head over ears in difficulty here, what with the weather, the expense, and Whymper.

I have tried to keep everything secret, but that fellow, whose life seems to depend on the Matterhorn, is here, suspiciously prying into everything. I have taken all the competent men away from him, and yet he is so enamoured of this mountain that he may go up with others and make a scene. He is here, in this hotel, and I try to avoid speaking to him.

In short, I will do my best to succeed, and I have hopes. Provided Aeolus be on our side!

I will write no more at present, hoping soon to send you a favourable sign. I trust this news from the Alps will refresh you somewhat in the heat of Turin and the oppression of ministerial affairs.

BREUIL HOTEL, July 14th

DEAR QUINTINO, – I am sending a telegram for you by express to St Vincent, seven hours walk from here; at the same time, to make assurance doubly sure, I send you this letter.

At 2 p.m. to-day I saw Carrel and Co. on the top peak of the Matterhorn; many others saw them as well as I; so success seems certain, notwithstanding that the day before yesterday the weather was very bad, so that the mountain was covered with snow. So start at once if you can, or else telegraph to me at St Vincent. Fancy, I do not even know whether you are at Turin! I have had no news from there for a week; so I am just writing on the chance. If you do not come or telegraph by tomorrow evening I shall go and plant our flag up there, that it may be the first. This is essential. I will, however, do all I can to wait for you, so that you may come yourself. Whymper has gone off to make the attempt on the other side, but I think in vain.

BREUIL, 15 July

DEAR QUINTINO, – Yesterday was a bad day, and Whymper, after all, gained the victory over the unfortunate Carrel. Whymper, as I told you, was desparate, and seeing Carrel climbing the mountain, tried his fortune on the Zermatt slope. Everyone here, and Carrel above all, considered the ascent absolutely impossible on that side; so we were all easy in our minds. On the 11th Carrel was at work on the mountain, and pitched his tent at a certain height. On the night between the 11th and 12th, and the whole of the 12th, the weather was horrible, and snow on the Matterhorn; on the 13th weather fair, and yesterday, the 14th, fine. On the 13th little work was done, and yesterday Carrel might have reached the top, and was perhaps only about 500 or 600 feet below, when suddenly, at about 2 p.m., he saw Whymper and the others already on the summit. Whymper must have promised a considerable sum to various Swiss guides if they could take him up, and having been favoured with an exceptionally fine day, he succeeded. I had, it is true, sent Carrel word of Whymper's proposed attempt, and had enjoined on him to get up at any cost, without loss of time to prepare the way, but my warning did not reach him in time, and moreover Carrel did not believe the ascent from the North to be possible. However, yesterday, as I saw some men on the Matterhorn, and was assured by everyone that they were our party, I sent off the telegram to you, bidding you come up. Poor Carrel, when he saw that he had been forestalled, had not the courage to proceed, and beat a retreat with his weapons and his baggage. He arrived here late this morning, and it was then that I sent off another telegram by express to stop you from coming. As you see, although every man did his duty, it is a lost battle, and I am in great grief.

I think, however, that we can play a counter-stroke by someone's making the ascent at once on this side, thus proving at any rate that the ascent is feasible this way; Carrel still thinks it possible. I was only vexed with him for bringing down the tents, the ropes, and all the other things that had been carried up with so much labour to a point so near the summit. He puts the blame on the party, who had completely lost heart, and on his fear that I would be unwilling to go to any further expense.

At any rate, in order not to return ridiculous as well as unsuccessful, I think that we ought at least to plant our flag on the summit. I at once tried to organize a fresh expedition, but hitherto, with the exception of Carrel and another, I have not found any men of courage whom I can trust. Some others might, perhaps, be found if I paid them extravagantly, but I do not think it wise to go to such expense; and then, if their courage is deficient, there would be no certainty of success.

I am therefore trying to fit out the expedition cheaply and will only give up if this one is unsuccessful. Now I shall not even have the satisfaction of going up myself, because Carrel says that, for the sake of quickness and in order to make the best of the short time we have at our disposal, it will be better that they should not have any traveller with them.

We must also remember that we are threatened by the weather, which is doubtful.

Just see how annoying it all is!

Yesterday the Val Tournanche was already *en fête* thinking that we were victorious; today we were disillusioned. Poor Carrel is to be pitied, the more so as part of the delay was due to his idea that Whymper would not be able to ascend from Zermatt. I am trying to act like Terentius Varro after the battle of Cannae.

PS – Notwithstanding what was happened, you might still make the first ascent from the Italian side, if you had the time; but till now Carrel has not assured me that the way is feasible right to the top. That is why I have not telegraphed to you again; perhaps I shall come to Turin myself in a couple of days.

On 16th July Carrel and three others made a fresh attempt, and on 17th Giordano was able to write in his diary:

Splendid weather: at 9.30 saw Carrel and his men on the Shoulder, after that saw nothing more of them. Then much mist about the summit. Lifted a bit about 3.30, and we saw our flag on the western summit of the Matterhorn. The English flag looked like a black shawl lying on the snow, in the centre . . .
July 18th. Great hilarity all day at the hotel and at Breuil, bonfires and songs. Amid the rejoicing, I alone was sad; I had not personally climbed the Matterhorn.

Felice Giordano, in Guido Rey, *The Matterhorn*

'Zermatt: To the Matterhorn'

Thirty-two years since, up against the sun,
Seven shapes, thin atomies to lower sight,
Labouringly leapt and gained thy gabled height,
And four lives paid for what the seven had won.

They were the first by whom the deed was done,
And when I look at thee, my mind takes flight
To that day's tragic deed of manly might,
As though, till then, of history thou hadst none.

Yet ages ere men topped thee, late and soon
Thou didst behold the planets lift and lower;
Saw'st, maybe, Joshua's pausing sun and moon,
And the betokening sky when Caesar's power
Approached its bloody end: yea, even that Noon
When darkness filled the earth till the ninth hour.

Thomas Hardy

CHAPTER 16

◆

People of the Valleys

The opening up of the Alps to tourists and mountaineers had profound effects on the inhabitants of the Alpine valleys. As has been seen from previous extracts, the typical attitude of the eighteenth-century tourist had been one of contempt for the mountain people. In the nineteenth century Ruskin's description of Alp dwellers is not a flattering one, but its tone is one of sympathy rather than contempt. Tourists complained, as tourists do everywhere, of the growth of mendicancy. The relationship between climbers and their guides varied between close comradeship and irritation at alleged exploitation. At Chamonix regulations were drawn up for the regulation of guides, partly to ensure competence, but also to enforce a closed shop and to institutionalize overmanning on the Alpine routes. The regulations survived the transfer of Chamonix (with the rest of Savoy) from Italian to French rule in 1860; but they remained unpopular with British visitors. None the less, some of the best climbers, like Leslie Stephen, retained an admiring affection for their guides. Towards the end of the century the advertisements which appear in Whymper's guidebooks illustrate the commercial development of the major resorts.

◆ ◆ ◆

The Mountain Gloom

The traveller on his happy journey, as his foot springs from the deep turf and strikes the pebbles gaily over the edge of the mountain road, sees with a glance of delight the clusters of nutbrown cottages that nestle among those sloping orchards, and glow beneath the boughs of the pines. Here it may well seem to him, if there be sometimes hardship, there must be at least innocence and peace, and fellowship of the human soul with nature. It is not so. The wild goats that leap along those rocks have as much passion of joy in all that fair work of God as the men that toil among them. Perhaps more. Enter the street of one of those villages, and you will find it foul with that gloomy foulness that is suffered only by torpor, or by anguish of soul. Here, it is torpor – not absolute suffering – not starvation or disease, but darkness of calm enduring; the spring known only as the time of the scythe, and the autumn as the time of the sickle, and the sun only as a warmth, the wind as a chill, and the mountains as a danger. They do not understand so much as the name of beauty, or of knowledge. They understand dimly that of virtue. Love, patience, hospitality, faith – these things they know. To glean their meadows side by side, so happier; to bear the burden up the breathless mountain flank, unmurmuringly; to bid the stranger drink from their vessel of milk; to see at the foot of their low deathbeds a pale figure upon a cross, dying, also patiently; – in this they are different from the cattle and from the stones, but in all this unrewarded as far as concerns the present life. For them, there is neither hope nor passion of spirit; for them neither advance nor exultation. Black bread, rude roof, dark night, laborious day, weary arm at sunset; and life ebbs away. No books, no thought, no attainments, no rest; except only sometimes a little sitting in the sun under the church wall, as the bell tolls thin and far in the mountain air; a pattering of a few prayers, not understood, by the altar rails of the dimly gilded chapel, and so back to the sombre home, with the cloud upon them still unbroken – that cloud of rocky gloom, born out of the wild torrents and ruinous stones, and unlightened, even in their religion, except by the vague promise of some better thing unknown, mingled with threatening, and obscured by an unspeakable horror, – a smoke, as it were, of martyrdom, coiling up with incense, and, amidst the images of tortured bodies and lamenting spirits in hurtling flames, the very cross, for them, dashed more deeply than for others, with gouts of blood.

Do not let this be thought a darkened picture of the life of these mountaineers. It is a literal fact. No contrast can be more painful than that between the dwelling of any well-conducted English cottager, and that of the equally honest Savoyard. The one, set in the midst of its dull flat fields and uninteresting hedgerows, shows in itself the love of brightness and beauty; its daisy studded garden-beds, its smoothly swept brick path to the threshold, its freshly sanded floor and orderly shelves of household furniture all testify to energy of heat, and happiness in the simple course and simple possessions of daily life. The other cottage, in the midst of an inconceivable, inexpressible beauty, set on some sloping bank of golden sward, with clear fountains flowing beside it, and wild flowers, and noble trees, and goodly rocks gathered round into a perfection as of Paradise, is itself a dark and plague-like stain in the midst of the gentle landscape. Within a certain distance of its threshold the ground is foul and cattle-trampled; its timbers are black with smoke, its garden choked with weeds and nameless refuse, its chambers empty and joyless, the light and wind gleaming and filtering through the crannies of their stones. All testifies that to its inhabitant the world is labour and vanity; that for him neither flowers bloom, nor birds sing, nor fountains glisten; and that his soul hardly differs from the grey cloud that coils and dies upon his hills, except in having no fold of it touched by the sunbeams.

Is it not strange to reflect that hardly an evening passes in London or Paris, but one of those cottages is painted for the better amusement of the fair and idle, and shaded with pasteboard pines by the scene-shifter; and that good and kind people, poetically-minded, delight themselves in imagining the happy life led by peasants who dwell by Alpine fountains, and kneel to crosses upon peaks of rock? – that nightly we give our gold, to fashion forth simulacra of peasants, in gay ribands and white bodices, singing sweet songs, and bowing gracefully to the picturesque crosses: and all the while the veritable peasants are kneeling, songlessly, to veritable crosses, in another temper than the kind and fair audiences deem of, and assuredly with another kind of answer than is got out of the opera catastrophe; an answer having reference, it may be in dim futurity, to those very audiences themselves? If all the gold that has gone to paint the simulacra of the cottages, and to put new songs in the mouths of the simulacra of the peasants, had gone to brighten the existent cottages, and to put new songs in the mouths of the existent peasants, it might, in the end, perhaps, have turned out better so, not only for the peasant, but for even the audience . . .

We paint the faded actress, build the lath landscape, feed our benevolence with fallacies of felicity, and satisfy our righteousness with poetry of justice. The time will come when, as the heavy-folded curtain falls upon our own stages of life, we shall begin to comprehend that the justice we loved was intended to have been done in fact, and not in poetry, and the felicity we sympathized in, to have been bestowed and not feigned. We talk much of money's worth, yet perhaps may one day be surprised to find that what the wise and charitable European public gave to one night's rehearsal of hypocrisy, – to one hours's pleasant warbling of Linda or Lucia – would have filled a whole Alpine valley with happiness, and poured the waves of harvest over the famine of many a Lammermoor.

John Ruskin, *Modern Painters*

The Lady Bountiful

My mother's sufferings from the heat led to our going from Geneva to Chamounix. On the way we slept at St Martin. As I was drawing there upon the bridge, a little girl came to beg, but beggars were so common that I paid no attention to her entreaties, till her queer expression attracted me, and a boy who came up at the same time described her as an *abandonée*, for her father was in prison, her sister dead, and her mother had deserted her and gone off to Paris. The child, who had scarcely an apology for being clothed, verified this in a touching and at the same time an elf-like way. Charlotte Leycester gave her four sous, with which she was so enchanted that she rushed away, throwing her hands into the air and making every demonstration of delight, and we thought we should see no more of her. However, in going home, we found her under a wall on the other side of the bridge, where she showed us with rapture the bread she had been able to buy with the money which had been given her. An old woman standing by told us about her – how wonderfully little the child lived on, sleeping from door to door, and how extraordinary her spirits still were. It was so odd a case, and there was something so interesting in the child, that we determined to follow her, and see where she would go to sleep. To our surprise, instead of guiding us through the village, she took her way straight up the woods on the mountain-side, by a path which she assured us was frequented by wolves. Meantime we had made out from the child that her name was Toinette, daughter of François Bernard, and that she once lived in the neighbouring village of Passey, where her home had been burnt to the ground, a scene which she described with marvellous gesticulations. She seemed to have conceived the greatest affection for Charlotte.

A great dog flew out of the cottage at us, but Toinette drove it away, and called out a woman who was standing in the doorway. The woman said she knew nothing of Toinette, but that she had implored to sleep there about three weeks before, and that she had slept there ever since; and then the child, caressing her and stroking her cheeks, begged to be allowed to do the same again. The woman offered to go with us to another house, where the people knew the child better. On arriving, we heard the inmates at prayers inside, singing a simple litany in responses. Afterwards they came out to speak to us. They said it was but for a very small matter François Bernard was imprisoned, as he had only stolen some bread when he was starving, but that, if he came back, he could do nothing for Toinette, and as her uncles were idiots, there was nobody to take care of her: if we wished to do anything for her, we had better speak to the Syndic, who lived higher up the mountain; so thither we proceeded, with Toinette and all her female friends in our train.

It was a strange walk, by starlight through the woods, and a queer companionship of rough kind-hearted people. Toinette, only seven years old, laughed and skipped over the stones, holding Charlotte's gown, and declaring she would never leave her. The Syndic was already in bed, but Madame, his wife, speedily got him up, and we held a parley with him on the wooden staircase, all the other people standing below. He said that there were no workhouses, no orphan asylums, and that though it was a bad case the commune had no funds; school did not open till October, and even if Toinette got work there was no lodging for her at night. However, when Charlotte promised to clothe her, he was so much enchanted with the *grandeur de sa charité*, that he said he would consult with the commune about Toinette. Meantime, in the morning Charlotte bought her some clothes, and settled something for her future; but before we left we saw that she must not be too much indulged, as she asked Charlotte, who had given her a frock, shoes, and a hat, to give her also some bonbons and a parasol!

We heard of Toinette Bernard for some years afterwards, and Charlotte Leycester sent annual remittances to her; but eventually she absconded, and utterly disappeared like a waif.

Augustus Hare, The Story of My Life

The Guides of Chamonix

In the month of May 1823, the organisation of the guides of Chamonix was undertaken by the Sardinian Government. They were formed into a Corporation by Royal Order, and a definite tariff for certain excursions was imposed. Further laws were promulgated in 1846 by Royal manifesto, the preamble of which was as follows:

'The increasing number of travellers who come to visit the Valley of Chamonix has shown the need of further regulating the service of guides established by our manifesto of the month of May, 1823, and of modifications for securing the safety of travellers and for rendering their excursions easy and agreeable.'

Additional rules were laid down in May, 1852. In the year 1846 the number of guides had been limited to sixty, but this limitation was now abolished. Every person domiciled in Chamonix was eligible to be placed on the guide-roll, if he had the necessary qualifications, which were defined as 'personal probity, combined with physical and intellectual aptitude.' These qualifications were to be tested by examination. No traveller was bound to take a guide even for the most dangerous excursion; but the days of climbing without guides had not begun, and the traveller was really forced to submit to the usual rules. When Savoy was ceded to France, the French Government continued to uphold the Society of Guides on the existing lines. Theoretically the object of the guide system as established by the Sardinian Government, and approved and amended by the Government of France, was to ensure the safety of travellers and to make their excursions 'easy and agreeable'. For this purpose security was to be taken for the competence of the guides. Let us see how it worked out. The examination was a mere farce, the rota was rigidly adhered to, and the traveller was also obliged to take as many guides as the Bureau in its wisdom might consider necessary for any particular expedition. Thus a trades' union of the worst form was established, and was perpetuated for many years. It seemed advantageous to the short-sighted natives, for it ensured the regular and systematic employment of most of the adult inhabitants; but it was really ruinous. It was hateful to mountaineers, who, wanting competent guides for some important expedition, had to take the first men on the roll, good or bad. Hence they either avoided Chamonix, or brought foreign guides with them into the valley. It tended to lower the quality of the guides themselves, the worst of whom might be cast for Mont Blanc, which possibly they had never climbed; whilst the best might have the bad luck to find no better employment than to accompany a mule to the Montanvert or to carry a lady's shawl to the Brévent or the Flégère.

No encouragement was given to special capacity. Why should a man cultivate the manners and practice the arts by which alone a guide really becomes great, if he was to be no better off than the most incompetent man upon the roll? The tendency of the system was to produce a dead level of mediocrity. The result might easily have been foreseen. The names of the old guides who worked unfettered at the time of Saussure's ascent, and for thirty years afterwards, stand out in the history of Chamonix like peaks above clouds. Their successors have sadly degenerated. It is a melancholy fact that of the three hundred men now on the Chamonix roll, those who could be relied upon in a grave emergency may be counted on the fingers of one hand.

Charles Edward Mathews, *The Annals of Mont Blanc*

A Guide on the Shreckhorn

On the night of August 13, 1861 I found myself the occupant of a small hole under a big rock near the foot of the Strahleck. Owing to bad diplomacy, I was encumbered with three guides – Peter and Christian Michel, and Christian Kaufmann – all of them good men, but one, if not two, too many. As the grey morning light gradually stole into our burrow, I woke up with a sense of lively impatience – not diminished, perhaps, by the fact that one side of me seemed to be permanently impressed with every knob in a singularly crossgrained bit of rock, and the other with every bone in Kaufmann's body. Swallowing a bit of bread, I declared myself ready. An easy start is of course always desirable before a hard day's work, but it rises to be almost agreeable after a hard night's rest.

This did not seem to be at all Peter Michel's opinion. He is the very model of a short, thick, broad mountaineer, with the constitution of a piece of seasoned oak; a placid, not to say stolid temper, and an illimitable appetite. He sat opposite me for some half-hour, calmly munching bread and cheese, and meat and butter, at four in the morning, on a frozen bit of turf, under a big stone, as if it were the most reasonable thing a man could do under the circumstances, and as though such things as the Shreckhorn and impatient tourists had no existence. A fortnight before, as I was told, he had calmly sat out all night, half way up the Eiger, with a stream of freezing water trickling over him, accompanied by an unlucky German, whose feet received frostbites on that occasion from which they were still in danger, while old Michel had not a chilblain.

And here let me make one remark to save repetition on the following pages. I utterly repudiate the doctrine that Alpine travellers are or ought to be the heroes of Alpine adventures. The true way to describe all my Alpine ascents is that Michel or Anderegg or Lauener succeeded in performing a feat requiring skill, strength, and courage, the difficulty of which was much increased by the difficulty of taking with him his knapsack and his employer. If any passages in the succeeding pages convey the impression that I claim any credit except that of following better men than myself with decent ability, I disavow them in advance and do penance for them in my heart. Other travellers have been more independent; I speak for myself alone.

Meanwhile I will only delay my narrative to denounce one other heresy – that, namely, which asserts that guides are a nuisance. Amongst the greatest of Alpine pleasures is that of learning to appreciate the capacities and cultivate the good will of a singularly brave and intelligent and worthy class of men. I wish that all men of the same class, in England and elsewhere, were as independent, well-informed, and trustworthy as Swiss mountaineers.

Leslie Stephen, *The Playground of Europe*

Advice for the Novice Traveller

The following remarks may be of some service to those who visit the Zermatt district for the first time.

Expenses. More will be got for money by settling down at a few places than by constantly moving from one place to another. *Pensionnaires* are taken at nearly all the hotels mentioned in this volume. Low rates are quoted at the beginning and at the end of the season.

Money. Take some Napoleons (20-franc pieces), a small quantity of French silver for wayside expenses, and the rest in sovereigns and £5 Bank of England notes. The notes can be changed at Geneva, Lausanne, or Zermatt. Sovereigns go everywhere except at the very smallest places. English silver is not understood, and will not pass. Beware of small Italian silver coins, which are supposed to be withdrawn from circulation.

Clothing. Woollen goods and flannels are most suitable. It answers better to have several changes of thin garments than to be provided with a few thick ones. *Mountain-boots* should be taken out, and got into use before starting. The *nailing* is best done on the spot. *Knickerbockers*. The musquitoes of the Rhone Valley display partiality for the calves of those who adopt this form of attire.

Rope. If excursions are contemplated on which it will be desirous to use rope, it will be best to take rope out. There is none in the market equal to the Manilla rope which is specially manufactured by Mr John Buckingham, 194–196 Shaftesbury Avenue, London, W.C. 1., which *ought* to be identified, (amongst other ways) by a red thread woven among the strands. It is to be regretted that there are several spurious imitations abroad, in which this red thread is fraudulently copied. Beware of them.

Ice-axes can be obtained at Zermatt at the establishment of Melchior Anderegg, or at Châtillon of Carrel (the maker).

Soap. There is a great opening for soap in Alpine regions, and at the present time it pays to carry a cake . . .

Religion. The Canton Valais is the most Catholic Canton in the Swiss Confederation. At the Census of 1888, 100,925 persons were returned as Catholic, and only 865 as Protestant. Protestantism is tolerated. English-speaking people, when in the Zermatt district, do not always recognise the fact that they are in a Catholic country, and sometimes do things which may excite differences of opinion.

Upon engaging Guides. The recommendations that I should make in regard to the choice of guides at Zermatt are just those which I should make in regard to guides at any other place. 1. Before engaging a guide, make enquiry as to his antecedents from those who know. 2. Avoid men notorious for accidents, and those who are addicted to drink. 3. For difficult or long excursions give preference to men of middle age rather than to the youngest or oldest.

There is no *Bureau des Guides* at Zermatt, and enquiries have to be made to learn what men are available. During 'the season', besides the Valaisan Guides whose names are given in the List in the Appendix, one often finds Oberlanders at Zermatt, or men from Macugnaga (Val Anzasca), from the Val Tournanche and other parts.

Some guides carry on the reprehensible practice of soliciting employment in the trains from Visp to Zermatt. *Those who introduce and recommend themselves are generally of an inferior class.*

I do not attempt to decide whether a traveller should employ guides. Some persons are competent to carry out by themselves all the excursions that are mentioned. A large number, however, are not equal to this. Inasmuch as I am unacquainted with the various capacities of my readers, I am unable to say whether they need not, or should, employ guides. Everyone must decide that for himself.

Mendicity. Before the Zermatt railway was constructed, mendicity had become a nuisance between Visp-Zermatt. Since the opening of the Railway, the *road* has been clear of beggars, *because it no longer pays to beg*. Cripples of sorts, however, have in the last few years broken out at Zermatt, and even at the Riffelalp. I am told that they do not belong to the

Village or even to the Valley. If they are not patronized, they will no doubt disappear. If they are encouraged, they will multiply.

Edward Whymper, *Guide to Zermatt and the Matterhorn*

Alpine Advertisements

CHAMONIX
GRAND HOTEL COUTTET

• • • • • •

A FIRST CLASS & MOST COMFORTABLE

HOTEL, HIGHLY RECOMMENDED

FINELY SITUATED IN A LARGE GARDEN,

WITH SPLENDID VIEWS OF MONT BLANC

• • • • • •

MUCH PATRONISED BY MEMBERS

OF THE ALPINE CLUB AND

BY ENGLISH FAMILIES.

• • • • • •

BATHS IN THE HOTEL

• • • • • •

ELECTRIC LIGHT

• • • • • •

OPEN ALL THE YEAR.

• • • • • •

IN THE WINTER SEASON, SKATING AND TOBOGGANING

• • • • • •

ENGLISH SPOKEN.

• • • • • •

F. Couttet Fils, Proprietor

ZERMATT

WOOD-CARVINGS, PHOTOGRAPHS, ALPENSTOCKS, ICE-AXES ETC

ESTABLISHMENT KEPT BY

MELCHIOR ANDEREGG

WOOD-CARVER AND MOUNTAIN-GUIDE OF ZAUN, MEYRINGEN

Musical boxes of all sizes ▪ Glove boxes ▪ Jewel Cases ▪ Mirrors ▪ Corks ▪ Thermometers ▪ Brushes ▪ Match boxes ▪ Salad forks and spoons ▪ Articles in horn ▪ Articles in silver (brooches, bells, pins, ornaments for watch-chains) ▪ Book-slides ▪ Letter and paper-racks ▪ Vases ▪ Paper-knives ▪ Bears ▪ Groups of chamois ▪ Eagles ▪ Bread-platters and bread-knives ▪ Easels ▪ Bookmarkers ▪ Penholders ▪ Watchstands ▪ Nutcrackers ▪ Needle-cases ▪ Frames for photographs ▪ Whymper's alpine photographs ▪ Alpenstocks of all sorts ▪ Ice-axes by the best makers ▪ Veils ▪ Snow-spectacles (blue, green, and neutral tint) ▪ Photographs of all the great peaks round Zermatt ▪ Whymper's guides.

ENGLISH, FRENCH, AND GERMAN SPOKEN.

Edward Whymper, *Guide to Zermatt and the Matterhorn*

◆

CHAPTER 17

The New World of Mountains

With the ascent of the last great unclimbed Alpine peak in 1865 the ambitions of Alpinists underwent a change: they sought no longer to reach a new summit, but to reach it by a new route, or at a new time of year. Winter climbing – which was eventually to lead to the introduction of skiing into the Alps – was pioneered by the American W.A.B. Coolidge. He is represented in this chapter, however, by an account of a different kind of pioneering: he was the first to take a dog to the top of Mont Blanc.

High mountains other than the Alps now became the destination of many of the most experienced mountaineers. Mountains in Scandinavia, the Caucasus, and Africa were explored, and the first ventures were made into the Himalayas. The extracts in this chapter illustrate different kinds of climbing in the New World: by the intrepid novice Isabella Bird Bishop in the Rockies, and by the rival veterans Edward Whymper and Jean-Antoine Carrel in the Ecuadorian Andes.

◆ ◆ ◆

The American and his Dog

I do not clearly recollect ever having heard of Tschingel till July 11, 1868. That month Almer had for the first time become guide to my aunt, the late Miss Brevoort, and myself. On July 8 we all three made our first high climb together (the Wetterhorn) and on July 11 started from the Little Scheidegg for the ascent of the Eiger. But the rocks (as often) were glazed, and we had to retreat. This disappointed me bitterly, for I was not quite eighteen years of age, and though I was in my fourth climbing season, I did not yet realise that even an easy mountain can sometimes become impossible owing to special circumstance. Almer sympathised much with me, and so, as we were walking down that afternoon to Grindelwald, tried to comfort me by promising to give me his dog Tschingel, as one of her sons, Bello by name, was now able to act as watchdog . . .

I have a vague idea that when Almer first brought Tschingel to us at our hotel the poor dog was very shy, and finally jumped out of the first floor window. But she certainly accompanied us when we and the guides left on July 17 in a carriage for Kandersteg . . .

Tschingel, though in no sense of pure breed, resembled generally either a small bloodhound or a large beagle. She had strong short legs and a tail that ended in a brush. She was smooth-haired, the colour of her coat being reddish-brown, inclining more to red. She had a white breast and stomach, with white stockings and muzzle. Her body was not handsome, being too thickset. But she had a very fine head, large and beautiful brown and most expressive eyes, and long dark brown *very* silky ears – in fact, my mother always said she would have a purse made out of these ears, but she died (1875) before Tschingel (1879). Her voice was deep and musical. She was very intelligent, and, though of course only used to Swiss German at first, soon got to understand English, but always showed a strong Teutonic reluctance to comprehend French! Of course she was a hunting dog by nature, and during our Alpine journeys was always going off on the chase after chamois, marmots, hares, foxes or what not. Once on the Ober Aletsch glacier in 1872 she left us for 2½ hrs. to pursue chamois, and then rejoined us at a much higher spot than where she had left us. She could not abide chicken as food, even chicken bones, though she might be very hungry, albeit she had a set of teeth with which she cracked great bones in an astonishing fashion. But from the very beginning she liked red wine, and later came to love weak tea and hot water, though this always had such an effect on her nerves that, after revelling in this drink, she would retire to a corner, sit down, and utter piercing howls – apparently of excessive and overwhelming pleasure, just as when she heard music. Until she became old she was very good tempered, save as regards cats, those mortal enemies of all dogs . . .

Her first great climb took place on July 18 1868, and was the *Blumalpis-horn* (12,044 ft.). She was very tired, and her paws were cut by the ice – this often happened, but she *would* not be left behind (once we had small leather shoes made to protect her poor paws, but she pulled them off at once). On the way up, however, her Alpine career nearly came to an end, for on the final slope she slipped, being still an inexperienced climber, and began to slide down the snow sloped towards the Oeschinen lake, but was luckily rescued by one of our porters, who caught hold of her collar in the nick of time . . .

Her final exploit during her first season's climbing was the passage of the *Mönchjoch* (11,680 ft.) from the old Faulberg hut to Grindelwald. I do not recollect whether it was on that occasion or in 1871 (perhaps the latter) that, the glacier on the Grindelwald side being very crevassed, a rope was tied round Tschingel's belly, and she was let down, resembling much the sheep shown on the insignia of the Order of the Golden Fleece. On glaciers she was always roped (coming immediately after my aunt), the rope passing through a ring in her work-a-day collar, which I still treasure, as well as her Sunday collar on the silver clasps of which are given the names of her mountain climbs, these becoming finally so numerous that silver pendants had to be attached to it all round . . .

[In 1875] I decided to take Tschingel up *Mont Blanc* (15,782 ft.) and this she achieved all right on July 24. It must be remembered that Tschingel was now ten years of age, so that her feat was all the more creditable to her. At the Grands Mulets she seemed to be unwilling to go on with us further . . . However, we persuaded her to start, and all went very well. There was a very high and cold wind blowing on the Bosses du Dromadaire. But this did not seem to inconvenience Tschingel at all, who ran ahead of us, barking loudly, till she reached the top, when she ran back to us to announce that we were not very far from it. It seems that at Chamonix the people looking up thought at first that she was a chamois! But she was only the first dog (so far as I am aware) to attain the summit *on her feet*, for one or two others have been carried up. On her return to Chamonix she was very warmly welcomed, and next day, lying on a sofa in a salon of the Hotel Couttet, held a sort of reception of admirers from all the other hotels.

W.A.B. Coolidge, *Alpine Studies*

A Lady's Life in the Rocky Mountains

A very pretty mare, hobbled, was feeding; a collie dog barked at us, and among the scrub, not far from the track, there was a rude, black, log cabin, as rough as it could be to be a shelter at all, with smoke coming out of the roof and window. The big dog lay outside it in a threatening attitude and growled. The mud roof was covered with lynx, beaver, and other furs laid out to dry, beaver paws were pinned out on the logs, a part of the carcass of a deer hung at one end of the cabin, a skinned beaver lay in front of a heap of peltry just within the door, and antlers of deer, old horseshoes, and offal of many animals, lay about the den.

Roused by the growling of the dog, his owner came out, a broad, thickset man about the middle height, with an old cap on his head, and wearing a grey hunting-suit much the worse for wear (almost falling to pieces, in fact), a digger's scarf sticking out of the breast-pocket of his coat; his feet, which were very small, were bare, except for some dilapidated moccasins made of horse hide. The marvel was how his clothes hung together, and on him. The scarf round his waist must have had something to do with it. His face was remarkable. He is a man about 45, and must have been strikingly handsome. He has large grey-blue eyes, deeply set, with well-marked eyebrows, a handsome aquiline nose, and a very handsome mouth. His face was smooth shaven except for a dense moustache and imperial. Tawny hair, in thin uncared-for curls, fell from under his hunter's cap and over his collar. One eye was entirely gone, and the loss made one side of the face repulsive, while the other might have been modelled in marble. 'Desperado' was written in large letters all over him. I almost repented of having sought his acquaintance.

His first impulse was to swear at the dog, but on seeing a lady he contented himself with kicking him, and coming up to me he raised his cap, showing as he did so a magnificently formed brow and head, and in a cultured tone of voice asked if there were anything he could do for me? I asked for some water, and he brought some in a battered tin, gracefully apologizing for not having anything more presentable. We entered into conversation, and as he spoke I forgot both his reputation and appearance, for his manner was that of a chivalrous gentleman, his accent refined, and his language easy and elegant. I inquired about some beavers' paws which were drying, and in a moment they hung on the horn of my saddle. Apropos of the wild animals of the region, he told me that the loss of his eye was owing to a recent encounter with a grizzly bear, which after giving him a death hug, tearing him all over, breaking his arm and scratching out his eye, had left him for dead. As we rode away, for the sun was sinking, he said, courteously, 'You are not an American. I know from your voice that you are a countrywoman of mine. I hope you will allow me the pleasure of calling on you.'

This man, known through the Territories and beyond them as 'Rocky Mountain Jim' or, more briefly, as 'Mountain Jim', is one of the famous scouts of the Plains, and is the original of some daring portraits in fiction concerning Indian frontier warfare. So far as I have at present heard, he is a man for whom there is now no room, for the time for blows and blood in this part of Colorado is now past, and the fame of many daring exploits is sullied by crimes which are not easily forgiven here . . .

Long's Peak, 14,700 feet high, blocks up one end of Estes Park, and dwarfs all the surrounding mountains. From it on this side rise, snow-born, the bright St Vrain and the Big and Little Thompson. By sunlight or moonlight its splintered grey crest is the one object which, in spite of wapiti and bighorn, skunk and grizzly, unfailingly arrests the eyes. From it come all storms of snow and wind, and the forked lightnings play round its head like a glory. It is one of the noblest of mountains, but in one's imagination it grows to be much more than a mountain. It becomes invested with a personality. In its caverns and abysses one comes to fancy that it generates and chains the strong winds, to let them loose in its fury. The thunder becomes its voice, and the lightnings do it homage. Other summits blush under the morning kiss of the sun, and turn pale the next moment; but it detains the first sunlight, and holds it round its head for an hour at least, till it pleases to change from rosy red to deep blue; and the sunset, as if spell-bound, lingers latest on its crest . . . Long's Peak, 'the American Matterhorn', as some call it, was ascended five years ago for the first time.

I thought I should like to attempt it, but up to Monday, when [my host] Evans left for Denver, cold water was thrown upon the project. It was too late in the season, the winds were likely to be strong etc; but just before leaving, Evans said that the weather was looking more settled, and if I did not get farther than the timber line it would be worth going. Soon after he left, 'Mountain Jim' came in, and he would go up as guide, and the two youths who rode here with me from Longmount and I caught at the proposal.

Mrs Edwards at once baked bread for three days, steaks were cut from the steer which hangs up conveniently, and tea, sugar and butter were bene-volently added. Our picnic was not to be a luxurious or 'well-found' one, for, in order to avoid the expense of a pack mule, we limited our luggage to what our saddle horses could carry. Behind my saddle I carried three pair of camping blankets and a quilt, which reached to my shoulders. My own boots were so much worn that it was painful to walk, even about the park, in them, so Evans had lent me a pair of his hunting boots, which hung to the horn of my saddle. The horses of the two young men were equally loaded, for we had to prepare for many degrees of frost. 'Jim' was a shocking figure; he had on an old pair of high boots, with a baggy pair of old trousers made of deer hide, held on by an old scarf tucked into them; a leather shirt, with three or four ragged unbuttoned waistcoats over it; an old smashed wideawake, from under which his tawny, neglected ringlets hung; and with his one eye, his one long spur, his knife in his belt, his revolver in his waistcoat pocket, his saddle covered with an old beaver skin, from which the paws hung down; his camping blankets behind him, his rifle laid across the saddle in front of him, and his axe, canteen, and other gear hanging to the horn, he was as awful-looking a ruffian as one could see. By way of contrast he rode a small Arab mare, of exquisite beauty, skittish, high-spirited, gentle, but altogether too light for him, and he fretted her incessantly to make her display herself . . .

From the dry, buff grass of Estes Park we turned off up a trail on the side of a pine-hung gorge, up a steep pine-clothed hill, down to a small valley, rich in fine, sun-cured hay about 18 inches high, and enclosed by high mountains whose deep hollow contains a lily-covered lake, fitly named 'The Lake of the Lilies'. Ah, how magical its beauty was, as it slept in silence, while there the dark pines were mirrored-motionless in its pale gold, and here the great white lively cups and dark green leaves rested on amethyst coloured water!

From this we ascended into the purple gloom of great pine forests which clothe the skirts of the mountains up to a height of about 11,000 feet, and from their chill and solitary depths we had glimpses of golden atmosphere and rose-lit summits, glimpses too, through a broken vista of purple gorges, of the illimitable Plains lying idealized in the late sunlight, their baked, brown expanse transfigured into the likeness of a sunset sea rolling infinitely in waves of misty gold.

We rode upwards through the gloom on a steep trail blazed through the forest, all my intellect concentrated on avoiding being dragged off my horse by impending branches, or having the blankets badly torn, as those of my companions were, by sharp dead limbs between which there was hardly room to pass – the horses breathless, and requiring to stop every few yards, though their riders, except myself, were afoot. The gloom of the dense, ancient, silent forest is to me awe-inspiring. On such an evening it is soundless, except for the branches creaking in the soft wind, the frequent snap of decayed timber, and a murmur in the pine tops as of a not distant waterfall, all tending to produce eeriness and a sadness 'hardly akin to pain'. There no lumberer's axe has ever run. The trees die when they have attained their prime, and stand there, dead and bare, till the fierce mountain winds lay them prostrate. The pines grew smaller and more sparse as we ascended, and the last stragglers wore a tortured, warring look. The timber line was passed, but yet a little higher a slope of mountain meadow dipped to the southwest towards a bright stream trickling under ice and icicles, and there a grove of the beautiful silver spruce marked our camping ground. The trees were in miniature, but so exquisitely arranged that one might well ask what artist's hand had planted them, scattering them here, clumping them there, and training their slim spires towards heaven. Looking east, gorges opened to the distant Plains, then fading into purple grey. Mountains with pine-clothed skirts rose in ranges, or, solitary, uplifted their grey summits, while close behind, but nearly 3000 feet above us, toward the bald white crest of Long's Peak, its huge precipices red with the light of a sun long lost to our eyes. Close to us, in the caverned side of the Peak, was snow that, owing to its position, is eternal. Soon the afterglow came on, and before it faded a big half-moon hung out of the heavens, shining through the silver-blue foliage of the pines on the frigid background of snow, and turning the whole into fairyland.

Unsaddling and picketing the horses securely, making the beds of pine shoots, and dragging up logs for fuel, warmed us all. 'Jim' built up a great fire, and before long we were all sitting around it at supper. It didn't matter much that we had to drink our tea out of the battered meat tins in which it was boiled, and eat strips of beef reeking with pine smoke without plates or forks.

'Treat Jim as a gentleman and you'll find him one', I had been told; and though his manner was certainly bolder and freer than that of gentlemen generally, no imaginable fault could be found. He was very agreeable as a man of culture as well as a child of nature; the desperado was altogether out of sight. He was very courteous and even kind to me, which was fortunate, as the young men had little idea of showing even ordinary civilities. That night I made the acquaintance of his dog Ring, said to be the best hunting dog in Colorado, with the body and legs of a collie, but a head approaching that of a mastiff, a noble face with a wistful human expression and the most truthful eyes I ever saw in an animal. His master loves him if he loves anything, but in his savage moods ill-treats him. Ring's devotion never swerves, and his truthful eyes are rarely taken off his master's face. He is almost human in his intelligence, and, unless he is told to do so, he never takes notice of anyone but 'Jim'. In a tone as if speaking to a human being, his master, pointing to me, said 'Ring, go to that lady, and don't leave her again tonight.' Ring at once came to me, looked into my face, laid his head on my shoulder, and then lay down beside me with his head on my lap, but never taking his eyes from 'Jim''s face . . .

A group of small silver spruces away from the fire was my sleeping place. It was thickly strewn with young pine shoots, and these, when covered with a blanket, with an inverted saddle for a pillow, made a luxurious bed. The mercury at 9 p.m. was 12 degrees below the freezing point. 'Jim', after a last look at the horses, made a huge fire and stretched himself out beside it, but Ring lay at my back to keep me warm. I could not sleep, but the night passed rapidly. I was anxious about the ascent, for gusts of ominous sound swept through the pines at intervals. Then wild animals howled, and Ring was perturbed in spirit about them . . .

Day dawned long before the sun rose, pure and lemon coloured. The rest were looking after the horses, when one of the students came running to tell me that I must come farther down the slope, for 'Jim' said he had never seen such a sunrise. From the chill, grey Peak above, from the everlasting snows, from the silvered pines, down through mountain ranges with their depths of tyrian purple, we looked to where the Plains lay cold, in blue-grey, like a morning sea against a far horizon. Suddenly, as a dazzling streak at first, but enlarging rapidly into a dazzling sphere, the sun wheeled above the grey line, a light and glory as when it was first created. 'Jim' involuntarily and reverently uncovered his head, and exclaimed, 'I believe there is a God!' I felt as if, Parsee-like, I must worship. The grey of the Plains changed to purple, the sky was all one rose-red flush, on which vermilion cloud-streaks rested; the ghastly peaks gleamed like rubies, the earth and heavens were new created. Surely 'the Most High dwelleth not in temples made with hands!' For a full hour those Plains simulated the ocean, down to whose limitless expanse of purple, cliff, rocks and promontories swept down.

By seven we had finished breakfast, and passed into the ghastlier solitudes above, I riding as far as what, rightly or wrongly, are called the 'Lava Beds', an expanse of large and small boulders, with snow in their crevices. It was very cold; some water which we crossed was frozen hard enough to bear the horse. 'Jim' had advised me against taking any wraps, and my thin Hawaiian riding-dress, only fit for the tropics, was penetrated by the keen air. The rarefied atmosphere soon began to oppress our breathing . . .

On arriving at the 'Notch' (a literal gate of rock), we found ourselves absolutely on the knifelike ridge or backbone of Long's Peak, only a few feet wide, covered with colossal boulders and fragments, and on the other side shelving in one precipitous, snow-patched sweep of 3000 feet to a picturesque hollow, containing a lake of pure green water. Other lakes, hidden among dense pine woods, were farther off, while close above us rose the Peak, which, for about 500 feet, is a smooth, gaunt, inaccessible-looking pile of granite. Passing through the 'Notch', we looked along the nearly inaccessible side of the Peak, composed of boulders and debris of all shapes and sizes, through which appeared broad, smooth ribs of reddish coloured granite, looking as if they upheld the towering rock mass above . . .

You know I have no head and no ankles, and never ought to dream of mountaineering; and had I known that the ascent was a real mountaineering feat I should not have felt the slightest ambition to perform it. As it is, I am only humiliated by my success, for 'Jim' dragged me up, like a bale of goods, by sheer force of muscle. At the 'Notch' the real business of the ascent began. Two thousand feet of solid rock towered above us, 4000 feet of broken rock shelved precipitously below; smooth granite ribs, with barely a foothold, stood out here and there; melted snow refrozen several times, presented a more serious obstacle; many of the rocks were loose and tumbled down when touched. To me it was a time of extreme terror. I was roped to 'Jim', but it was of no use; my feet were paralysed and slipped on the bare rock, and he said it was useless to try to go that way, and we retraced our steps. I wanted to return to the 'Notch', knowing that my incompetence would detain the party, and one of the young men said almost plainly that a woman was a dangerous encumbrance, but the trapper replied shortly that if it were not to take a lady up he would not go up at all. He went on to explore, and reported that further progress on the correct line of ascent was blocked by ice; and then for two hours we descended, lowering ourselves by our hands from rock to rock along a boulder-strewn sweep of 4000 feet, patched with ice and snow, and perilous from rolling stones. My fatigue, giddiness and pain from bruised ankles, and arms half pulled out of their sockets, were so great that I should never have gone half-way had not 'Jim', *nolens volens*, dragged me along with a patience and skill, and withal a determination that I should ascend the Peak, which never failed. After descending about 2000 feet to avoid the ice, we got into a deep ravine with inaccessible sides, partly filled with ice and snow and partly with large and small fragments of rock, which were constantly giving away, rendering the footing very insecure. That part to me was two hours of painful and unwilling submission to the inevitable; of trembling, slipping, straining, of smooth ice appearing when it was least expected, and of weak entreaties to be left behind while the others went on. 'Jim' always said that there was no danger, that there was only a short bad bit ahead, and that I should go up even if he carried me.

Slipping, faltering, gasping from the exhausting toil in the rarefied air, with throbbing hearts and panting lungs, we reached the top of the gorge and squeezed ourselves between two gigantic fragments of rock by a passage called the 'Dog's Lift', when I climbed on the shoulders of one man and then was hauled up. This introduced us by an abrupt turn round the southwest angle of the Peak to a narrow shelf of considerable length, rugged, uneven, and so overhung by the cliff in some places that it is necessary to crouch to pass at all. Above, the Peak looks nearly vertical for 400 feet; and below, the most tremendous precipice I have ever seen descends in one unbroken fall. This is usually considered the most dangerous part of the ascent, but it does not seem so to me, for such foothold as there is is secure, and one fancies that it is possible to hold on with the hands. But there, and on the final, and to my thinking, the worst part of the climb, one slip and a breathing, thinking, human being would lie 3000 feet below, a shapeless, bloody heap! Ring refused to traverse the ledge, and remained at the 'Lift' howling piteously.

As we crept from the ledge round a horn of rock I beheld what made me perfectly sick and dizzy to look at – the terminal Peak itself – a smooth, cracked face or wall of pink granite, as nearly perpendicular as anything could well be up which it was possible to climb.

Scaling, not climbing, is the correct term for this last ascent. It took one hour to accomplish 500 feet, pausing for breath every minute or two. The only foothold was in narrow cracks or on minute projections on the granite. To get a toe in these cracks, or here and there on a scarcely obvious projection, while crawling on hands and knees, all the while tortured with thirst and gasping and struggling for breath, this was the climb; but at last the Peak was won. A grand, well-defined mountain top it is, a nearly level acre of boulders, with precipitous sides all round, the one we came up being the only accessible one.

It was not possible to remain long. One of the young men was seriously alarmed by bleeding from the lungs, and the intense dryness of the day and the rarefaction of the air, at a height of nearly 15,000 feet, made respiration very painful. There is always water on the Peak, but it was frozen hard as a rock, and the sucking of ice and snow increases thirst. We all suffered severely from the want of water, and the gasping for breath made our mouths and tongues so dry that articulation was difficult and the speech of all unnatural . . .

We placed our names, with the date of ascent, in a tin within a crevice, and descended to the ledge, sitting on the smooth granite, getting our feet into cracks and against projections, and letting ourselves down by our hands, 'Jim' going before me, so that I might steady my feet against his powerful shoulders. I was no longer giddy, and faced the precipice of 3500 feet without a shiver. Repassing the ledge and 'Lift', we accomplished the descent through 1500 feet of ice and snow, with many falls and bruises, but no worse mishap, and there separated, the young men taking the steepest but most direct way to the 'Notch', with the intention of getting ready for the march home, and 'Jim' and I taking what he thought the safer route for me – a descent over boulders for 2000 feet, and then a tremendous ascent to the 'Notch'. I had various falls, and once hung by my frock, which caught on a rock, and 'Jim' severed it with his hunting-knife, upon which I fell into a crevice full of soft snow. We were driven lower down the mountains than he had intended by impassable tracts of ice, and the ascent was tremendous. For the last 200 feet the boulders were of enormous size, and the steepness fearful. Sometimes I drew myself up on hands and knees, sometimes crawled; sometimes 'Jim' pulled me up by my arms or a lariat, and sometimes I stood on his shoulders, or he made step for me of his feet and hands, but at six we stood on the 'Notch' in the splendour of the sinking sun, all colour deepening, all peaks glorifying, all shadows purpling, all perils past . . .

With great difficulty and much assistance I recrossed the Lava Beds, was carried to the horse and lifted upon him, and when we reached the camping ground I was lifted off him, and laid on the ground wrapped up in blankets, a humiliating termination of a great exploit. The horses were saddled, and the young men were all ready to start, but 'Jim' quietly said, 'Now, gentlemen, I want a good night's rest, and we shan't stir from here tonight.' I believe they were really glad to have it so, as one of them was quite finished. I retired to my arbour, wrapped myself in a roll of blankets, and was soon asleep.

When I woke, the moon was high shining through the silvery branches, whitening the bald Peak above, and glittering on the great abyss of snow behind, and pine logs were blazing like a bonfire in the cold still air . . . 'Jim', or Mr Nugent as I always scrupulously called him, told stories of his early youth, and of a great sorrow which had led him to embark on a lawless and desperate life. His voice trembled, and tears rolled down his cheek. Was it semi-conscious acting, I wondered, or was his dark soul really stirred to its depths by the silence, the beauty, and the memories of youth?

We reached Estes Park at noon of the following day. A more successful ascent of the Peak was never made.

Isabella Bird Bishop, *This Grand Beyond*

Mountain-sickness on Chimborazo

Neither of the two Carrels, nor I myself, had ever experienced the least symptom of mountain-sickness. None of us, however, prior to this journey had been 16,000 feet high; and, probably, had never sustained so low a pressure as 17 inches. I had at various times been in the company of persons who said they were affected by 'rarefaction of the air', and who were unable to proceed; but their symptoms, so far as I observed them, might have been produced by fatigue and unfamiliarity with mountaineering, and were not of the more acute kind. Although I attached little importance to such cases as had come under my own personal observation, I had never felt disposed to question the *reality* of mountain-sickness; and on the contrary had frequently maintained that it is reasonable to expect some effects should be produced upon men who experience much lower atmospheric pressures than those to which they are accustomed; and that it is much more remarkable to find that *apparently*, no effects of a detrimental kind are caused on many persons who ascend to the height of 14–15,000 feet (or, say, sustain a pressure of seventeen and a half inches), than it is to learn that others have suffered at slightly lower pressures. The thing that seemed most puzzling was that at the greatest heights I had reached, instead of appearing to suffer any injurious effects, the effects seemed positively beneficial; and from this I thought it was not unlikely that we should be able to reach much more considerable heights, and to sustain considerably lower pressures, without being adversely affected.

Some of my friends, however, who had been as high as 17–18,000 feet, competent mountaineers, and men who could speak without exaggeration, told me that they had not been at all comfortable at such elevations. It seemed certain that sooner or later we should suffer like the rest of the world, but I proposed to put off the evil day as long as possible; to mount gradually and leisurely, by small stages, so that there should be no abrupt transition; and to get to the lowest attainable pressures (the greatest heights) by the simplest means that could be devised, and by the easiest routes that could be found, in order that extreme exertion and fatigue should take no part in anything that might happen . . .

As it would be impossible to retain natives at our higher camps and we ourselves might be detained at them by bad weather or from other causes even for weeks at a time, it was necessary to be well provided with food; and as it could not be expected that we should be able to obtain on the spot provisions which would keep for a length of time, I concluded, before leaving Europe, that to work with certainty we must make ourselves entirely independent of the resources of the country in the matter of the food which would be consumed at the greatest heights. A large quantity of the most portable and most condensed provisions accordingly went out for our use.

These provisions were packed in boxes measuring 28¼ × 11¼ × 10¼ inches, weighing about 72 lbs apiece. Each of these boxes contained three tin cases, measuring 9¼ × 9 × 8¼ inches, and each tin case held food for four men for one day. The tins, being thoroughly soldered down, could be

left exposed in the worst weather, or dipped in water without taking harm.
The contents comprised nearly everything that was requisite except water
and firing. A great saving of time was effected in the field by arranging the
food in this manner, and it relieved me from the necessity of continual
calculations, and from apprehensions that some of the minor requisites
might be forgotten.

(Each tin case contained:- Ox-cheek, 2 lbs; Mutton, 2 lbs; Beef, 2 lbs;
Potted ham, one tin; Liebig's extract, 2 ozs, in tin; Preserved soup, 2 pint
tins; Cocoa and milk, one tin; Condensed milk, one tin; Sugar, 4 ozs;
Mustard, 1 oz; Salt, 2 ozs; Pepper, 1 oz; Biscuits, about 2 lbs, in tin;
Lemonade powder, in tin; Seidlitz powders, in tin; 3 pills; small bottle of
Chlorodyne; Black-currant and cayenne lozenges, 2 ozs; muscatelles, 12 ozs;
Tea, 3 ozs. These quantities were found sufficient, or more than enough,
with the exception of sugar.)

For a thousand feet above the first camp, our reladen caravan progressed
at a fair pace, and then (pressure being about 17.25 inches) struggling
commenced. My own mule reached the head of the *vallon* (about 16,000
feet above the sea) without shewing signs of exhaustion. It then struck work,
and I dismounted. So far, the bed of the *vallon* was loose, sandy soil, with
little vegetation. Our course then turned to the right, that is towards the
east, up the western slopes of the south-west ridge of Chimborazo, and led
by steeper gradients over firm ground, covered with shattered blocks of lava
fallen from the arête above. I patted and coaxed my animal on for a few
yards, and then it stopped again. It clearly found difficulty supporting its
own weight. By continued encouragement, it was induced to advance a few
steps at a time; but the halts became more frequent, and, impatient of
delay, I pushed on, and left it to pursue its course by itself. Looking back,
to see how the rest were progressing, I found that they were scattered over
about half-a-mile, and that all the animals were in difficulties, though none
carried more than one hundred and sixty pounds.

Carrel had selected a position for the second camp with much judgment,
at the foot of a wall of lava, which perfectly protected the tent on one side.
The place was easy of access, and the highest point to which mules could be
taken; with snow-beds in its vicinity that would yield water, and ground
round about it upon which we could exercise. The baggage animals struggled upwards one by one, and by 5.30 p.m all had arrived. The barometer
stood at this place at sixteen inches and a half.

We were all in high spirits. The weather had been fine, and the move had
been successfully effected. It was arranged that one of the arrieros should
sleep at Tortorillas, and come up daily to learn what was needed; and all the
rest of the troop were sent back to Guaranda. They left us very gladly; for
although we had succeeded in establishing our camp at the selected spot,
it had only been done by great exertions on the part of my people and their

beasts. The mules were forced up to the last yard they could go, and staggering under their burdens (which were scarcely more than half the weight they were accustomed to carry), stopped repeatedly, and by their trembling, falling on their knees, and by their general behaviour, showed that they had been driven to the verge of exhaustion. When we others arrived at the second camp, we ourselves were in good condition – which was to be expected, as we had ridden most of the way; but in about an hour I found myself lying on my back, along with both the Carrels, placed *hors de combat*, and incapable of making the least exertion. We knew that the enemy was upon us, and that we were experiencing our first attack of mountain-sickness.

We were feverish, had intense headaches, and were unable to satisfy our desire for air, except by breathing with open mouths. This naturally parched the throat, and produced a craving for drink, which we were unable to satisfy, – partly from the difficulty in obtaining it, and partly from trouble in swallowing it. When we got enough, we could only sip, and not to save our lives could we have taken a quarter of a pint at a draught. Before a mouthful was down, we were obliged to breathe and gasp again, until our throats were as dry as ever. Besides having our normal rate of breathing largely accelerated, we found it impossible to sustain life without every now and then giving spasmodic gulps, just like fishes when taken out of water. Of course there was no inclination to eat; but we wished to smoke, and found that our pipes almost refused to burn, for they, like ourselves, wanted more oxygen.

This condition of affairs lasted all night, and all the next day, and I then managed to pluck up spirit enough to get out some chlorate of potash, which by the advice of Dr W. Marcet had been brought out in case of need . . . Ten grains to a wine glass of water was the proportion he recommended, – the dose to be repeated every two or three hours if necessary. It appeared to me to operate beneficially, though it must be admitted that it was not easy to determine, as one *might* have recovered just as well without taking it at all. At all events, after taking it, th : intensity of the symptoms diminished, there were fewer gaspings, and in some degree a feeling of relief.

Louis Carrel also submitted himself to experiment, and seemed to derive benefit; but Jean-Antoine sturdily refused take any 'doctor's stuff' which he regarded as an insult to intelligence. For all human ills, for every complaint, from dysentery to want of air, there was, in his opinion, but one remedy; and that was wine; most efficacious always if taken hot, more especially if a little spice and sugar were added to it.

The stories that he related respecting the virtues of Red wine would be enough to fill a book. The wine must be Red – 'White wine,' he used to say dogmatically, 'is bad, it cuts the legs.' Most of these legends I cannot remember, but there was one which it was impossible to forget, commencing thus. 'Red wine when heated and beaten up with raw eggs is good for many complaints – particularly at the Eve of St John, when the moon is at the full, for women who are in the family way; provided it is drunk whilst looking over the left shoulder, and' – I never heard the end of that story because I laughed too soon.

His opinions upon things in general were often very original, and I learned much whilst in his company; amongst the rest, that for the cure of headache, nothing better can be mentioned than keeping the head *warm* and the feet *cold*. It is only fair to say that he practised what he preached. I can remember no more curious sight than that of this middle-aged man, lying nearly obscured under a pile of ponchos, with his head bound up in a wonderful arrangement of handkerchiefs, vainly attempting to smoke a short pipe whilst gasping like a choking cod-fish, his naked feet sticking out from underneath his blankets when the temperature in the tent was much below the freezing point . . .

Our symptoms did not differ in any material point from those which have already been recorded by persons deserving of credence, and, so far, the experience was not unexpected; but they appeared earlier than was anticipated, and when I got into a condition to think, I was greatly surprised at the suddenness with which we were overtaken, and at the fact that we succumbed nearly simultaneously. It is scarcely exaggeration to say that in one hour we were all right and that in the next we were all wrong. Two out of the three had already visited the place without being attacked.

The symptoms come under the three heads, headache, disturbance of the natural manner of respiration, and feverishness. Headache with all three of us was intense, and rendered us almost frantic or crazy. Before 6 p.m. on Dec. 27, we had, I believe, been entirely free from headache in Ecuador. My own continued acute until the 30th and then it disappeared gradually. With Louis it did not last quite so long, and Jean-Antoine got better sooner than his cousin. When it was at its maximum we all seemed to be about equally afflicted. The interference with our natural manner of respiration was even more troublesome. At 6 p.m. we could move about, talk, or eat and drink freely, while at 8 p.m. and throughout the night of the 27th, eating would have been impossible, and to talk or drink was difficult. We could only gasp ejaculations, or a few words at a time, and efforts at conversation were cut short by irrepressible, spasmodic gulps; while, during the whole time, respiration was effected though open mouths, the ordinary amount of air taken in through the nostrils being found inadequate. We were all feverish, but no observations were made until 1 p.m. on the 28th, when my own temperature was found to be 100.4 degrees Fahrenheit. It was no doubt considerably higher in the previous night. On this head, nothing can be said in regard to the Carrels; for, though they spoke of feverishness, they positively declined both then and at all times to have their temperatures taken.

It will be understood from what has just been said that our 'incapacity' was neither due to exhaustion or to deficiency of bodily strength, nor was owing to inability to cope with mountaineering difficulties or to weakness from want of food, but was caused by the whole of our attention being taken up in efforts to get air; and my two assistants, spontaneously and without any questioning on my part, attributed the condition in which we found ourselves to the 'rarity of the air' at our second camp. There is evidence of my own inability to perform my regular work in the blanks in my journals at this date, and further evidence of the reality of the attack in the fact that we could not smoke. Two out of the three were habitual consumers of tobacco, and had become slaves to this vice to such an extent that they smoked conscientiously upon every opportunity. When such persons put aside their beloved pipes there is certainly something wrong. All three found smoking too laborious, and ceased their efforts in despair. But it should not be understood, from anything which may have been said, that I discussed the subject with the Carrels, for I considered it best to leave them in ignorance of the fact that they were the subjects of scientific inquiry.

Edward Whymper, *Travels Among the Great Andes of the Equator*

CHAPTER 18

◆

Once More to the Volcano

Volcanoes retained their fascination in the nineteenth century no less than in the ancient world. The extracts in this chapter show how that fascination was expressed by literary tourists (John Henry Newman and Mark Twain), by poets (Matthew Arnold) and by scientific mountaineers (Edward Whymper).

◆ ◆ ◆

Newman in Ashes

To Jemima Newman, April 1833

. . . I shall try, while it is fresh in my memory to give you some account of my going up Vesuvius yesterday, the painful and joyful 12th – an expedition which has introduced me to the most wonderful sight I have seen abroad, and which is well worth my coming to Naples, if I went back again straight – and in which I have undergone more labour and *active* pain, as well as unusual enjoyment, I ever recollect my having.

Mr Bennett, Anderson, and I started about ½ past 11 (just as the names of the new Fellows were giving out) and on arriving at Resina, five miles from Naples, mounted mules and asses which brought us up to the foot of the cone. There is not much remarkable so far. You go first a long way between two walls, the boundaries of vineyards – then over the lava, which is like a plough field in colour and shape, petrified – only more wild and on a larger scale – properly I believe it is the scoria or ashes which lies *on* the lava or into which the lava on the surface is converted – I forget – On dismounting you address yourself to the task of ascending the cone, which does not appear much too high to run up, tho' certainly steep – However it *is* too high to run up when you try, being 800 feet high. The material is fine ashes, with a few lumps of lava scattered about it, which serve little other purpose than to fall upon one's shins. Well, we set to – and a tug it was. The first ascent is 600 feet (for they take you by the lowest entrance) and when half up I confess I did for a ½ minute repent of the undertaking, tho' there was no sun and but little wind – for my feet slipped back about ¾ of the strides they made. One's only consolation was that one must get to the top sometime or other, and this I made. At length we were landed – and sitting down on the ashes at the top (which are so dry as to be remarkably clean) we cooked some beef and drunk some delicious wine, tho' it seems this same wine is so common as hardly to be drinkable any where else. Then we began our rambles. First we went over some sulphur beds, which are of a bright greenish yellow in the midst of the black and then commenced the ascent of the second cone, which is inside the first crater and is about 150 feet high. The material is the same loose ash. When at the top we found an awful sight – the vast expanse of the true crater, broken into many divisions and recesses, up and down (but with no bottomless cavities) and resplendent with all manner of the most beautiful colours from the sulphur, – clouds of which were steaming out here and there from holes in the crust, and almost insupportably strong. The utter silence increased the imposing effect, which became quite fearful, when, on putting the ear to a small crevice, you hear a rushing sound, deep and hollow, part of wind and part of the internal commotion of the mountain. Then we began to descend the crater – which is *very* steep, and at times suffocating from the sulphur puffs – After various turns and windings across the crater, we saw before us the pit from which the chief eruption proceeds at present (for it varies year by year – the *whole* of this second cone has been thrown up by the comparatively insignificant eruption of the past year) and we began to descend into it – here I suffered – for having shoes not sufficiently tight for my feet, they filled (as by the by they did all the time ascending and descending) with the hot ashes which were intolerable, so that I was obliged to cling by my hands. I can only say that I found both my hands and the soles of my feet blistered all over on my return home, besides my hands being torn in various places – I assure you, I quite cried out with the pain. At length I got down – At the bottom it is tolerably cool – a cold wind proceeds from the hole which is not very large, and blocked up with lava. After ascending and again descending this inner cone, we commenced our circuit of the outer one, which is laborious, being besides 3 miles around, the greater part of which we traversed. First we ascended the remaining 200 feet of the 800 and then kept up and down an irregular ridge till we descended to where we had lunched. It was all still of ashes. The view is very striking. The vast plain of Naples, which is covered with innumerable vines, was so distant as to look like a greenish marsh – we could see Pompeii and its amphitheatre very distinctly at a little distance, and in the same direction various streams of lava (their age indicated by their successive shades of blackness) in widening course at the foot of the mountain. It was grand too to look down a sheer descent of 800 feet, which began at one's feet, the walking place being a narrow ledge going off on each side at a very sharp angle from the perpendicular. After getting to the luncheon place, we commence our descent, which is a regular tumble – the

600 feet ought to be done in 3 minutes – but my shoes obliged me to stop every 20 or 30 steps – however it was very curious and amusing. At length we mounted our animals, and in turn entered our carriage – and got home by 8 pm to dinner. The best part is that the whole expedition only cost me a piaster (4 shillings) – I have given you a very true account – but I am tired and want to go to bed. It is unpleasant to be uncertain about tomorrow. Only think of people, nay ladies, ascending the first cone *at night* to see the eruption!

John Henry Newman, *Letters*

Songs of Callicles

How gracious is the mountain at this hour!
A thousand times have I been here alone,
Or with the revellers from the mountain-towns,
But never on so far a morn; the sun
Is shining on the brilliant mountain-crests,
And on the highest pines; but farther down,
Here in the valley, is in shade; the sward
Is dark, and on the stream the mist still hangs;
One sees one's footprints crushed in the wet grass,
One's breath curls in the air; and on these pines
That climb from the stream's edge, the long grey tufts,
Which the goats love, are jewell'd thick with dew . . .

The track winds down to the clear stream,
To cross the sparkling shallows; there
The cattle love to gather, on their way
To the high mountain-pastures, and to stay
Till the rough cow-herds drive them past,
Knee-deep in the cool ford; for 'tis the last
Of all the woody, high, well-water'd dells
On Etna; and the beam
Of noon is broken there by chestnut-boughs
Down its steep verdant sides; the air
Is freshen'd by the leaping stream, which throws
Eternal showers of spray on the moss'd roots
Of trees, and veins of turf, and long dark shoots
Of ivy-plants, and fragrant hanging bells
Of hyacinths, and on late anemonies,
That muffle its wet banks; but glade,
And stream, and sward, and chestnut-trees,

End here; Etna beyond, in the broad glare
Of the hot noon, without a shade,
Slope behind slope, up to the peak, lies bare;
The peak, round which the white clouds play . . .

Through the black, rushing smoke-bursts,
Thick breaks the red flame;
All Etna heaves fiercely
Her forest-clothed frame.

Not here, O Apollo!
Are haunts meet for thee.
But, where Helicon breaks down
In cliff to the sea,

Where the moon-silver'd inlets
Send far their light voice
Up the still vale of Thisbe,
O speed and rejoice!

On the sward at the cliff-top
Lie strewn the white flocks,
On the cliff-side the pigeons
Roost deep in the rocks.

In the moonlight the shepherds,
Soft lulled by the rills,
Lie wrapt in their blankets
Asleep on the hills.

What forms are these coming
So white through the gloom?
What garments out-glistening
The gold-flower'd broom?

What sweet-breathing presence
Out-perfumes the thyme?
What voices enrapture
The night's balmy prime?

'Tis Apollo comes leading
His choir, the Nine.
– The leader is fairest
But all are divine.

They are lost in the hollows!
They stream up again!
What seeks on this mountain
The glorified train?

They bathe on this mountain
In the spring by their road;
Then on to Olympus,
Their endless abode.

Whose praise do they mention?
Of what is it told?
What will be for ever;
What was from old.

First hymn they the Father
Of all things; and then,
The rest of immortals
The action of men.

The day in his hotness,
The strife with the palm,
The night in her silence,
The stars in their calm.

Matthew Arnold, 'Empedocles on Etna'

A Virginian on Vesuvius

At the Hermitage we were about fifteen or eighteen hundred feet above the sea, and thus far a portion of the ascent had been pretty abrupt. For the next two miles the road was a mixture – sometimes the ascent was abrupt and sometimes it was not: but one characteristic it possessed all the time, without failure, without modification – it was all uncompromisingly and unspeakably infamous. It was a rough, narrow trail, and led over an old lava flow – a black ocean which was tumbled into a thousand fantastic shapes – a wild chaos of ruin, desolation, and barrenness – a wilderness of billowy upheavals, of furious whirlpools, of miniature mountains rent asunder – of gnarled and knotted, wrinkled and twisted masses of blackness that mimicked branching roots, great vines, trunks of trees, all interlaced and mingled together: and all these weird shapes, all this turbulent panorama, all this stormy, far-stretching waste of blackness, with its thrilling suggestiveness of life, of action, of boiling, surging, furious motion, was petrified! –

all stricken dead and cold in the instant of its maddest rioting! fettered, paralysed, and left to glower at heaven in impotent rage for evermore!

Finally we stood in a level, narrow valley (a valley that had been created by the terrific march of some old time irruption) and on either hand towered the two steep peaks of Vesuvius. The one we had to climb – the one that contains the active volcano – seemed about eight hundred or one thousand feet high, and looked almost too straight up and down for any man to climb, and certainly no mule could climb it with a man on his back. Four of these native pirates will carry you to the top in a sedan chair, if you wish it, but suppose they were to slip and let you fall, – is it likely that you would ever stop rolling? Not this side of eternity, perhaps. We left the mules, sharpened our finger nails, and began the ascent I have been writing about so long, at twenty minutes to six in the morning. The path led straight up a rugged sweep of loose chunks of pumice-stone, and for about every two steps forward we slid back one. It was so excessively steep that we had to stop, every fifty or sixty steps, and rest a moment. To see our comrades, we had to look nearly straight up at those above us, and very nearly straight down at those below. We stood on the summit at last – it had taken an hour and fifteen minutes to make the trip.

What we saw there was simply a circular crater – a circular ditch, if you please – about two hundred feet deep, and four or five hundred feet wide, whose inner wall was about half a mile in circumference. In the centre of the great circus ring thus formed, was a torn and ragged upheaval a hundred feet high, all snowed over with a sulphur crust of many and many a brilliant and beautiful colour, and the ditch enclosed this like the moat of a castle, or surrounded it as a little river does a little island, if the simile is better. The sulphur coating of that island was gaudy in the extreme – all mingled together in the richest confusion were red, blue, brown, black, yellow, white – I do not know that there was a colour, or shade of a colour, or combination of colours, unrepresented – and when the sun burst through the morning mists and fired this tinted magnificence, it topped imperial Vesuvius like a jewelled crown!

The crater itself – the ditch – was not so variegated in colouring, but yet, in its softness, richness, and unpretentious elegance, it was more charming, more fascinating to the eye. There was nothing 'loud' about its well-bred and well-dressed look. Beautiful? One could stand and look down upon it for a week without getting tired of it. It had the semblance of a pleasant meadow, whose slender grasses and whose velvety mosses were frosted with a shining dust, and tinted with palest green that deepened gradually to the darkest hue of the orange leaf, and deepened yet again into gravest brown, then faded into orange, then into brightest gold, and culminated in the delicate pink of a new blown rose. Where portions of the meadow had sunk, and where other portions had been broken up like an ice-flow, the cavernous openings of the one, and the ragged upturned edges exposed by the other, were hung with a lace work of soft-tinted crystals of sulphur that changed their deformities into quaint shapes and figures that were full of grace and beauty.

The walls of the ditch were brilliant with yellow banks of sulphur and with lava and pumice-stone of many colours. No fire was visible anywhere, but gusts of sulphurous steam issued silently and invisibly from a thousand little cracks and fissures in the crater, and were wafted to our noses with every breeze. But so long as we kept our nostrils buried in our handkerchiefs, there was small danger of suffocation.

Some of the boys thrust long strips of paper down into holes and set them on fire, and so achieved the glory of lighting their cigars by the flames of Vesuvius, and others cooked eggs over fissures in the rocks and were happy.

Mark Twain, *The Innocents Abroad*

The Ascent of Cotopaxi

We had learned on Chimborazo that mountain-sickness was a reality. Although the more acute symptoms had disappeared, whilst remaining at low pressures, it was not certain that they would not reappear; still less that they would not recur if we remained continuously at a yet lower pressure than we had experienced at the third camp, namely about 16 inches. To settle this matter, so far as it could be done in Ecuador, I had intended to ascend Chimborazo again, perhaps several times, and had even projected a residence on the snow plateau at its summit. This now could not be done. The stores and baggage which had cost so much time and trouble to take up had all been brought down again, the camps were broken up, and the information which was desired could only be obtained by beginning afresh in some other quarter.

All the other Great Andes of the Equator were believed to be lower than Chimborazo, and consequently we were not likely to add materially to what we had already learned concerning the effects of diminished atmospheric pressure by simple ascents and descent of them. Moreover, two of the loftiest – Antisana and Cayambe – were as yet unclimbed, and, even should we get up them, it was probable that we should be unable to remain on the summits. So my thoughts naturally turned to the great volcano Cotopaxi. It was reported that there was a large slope of ash at the apex of its terminal cone, and I proposed to encamp upon it, close to the top of the mountain. If this could be done, and if we should find that we could remain at this height (19,500 feet) for a length of time without suffering inconvenience from the low reigning pressure, it would substantially advance our information, and would give good grounds for hope that one might carry exploration elsewhere as high as 24,000 or 25,000 feet above the level of the sea; though it would still leave in uncertainty the possibility of attaining the very highest summits in the world. It is idle to suppose that men will ever reach the loftiest points on the globe, unless they are able to camp out at considerably greater elevations than twenty thousand feet.

The chance of having a nocturnal view of the interior of the crater, though a secondary, was a powerful attraction. Those who had hitherto ascended Cotopaxi had remained a very short time on the top, and had only obtained fragmentary views of the crater, and had given rather divergent accounts of it. Opportunities do not often occur of looking by night into the bowels of a first-rate, active volcano, and the idea of camping upon the apex of the cone grew upon me, the more I thought about it. By doing so, I proposed to kill two birds with one stone . . .

Cotopaxi is an ideal volcano. It comports itself, volcanically speaking, in a regular and well-behaved manner. It is not one of the provoking sort – exploding in paroxysms and going to sleep directly afterwards. It is in a state of perpetual activity, and has been so ever since it has had a place in history. There are loftier mountains which have been volcanoes, and there are active volcanoes with larger craters, yielding greater quantities of lava, but the summit of Cotopaxi, so far as is known, has the greatest absolute elevation above the level of the sea of all volcanoes that are in working order . . .

The ascent to Cotopaxi, by the route we followed, was a walk; and the direction that we took is best indicated by saying that we kept along the crest of the rather ill-defined ridge which descends almost continuously from the summit towards the mountain Ruminahui. No climbing whatever was necessary. The lower camp was distant about 8600 feet from the nearest part of the crater, and in this distance we rose 4500 feet. Isolated snow-patches commenced at about 15,400 feet, and a little higher we were able to follow snow uninterruptedly right up to the slope upon which I proposed to encamp. In order to ensure regularity in the march, we tied up in line, a proceeding that our natives did not at all comprehend, and they wondered still more at the use of the axe in cutting steps in the snow, to facilitate progress. The most interesting feature I noticed upon this section of the mountain was the existence of glaciers upon the upper part of the cone. They occurred on each side of us, and in some places extended to within 500 feet of the top; but, through being much covered by ash, it was not possible to say exactly where they commenced or terminated, and for the same reason they were quite unrecognizable at a distance.

At 11 a.m. we arrived at the foot of the great slope of ash upon the western side of the summit, which leads right up to the edge of the crater, and we found this was the steepest and most laborious part of the ascent. I estimate it to be 750 feet high, and 1100 feet long. It was composed of the materials which are being daily, even hourly ejected (mainly of particles weighing about 500 to a grain, with an admixture of angular fragments of lava up to a quarter of an inch in diameter), and it was piled up nearly to the maximum angle at which it would stand. I know experimentally that its materials will stand at 41°, but the face of the slope was not I think steeper than 37°. We deposited our baggage at the foot of it until we had completed the ascent, and found that occasional streaks of ice gave some stability to the mass, which would otherwise have slipped down in large quantities at every step.

We hurried up this unstable slope as fast as we could do, and reached the western edge of the summit rim exactly at midday. The crater was nearly filled with smoke and steam, which drifted about and obscured the view. The opposite side could scarcely be perceived, and the bottom was quite concealed. As the vapours were wafted hither and thither, we gained a pretty good idea of the general shape of the crater, though as a whole it was not seen until night-time.

A few minutes after our arrival, a roar from the bottom told us that the 'animal' (Carrel's term for the volcano) was alive. It had been settled beforehand that every man was to shift for himself if an eruption occurred, and that all our belongings were to be abandoned. When we heard the roar, there was an 'it is time to be off' expression clearly written on all our faces; but before a word could be uttered we found ourselves enveloped only in a cloud of cool and quite unobjectionable steam, and we concluded to stop.

The establishment of the tent was the first consideration. It was unanimously decided that it was not desirable to camp at the top of the slope, close to the rim or lip of the crater, on account of wind and the liability to harm from lightning, and the more I examined the slope itself the less I liked it. It was naked, exposed, and slipped upon the slightest provocation. Jean-Antoine and I therefore set out on a tour to look for a better place, but after spending several hours in passing round about a quarter of the crater, without result, we returned to the others, and all hands set to work to endeavour to make a platform upon the ash. This proved to be a long and troublesome business. Unlike snow, it gained no coherence by being beaten or trampled down, and the more they raked to extend our platform the more slipped down from above. Ultimately it was made sufficiently secure by scooping channels in the portion of the slope which was above and tenderly pouring many tons upon the slope below, so as to strengthen the base. The tent-ropes were secured to large blocks of lava, which had to be brought from long distances and buried in the ash. For additional security four ropes were run out besides the usual ones, and we rigged up our long rope as a sort of handrail to the nearest convenient point of the rim of the crater, from which we were distant 250 feet. When this was done, the natives were sent back to the lower camp, and the Carrels and I remained alone.

We had scarcely completed our preparations when a violent squall arose, which threatened to carry the whole establishment away, and during an hour it was a great question whether our abode would weather the storm. The squall passed away as suddenly as it arose, and for the rest of our stay we were not much troubled by wind. While this was occurring there was another cause for alarm. A great smell of indiarubber commenced to arise, and on putting my hand to the floor of the tent I found that it was on the point of melting. On placing a maximum thermometer on the floor, it indicated 110° Faht. As my feet did not feel at all warm I tried the temperature at the other side of the tent and found it was only 50° and in the middle it was 72.5°. These temperatures were maintained during our stay on this spot. Outside, even during the daytime, the air was intensely cold; and the minimum of the night of February 18, registered by a thermometer placed four feet above the ground, and four feet from the tent on its windward side, was 13° Faht., which was the lowest temperature that was observed during the whole of the journey.

When daylight began to fail, we settled down in the tent, and it is now time to recur to the motive which had taken us to the summit of Cotopaxi. There were three principal questions to which I desired answers. 1. Shall we, upon again reaching the elevation, and experiencing the diminution in pressure which had rendered us incapable on Chimborazo, have a recurrence of our experiences upon that mountain? 2. Or, are we now habituated to a pressure of 16 inches? 3. If we are habituated to a pressure of 16 inches, shall we now be able to remain some time at a considerably lower pressure without being rendered incapable?

During the ascent I had watched my people with mingled feelings of curiosity and anxiety. Their pace was rather slow, but it was steadily maintained. At one point, when between 18,000 and 19,000 feet above the level of the sea, they went up 360 steps without stopping. I noticed nothing unusual during the ascent, nor upon the summit, except the overpowering desire to sit down, which always mastered us when we were at great elevations (low pressures) and the disposition to breathe through open mouths. The collapse on Chimborazo had, however, occurred very suddenly. We were all right in one hour and all wrong in the next. It came upon us, so it seemed, without premonition. All at once, we found ourselves with intense headaches (not having had any before), gasping for air, and half asphyxiated. Hour after hour went by on the summit of Cotopaxi without anything of the kind happening again . . .

When night fairly set in we went up to view the interior of the crater. The atmosphere was cold and tranquil. We could hear the deadened roar of the steam-blasts as they escaped from time to time. Our long rope had been fixed both to guide in the darkness and to lessen the chance of disturbing the equilibrium of the slope of ash. Grasping it, I made my way upwards, prepared for something dramatic, for a strong glow on the under sides of the steam-clouds showed that there was fire below. Crawling and grovelling as the lip was approached, I bent eagerly forward to peer into the unknown, with Carrel behind, gripping my legs.

The vapours no longer concealed any part of the vast crater, though they were there, drifting about, as before. We saw an amphitheatre 2300 feet in diameter from north to south, and 1650 feet across from east to west, with a rugged and irregular crest, notched and cracked; surrounded by cliffs, by perpendicular and even overhanging precipices, mixed with steep slopes, some bearing snow, and others apparently encrusted with sulphur. Cavernous recesses belched forth smoke; the sides of cracks and chasms no more than half-way down shone with ruddy light; and so it continued on all sides, right down to the bottom, precipice alternating with slope, and the fiery fissures becoming more numerous as the bottom was approached. At the bottom, probably twelve hundred feet below us, and towards the centre, there was a rudely circular spot, about one tenth of the diameter of the crater, the pipe of the volcano, its channel of communication with lower regions, filled with incandescent if not molten lava, glowing and burning; with flames travelling to and fro over its surface, and scintillations scattering as from a wood-fire; lighted by tongues of flickering flame which issued from the cracks in the surrounding slopes.

At intervals of about half an hour the volcano regularly blew off steam. It rose in jets with great violence from the bottom of the crater, and boiled over the lip, continually enveloping us. The noise on these occasions resembled that which we hear when a huge ocean liner is blowing off steam. It appeared to be pure, and we saw nothing thrown out, yet in the morning the tent was almost black with matter which had been ejected . . .

We were up again before daylight on the 19th, and then measured 600 feet on the western side of the crater, and took angles to gain an idea of its dimensions. I photographed it, and made final observations of the mercurial barometer to determine its altitude. From the mean of the whole, its summit appears to be 19,613 feet above the sea. In 1872–3, Messrs Reiss and Stübel (by angles taken from various barometrically measured bases) made its height 19,498 feet; and by the same method La Condamine, in the early part of last century, found that its height was 18,865 feet. As there is not much probability of considerable error in any of the determinations, it would seem that Cotopaxi has materially increased its elevation in the course of the last century and a half.

The time to descend had now arrived, and at 11.30 a.m. our Ecuadorians should have remounted, to assist in carrying our baggage down again. The weather, however, was abominable, and they preferred to leave the work to us. After depositing our more bulky stores at the foot of the great slope of ash, we tramped down to the first camp. The feet of Louis were still in a very tender state, and he could not take part in racing; but Jean-Antoine and I went down as hard as we could, and descended the 4300 feet in 110 minutes. Two days more elapsed before animals could be brought from Machachi for the retreat, and it was later on the 21st before we got clear of Cotopaxi. The night was dark, and the path invisible; but guided by the bells we gained the hamlet, and encamped once more in the chapel of Pedregal.

The rest of my Machachi men now returned home, and the authorities lost no time in interviewing them, for these poor noodles were possessed with the idea that we were in search of gold. 'Tell us, what did they do?' Said my men, 'The Doctor, dressed like a king, went from one place to another, looking about; but after a time Señor Juan and Señor Luis seemed afraid of him, for they tied him up with a rope.' 'Enough of this; tell us, did they find treasure?' 'We think they did. They went down on their hands and knees searching for it, and they wrapped what they took in paper and brought it away.' 'Was it gold?' 'We do not know, but it was very heavy.' This, though true, was rather misleading. The 'royal' attire which so impressed them consisted of the Ulster coat and dressing gown underneath, crowned by the Dundee whaling-cap; and the 'treasures' we carried away were samples of the jagged crest and debris of the terminal slope.

Cotopaxi shews no signs of approaching decrepitude, and for many centuries yet to come it may remain the highest active volcano in the world; or perchance the imprisoned forces may find an easier outlet, through barriers offering less resistance, and either Sangai, Tunguragua, or Pichincha may become the premier volcano of the Equator. Whilst the great cone which has so often trembled with subterranean thunders – buried beneath glaciers more extensive than those of Cayambe or Antisana – will echo with the crash of the ice-avalanche; its crater will disappear, and over its rugged floor and its extinguished fires, soft snowflakes will rear a majestic dome loftier than Chimborazo.

Edward Whymper, *Travels Among the Great Andes of the Equator*

The Spoils of the Volcanoes

VOLCANIC DUSTS
FROM THE GREAT ANDES OF THE EQUATOR
COLLECTED BY EDWARD WHYMPER.

1. VOLCANIC DUST FROM COTOPAXI, Eruption of June 26, 1877, which fell at Quito after an aerial voyage of 34 miles. See *Travels Among the Great Andes,* ch. vi. ['in the brown glass chips vacuoles are abundant, many of them range from about .001 to .002 inch in diameter, but some are still smaller.' Prof. T.G. Bonney, *Proc. Royal. Soc.*, June 1884]

2. VOLCANIC DUST FROM COTOPAXI, Eruption of July 3, 1880, which was ejected to a height of 40,000 feet above the level of the sea, and fell on CHIMBORAZO after an aerial voyage of 64 miles. See *Travels Among the Great Andes*, chapter xviii. The finest particles weigh less than one twenty-five thousandth part of a grain.

3. VOLCANIC DUST FROM THE TERMINAL SLOPE OF COTOPAXI, 19,500 feet above the level of the sea. This is the matter which is ejected daily by the Volcano. See *Travels Among the Great Andes*, chapter vii.

4. VOLCANIC DUST FROM 15,300 FEET ON COTOPAXI, about 2000 particles to a grain. See *Travels Among the Great Andes*, chapter vii. ['The granules commonly range from .01 to .015 inch in diameter. The most abundant are minute lapilli of scoriaceous aspect; in less numbers are glassy whitish and reddish granules – with these occur fragments of felspar, augite and hypersthene.' Prof T.G. Bonney, *Proc. Royal Soc.*, June 1884].

5. LAPILLI FROM 15,000 FEET ON COTOPAXI. See *Travels Among the Great Andes*, chapter vii. ['Pumiceous lapilli; pulverised glass; and mineral fragments.' Prof. T.G. Bonney, *Proc. Royal Soc.* June 1884]

6. LAPILLI FROM AMBATO (8600 FEET). Mainly colourless, vesicular pumice. Many of the fragments have entangled with them small microliths, and also plates of a pale greenish mica. The town of Ambato is built upon this deposit. See *Travels Among the Great Andes*, chap. iv.

7. FINE VOLCANIC DUST FROM MACHACHI (9800 FEET), existing as a continuous stratum ten inches thick, the product of some unrecorded eruption of great intensity. Consists largely of felspar and horneblende. The finest particles are felspar and pumice. 'Almost as soft to the touch as cotton wool.' See *Travels Among the Great Andes*, chap. v.

8. FINE PUMICE DUST FROM MACHACHI (9800 FEET). This forms beds many feet in thickness, and consists mainly of clear, colourless, vesicular pumice, which includes greenish mica, some in minute hexagonal plates. See *Travels Among the Great Andes*, chap. v.

These Volcanic Dusts are perfectly pure, and form most interesting and instructive objects for the Microscope.

Sold in bottles, price 1s 6d. each. Each sample contains one grain and upwards.

Sent post free on receipt of Postal Order for 1s 7d., or the set of eight specimens, in a box, post free for 10s.

JAMES R. GREGORY & CO., MINERALOGISTS &C,

1 KELSO PLACE, KENSINGTON, LONDON

Edward Whymper, *A Guide to Zermatt and the Matterhorn*

CHAPTER 19

◆

Soaped Poles

Not everyone was favourably impressed by the development of mountaineering in the nineteenth century, and opposition to the cult of climbing was expressed even by many who had shown their own love of the mountains in other ways. Tennyson's shepherd, in language which shows a keen appreciation of mountain beauty, sings the praises of the valleys. Ruskin's denunciation of the desecration of the Alps is more seriously intended, and was taken seriously enough to call forth many a reply from mountaineers, as will be seen in the next chapter. Hilaire Belloc in prose, and an unknown writer in the Wasdale Head Visitor's Book in verse, express eloquently the advantages of looking up at mountains from below rather than ascending them to the summit. Arnold Lunn, no mean mountaineer himself, concedes that at least in the literary field, the mountain lovers have won the palm from the mountaineers.

◆ ◆ ◆

Love is of the Valley

Come down, O maid, from yonder mountain height
What pleasure lives in height (the shepherd sang),
In height and cold, the splendour of the hills?
But cease to move so near the Heavens, and cease
To glide a sunbeam by the blasted Pine,
To sit a star upon the sparkling spire;
And come, for Love is of the valley, come,
For Love is of the valley, come thou down
And find him; by the happy threshold, he,
Or hand in hand with Plenty in the maize,
Or red with spirted purple of the vats,
Or foxlike in the vine; nor cares to walk
With Death and Morning on the silver horns,
Nor wilt thou snare him in the white ravine,
Nor find him dropt upon the firths of ice,
That huddling slant in furrow-cloven falls

To roll the torrent out of dusky doors:
But follow; let the torrent dance thee down
To find him in the valley; let the wild
Lean-headed Eagles yelp alone, and leave
The monstrous ledges there to slope, and spill
Their thousand wreaths of dangling water-smoke,
That like a broken purpose waste in air:
So waste not thou; but come; for all the vales
Await thee: azure pillars of the hearth
Arise to thee; the children call, and I
Thy shepherd pipe, and sweet is every sound,
Sweeter thy voice, but every sound is sweet;
Myriads of rivulets hurrying through the lawn,
The moan of doves in immemorial elms,
And murmuring of innumerable bees.

Alfred Tennyson, 'The Princess'

The Desecration of the Alps

It is not therefore strange, however much to be regretted, that while
no gentleman boasts in other cases of his sagacity or his courage – while no
good soldier talks of the charge he led, nor any good sailor of the helm he
held, – every man among the Alps seems to lose his senses and his modesty
with the fall of the barometer, and returns from his Nephelococcygia
brandishing his ice-axe in everybody's face. Whatever the Alpine Club have
done, or may yet accomplish, in a sincere thirst for mountain knowledge, and
in happy sense of youthful strength, and play of animal spirit, they have
done, and will do, wisely and well; but whatever they are urged to do by mere
sting of competition and itch of praise, they will do, as all vain things must
be done for ever, foolishly and ill. It is a strange proof of that absence of any
real national love of science, of which I have had occasion to speak in the text,
that no entire survey of the Alps has yet been made by properly qualified
men; and that, except of the chain of Chamouni, no accurate maps exist, nor
any complete geological section even of that. But Mr Reilly's survey of that
central group, and the generally accurate information collected in the guide-
book published by the Club, are honourable results of English adventure;
and it is to be hoped that the continuance of such work will gradually put
an end to the vulgar excitement which looked upon the granite of the Alps
only as an unoccupied advertisement wall for chalking names upon . . .

Granting, however, such praise and such sphere of exertion as we thus
justly may, to the spirit of adventure, there is one consequence of it, coming
directly under my own cognizance, of which I cannot but speak with utter

regret, – the loss, namely, of all real understanding of the character and beauty of Switzerland, by the country's being now regarded as half watering-place, half gymnasium. It is indeed true that under the influence of the pride which gives poignancy to the sensations which others cannot share with it (and a not unjustifiable zest to the pleasure which we have worked for), an ordinary traveller will usually observe and enjoy more on a difficult excursion than on an easy one; and more in objects to which he is unaccustomed than in those with which he is familiar. He will notice with extreme interest that snow is white on the top of a hill in June, though he would have attached little importance to the same peculiarity in a wreath at the bottom of a hill in January. He will generally find more to admire in a cloud underneath his feet, than in one over his head; and, oppressed by the monotony of a sky which is prevalently blue, will derive extraordinary satisfaction from its approximation to black. Add to such grounds of delight the aid given to the effect of whatever is impressive in the scenery of high Alps, by the absence of ludicrous or degrading concomitants; and it ceases to be surprising that Alpine excursionists should be greatly pleased, or that they should attribute their pleasure to some true and increased apprehension of the nobleness of natural scenery. But no impression can be more false. The real beauty of the Alps is to be seen, and seen only, where all may see it, the child, the cripple, and the man of grey hairs. There is more true loveliness in a single glade of pasture shadowed by pine, or gleam of rocky brook, or inlet of unsullied lake, among the lower Bernese and Savoyard hills, than in the entire field of jagged gneiss which crests the central ridge from the Schreckhorn to the Viso. The valley of Cluse, through which unhappy travellers consent now to be invoiced, packed in baskets like fish, so only that they may cheaply reach, in the feverous haste which has become the law of their being, the glen of Chamouni whose every lovely foreground rock has now been broken up to build hotels for them, contains more beauty in half a league of it, than the entire valley they have devastated, and turned into a casino, did in its uninjured pride; and that passage of the Jura by Olten (between Basle and Lucerne), which is by the modern tourist triumphantly effected through a tunnel in ten minutes, between two piggish trumpet grunts proclamatory of the ecstatic transit, used to show from every turn and sweep of its winding ascent, up which one sauntered, gathering wild-flowers for half a happy day, diviner aspects of the distant Alps than ever were achieved by toil of limb, or won by risk of life . . .

You have despised nature; that is to say, all the deep and sacred sensations of natural scenery. The French revolutionists made stables of the cathedrals of France; you have made racecourses of the cathedrals of the earth. Your *one* conception of pleasure is to drive in railroad carriages round their aisles, and eat off their altars. You have put a railroad bridge over the falls of Schaffhausen. You have tunnelled the cliffs of Lucerne by Tell's chapel;

you have destroyed the Clarens shore of the Lake of Geneva; there is not a quiet valley in England that you have not filled with bellowing fire; there is no particle left of English land which you have not trampled coal ashes into – nor any foreign city in which the spread of your presence is not marked among its fair old streets and happy gardens by a consuming white leprosy of new hotels and perfumers' shops: the Alps themselves, which your own poets used to love so reverently, you look upon as soaped poles in a bear-garden, which you set yourselves to climb, and slide down again, with 'shrieks of delight'. When you are past shrieking, having no articulate voice to say you are glad with, you fill the quietude of their valleys with gunpowder blasts, and rush home, red with cutaneous eruption of conceit, and voluble with convulsive hiccough of self-satisfaction.

John Ruskin, *Sesame and Lilies*

The Alps from a Distance

The wood went up darkly and the path branched here and there so that I was soon uncertain of my way, but I followed generally what seemed to me the most southerly course, and so came at last up steeply through a dip or ravine that ended high on the crest of the ride.

Just as I came to the end of the rise, after perhaps an hour, perhaps two, of that great curtain of forest which had held the mountain side, the trees fell away to brushwood, there was a gate, and then the path was lost upon a fine open sward which was the very top of the Jura and the coping of that multiple wall which defends the Swiss Plain. I had crossed it straight from edge to edge, never turning out of my way.

It was too marshy to lie down on it, so I stood a moment to breathe and look about me.

It was evident that nothing higher remained, for though a new line of wood – firs and beeches – stood before me, yet nothing appeared above them, and I knew that they must be the fringe of the descent. I approached this edge of wood, and saw that it had a rough fence of post and rails bounding it, and as I was looking for the entry of a path (for my original path was lost, as such tracks are, in the damp grass of the little down) there came to me one of those great revelations which betray to us suddenly the higher things and stand afterwards firm in our minds.

There, on this upper meadow, where so far I had felt nothing but the ordinary gladness of The Summit, I had a vision.

What was it I saw? If you think I saw this or that, and if you think I am inventing the words, you know nothing of men.

I saw between the branches of the trees in front of me a sight in the sky that made me stop breathing, just as great danger at sea, or great surprise in love, or a great deliverance will make a man stop breathing. I saw something I had known in the West as a boy, something I had never seen so grandly discovered as was this. In between the branches of the trees was a great promise of unexpected lights beyond.

I pushed left and right along that edge of the forest and along the fence that bound it, until I found a place where the pine-trees stopped, leaving a gap, and where on the right, beyond the gap, was a tree whose leaves had failed; there the ground broke away steeply below me, and the beeches fell, one below the other, like a vast cascade, towards the limestone cliffs that dipped down still further, beyond my sight. I looked through this framing hollow and praised God. For there below me, thousands of feet below me, was what seemed an illimitable plain; at the end of that world was an horizon, and the dim bluish sky that overhangs an horizon.

There was brume in it and thickness. One saw the sky beyond the edge of the world getting purer as the vault rose. But right up – a belt in that empyrean – ran peak and field and needle of intense ice, remote, remote from the world. Sky beneath them and sky above them, a steadfast legion, they glittered as though with the armour of the immovable armies of Heaven. Two days' march, three days' march away, they stood up like the walls of Eden. I say it again, they stopped my breath. I had seen them.

So little are we, we men: so much are we immersed in our muddy and immediate interests that we think, by numbers and recitals, to comprehend distance or time, or any of our limiting infinities. Here were these magnificent creatures of God, I mean the Alps, which now for the first time I saw from the height of the Jura; and because they were fifty or sixty miles away, and because they were a mile or two high, they were become something different from us others, and could strike one motionless with the awe of supernatural things. Up there in the sky, to which only clouds belong and birds and the last trembling colours of pure light, they stood fast and hard; not moving as do the things of the sky. They were as distant as the little upper clouds of summer, as fine and tenuous; but in their reflection and in their quality as it were of weapons (like spears and shields of an unknown array) they occupied the sky with a sublime invasion: and the things proper to the sky were forgotten by me in their presence as I gazed.

To what emotion shall I compare this astonishment? So, in first love one finds that *this* can belong to *me*.

Their sharp steadfastness and their clean uplifted lines compelled my adoration. Up there, the sky above and below them, part of the sky but part of us, the great peaks made communion between that homing creeping part of me which loves vineyards and dances and a slow movement among pastures, and that other part which is only properly at home in Heaven. I say that this kind of description is useless, and that it is better to address prayers to such things than to attempt to interpret them for others.

These, the great Alps, seen thus, link one in some way to one's immortality. Nor is it possible to convey, or even to suggest, those few fifty miles, and those few thousand feet; there is something more. Let me put it thus: that from the height of Weissenstein I saw, as it were, my religion. I mean, humility, the fear of death, the terror of height and of distance, the glory of God, the infinite potentiality of reception whence springs that divine thirst of the soul; my aspiration also towards completion, and my confidence in the dual destiny. For I know that we laughers have a gross cousinship with the most high, and it is this contrast and perpetual quarrel which feeds a spring of merriment in the soul of a sane man.

Since I could now see such a wonder and it could work such things in my mind, therefore, some day I should be part of it. That is what I felt.

This it is also, which leads some men to climb mountain-tops, but not me, for I am afraid of slipping down.

Hilaire Belloc, *The Path to Rome*

The Repentant Climber

Of Scawfell Pike I clomt the height;
  And when I got upon it,
With all my soul, with all my might,
  I wished I hadn't done it.

My blythe companion lay at ease,
  No heights had he to scale!
And smoked the pipe of utter peace,
  Reclining down the vale.

Woe to the man on clambering bent!
  He finds but falls and strains,
And mists, and much bewilderment,
  And divers aches and pains.

But well for him who, in the vale,
  Reclining smokes in peace;
No strains are his, no heights to scale,
  Body and mind at ease.

I scrambled down; my limbs, though sound,
  Were most severely shaken;
Oft when I thought I'd reached smooth ground,
  I found I was mistaken!

> Let he who wills go climb the hills,
> My taste with his don't tally;
> Let he who wills go climb the hills,
> But I'll stay in the valley!

Wasdale Head Farm Visitors' Book

Mountaineers vs Mountain Lovers

With a few great exceptions, the literature of mountaineers is not as fine as
the literature of mountain lovers . . . The contrast is rather too marked
between the work of those who loved mountains without climbing them and
the literature of the professional mountaineers. Even writers like Mr
Kipling, who have only touched mountains in a few casual lines, seem to
have captured the mountain atmosphere more successfully than many a
climber who has devoted articles galore to his craft. Of course, Mr Kipling
is a genius and the average Alpine writer is not; but surely one might not
unreasonably expect a unique literature from those who know the mountains in all their changing tenses, and who by service of toil and danger have
wrung from them intimate secrets unguessed at by those who linger outside
the shrine.

Mountaineering has, of course, produced some great literature. There is
Leslie Stephen, though even Stephen at his best is immeasurably below
Ruskin's finest mountain passages. But Leslie Stephens are rare in the history
of Alpine literature, whereas the inarticulate are always with us.

In some ways, the man who can worship a mountain without wishing to
climb it has a certain advantage. He sees a vision, where the climber too
often sees nothing but a variation route. The popular historian has often a
more vivid picture of a period than the expert, whose comprehensive knowledge of obscure charters sometimes blinds him to the broad issues of
history. Technical knowledge does not always make for understanding. The
first great revelation of the mountains has a power that is all its own. To the
man who has yet to climb, every mountain is virgin, every snow-field a
mystery, undefiled by traffic with man. The first vision passes, and the love
that is based on understanding supplants it. The vision of unattainable
snow translates itself into terms of memory – that white gleam that once
belonged to dreamland into an ice-wall with which you have wrestled
through the scorching hours of a July afternoon. You have learned to spell
the writing on the wall of the mountains. The magic of first love, with its
worship of the unattainable, is too often transformed into the soberer
affection founded, like domestic love, on knowledge and sympathy; and the
danger would be greater if the fickle hills had not to be wooed afresh every
season. Beyond the mountain that we climbed and seem to know, lurks ever

the visionary peak that we shall never conquer; and this unattainable ideal gives an eternal youth to the hills, and a never-failing vitality to our Alpine adventure. Yet when we begin to set down our memories of the mountains, it seems far easier to recall those objective facts, which are the same for all comers, the meticulous details of route, the conditions of snow and ice, and to omit from our epic that subjective vision of the mountain, that individual impression which alone lends something more than a technical interest to the story of our days among the snow. And so it is not altogether surprising that the man who has never climbed can write more freely and more fully of the mountains, since he has no expert knowledge to confuse the issue, no technical details to obscure the first fine careless rapture.

The early mountaineers entered into a literary field that was almost unexplored. They could write of their hill journeys with the assurance of men branching out into unknown byways. They could linger on the commonplaces of hill travel, and praise the freedom of the hills, with the air of men enunciating a paradox. To glorify rough fare, simple quarters, a bed of hay, a drink quaffed from the mountain stream, must have afforded Gesner the same intellectual pleasure that Mr Chesterton derives from the praise of Battersea and Beer. And this joy in emotions which had yet to be considered trite lingers on even into the more sedate pages of *Peaks, Passes and Glaciers*. The contributors to those classic volumes were rather frightened of letting themselves go; but here and there one lights on some spontaneous expression of delight in the things that are the very flesh and blood of our Alpine experience – the bivouac beneath the stars, the silent approach of dawn, the freemasonry of the rope, the triumph of the virgin summit. 'Times have changed since then,' wrote Donald Robertson in a recent issue of *The Alpine Journal*, 'and with them Alpine literature. Mountaineering has become a science, and as in other sciences, the professor has grown impatient of the average intelligence, and evolved his own tongue.' . . .

A great deal of Alpine literature appeals, and rightly appeals, only to the expert. Such contributions are not intended as descriptive literature. They may, as the record of research into the early records of mountaineering and mountains, supply a much-needed link in the history of the craft. As the record of new exploration, they are sure to interest the expert, while their exact description of routes and times will serve as the material for future climbers' guides. But this is not the whole of Alpine literature, and the danger is that those who dare not attempt the subjective aspects of mountaineering should frighten off those who have the necessary ability by a tedious repetition of the phrase 'fine writing', that facile refuge of the Philistine. The conventional Alpine article is a dreary affair. Its humour is antique, and consists for the most part in jokes about fleas and porters, and in the substitution of long phrases for simple ones. Its satire is even thinner.

The root assumption that the Alpine climber is a superior person, and that social status varies with the height above sea level, recurs with monotonous regularity. The joke about the tripper is as old as the Flood, and the instinct that resents his disturbing presence is not quite the hall-mark of the aesthetic soul that some folk seem to think. It is as old as the primitive man who espied a desirable glade, and lay in wait for the first tourist with a club . . .

There are many writers who have captured the romance of mountaineering, far fewer who have the gift for that happy choice of words that gives the essence of a particular Alpine view. Pick up any Alpine classic at a venture, and you will find that not one writer in fifty can hold your attention through a long passage of descriptive writing. The average writer piles on his adjectives. From the Alpine summit you can see a long way. The horizon seems infinitely far off. The valleys sink below into profound shadows. The eye is carried from the dark firs upward to the glittering snowfields. 'The majestic mass of the . . . rises to the north, and blots out the lesser ranges of the . . . The awful heights of the . . . soar upwards from the valley of . . . In the east, we could just catch a glimpse of the . . . and our guides assured us that in the west we could veritably see the distant snows of our old friend the . . .' And so on, and so forth. Fill in the gaps, and this skeleton description can be made to fit the required panorama. It roughly represents nine out of ten word pictures of Alpine views.

Arnold Lunn, *The Alps*

CHAPTER 20

◆

Aesthetics and Ascetics

The extracts in this chapter illustrate the response of mountaineers to the criticisms of Ruskin and his followers. Sir Leslie Stephen claims that even from a strictly aesthetic point of view, the mountaineer has a greater appreciation of mountain scenery than the non-mountaineer. His argument is backed up by A.F. Mummery, that mountaineer's mountaineer, whom many regard as the inventor of serious modern rock-climbing, and by Guido Rey in a piece which contains a moving description of his glimpse of the aged Whymper revisiting the Matterhorn. Arnold Lunn sums up the case for the defence in this chapter as in the last he summed up the case for the prosecution: for him the twentieth-century mountaineer is an ascetic, in the tradition of the mountain saints of the early church.

◆ ◆ ◆

The Mountaineer's Experimental Faith

I am standing at the foot of what, to my mind, is the most glorious of all Alpine wonders – the huge Oberland precipice, on the slopes of the Faulhorn or the Wengern Alp. Innumerable tourists have done all that tourists can do to cocknify (if that is the right derivative from cockney) the scenery; but, like the Pyramids or a Gothic cathedral, it throws off the taint of vulgarity by its imperishable majesty. Even on turf strewn with sandwich papers and empty bottles, even in the presence of hideous peasant-women singing 'Stand-er-auf' for five centimes, we cannot but feel the influence of Alpine beauty. When the sunlight is dying off the snows, or the full moon lighting them up with ethereal tints, even sandwich papers and singing women may be forgotten. How does the memory of scrambles along snow arêtes, of plunges – luckily not too deep – into crevasses, of toils through long snowfields, towards a refuge that seemed to recede as we advanced – where, to quote Tennyson with due alteration, to the traveller toiling in immeasurable snow –

> Sown in a wrinkle of the monstrous hill
> The chalet sparkles like a grain of salt; –

how do such memories as these harmonise with the sense of superlative sublimity?

One element of mountain beauty is, we shall all admit, their vast size and steepness. That a mountain is very big, and is faced by perpendicular walls of rock, is the first thing which strikes everybody, and is the whole essence and outcome of a vast quantity of poetical description. Hence the first condition towards a due appreciation of mountain scenery is that these qualities should be impressed upon the imagination. The mere dry statement that a mountain is so many feet in vertical height above the sea, and contains so many tons of granite, is nothing. Mont Blanc is about three miles high. What of that? Three miles is an hour's walk for a lady – an eighteen penny cab-fare – the distance from Hyde Park Corner to the Bank – an express train could do it in three minutes, or a race-horse in ⁵ive. It is a measure which we have learnt to despise, looking at it from a horizontal point of view; and accordingly most persons, on seeing the Alps for the first time, guess them to be higher, as measured in feet, than they really are. What, indeed, is the use of giving measures in feet to any but the scientific mind? Who cares whether the moon is 250,000 or 2,500,000 miles distant? Mathematicians try to impress upon us that the distance of the fixed stars is only expressible by a row of figures which stretches across a page; suppose it stretched across two or across a dozen pages, should we be any the wiser, or have, in the least degree, a clearer notion of the superlative distances? We civilly say, 'Dear me!' when the astronomer looks to us for the appropriate state, but we only say it with our mouth; internally our remark is 'You might as well have multiplied by a few more millions whilst you were about it.' . . .

We feel a similar need in the case of mountains. Besides the bare statement of figures, it is necessary to have some means for grasping the meaning of the figures. The bare tens and thousands must be clothed with some concrete images. The statement that a mountain is 15,000 feet high is, by itself, little more impressive than that it is 3,000; we want something more before we can mentally compare Mont Blanc and Snowdon . . .

Nothing is more common than for tourists to mistake some huge pinnacle of rock, as big as a church tower, for a traveller. The rocks of the Grands Mulets, in one corner of which the chalet is hidden, are often identified with a party ascending Mont Blanc; and I have seen boulders as big as a house pointed out confidently as chamois. People who makes these blunders must evidently see the mountains as mere toys, however many feet they may give them at a random guess. Huge overhanging cliffs are to them steps within the reach of human legs; yawning crevasses are ditches to be jumped; and foaming waterfalls are like streams from penny squirts. Every one knows the avalanches on the Jungfrau, and the curiously disproportionate appearance of the little puffs of white smoke, which are said to be the cause of the thunder; but the disproportion ceases to an eye that has learnt really to measure distance, and to know that these smoke-puffs represent a cataract of crashing blocks of ice.

Now the first merit of mountaineering is that it enables one to have what theologians would call an experimental faith in the size of mountains – to substitute a real living belief for a dead intellectual assent. It enables one, first, to assign something like its true magnitude to a rock or snow-slope; and, secondly, to measure that magnitude in terms of muscular exertion instead of bare mathematical units . . . [A mountaineer] can translate 500 or 1,000 feet of snow-slope into a more tangible unit of measurement. To him, perhaps, they recall the memory of a toilsome ascent, the sun beating on his head for five or six hours, the snow returning the glare with still more parching effect; a stalwart guide toiling all the weary time, cutting steps in hard blue ice, the fragments hissing and spinning down the long straight grooves in the frozen snow till they lost themselves in the yawning chasm below; and step after step taken along the slippery staircase, till at length he triumphantly sprang upon the summit of the tremendous wall that no human foot had scaled before. The little black knobs that rise above the edge represent for him huge impassable rocks, sinking on one side in scarped slippery surfaces towards the snowfield, and on the other stooping in one tremendous cliff to a distorted glacier thousands of feet below.

The faint blue line across the upper nevé, scarcely distinguishable to the eye, represents to one observer nothing but a trifling undulation; a second, perhaps, knows that it means a crevasse; the mountaineer remembers that it is the top of a huge chasm, thirty feet across, and perhaps ten times as deep, with perpendicular sides of glimmering blue ice, and fringed by thick rows of enormous pendent icicles. The marks that are scored in delicate lines, such as might be ruled by a diamond on glass, have been cut by innumerable streams trickling in hot weather from the everlasting snow, or ploughed by succeeding avalanches that have slipped from the huge upper snowfields above . . .

Hence, if mountains owe their influence upon the imagination in great degree to their size and steepness, and apparent inaccessibility – as no one can doubt that they do, whatever may be the explanation of the fact that people like to look at big, steep, inaccessible objects – the advantages of the mountaineer are obvious. He can measure those qualities on a very different scale from the ordinary traveller. He measures the size, not by the vague abstract term of so many thousand feet, but by the hours of labour, divided into minutes – each separately felt – of strenuous muscular exertion. The steepness is not expressed in degrees, but by the memory of the sensation produced when a snow-slope seems to be rising up and smiting you in the face; when, far away from all human help, you are clinging like a fly to the slippery side of a mighty pinnacle in mid-air. And as for the inaccessibility, no one can measure the difficulty of climbing a hill who has not wearied his muscles and brain in struggling against the opposing obstacles. Alpine travellers, it is said, have removed the romance from the mountains by climbing them. What they have really done is to prove that there exists a narrow line by which a way may be found to the top of any given mountain; but the clue leads through innumerable inaccessibilities; true, you can follow one path, but to right and left are cliffs which no human foot will ever tread, and whose terrors can only be realized when you are in their immediate neighbourhood. The cliffs of the Matterhorn do not bar the way to the top effectually, but it is only by forcing a passage through them that you can really appreciate their terrible significance.

Hence, I say, that the qualities which strike every sensitive observer are impressed upon the mountaineer with tenfold force and intensity. If he is as accessible to poetical influences as his neighbours – and I don't know why he should be less so – he has opened new avenues of access between the scenery and his mind. He has learnt a language which is but partially revealed to ordinary men. An artist is superior to an unlearned picture-seer, not merely because he has greater natural sensibility, but because he has improved it by methodical experience; because his senses have been sharpened by constant practice, till he can catch finer shades of colouring, and more delicate inflexions of line; because, also, the lines and colours have acquired new significance, and been associated with a thousand thoughts with which the mass of mankind have never cared to connect them. The mountaineer is improved by a similar process. But I know some sceptical critics will ask, does not the way in which he is accustomed to regard mountains rather deaden their poetical influence? Doesn't he come to look at them as mere instruments of sport, and overlook their more spiritual teaching? Does not all the excitement of personal adventure and the noisy apparatus of guides, and ropes, and axes, and tobacco, and the fun of climbing, rather dull his perceptions and incapacitate him from perceiving –

> The silence that is in the starry sky.
> The sleep that is among the lonely hills?

Well, I have known some stupid and unpoetical mountaineers; and since I have been dismounted from my favourite hobby, I think I have met some similar specimens amongst the humbler class of tourists. There are persons, I fancy, who 'do' the Alps; who look upon the Lake of Lucerne as one more task ticked off from their memorandum-book, and count up the list of summits visible from the Gornergrat without being penetrated with any keen sense of sublimity. And there are mountaineers who are capable of making a pun on the top of Mont Blanc – and capable of nothing more. Still I venture to deny that even punning is incompatible with poetry, or that those who make the pun can have no deeper feeling in their bosoms which they are perhaps too shamefaced to utter.

The fact is that that which gives its inexpressible charm to mountaineering is the incessant series of exquisite natural scenes which are for the most part enjoyed by the mountaineer alone. This is, I am aware, a round assertion; but I will try to support it by a few of the visions which are recalled to me by these Oberland cliffs, and which I have seen profoundly enjoyed by men who perhaps never mentioned them again, and probably in describing their adventures scrupulously avoided the danger of being sentimental.

Thus every traveller has occasionally done a sunrise, and a more lamentable proceeding than the ordinary view of a sunrise can hardly be imagined. You are cold, miserable, breakfastless; have risen shivering from a warm bed, and in your heart long only to creep into bed again. To the mountaineer all this is changed. He is beginning a day full of the anticipation of a pleasant excitement. He has, perhaps, been waiting anxiously for fine weather, to try conclusions with some huge giant not yet scaled. He moves out with something of the feeling with which a soldier goes to the assault of a fortress, but without the same probability of coming home in fragments; the danger is trifling enough to be merely exhilatory, and to give a pleasant tension to the nerves; his muscles feel firm and springy, and his stomach – no small advantage to the enjoyment of scenery – is in excellent order. He looks at the sparkling stars with keen satisfaction, prepared to enjoy a fine sunrise with all his faculties at their best, and with the added pleasure of a good omen for his day's work. Then a huge dark mass begins to mould itself slowly out of the darkness, the sky begins to form a background of deep purple, against which the outline becomes gradually more definite; one by one, the peaks catch the exquisite Alpine glow, lighting up in rapid succession, like a vast illumination; and when at last the steady sunlight settles upon them, and shows every rock and glacier, without even a delicate film of mist to obscure them, he feels his heart bound, and steps out gaily to the assault – just as the people on the Rigi are giving thanks that the show is over and that they may go to bed. Still grander is the sight when the mountaineer has already reached some lofty ridge, and, as the sun rises, stands between the day and the night – the valley still in deep sleep, with the mists lying between the folds of the hills, and the snow-peaks standing out clear and pale white just before the sun reaches them, whilst a broad band of orange light runs all round the vast horizon. The glory of sunsets is equally increased in the thin upper air. The grandest of all such sights that live in my memory is that of a sunset from the Aiguille de Gouter. The snow at our feet was glowing with rich light, and the shadows in our footsteps a vivid green by the contrast. Beneath us was a vast horizontal floor of thin level mists suspended in mid air, spread like a canopy over the whole boundless landscape, and tinged with every hue of sunset. Through its rents and gaps we could see the lower mountains, the distant plains, and a fragment of the Lake of Geneva lying in a more sober purple. Above us rose the solemn mass of Mont Blanc in the richest glow of an Alpine sunset. The sense of lonely sublimity was almost oppressive, and although half our party was suffering from sickness, I believe even the guides were moved to a sense of solemn beauty . . .

I might go on indefinitely recalling the strangely impressive scenes that frequently startle the traveller in the waste upper world; but language is feeble indeed to convey even a glimmering of what is to be seen to those who have not seen it for themselves, whilst to them it can be little more than a peg upon which to hang their own recollections. These glories, in which the mountain Spirit reveals himself to his true worshippers, are only to be gained by the appropriate service of climbing – at some risk, though a very trifling risk, if he is approached with due form and ceremony – into the furthest recesses of his shrines. And without seeing them, I maintain that no man has really seen the Alps.

The difference between the exoteric and the esoteric school of mountaineers may be indicated by their different view of glaciers. At Grindelwald, for example, it is the fashion to go and 'see the glaciers' – heaven save the mark! Ladies in costumes, heavy German professors, Americans doing the Alps at a gallop, Cook's tourists, and other varieties of a well known genus, go off in shoals and see – what? – a gigantic mass of ice, strangely torn with a few exquisite blue crevasses, but defiled and prostrate in dirt and ruins. A stream foul with mud oozes out from the base; the whole mass seems to be melting fast away; the summer sun has evidently got the best of it in these lower regions, and nothing can resist him but the great mounds of decaying rock that strew the surface in confused lumps. It is as much like the glacier of the upper regions as the melting fragments of snow in a London street are like the surface of the fresh snow that has just fallen in a country field. And by way of improving its attractions a perpetual picnic is going on, and the ingenious natives have hewed a tunnel into the ice, for admission to which they charge certain centimes. The unlucky glacier reminds me at his latter end of a wretched whale stranded on a beach, dissolving into masses of blubber, and hacked by remorseless fishermen, instead of plunging at his ease in the deep blue water. Far above, where the glacier begins his course, he is seen only by the true mountaineer. There are vast amphitheatres of pure snow, of which the glacier known to tourists is merely the insignificant drainage, but whose very existence they do not generally suspect. They are utterly ignorant that from the top of the ice-fall which they visit you may walk for hours on the eternal ice. After a long climb you come to the region where the glacier is truly at its noblest; where the surface is a spotless white; where the crevasses are enormous rents sinking to profound depths, with walls of the purest blue; where the glacier is torn and shattered by the energetic forces which mould it, but has an expression of superabundant power, like a full stream fretting against its banks and plunging through the vast gorges that it has hewn for itself in the course of centuries. The bases of the mountains are immersed in a deluge of cockneyism – fortunately a shallow deluge – whilst their summits rise high into the bracing air, where everything is pure and poetical.

The difference which I have thus endeavoured to indicate is more or less traceable in a wider sense. The mountains are exquisitely beautiful, indeed, from whatever points of view we contemplate them; and the mountaineer would lose much if he never saw the beauties of the lower valleys, of pasturages deep in flowers, and dark pine-forests with the summits shining from far off between the stems. Only, as it seems to me, he has the exclusive prerogative of thoroughly enjoying one, and that the most characteristic, though by no means the only element, of the scenery. There may be a very good dinner spread before twenty people; but if nineteen of them were teetotalers, and the twentieth drank his wine like a man, he would be the only one to do it full justice; the others might praise the meat or the fruits, but he would alone enjoy the champagne; and in the great feast which Nature spreads before us (a stock metaphor, which emboldens me to make the comparison) the high mountain scenery acts the part of the champagne. Unluckily too, the teetotalers are very apt, in this case also, to sit in judgement upon their more adventurous neighbours. Especially are they pleased to carp at the views from the high summits. I have been constantly asked, with a covert sneer, 'Did it repay you?' – a question which involves the assumption that one wants to be repaid, as though the labour were not itself part of the pleasure, and which implies a doubt that the view is really enjoyable. People are always demonstrating that the lower views are the most beautiful; and at the same time complaining that mountaineers frequently turn back without looking at the view from the top, as though that would necessarily imply that they cared nothing for scenery. In opposition to which I must first remark that, as a rule, every step of an ascent has a beauty of its own, which one is quietly absorbing even when one is not directly making it a subject of contemplation, and that the view from the top is generally the crowning glory of the whole.

Leslie Stephen, *The Playground of Europe*

The True Mountaineer is a Wanderer

It is true that extraordinary progress has been made in the art of rock climbing, and that consequently any given rock climb is much easier now than thirty years since, but the essence of the sport lies, not in ascending a peak, but in struggling with and overcoming difficulties. The happy climber, like the aged Ulysses, is one who has 'Drunk delight of battle with his peers' and this delight is only attainable by assaulting cliffs which tax to their utmost limits the powers of the mountaineers engaged. This struggle involves the same risk, whether early climbers attacked what we now call easy rock, or whether we moderns attack formidable rock, or whether the ideal climber of the future assaults cliffs which we now regard as hopelessly inaccessible . . . Regarded as a sport, some danger is, and always must be, inherent in [mountaineering]; regarded as a means of exercise amongst noble scenery, for quasi-scientific pursuits, as the raw material for interesting papers, or for the purposes of brag and bounce, it has become as safe as the ascent of the Rigi or Pilatus was to the climbers of thirty years since. But these pursuits are not mountaineering in the sense in which the founders of the Alpine Club used the term, and they are not mountaineering in the sense in which the elect – a small, perchance even a dwindling body – use it now. To set one's utmost faculties, physical and mental, to fight some grim precipice, or force some gaunt, ice-clad gully, is work worthy of men; to toil up long slopes of screes behind a guide who can 'lie in bed and picture every step of the way up, with all the places for hand and foot' is work worthy of the fibreless contents of fashionable clothes, dumped with all their scents and ointments, starched linen and shiny boots, at Zermatt by the railway.

The true mountaineer is a wanderer, and by a wanderer I do not mean a man who expends his whole time in travelling to and fro in the mountains on the exact tracks of his predecessors – much as a bicyclist rushes along the turnpike roads of England – but I mean a man who loves to be where no human being has been before, who delights in gripping rocks that have previously never felt the touch of human fingers, or in hewing his way up ice-filled gullies whose grim shadows have been sacred to the mists and avalanches since 'Earth rose out of chaos'. In other words, the true mountaineer is the man who attempts new ascents. Equally, whether he succeeds or fails, he delights in the fun and jollity of the struggle. The gaunt, bare slabs, the square, precipitous steps in the ridge, and the black, bulging ice of the gully, are the very breath of life to his being. I do not pretend to be able to analyse this feeling, still less to be able to make it clear to unbelievers. It must be felt to be understood, but it is potent to happiness and sends the blood tingling through the veins, destroying every trace of cynicism and striking at the very roots of pessimistic philosophy.

Our critics, curiously enough, repeat in substance Mr Ruskin's original taunt, that we regard the mountains as greased poles. I must confess that a natural and incurable denseness of understanding does not enable me to feel the sting of this taunt. Putting aside the question of grease, which is offensive and too horrible for contemplation in its effects on knickerbockers – worse even than the structure-destroying edges and splinters of the Grepon ridge – I do not perceive the enormity of the sin of climbing poles. At one time, I will confess, I took great delight in the art, and, so far as my experience extends, the taste is still widespread amongst English youth. The sting of the taunt is presumably meant to lurk in the implication that the climber is incapable of enjoying noble scenery; that, in the jargon of certain modern writers, he is a '*mere* gymnast'. But why should a man be assumed incapable of enjoying aesthetic pleasures because he is also capable of the physical and non-aesthetic pleasures of rock-climbing?

A well-known mountaineer asserts that the fathers of the craft did not regard 'the overcoming of physical obstacles by means of muscular exertion and skill' as 'the chief pleasure of mountaineering'. But is this so? Can any one read the great classic of mountaineering literature, *The Playground of Europe*, without feeling that the overcoming of these obstacles was a main factor of its author's joy? Can any one read *Peaks, Passes and Glaciers* and the earlier numbers of the *Alpine Journal* without feeling that the various writers gloried in the technique of their craft? Of course the skilful interpolation of 'chief' gives an opening for much effective dialectic, but after all, what does it mean? How can a pleasure which is seated in health and jollity and the 'spin of the blood' be measured and compared with a purely aesthetic feeling? It would appear difficult to argue that as a man cultivates and acquires muscular skill and knowledge of the mountains, he correspondingly dwarfs and impairs the aesthetic side of his nature. If so, we magnify the weak-kneed and the impotent, the lame, the halt and the blind, and brand as false the Greek ideal of the perfect man. Doubtless a tendency in this direction may be detected in some modern thought, but, like much else similarly enshrined, it has no ring of true metal. Those who are so completely masters of their environment that they can laugh and rollick on the ridges, free from all constraint of ropes or fear of danger, are far more able to appreciate the glories of the 'eternal hills' than those who can only move in constant terror of their lives, amidst the endless chatter and rank tobacco smoke of unwashed guides.

The fact that a man enjoys scrambling up a steep rock in no way makes him insensible of all that is beautiful in nature. The two sets of feelings are indeed wholly unconnected. A man may love climbing and care naught for mountain scenery; he may love the scenery and hate climbing; or he may be equally devoted to both. The presumption obviously is that those who are most attracted by the mountains and most constantly return to their fastnesses, are those who to the fullest extent possess both these sources of enjoyment – those who can combine the fun and frolic of a splendid sport with that indefinable delight which is induced by the lovely form, tone, and colouring of the great ranges.

I am free to confess that I myself should still climb, even though there were no scenery to look at, even if the only climbing attainable were the dark and gruesome pot-holes of the Yorkshire dales. On the other hand, I should still wander among the upper snows, lured by the silent mists and the red blaze of the setting sun, even though physical or other infirmity, even though in after aeons the sprouting of wings and other angelic appendages, may have sunk all thought of climbing and cragsmanship in the whelming past.

A.F. Mummery, *My Climbs in the Alps and Caucasus*

Beyond Platonic Love

The Jomein is the furthest point to which platonic lovers of the mountains venture. Some come up to see the Matterhorn and return leaving their names inscribed in the hotel register, as in the hall of a prince's palace. Others come back every year for the fresh, healthgiving air and for the untrammelled freedom of the place. Once here they too fall under the giant's spell; they witness the departure of parties of climbers, they follow their vicissitudes with the telescope, they thrill with emotion as they make out tiny men climbing at an enormous altitude, on the rope ladder; and seeing that they look so small and proceed so slowly, they understand that the mountain is vast and the way difficult; when the climbers return they crowd round them with curiosity and respect, and listen with pleasure to the narrative of those who have trodden every stone on the mysterious mountain which they contemplate all day from below, and which has at last cast its spell about them. All honour to these honest pagans who do not mock at mountain worship.

Only once did I happen to meet at the Jomein with a gentleman, an educated and otherwise right-thinking citizen, who had brought with him in his luggage, among his bundles of newspapers, that cordial dislike for climbers which is the current coin in our cities. He gave vent to his antipathy in the following remarks, which were full of practical common sense. He liked the mountains as far as one could go in a carriage, or at most with a mule; all the rest was vanity or lunacy. He said that for the last twenty years he had spent the summer in the mountains, at the best hotels, admiring Alpine scenery at his ease. That this was much better than our plan of starting off for our climb directly after arriving at the hotel, even by night in the dark. That when climbing we pay much more attention to the place where we are to put our feet than to admiring the view. That on the top we are so tired that we can think of nothing but our food, and that as soon as we get there we are already thinking of the descent. The day slips by, we slide down the ropes, we plunge panting and trembling down the steep rocks, and do not pause until we are in safety once more. 'You have performed marvellous feats of endurance,' he said, 'you can boast of having done the Matterhorn, but in what way have you appreciated its wondrous beauty, or heard the mysterious voice of Nature on those heights?' And he ended by declaring that he was familiar with the beauties of the mountains without ever having risked his neck. In my heart of hearts I pitied that gentleman. I likened him to one who fancies himself a sailor though he has never left the beach, or believes he has possessed a woman when he has only serenaded her under her windows.

But the mountains are so kindly and so great that they reject none of those who turn to them, and they are good to all: to the men of science who come to study them; to the painters and poets who seek an inspiration in them; to the sturdy climbers who zealously seek violent exercise, and to the weary who flee from the heat and the turmoil of the city to refresh themselves at this pure source of physical and moral health. Mountaineering is merely a more vigorous, more complete form of this health . . .

I wish that sceptics could experience the good affects that a great ascent produces in us. The vanities which filled our minds before we started now seem trivial to us. Now we appreciate the comforts to which use had made us indifferent. We feel a greater love for our home and our family which awaits us there. For we climbers also have our affections, and they are much more vividly present to our minds in moments of danger than to others who are leading their customary lives; and when we come down from the mountains we rejoice to bring back and display to our dear ones the equanimity wc have acquired in the heights, and to see them smiling upon us because the mountain has restored to them a healthier, stronger, more affectionate son, brother, or friend.

The climbing is a means, not an end in life: a means to temper the character of youth for the coming struggle, to preserve the vigour of manhood, to check the flight of years, and to prepare for old age a treasury of memories that shall be untroubled and free from remorse. I have seen white-haired men deeply moved at the thought of their early ascents. Happy are those simple minds that retain their capacity to thrill as on the first day in the presence of the beauties of the mountains! My heart goes out in intimate fellow-feeling to those who return year by year to some familiar corner of the Alps and climb ten times over, as long as their legs will carry them, the same peak which was their first Alpine love.

I found one of these sublimely obstinate veterans one fine day at the foot of the Matterhorn.

I was descending from the Theodul. Half-way between the Col and the Jomein I saw coming slowly up towards me a fine, tall old man, with a ruddy countenance, clean-shaven, clear-eyed, and with snow-white hair. His face bore the impress of an iron will; his body straight as a dart notwithstanding his years, was full of vigour; his long, rhythmical gait testified to his familiarity with the mountains. As I passed him I took off my hat to him, as is the polite custom of those who meet in the mountains. He returned my bow and passed on. My guide had stopped to talk to his. When he rejoined me he whispered, 'Do you know who that is?' I answered that I did not. 'Monsieur Whymper!' And he pronounced the name in a tone of respect. I was as much moved as if I were in the presence of a ghost. I had never seen Whymper except in photographs. I at once turned round to look at him. He had stopped too and was looking at the Matterhorn, whose aspect was one of marvellous grandeur from this point.

I cannot describe how much I was impressed by that meeting in that spot. It was not a man I saw, but the idealized image of the perfect mountaineer, whom I and others have so often dreamed of imitating. They were there, the Matterhorn and Whymper, the two great rivals, and the sight of them in each other's presence brought home to one the superiority of the tiny conqueror to the conquered giant. He had come back after thirty years to see once more the mountain that had made him famous. He found none of his former comrades there. Croz lay at Zermatt, Carrel at Valtournanche; only the Matterhorn stood unchangeable, everlasting. He was looking at it, and was perhaps recalling the deeds of daring he had performed on the stubborn peak in the vigour of his youthful years.

I watched, without his noticing it, and with a kind of veneration, that man who had not feared the Matterhorn when the Matterhorn was a mystery, and who loved it still though the crowd had made it commonplace. I saw his snow-white hair flowing beneath the brim of his grey felt hat, and it seemed to me that it must have begun to turn white on the terrible day of victory and disaster. I myself was harrowed by the thought of what he must have suffered on that day and afterwards. The Matterhorn had cost him dear! It was not, however, the struggle with the mountain that had saddened him, but the contest with his fellow-men which followed his victory.

I would fain have made some sign, have shown him some act of reverence, some proof of my sympathetic interest; have told him that I had read his book again and again, that it had done me good, because it had brought me also up into these places . . .

Whymper started again, and slowly continued his ascent, and I was left with my wish unsatisfied. But I too shall return in my old age to the foot of the Matterhorn. I shall struggle up step by step, leaning on my now useless axe, to these dear haunts, seeking comfort in the contemplation of the familiar peaks. I shall enjoy the final pleasures of Alpine life, the cool spring that quenches thirst, the refreshing cup of warm milk, the colour of a little flower, a breath of the wholesome odour of pines wafted up by the winds from the neighbouring forest, the silvery sound of bells which rises in the evening from the peaceful pastures. On the way I shall find my old guides, once my companions in the happy days of strenuous effort, and I shall stop to talk with them, and to recall old memories. Seated on the hotel terrace in the pleasant mountain sunshine I shall look out down the valley, over the long basin of the Breuil, for the arrival of parties of climbers. Young men will appear, full of courage and hope. Perhaps Fasano, the faithful waiter at the Jomein, will point me out to them and say: 'That gentleman over there was a great climber in his day; he has passed many a night up on the mountain here.' The young men will look at me incredulously while I shall straighten my bent back, at the prompting of my last shreds of vanity; and I shall take aside those who are kind enough to listen to me, and bare my arm like a veteran of many battles, to show them secretly an old wound received up in the mountains, and shall encourage them to make attempts and exhort them to be prudent. Then I shall be content if I note in them traces of the emotion I felt the first time I saw the Matterhorn.

Guido Rey, *The Matterhorn*

Alpine Mysticism and Cold Philosophy

The mountaineer has a great advantage over the non-mountaineer. He has chosen the ascetic way to mountain understanding, and among the hills, as elsewhere, asceticism is the key to the higher forms of mystical experience. One need not question the sincerity of Ruskin's condemnation of those who had transformed the mountain cathedrals into arenas for athletic feats, but I have sometimes suspected that the peculiar venom of his attack may have been due to the fact that the mountaineer provoked an uneasy and unformulated doubt as to the quality of his own life, which was essentially non-ascetic and soft. He had been privately educated and thus deprived of the ascetic experiences which the Victorian public schools so generously provided. He played no games, took part in no sports. He inherited a comfortable income from his father, which insured him against the necessity of uncongenial work. His life from birth to death was a stranger to the discipline of pain, danger or discomfort.

Asceticism is often confused with puritanism. The Puritan condemns pleasure as wicked, and the ascetic abstains from certain pleasures, which he admits to be innocent, as the price to be paid for the higher forms of happiness. An ascetic may confine his drinks to water, but he does not deserve to be branded a Puritan so long as he makes no attempt to prevent other people from drinking wine. An ascetic might be defined as one who sacrifices pleasure to happiness, for pleasure and happiness are not identical . . .

To the Greek the athlete was the typical ascetic, for he exercised his body by sacrificing the pleasures of self-indulgence to the happiness of self-discipline. He was, as St Paul said, temperate in all things to win a corruptible crown. No illustration, as St Paul knew, was more calculated to impress his hearers with the reasonableness of Christian asceticism; for where institutional religion declines, as in the pagan world, the ascetic instinct finds expression in strenuous sport. If it were not for this peculiar form of happiness, which is the reward of the ascetic, there would be no boat-racing and no rock-climbing and no ski-racing. No ski racer can reach the international class unless he is prepared to risk fall after fall when practising or racing, at a speed which often attains to sixty miles an hour. There is no pleasure in such skiing, but there is a queer kind of happiness.

'The racer's mind must overcome the physical reactions, which shrink from the fastest line on steep slopes, and must keep the body under the control necessary for performing turns with complete precision.

'When the racer is ski-ing well there come moments when he knows that his mind has won, and for a few brief seconds he has complete control over his body. Such moments are rare, but it is for them that men endure the physical discomforts attendant upon all ascetic sports, for they then experience a happiness, almost an ecstasy, which has nothing in common with pleasure or enjoyment as those terms are normally understood.

'It is this spiritual, perhaps almost mystical, thrill, this fleeting glimpse of the paradise of Eden, which causes men to encounter gladly the dangers and hardships of mountaineering, to endure the acute physical agony of rowing and long-distance running, and to overcome the physical difficulties attendant on all sports.' [From *High Speed Ski-ing*, by Peter Lunn.]

The happiness of the rock-climber is derived from the same source as the happiness of the racer – from the dominion, that is, of the mind over the body . . . There is no sport which illustrates more perfectly the ascetic principle that happiness must be paid for by pain, and that the degree of happiness is in proportion to the price paid. Few sports offer their devotees a wider range of disagreeable moments. The agony of the half-slip when one is leading on an exposed climb, the desparate struggle to regain balance, a struggle which is a matter of infinitely small readjustments on a battle-ground measured in inches, are the price which the cragsman pays, not only for the exquisite relief of safety after peril, but also for the quasi-mystical happiness of those moments when his mind has established complete dominion over his body, moments when the effortless rhythm of the upward movement transforms the accident of crack and ledge into an ordered sequence of harmonious movement.

Many mountaineers who have lost all contact with institutional religion have discovered among the hills the satisfaction of certain aspirations which others have fulfilled within the framework of the religious life. They have caught the reflection of eternal beauty in the temporal loveliness of the hills. They have been initiated into the secret of the ascetic, and have found the happiness which is the by-product of pain and danger. But when we have said this we have said all that can usefully be said on the relation of mountaineering to religion. Points of contact do not suffice to establish their identity. Boxing involves asceticism, but no one has yet claimed that there is a religion of the Ring . . .

It is foolish to invite the ridicule of the discerning by making claims for mountaineering which cannot be substantiated. Mountaineering is neither a substitute for religion nor a civic duty. It is a sport; for we climb, not to benefit the human race, but to amuse ourselves. In so far as mountaineering is something more than a sport we must base this claim on the fact that it is carried out in surroundings which suggest spiritual truths even to the unspiritual. Ruskin compared mountains to cathedrals, and the comparison is sound; for one does not worship cathedrals, though one may worship in the cathedrals of man or among the cathedrals of nature.

All evil, as a great mediaeval thinker remarked, is the result of mistaking means for ends. Mountaineering is not an end in itself, but a means to an end. 'For it is true' as the first mountaineer to ascend the throne of St Peter (Pius XI) remarked:

'For it is true that, of all innocent pleasures, none more than this one (excepting where unnecessary risks are taken) may be considered as being helpful mentally and physically, because, through the efforts required for climbing in the rarefied mountain air, energy is renewed; and owing to the difficulties overcome the climber thereby becomes better equipped and strengthened to resist the difficulties encountered in life, and by admiring the beauties and grandeur of the scenery as seen from the mighty peaks of the Alps his spirit is uplifted to the Creator of all.'

Arnold Lunn, *Mountain Jubilee*

CHAPTER 21

◆

Falls and Fatalities

The possibility of death by falling, whether through a slip or because of an avalanche, is always in the mind of a mountaineer, however far back it may be pushed for most of the time. The deaths on the first ascent of the Matterhorn must be the most famous of mountain fatalities: but Whymper himself, on a previous attempt on the mountain from the Italian side, had already had a fall which came very near to being fatal. His rival Carrel was also to die on the Matterhorn, but in circumstances which many mountaineers and guides might consider the ideal way to die. Arnold Lunn, like Whymper, survived a dangerous fall: unlike Whymper, he was handicapped in future climbing and became instead a champion skier. One of the most grisly stories of mountain death comes from the hills of Wales, and is told by F.S. Smythe, the Everest climber.

◆ ◆ ◆

'In attempting to pass the corner I slipped and fell'

Out of curiosity I wandered to a notch in the ridge, between two tottering piles of immense masses, which seemed to need but a few pounds on one or the other side to make them fall; so nicely poised that they would literally have rocked in the wind, for they were put in motion by a touch; and based on support so frail that I wondered they did not collapse before my eyes. In the whole range of my Alpine experience I have seen nothing more striking than this desolate, ruined, and shattered ridge at the back of the Great Tower. I have seen stranger shapes – rocks which mimic the human form, with monstrous leering faces – and isolated pinnacles, sharper and greater than any here; but I have never seen exhibited so impressively the tremendous efforts which may be produced by frost, and by the long-continued action of forces whose individual efforts are imperceptible.

It is needless to say that it is impossible to climb by the crest of the ridge at this part; still one is compelled to keep near to it, for there is no other way. Generally speaking, the angles on the Matterhorn are too steep to allow the formation of considerable beds of snow, but here there is a corner which permits it to accumulate, and it is turned to gratefully, for, by its assistance, one can ascend four times as rapidly as upon the rocks.

The Tower was now almost out of sight, and I looked over the central Pennine Alps to the Grand Combin, and to the chain of Mont Blanc. My neighbour, the Dent d'Hérens, still rose above me, although but slightly, and the height which had been attained could be measured by its help. So far, I had no doubts about my capacity to descend that which had been ascended; but, in a short time, on looking ahead, I saw that the cliffs steepened, and I turned back (without pushing on to them, and getting into inextricable difficulties) exulting in the thought that they would be passed when we returned together, and that I had, without assistance, got nearly to the height of the Dent d'Hérens, and considerably higher than anyone had been before. My exultation was a little premature.

About 5 p.m. I left the tent again, and thought myself as good as at Breuil. The friendly rope and claw had done good service, and had smoothened all the difficulties. I lowered myself through the Chimney, however, by making a fixture of the rope, which I then cut off, and left behind, as there was enough and to spare. My axe had proved a great nuisance in coming down, and I left it in the tent. It was not attached to the baton, but was a separate affair, – an old navy boarding-axe. While cutting up the different snow-beds on the ascent, the baton trailed behind fastened to the rope; and, when climbing, the axe was carried behind, run through the rope tied round my waist, and was sufficiently out of the way; but in descending, when coming down face outwards (as is always best where it is possible) the head or the handle of the weapon caught frequently against the rocks, and several times nearly upset me. So, out of laziness if you will, it was left in the tent. I paid dearly for the imprudence.

The Col du Lion was passed, and fifty yards more would have placed me on the 'Great Staircase' down which one can run. But on arriving at an angle of the cliffs of the Tête du Lion, while skirting the upper edge of the snow which abuts against them, I found that the heat of the two past days had nearly obliterated the steps which had been cut when coming up. The rocks happened to be impracticable just at this corner, so nothing could be done except make the steps afresh. The snow was too hard to beat or tread down, and at the angle it was all but ice; half-a-dozen steps only were required, and then the ledges could be followed again. So I held to the rock with my right hand, and prodded at the snow with the point of my stick until a good step was made, and then, leaning round the angle, did the same for the other side. So far well, but in attempting to pass the corner (to the present moment I cannot tell how it happened) I slipped and fell.

The slope was steep on which this took place, and was at the top of a gully that led down through two subordinate buttresses towards the Glacier du Lion – which was just seen, a thousand feet below. The gulley narrowed and narrowed, until there was a mere thread of snow lying between two walls of rock, which came to an abrupt termination at the top of a precipice that intervened between it and the glacier. Imagine a funnel cut in half through its length, placed at an angle of 45 degrees, with its point below and its concave side uppermost, and you will have a fair idea of the place.

The knapsack brought my head down first, and I pitched into some rocks about a dozen feet below; they caught something and tumbled me off the edge, head over heels, into the gully; the baton was dashed from my hands, and I whirled downwards in a series of bounds, each longer than the last; now over ice, now into rocks; striking my head four or five times, each time with increased force. The last bound sent me spinning through the air, in a leap of fifty or sixty feet, from one side of the gully to the other, and I struck the rocks, luckily, with the whole of my left side. They caught my clothes for a moment, and I fell back on to the snow with motion arrested; my head fortunately came the right side up, and a few frantic catches brought me to a halt, in the neck of the gully, and on the verge of the precipice. Baton, hat, and veil skimmed by and disappeared, and the crash of the rocks which I had started, as they fell on to the glacier, told how narrow had been the escape from utter destruction. As it was I fell nearly 200 feet in seven or eight bounds. Ten feet more would have taken me in one gigantic leap of 800 feet on to the glacier below.

The situation was still sufficiently serious. The rocks could not be let go for a moment, and the blood was spurting out of more than twenty cuts. The most serious ones were in the head, and I vainly tried to close them with one hand, while holding on with the other. It was useless; the blood jerked out in blinding jets at each pulsation. At last, in a moment of inspiration, I kicked out a big lump of snow, and stuck it as a plaster on my head. The idea was a happy one, and the flow of blood diminished; then, scrambling up, I got, not a moment too soon, to a place of safety, and fainted away. The sun was setting when consciousness returned, and it was pitch dark before the Great Staircase was descended; but, by a combination of luck and care, the whole 4800 feet of descent to Breuil was accomplished without a slip, or once missing the way. I slunk past the cabin of the cowherds, who were talking and laughing inside, utterly ashamed of the state to which I had been brought by my imbecility, and entered the inn stealthily, wishing to escape to my room unnoticed. But Favre met me in the passage, demanded 'Who is it?' screamed with fright when he got a light, and aroused the household. Two dozen heads then held solemn council over mine, with more talk than action. The natives were unanimous in recommending that hot wine (syn. vinegar), mixed with salt, should be rubbed into the cuts. I protested, but they insisted. It was all the doctoring they received. Whether their rapid healing was to be attributed to that simple remedy, or to a good state of health, is a question; they closed up remarkable quickly, and in a few days I was able to move again.

As it seldom happens that one survives such a fall, it may be interesting to record what my sensations were during its occurrence. I was perfectly conscious of what was happening, and felt each blow; but, like a patient under chloroform, experienced no pain. Each blow was, naturally, more severe than that which preceded it, and I distinctly remember thinking, 'Well, if the next is harder still, that will be the end!' Like persons who have been rescued from drowning, I remember that the recollection of a multitude of things rushed through my head, many of them trivialities or absurdities, which had been forgotten long before; and, more remarkable, this bounding through space did not feel disagreeable. But I think that in no very great distance more, consciousness as well as sensation would have been lost, and upon that I base my belief, improbable as it seems, that death by a fall from a great height is as painless an end as can be experienced.

The battering was very rough, yet no bones were broken. The most severe cuts were one of four inches long on the top of the head, and another of three inches on the right temple: this latter bled frightfully. There was a formidable-looking cut, of about the same size as the last, on the palm of the left hand, and every limb was grazed, or cut, more or less seriously. The tips of the ears were taken off, and a sharp rock cut a circular bit out of the side of the left boot, sock, and ankle at one stroke. The loss of blood, although so great, did not seem to be permanently injurious. The only serious effect has been the reduction of a naturally retentive memory to a very common-place one; and although my recollections of more distant occurrences remain unshaken, the events of that particular day would be clean gone but for the few notes which were written down before the accident.

Edward Whymper, *Scrambles in the Alps*

The Death of Carrel

We started for the Cervin at 2.15 a.m. on the 23rd, in splendid weather, with the intention of descending the same night to the hut at the Hörnli in the Swiss side. We proceeded pretty well, but the glaze of ice on the rocks near the Col du Lion retarded our march somewhat, and when we arrived at the hut at the foot of the Great Tower, prudence counselled the postponement of the ascent until the next day, for the sky was becoming overcast. We decided upon this, and stopped.

Here I ought to mention that both I and Gorret noticed with uneasiness that Carrel showed signs of fatigue upon leaving the Col du Lion. I attributed this to temporary weakness. As soon as we reached the hut he lay down and slept profoundly for two hours, and awoke much restored. In the meantime the weather was rapidly changing. Storm clouds coming from the direction of Mont Blanc hung over the Dent d'Hérens, but we regarded them as transitory, and trusted to the north wind, which was still continuing to blow. Meanwhile, three of the Maquignazs and Edward Bich, whom we found at the hut, returning from looking after the ropes, started downwards for Breuil, at parting wishing us a happy ascent, and holding out hopes of a splendid day for the morrow.

But, after their departure, the weather grew worse very rapidly; the wind changed, and towards evening there broke upon us a most violent hurricane of hail and snow, accompanied by frequent flashes of lightning. The air was so charged with electricity that for two consecutive hours in the night one could see in the hut as in broad daylight. The storm continued to rage all night, and the day and night following, continously, with incredible violence. The temperature in the hut fell to − 3 degrees.

The situation was becoming somewhat alarming, for the provisions were getting low, and we had already begun to use the seats of the hut as firewood. The rocks were in an extremely bad state, and we were afraid that if we stopped longer, and the storm continued, we should be blocked up in the hut for several days. This being the state of affairs, it was decided among the guides that if the wind should abate we should descend on the following morning; and as the wind did abate somewhat on the morning of the 25th (the weather, however, still remaining very bad), it was unanimously settled to make a retreat.

At 9 a.m. we left the hut. I will not speak of the difficulties and dangers in descending the arête to the Col du Lion, which we reached at 2.30 p.m. The ropes were half frozen; the rocks were covered with a glaze of ice, and fresh snow hid all points of support. Some spots were really as bad as could be, and I owe much to the prudence and coolness of the two guides that we got over them without mishap.

At the Col du Lion, where we hoped the wind would moderate, a dreadful hurricane recommenced, and in crossing the snowy passages we were nearly *suffocated* by the wind and snow which attacked us on all sides. Through the loss of a glove, Gorret, half an hour after leaving the hut, had already got a hand frost-bitten. The cold was terrible here. Every moment we had to remove the ice from our eyes, and it was with the utmost difficulty that we could speak so as to understand one another.

Nevertheless, Carrel continued to direct the descent in a most admirable manner, with a coolness, ability, and energy above all praise. I was delighted to see the change, and Gorret assisted him splendidly. This part of the descent presented unexpected difficulties, and at several points great dangers, the more so because the *tourmente* prevented Carrel from being sure of the right direction, in spite of his consummate knowledge of the Matterhorn. At 11 p.m. (or thereabouts – it was impossible to look at our watches, as all our clothes were half frozen) we were still toiling down the rocks. The guides sometimes asked each other where they were; then we went forward again – to stop, indeed, would have been impossible. Carrel at last, by marvellous instinct, discovered the passage up which we had come, and in a sort of grotto we stopped a minute to take some brandy.

While crossing some snow we saw Carrel slacken his pace and then fall two or three times to the ground. Gorret asked him what was the matter, and he said 'Nothing', but he went on with difficulty. Attributing this to fatigue through the excessive toil, Gorret put himself at the head of the caravan, and Carrel, after the change, seemed better and walked well, though with more circumspection than usual. From this place a short and steep passage takes one down to the pastures, where there is safety. Gorret descended first, and I after him. We were nearly at the bottom when I felt the rope pulled. We stopped, awkwardly placed as we were, and cried out to Carrel several times to come down, but we received no answer. Alarmed, we went up a little way, and heard him say, in a faint voice, 'Come up and fetch me, I have no strength left.'

We went up and found that he was lying with his stomach to the ground, holding on to a rock, in a semi-conscious state, and unable to get up or to move a step. With extreme difficulty we carried him up to a safe place and asked him what was the matter. His only answer was 'I know no longer where I am.' His hands were getting colder and colder, his speech weaker and more broken, and his body more still. We did all we could for him, putting with great difficulty the rest of the cognac into his mouth. He said something, and appeared to revive, but this did not last long. We tried rubbing him with snow, and shaking him, and calling to him continually; but he could only answer with moans.

We tried to lift him, but it was impossible – he was getting stiff. We stooped down, and asked in his ear if he wished to commend his soul to God. With a last effort he answered 'Yes', and then fell on his back, dead upon the snow.

Leone Sinigaglia, edited by Whymper, *Guide to Zermatt and the Matterhorn*

The Golden Moments before the Fall

Two days after I first arrived at Tallylyn in 1909, I wandered up to Llyn Cae, surely the loveliest of all the Welsh tarns. A magnificent gully seamed the face of the dark cliffs beyond the lake. I did not then know that this was the Great Gully of Craig y Cae, Owen Glynne Jones's favourite Welsh climb. Had I known this I should not have started the ascent at 5 p.m.

Since then a miniature landslide has converted the famous cave pitch into an easy scramble, which is a pity. But when I first climbed the gully I could have dispensed with unnecessary difficulties, for I began the climb far too late in the day. Like most men who have learned to climb in the Alps, I tended to underestimate the necessary allowance of time for a great Welsh gully, and before long I realized that if the last pitches should prove severe, I should not reach the top that night. Luckily, the last stages were interesting but straightforward, and as the light failed I scrambled out of the narrow exit of the final crag. I enjoyed that climb, and I have seen few more impressive sights than the black waters of the tarn far below, framed between the dark smooth cliffs which confine the recesses of the gully.

On the following day I met two friends, a little distance above Tallylyn. One of them was carrying a fisherman's rod, but the other was wearing well-nailed boots. This looked more hopeful, so I asked them whether they would like to join me some day on a climb. Mr Syme, the owner of the boots, had climbed before. His friend, Mr Warren, was quite prepared to sample a Welsh gully, and they both agreed to meet me next day.

That night C. Scott Lindsay arrived, and next morning the four of us – Lindsay, my new friends and I – set out to climb the Great Gully. A casual remark of Mr Syme's revealed the fact that Mr Warren was a rising surgeon on the staff of the London Hospital. Another casual remark disclosed the name of the small village where Warren and Syme were staying. I should at this moment be wearing an artificial leg but for this lucky series of accidents, beginning with the nailed boots which Syme was wearing and which had effected our introduction.

On the following day Lindsay felt like a rest, so I set off alone and climbed the east ridge of Cyfrwy, off which I fell two days later. It is an interesting climb, not very difficult judged by modern standards, but quite amusing. A steep face looks sensational but is really quite easy. The best thing on the ridge is a miniature Mummery crack which calls for skill if one wishes to climb it without disproportionate effort.

On August 28th I started for my last climb. Lindsay was not feeling fit, and he left me near the top of Cader Idris. I decided to descend the east and to climb the north ridge of Cyfrwy. I was carrying a short rope which I had brought along on the chance that Lindsay might join me.

The day was perfect. The burnished silver of the sea melted into a golden haze. Light shadows cast by scudding clouds drifted across the blue and distant hills. The sun flooded down on the rocks. I slid down the crack and reached the top of the steep face of rock above 'the Table'. The usual route dodges the top fifteen feet of this face, and by an easy traverse reaches a lower ledge. But on that glorious afternoon I longed to spin out the joys of Cyfrwy, and I found a direct route from the top to the bottom of this wall, a steep but not very severe variation.

It was one of those days when to be alive is 'very heaven'. The feel of the warm, dry rocks and the easy rhythm of the descending motion gave me an almost sensuous pleasure. One toyed with the thought of danger, so complete was the confidence inspired by the firm touch of the wrinkled rocks.

In this short span
Between my finger tips and the smooth edge
And these tense feet cramped to a crystal ledge,
    I hold the life of man.

Consciously I embrace,
Arched from the mountain rock on which I stand
To the firm limit of my lifted hand,
    The front of time and space;

For what is there in all the world for me
    But what I know and see?
And what remains of all I see and know
    If I let go?

[Geoffrey Winthrop Young]

I was glad to be alone. I revelled in the freedom from the restraints of the rope, and from the need to synchronize my movements with the movements of companions.

I have never enjoyed rock-climbing more. I have never enjoyed rock-climbing since. But, at least, the hills gave me of their best, full measure and overflowing, in those last few golden moments before I fell.

A few moments later Lindsay, who was admiring the view from Cader, was startled by the thunder of a stone avalanche. He turned to a stray tourist, urging him to follow, and dashed off in the direction of Cyfrwy.

And this is what had happened. I had just lowered myself off the edge of 'the Table'. There was no suggestion of danger. Suddenly the mountain seemed to sway, and a quiver ran through the rocks. I clung for one brief moment of agony to the face of the cliff. And then suddenly a vast block, which must have been about ten feet high and several feet thick, separated itself from the face, heeled over on top of me, and carried me with it into space. I turned a somersault, struck the cliff some distance below, bounded off once again and, after crashing against the ridge two or three times, landed on a sloping ledge about seven feet broad. The thunder of the rocks falling through the hundred and fifty feet below my resting-point showed how narrow had been my escape.

I had fallen a distance which Lindsay estimated at a hundred feet. It was not a sliding fall, for except when I struck and rebounded I was not in contact with the ridge. The fall was long enough for me to retain a very vivid memory of the thoughts which chased each other through my brain during those few crowded seconds. I can still feel the clammy horror of the moment when the solid mountain face trembled below me, but the fall, once I was fairly off, blunted the edge of fear. My emotions were subdued, as if I had been partially anaesthetized. I remember vividly seeing the mountains upside down after my first somersault. I remember the disappointment as I realized that I had not stopped and that I was still falling. I remember making despairing movements with my hands in a futile attempt to check my downward progress.

The chief impression was a queer feeling that the stable order of nature had been overturned. The tranquil and immobile hills had been startled into a mood of furious and malignant activity, like a dangerous dog roused from a peaceful nap by some inattentive passer-by who has trodden on him unawares. And every time I struck the cliff only to be hurled downwards once again, I felt like a small boy who is being knocked about by a persistent bully – 'Will he never stop? – surely he can't hit me again – surely he's hurt me enough.'

When at last I landed, I tried to sit up, but fell back hurriedly on seeing my leg. The lower part was bent almost at right angles. It was not merely broken, it was shattered and crushed.

I shouted and shouted and heard no reply. Had Lindsay returned home? Would I have to wait for hours before help came?

Solitude had lost its charm. I no longer rejoiced in my freedom from intrusion. On the contrary, I raised my voice, and called upon society to come to my assistance. I set immense store on my membership of the Human Club, and very urgently did I summon my fellow-members to my assistance.

And then suddenly I heard an answering cry, and my shouts died away in a sob of heartfelt relief.

And while I waited for help, I looked up at the scar on the cliff where the crag had broken away, and I realized all that I was in danger of losing. Had I climbed my last mountain?

During the war the cheery dogmatism of some second lieutenant home from the front was extremely consoling, for the human mind is illogical and the will to believe very potent. And so when Lindsay arrived and replied with a hearty affirmative when I asked him whether I should ever climb again, I was greatly comforted, even though Lindsay knew less of broken legs than the average subaltern of the chances of peace.

Lindsay was preceded by an ancient man who keeps the hut on Cader. He examined my leg with a critical eye and informed me that it was broken. He then remarked that I had been very ill-advised to stray off the path on to 'rough places' where even the natives did not venture. He grasped my leg, and moved it a little higher on to the ledge. This hurt. He then uncoiled my rope and secured me to a buttress which overhung my narrow perch.

Then Lindsay staggered on to the ledge, gave one glance at my leg, turned a curious colour, and sat down hurriedly. He suggested breaking off a gate, and carrying me down on it. The ancient man of Cader hazarded a tentative suggestion in favour of sacks. I demurred, for a sack may be appropriate to a corpse but is not conducive to the comfort of a wounded man.

Lindsay, by a lucky accident, remembered Warren's address, and so I sent him off to find him. He left me in charge of the tourist who had followed him, and departed with the man of Cader.

Lindsay's chance companion was useful while he stayed, for I was lying on a sloping ledge, and was glad of his shoulder as a pillow. Ten minutes passed, and my companion remarked that he thought he ought to be going. I protested, but could not move him. His wife, he said, would be getting anxious. I hinted that his wife's anxiety might be ignored. 'Ah, but you don't know my wife,' he replied, and, so saying, he left me.

He consented to leave his cap behind as a pillow. A month later he wrote and asked me why I had not returned it. This struck me as unreasonable, but – as he justly observed – I did not know his wife.

I fell at 4 p.m. About 7.30 it became colder, and shivering made the pain worse. About 7.45 the old man of Cader returned with some warm tea which he had brewed for me, and for which I was more than grateful. Half-an-hour later the local policeman arrived with a search party and a stretcher.

Luckily the ledge ran across on to easy ground, but it was not until midnight – eight hours after my fall – that I reached the Angel Hotel.

My leg was broken, crushed and comminuted. Twice the preparations were made for amputation. Twice my temperature fell in the nick of time. At the end of a week I was taken home, and lay on my back for four months, much consoled by a Christian Scientist who assured me that my leg was intact. But it was not to Mrs Eddy, but to the vain hope of the hills that I turned for comfort in the long nights when pain had banished sleep.

Four months after I fell I left my bed and began to walk again with the help of a splint. My right leg was slightly crooked and was two inches shorter than the left. An open wound on the shin did not disappear for eleven years, but in spite of these and other defects, Warren's skill had left me with a very serviceable leg.

I began to ski again fifteen months after the accident. Unfortunately, I wasted two seasons trying to ski with ordinary bindings, and it was not until I secured spring bindings that I began to feel reasonably confident . . .

Two years after my fall I climbed the Dent Blanche. I ought to have chosen an easier and shorter expedition, for I was very heartily sick with pain and weariness long before I reached the top. But the moment of arrival on the summit stands out – unique in my mountain memories. Nothing mattered now that I had finally routed the fears which had haunted me for two long years. I could still climb, could still say:

> I have not lost the magic of long days;
> I live them, dream them still;

Still am I master of the starry ways
And freeman of the hill
Shattered my glass ere half the sands were run,
I hold the heights, I hold the heights I won.

[Geoffrey Winthrop Young]

Arnold Lunn, *The Mountains of Youth*

Death by Misadventure?

One of the best climbs of its kind in Britain is the Great Gully, a wall sided cleft in which numerous pitches of varying difficulty must be surmounted, a job of four hours or more to most parties. The length and difficulty of the Great Gully were indirectly responsible for the worst catastrophe that has befallen British mountaineering, not the worst as regards numbers – in that respect the accident on the face of Scawfell Pinnacle in 1903 when four lives were lost takes precedence – but the worst as regards the circumstances in which it took place.

One cold damp November day in 1927 four young men, Messrs. Giveen, Stott, Taylor and Tayleur left the Climbers' Club Hut at Helyg by the Ogwen road to make the ascent. Of the four only Giveen was an experienced rockclimber, the remaining three were novices. In short the party was far too weak for such an arduous expedition and it seems likely that the preliminary trudge of two hours through wind and rain to the foot of the climb proved fatiguing to all but Giveen. The Gully, with its pitches turned into incipient waterfalls by the rain, proved a most difficult and arduous business; it involved long delays, wet clothes, and chilled bodies. So slow were the four that darkness overtook them on the climb, and only good leadership on the part of Giveen extricated them. They arrived on the crest of Craig yr Ysfa by the light of a lantern.

Then began the trudge back to the hut. The three novices were tired and faint from their exertions and want of food, and the party stumbled painfully down the rough slopes towards the small lake known as Ffynnon Lugwy which lies to the south of Craig yr Ysfa at an elevation of 1786 feet. They had a compass but accidentally dropped and lost it. Then the lantern failed. Unable to see anything in the mist and rain Stott and Taylor walked into the lake. Stott managed to scramble out, but hearing Taylor, who was no swimmer, still struggling in the icy water he very bravely dived back and after a terrible struggle managed to rescue him. This effort so exhausted the two that they collapsed face downwards on the boggy shore of the lake. The situation, merely unpleasant before, had suddenly become dangerous. It was up to Giveen to save his party. There were two courses open to him.

One was to get the two exhausted men to the driest and most sheltered spot, to give them all the clothing he could spare, restore their circulation as best he could, and leaving Tayleur to tend them, race for the nearest farm several of which are situated close to the hut half an hour or forty minutes distant from the lake. The other was to remain himself with Stott and Taylor and send Tayleur for help. The former course was best because Giveen knew the countryside better than Tayleur who was tired and might be slow in summoning assitance. What did he in fact do? He left Stott and Taylor lying where they had fallen and accompanied by Tayleur set off for the hut. Now comes the worst part of a story unsurpassed for callousness in the annals of mountaineering, so much so that it is only possible and charitable to conclude that Giveen was out of his mind. On reaching the hut he and Tayleur ate supper and went to bed. They woke some hours later and finding that Stott and Taylor had not arrived decided that something ought to be done! Their obvious course was to rouse the neighbouring farmers; instead they motored to an hotel several miles distant to seek help arriving there twelve hours after Stott and Taylor had fallen exhausted. The rescue party was immediately organised but arrived to find Stott and Taylor dead.

The story told by Giveen at the inquest was very different to this. He had done everything possible for his companions and had only accompanied Tayleur because of the latter's exhaustion. On arriving at the hut he had at once set off for help. A colourless verdict was passed; indeed sympathy was expressed for Giveen. But there was one who remained gravely dissatisfied, Stott's father. In response to his request a party examined the scene of the accident. On the shore of the lake they found Stott's watch. Its hands had been stopped by immersion at 6.40. Giveen and Tayleur were now challenged to explain away the twelve hours that had elapsed between the accident and the summoning of help. Finally, Tayleur admitted that he had not been particularly exhausted, that Giveen had hurried him off from Stott and Taylor, who had been found with their rucksacks still on their backs, their faces in the boggy ground so that Taylor had been actually drowned. Finally the whole wretched story became apparent. Giveen must have been insane at the time for later he entered a mental home. On his release he committed suicide. Tayleur, it would seem, apart from being a novice in mountaineering, was overawed and overruled by his leader.

In case it should seem to some unnecessary to have included this tragic and unsavoury story I have only done so because in the days when mountaineering and rock climbing are rapidly increasing in popularity among all classes and types of persons it cannot be too often stated that a sense of responsibility is, and must always be, the underlying note in mountaineering, the responsibility of the leader in the selection of a climb and the method in which it is carried out and responsibility of each member of a party towards his companions. This sense of responsibility more than anything else promotes good comradeship and sound mountaineering.

Frank S. Smythe, *Over Welsh Hills*

CHAPTER 22

◆

Amateurs and Gentlemen

The typical climber of the nineteenth century was a visitor to the mountains who employed guides from the local population. In the twentieth century, especially among British climbers, guideless climbing became much more popular. Hand in hand with this development it became essential to have written or unwritten codes of practice for the amateur climbers.

In this chapter, F.S. Smythe's light-hearted piece illustrates the problems which guideless climbers might bring upon themselves. G.W. Young provides the most explicit attempt ever made to devise a code of conduct for the amateur mountaineer. Eric Shipton tells the bizarre story of a complete amateur who ended his life nearer the summit of the highest mountain than any other solo climber has ever reached.

◆ ◆ ◆

A Night Adventure in the Dolomites

We had arrived at the hut soon after midday and were anxious for a taste of Dolomite rock climbing. So at 3 p.m. we set off for a practice scramble on the Langkofelkarspitze. This peak, which must not be confused with its larger neighbour, the Langkofel, rises directly behind the hut, in the very centre of the great rock amphitheatre sweeping round from the Plattkofel to the Langkofel.

For the subsequent events I am alone to blame. Our sole guide-book was Baedeker, who described the Langkofelkar as being an easy walk of half an hour to the west of the hut. So it is; but the Langkofelkar is the scree-filled hollow to the west of the Langkofelkarspitze and a very different proposition from the latter. My mistake was in thinking that, having attained the summit, a walk down to the west would bring us back to the hut.

Once on the rocks, Bell went ahead at a great pace. He is always in good rock-climbing form, but personally I must confess to a certain temperamentality at the start of a difficult rock climb. Like a motor car, I require to be warmed up – a condition that requires nursing for a while. In this particular instance we had not proceeded far before I had insisted that we should don the rope.

Dolomite climbing has certain peculiarities, dangers, and fascinations all its own. In British or Alpine rock climbing the difficulty above the angle of adhesion (i.e. the greatest angle up which it is possible to crawl, utilising friction only) is limited by the number, distribution and size of the holds. In the Dolomites the difficulty of a climb usually depends upon the angle, for the rock is extraordinarily rough and the holds embarrassing in their profusion. The roughness of the rock is also responsible for a certain tenderness in the tips of the fingers after a day or two, often developing to a painful rawness like frostbite.

Owing to its brittle nature, Dolomite rock is unsound in the most dangerous sense of the word, and it is often impossible to tell whether or not a hold will break away until the whole weight is upon it, whilst masses of unstable rock, ready to come away at a touch, are common on seldom climbed routes. Perhaps the most subtle trap that I have ever encountered was on the ordinary route up the most famous of Dolomite peaks, the Fünffingerspitze, where a hold, which I had tested, as I thought, in every direction, slid away from its parent rock like a drawer. Only a fingerhold with the other hand prevented me from joining it in its flight through space.

The fascination of Dolomite climbing lies in its steepness and complexity. There is an allurement beyond words in these immense peaks that soar from the emerald pastures – in their intricacies of detail; the chimneys, cracks, ledges, ribs, ridges and edges hidden on their apparently featureless precipices. There is a joy in the direct defiance of nature's primary law; in the confident uplifting of the body by well-trained nerve and sinew; of balancing, edging, crawling, clambering up and up the lofty yellow walls.

The rocks of the Langkofelkarspitze afford typical Dolomite climbing. In some places they are steep and exposed, in others loose and easy. Vertical pitches alternate with ledges, chimneys, faces and traverses, admitting of much variation, but always interesting.

The last difficulty was a sheer wall. A little ledge ran across; a steep crack led upwards from the end of the ledge – an airy place with an immense cliff below. A knife-edged ridge followed. We scrambled along it and stepped on to a tiny summit. But what were we on? A deep cleft separated us from the main mass of the Langkofelkarspitze, which rose two or three hundred feet above it. Our summit was only a subsidiary summit – the north-west peak, as we discovered afterwards. We looked at our watches and were amazed to find it 6 p.m. Time is surely bewitched on the mountains. To us an hour at most had passed. There was less than two hours of daylight left, and no time to lose if we were to get off the peak by nightfall.

We were loth to descend by the way we had come. A little insistent demon whispered 'An easy way! An easy way!' But where? Evidently to the west, where long stretches of broken rocks, set at a moderate angle, seemed to offer little more than a scramble. It was a carefully baited trap, and our eventual decision to descend them was one which neither of us has since been able to understand. To attempt the descent of an unknown rock face with less than two hours of daylight remaining is at variance with the most elementary principles of common-sense and rank bad mountaineering withal. Perhaps we were subconsciously influenced by the guide-book; perhaps the ease with which we had ascended had gone to our heads; perhaps . . . But why moralise?

I have a recollection, as we turned to descend, of glancing round at peaks warming in the glow of the westering sun, of fairy pinnacles and fretted spires rising from dusky depths. Most extraordinary peak of all is the overhanging Zahnkofel, lurching over like a monstrous tidal wave about to break on some doomed shore.

At first all went well, and keeping close together we scrambled rapidly down long stretches of easy broken rocks, but presently the angle steepened to a wall dropping far away into the depths of a gully. We now had a first sight of what lay in store, and, had we still not been possessed with a species of madness, we should have returned and spent the night on the line of ascent. The wall was impossible, and a traverse to the right necessary to avoid it. It was an exposed and difficult piece of work on nearly vertical and treacherously loose rocks.

Bell went first, climbing in his ever neat and methodical way, testing every hold, moving with a perfect precision. And as I watched, holding the rope, the last flare of sunset died around us, and a cold deathly greyness came to the world.

There is but little twilight in these latitudes; night's hosts follow hard on the chariot of the setting sun; and it was almost dark by the time we were reunited on easier ground. There we halted a few moments to decide on our plan of campaign. We were on a sloping shelf – an excellent site for a bivouac – and the wisest thing was to have stopped there, but not only had we had nothing to eat since mid-day, but we had foolishly brought no food with us, and a night of enforced abstinence might well leave us in unfit condition for severe rock climbing on the morrow. We could not be far now from the foot of the peak; a few hundred feet more would see us safely down. So we argued, and continued the descent.

There were two alternatives: to keep to the face, or to take to the gully that falls from the gap between the north-west and main peaks of the Langko-felkarspitze. It was almost completely dark now, but the great rift of the gully seemed darker still, whilst the sounds of a falling stream in its depths spoke eloquently of large and probably impossible pitches. The face, on the other hand, offered less restriction of movement and more alternatives. We were soon undeceived. Below the stretch of easy rocks the angle steepened again – steepened to the vertical – and finally dropped, a hopeless overhang, into the gully.

Sitting on a ledge, I slowly paid out the rope as Bell descended out of sight. Presently I heard him shout –

'I'm on a small ledge from which we can rope down into the gully – come on!'

I came on. The climbing was terribly steep and exposed, and I was glad to place the doubled rope around a small knob of rock and use it as a handhold. I soon reached the ledge, which was about thirty feet below, where I found that Bell had moved along it some ten yards to the right and was firmly secured to a large rock spike. The ledge is but a few inches broad and formed the one wrinkle in the wall.

Holding on to the rocks with one hand, I jerked the doubled rope with the other to detach it from the knob of rock above, but it refused to come. This was exceedingly serious; without it, further progress was impossible. I jerked harder, sending waves up the rope, but still it obstinately adhered to the knob. Suddenly, after a particularly vicious jerk, there was a clatter above. I heard a shout of 'Look out – stone!' from Bell. Nothing was visible in the gloom, and there was no time to do anything save to duck my head down close to the rocks, so that the chunk of dolomite, instead of braining me, merely grazed the back of my head. But it was a stunning blow, and for an instant I swayed back. There were some twenty feet of slack rope between me and the knob, and had I fallen over the overhang the rope must inevitably have broken or been pulled off the knob. Neither could Bell, from his position horizontally ten yards away, have held me, and he would have been left alone in as desperate a situation as could be imagined. Our guardian angels were very near us that night. As though from a great distance, I heard Bell's voice –

'Are you all right?'

A minute or two's rest, and I could assure him that I was. Curiously enough, there were no nervous or physical effects either then or afterwards.

But the problem of the rope remained. The only solution was to climb up, loosen it, and return without its aid. Bell could not pass me on the ledge, and the job rested with me.

The moon had risen behind our peak, and the reflected light revealed the way to some extent. For the rest, it was grope, and feel, and test, step by step, and from balance to balance.

I shall not easily forget that solitary climb in the dark. Perhaps it was the blow from the stone, or the innate capacity for resignation possessed by man, for I remember no excitement or fear, but rather an extraordinary detached sensation: things seemed to be moving in a dream. The black gulf of the gully beneath; the pinnacles and cliffs of the Plattkofel steeped in moonlight; the ghostly sheen of the snow patches in the Langkofelkar like uneasy spirits; the utter peace and stillness of that July night gave me a feeling of unreality – I had only to let go to awake in bed. Yet through these false imaginings a little voice whispered, 'You've got to get down! You've got to get down!'

It was impossible, of course, to use the rope as a handhold; it might well be on the point of coming off the knob after the jerkings it had undergone. Without further adventures I reached the knob, released the rope, climbed down to the ledge again, and, moving along, joined Bell. As far as we could judge, the doubled 100-feet rope just reached the sloping bed of the gully, and there was a substantial rock to put it round. This time there seemed nothing to prevent the rope from being jerked off the spike from below, but nevertheless it would have been wiser, had we thought of it, to have cut a small portion and made a loop through which the rope could have been pulled with certainty.

It was an eerie business sliding down the rope into the black maw of the gully, with its invisible splashing water. There was little rope to spare, but it just reached, and soon we stood together in the damp stream bed, feeling that the worst was over. But our luck was tempered by a devil of misfortune. We had tested the rope in every conceivable way before the descent, yet once again it resolutely refused to be jerked off the belay, and this time there was no return.

Three hundred feet of climbing remained, and for this we took off our boots and, tying them together by their laces, hung them round our necks.

A few feet lower the gully dropped in an overhang, and from far beneath came the sound of its dashing stream. The only hope was on the left, where a long and steep rib of rock slanted down. This was difficult, but climbable; but darkness has one advantage – it eliminates the sensational. Slowly and methodically we groped our way down to safety, stockinged feet feeling for holds at every step, and at long last jumped down to the snow and scree at the foot of the peak. There we halted a moment.

Our sensations are difficult to describe. We were not elated, nor yet – at the time – thankful. The detached impersonal impression dominated all. It was almost as though we had been acting as the unwilling puppets of some satanic stage manager to the audience of demons, goblins, and witches who haunt the craggy amphitheatre. How they must have jeered at our discomfiture! but now they were very silent – no doubt our 'turn' was a very poor one. But listen! What was that faint murmuring in the 'whispering galleries' of the rocks? – that undercurrent of sound as though from some vast uneasy concourse, part hushed, but not silent? Nothing more than the splash of a stream from the gaunt bastions behind us. Hark! A sudden crash, a mad roar of fiendish merriment, a thousand chuckles pulse and die around the cirque. An invisible curtain falls on – Silence.

What foolish fancies are these – have you never heard a falling stone? Down we ran to the hut.

F.S. Smythe, *Climbs and Ski Runs*

Management and Leadership on the Mountains

A party consists usually of from two to four climbers, exclusive of guides. A larger number inevitably divides into two or more units for mountaineering purposes. The management devolves upon the most experienced mountaineer. His selection as leader, in this sense, is more often than not tacit and unexpressed, especially among British climbers.

Over-management is fatal to the effective co-operation of a party; and a formal selection of a leader, or a precise insistence upon the performance of individual duties by individual members, may only disturb the pleasant relationship of friends on a climbing holiday. If a man is not felt to be qualified as leader by personality and experience, no vote will make him so.

Large or democratic parties, of equal experience, can carry out very delightful sub-alpine wanderings without leadership. If they attempt serious mountaineering, it is usually at the cost to their friends of sleepless nights and of expensive search parties.

Among men of equal experience, equally able to grasp a situation and to co-operate without words of command, the duties of leadership are slight and their operation never obtrusive. Experience teaches them to accept, as a matter of convenience, the management of their daily routine by some one of their number, and to acknowledge, as a matter of security and economy of time, the leadership of the most expert in the incidents of the climbing day. In a pursuit so exacting as mountaineering, charged with the unexpected and dependent upon continuous harmony of action for its ordinary progress, some such voluntary subordination is essential. The leader may be only the focus of the collective opinion of an experienced party: like the conductor of an orchestra he may not be equally competent to play all the instruments he directs; but if there is no one to whom to look for the word, in mountaineering as in music the time is lost and harmony vanishes for easy and for difficult passages alike . . .

Management in Anticipation

Three things only are necessary for the salvation of a mountaineering holiday: good health, good fellowship and good climbing. These three conditions are mutually contributory and interdependent; and the last, the declared object of the association, is only attainable when the other two are secure.

It goes without saying that a good leader must be able to design and direct an ascent so far as the actual climbing is concerned; but he will discount beforehand half his chances of successful performance unless he has learned how to bring his party on to the glacier at four in the morning, fit in health and on good terms with themselves and one another.

Fortunately, in dealing with healthy men, special attention to the first condition of health is confined to the first two or three days of a tour. After these are safely passed, air and exercise and increasing fitness take over medical charge and deal summarily with the beginnings of any lesser or local ailments.

There is no need to bother overmuch about the party before the tour commences. Of course men, for their own sakes, will come as fit as they can. Attention to the diet and, if it can be got, some regular exercise in the open air – walking, running or tennis – may be suggested; but I have never seen any particular benefit accrue from exercising particular sets of climbing muscles. I return to this elsewhere; and I would only make one exception here, for a leader's attention. Some men, especially as they get on in years, are liable to cramp in the trunk muscles from the fatigue of general climbing, and in the hands after severe rock work. In these cases it is well worth recommending anticipatory 'local' exercises for the hand and forearm and for the walls of the trunk, to keep the muscles supple and 'long'. Dancing, skipping, fencing and wood-chopping are all worth mentioning to men who cannot get into the open air. And above all, the morning cold bath!

The first few days of the tour, however, are vital. Mountaineers are sound men, and have usually only two weak points, the feet and the stomach. New boots or overwork attack the first; unaccustomed food, changing atmospheric pressures, and revolutionary hours of sleep, food and exercise upset the second. For the feet precautionary measures are the safest. In ordinary life, we accept their constant service unconsciously, and it requires an effort to give our own and, even more, other men's feet the additional attention they require on the first few days of any tour. To see that the boots fit, on the second day even more than the first; to make sure that one or even two extra pairs of socks are put on if any boot has become stretched after wetting; to discover if there is any beginning of rub or blister, and to check it by boracic powder or other ointment in the sock at once, even if this means a halt in the middle of a climb; to suggest bracing with cold water in the evening or whenever opportunity offers; in the case of anyone whose skin is tender, to double these precautions: these are some of the first duties of management . . .

Care in the choice of food, discouragement of the inclination to starve during the day and to overeat in the evenings, insistence upon a regimen to get the subconscious stomach working by its new time-table, and, in case of failure, the employment of the simple domestic remedies at once and in time, these are all indispensable during the first days. But their observance cannot be left without prompting to the individual discretion. Especially is this the case in looking after young mountaineers, who are unacquainted with the treacherous dealings of odd meals and broken sleep at high altitudes.

In the matter of the choice of food the leader has to overcome the repugnance natural after a satisfying evening meal to attend himself to all the rather messy details of provisioning for the next day.

No guide or hotel-keeper can be trusted to do this. During the first days of hard exercise the average man will eat but little solid food, and turns from meats and tins such as hotels love to load into the sacks. He has to be tempted with sweet-stuffs, jams (the small tins are irresistible), chocolate and meat-essences and eggs for support. The disposition to eat little during the effort of the first days, and to eat largely in the reaction of the evenings, has to be countermined by the offer, at not infrequent intervals, of pleasant luxuries that go down easily. It is old-fashioned, and entirely wrong, especially with young people, to give them only what used to be termed wholesome, nourishing food. In healthy open-air conditions the body knows what it wants, and the palate interprets the desire. Food that is not palatable or eaten with pleasure is of little benefit, and cloying sugar compounds, the best muscle fuel, become again surprisingly attractive . . .

Thirst is another difficulty at the beginning of a tour. To a large extent such thirst is merely feverish; it is impossible of satisfaction, and to indulge it swamps and upsets the human machinery. Some resolute men, to avoid the delicious temptation, train themselves not to drink at all during the day; and then make it up in the evening. But a certain amount of liquid is as essential, in action, as a certain amount of food, and the moderate habit has to be acquired by practice. The exact amount necessary, as distinguished from acceptable, varies with the individual. The merely feverish thirst of the first day can be dodged by letting water run through the mouth, swallowing, as a special indulgence, only a mouthful or so. Sucking a prune-stone, or even a pebble, keeps the saliva flowing and is a consolation on hot snowy tramps. To the same end, of prolonging the pleasant assuaging process, devices such as sipping water slowly from a pearl-shell or cup cool to the eye, chewing orange peel, sucking a lemon or tea or wine slowly through lumps of sugar, or crushing a handful of snow till it becomes an ice-pear in the hand and then sucking the end of it, are all worth remembering.

Meat-fed men do not require strong stimulants. A little wine in the water, chilled by snow, is often pleasanter to the taste than water alone. Mountain water has often a flat favour of cold stone, or recalls the flask or pouch in which it has been carried. Wine removes the suspicion. Spirits should be kept for a last resource, for cases of injury or collapse, and then used only if the head is not affected. Their stimulus, under the conditions of climbing, is too evanescent to be of any service; the reaction is almost immediate, and the resulting condition worse than before. Cold tea and cold coffee are popular beverages: or the juice of many lemons can be carried in a small aluminium flask, to mix with the chosen blend. Sugar lessens the quenching power. If sugar cannot be dispensed with, a lemon squeezed into the tea restores its effect upon the saliva ducts of the mouth. Snow, crushed ice or water can be added as the supply diminishes . . .

Smoking I believe to be a question for personal decision. I have never found the moderate indulgence in pipes or cigars affect wind or training in the slightest degree during the hardest days. The rule that halts should be few and short ensures moderation; for smoking during actual climbing is all but impossible. One famous mountaineer prefers to light a pipe before any particularly hard problem, but experiment suggests that the art is not worth learning. It is uncomfortable for the lungs and costly in pipe-stems. A pipe makes a good temporary substitute for food, drink, or sleep. It comforts many cold moments of waiting and makes a soothing counsellor in difficulties. Ability to smoke, and consequently to sustain his part in the effortless silence which characterizes the true comradeship of mountaineering, should be among the qualifications of any climbing companion.

A manager's functions are precautionary rather than corrective. It is well that he should know something of medical treatment and of first aid. But advice under these headings is best obtained from the many good handbooks. From them he will learn how to use the contents of the pocket medical and surgical cases without which no party should ever attempt to climb . . .

Leadership in Action

The manager as leader has a special responsibility to himself. He is the stroke of the party. Like a good stroke, while exerting himself to the utmost, he has always to keep some strength, nervous and physical, in reserve, to meet a sudden emergency, or to vitalize unexpectedly depressing hours of dull return. As a duty to the party he should save himself by making use of the stronger members, should there be any, to take something of his share of the more laborious and less vital labour. A party which knows his value as reserve and management will save him, for instance, some part of his portion in the work of carrying, of leading in soft snow, or of easy step-cutting. They too must recognize he has always to keep something in reserve for a crisis.

At the same time, no matter what the crisis or his private doubts, he must never appear, if he can possibly help it, to have called out his last reserves, or to be feeling any diminished confidence in his own ability, or in that of his party, to force a successful issue. He must, too, avoid mystery. Nothing is more nerve-trying in critical moments, to men whose experience cannot measure the extent of a crisis, than tense silence or too obvious self-control on the part of those who can. It is better, if the situation is genuinely serious, to bring it down to a human level by blowing off a few words of violent commonplace expletive, than to leave it in that daunting remoteness of gravity for which words are inadequate. The more crucial the occasion, the more does the nerve of the party centre in the leader. Their confidence in his confidence is a more important asset than their confidence in his skill . . .

To keep in touch with every one of a party of friends, so as to continue aware of the way in which their minds and their bodies are being affected by the circumstances, is not easy. On severe climbs it is all but impossible to prevent the rear men, separated by lengths of rope and interruptions of difficult ground, from remaining in ignorance of what is being done in front, or of what is guiding the choice of problems which they are expected in their turn to surmount. For this reason it is helpful to break the habit of silence which falls upon men dealing with serious work, – and which, like the inclination to whisper in a dark room, seems to have behind it some primitive feeling of fear of provoking further attention from unseen but very present forces, – and talk down the rope occasionally, passing question and answer up and down, and cheering the tail with a renewed feeling of unity and confidence drawn from the confidence of the leader. With the same object in view, wherever the climb allows it, the party should be allowed to collect for a moment and forget in talk the depression or doubt inevitable to solitude, before the leaders start again . . .

A mountaineering party, when in action, is dependent for its good-humoured and hearty co-operation on more than the external interests of the climbs, however well selected beforehand and sustained, on more even than its good health and food, however well cared for. It has to be welded into a fine instrument: its temper is its strength; and its temper has to be kept at just the right heat. Hot words on occasion will do it little harm. Men in a state of primitive well-being are apt to become elemental in temper. A sudden crisis sets off a shower of sparks of language. These do no harm. No experienced man looks upon them as personally directed, or remembers them when the crisis is past. What has really to be guarded against is the effect of monotony in any form, even the irritating repetition of some small unconscious personal trick. Slight resentments become magnified grotesquely during the long hours of silent effort, especially of monotonous effort, on snow, glaciers, or path. Any ordinary mountaineer will probably remember occasions when some trifling habit of a good friend, some unintentional or momentary lack of consideration, has taken advantage of the dull ending of a strenuous day to come back upon him irresistibly, and fill him unaccountably with sullen growing resentment. He may realize its foolishness, but like the similar insistence of the refrain of some silly comic song, it becomes part of the mechanical movement in which his whole being is for the time absorbed.

If he has been fortunate enough to escape such an attack himself, he must at times have been aware of the dangerous electricity accumulating in some one or other of the members of a tired party. It is the commonest symptom of fatigue. A manager has to look out for this. Its consciousness will disappear with the sight of the hotel door, and be secretly regretted on the morrow, but in the meantime he has to prevent the unforgettable being said. Silence is his chief enemy. It is useless to try and tempt tired men, usually tramping in single file, into agreeable conversation, unless some happy accident of the way rests the mind with a new distraction, but he has to seize any desperate occasion for casual remarks. It does not signify what he chatters, provided he is not inappropriately cheerful, and shows himself at least to be completely and seemingly idiotically unconscious of any strain in the situation. Even if he draws the discharge of temper on himself, he has averted all serious danger. Song is the best outlet since it fits in with the mechanical movement while it withdraws attention from it; but song can only be employed when the ground allows of the feet moving in accord . . .

Social Composition of the Party

A mountaineer, in the composition and management of his party, cannot afford to neglect the action of health and condition upon temper, or of temperament and mood upon achievement. He must select men, therefore, not by their promise of the plains, but by what he knows or concludes will be their conduct under the harder test of the heights. If he has to take anyone on chance, he must be on the watch from the first, and if he finds he has made a mistake, content himself with a less ambitious programme. In big mountaineering no man has more than a momentary margin. In less exacting work no man has a continuous margin of will-power, nerve and temper, to say nothing of skill, for more than himself and one other. Every party of more than two should contain two men of tried nerve – that is, of an experience that has learned to control the effects of shock or of fatigue upon the nerves. Every party, for its own peace, should contain one expert rock climber and one reliable iceman. A good second-man, or 'backer-up', and a weight carrier are invaluable assets. These parts may, of course, be doubled in a single individual. The ability to heal, or cook, or sing may be allowed to outweigh some minor defects – but not temper, clumsiness, or a sluggish vitality.

A manager has also to remember that that party earns the best success which works with the most collective good-humour and good-will. With the object of maintaining the genial atmosphere that best resists local disturbances, mental or physical, one member of a party of three or four may well be either younger or less experienced than the rest. Rowing eights in training have discovered the merits of a mascot or protégé, whom the rest can look after and laugh with or at. No party of men or women can quarrel if there are children (not belonging to them) of their number. One considerably younger member of a party, or one younger in the sense that he or she is a novice to the work, and in so far is a child, gives the climbing group the pleasant sense of centring round some one as a common care. He is a permanent distraction. In moments of excitement, pleasure or fatigue, every member of such a party unconsciously puts himself first into the newcomer's attitude of mind, and speculates how the sensation will present itself to him. The process provides our individual consciousness with an external interest that diverts us from the oppression of absorption in ourselves.

In a holiday party of four, which is the best number for serious guideless climbing, enabling the break into the ideal pairs for rock climbing, and the safer combination for glaciers, one member may well be an 'infant' or beginner of this sort; but if such an element is included, the 'breaking' must be confined to very safe passages. In a party of three, provided that two are thorough experts, and one of these possibly a first-class guide, and provided that no severe climbing is contemplated, maleficent psychic influences may be combated by the inclusion of our less responsible third. If serious work is in prospect, the third must be at least strong and efficient; in fact, in parties of less than four, considerations of skill or experience must always take precedence of purely social qualifications. In a party of two, for rock climbing, both must be, primarily, expert, and our social selection must be confined to this class. For glacier work any party of two, even though, socially, they speak with the tongues of angels, must always be unsound . . .

Walking Manners

There are several points of what may be termed walking manners, common to all types of long mountain walking and not only to climbing, whose observance contributes a great deal to the individual peace of mind during the early and late hours of a long alpine day. Men when they are off the rope, or who have never been on a rope, almost universally neglect them, and are blind to the cumulative effect upon a tired companion's temper or upon their own humour. Every one thinks he can walk, and most men never bother to discover why the excellent companion of the Sunday afternoon ramble proved a failure on a long walking tour.

The first point of manners for the man in control is that of pace. Most climbers suffer from the weakness of increasing the pace the moment they take the lead on a path, slope, or glacier. This is trying to the party, consciously or not, and wasteful. A manager should either block the way himself, or, if he is behind, keep consistently to what he considers the right tempo. It is better that he should be thought to be getting old or lazy than that the party should be rushed inopportunely.

A second and frequent failing is the 'half step' trick. Some fifty per cent of fast walkers, whenever they walk abreast on road or path or hill, persistently keep half a stride in front, their shoulder just clear of their companion. It may be due to some half-formed feeling of satisfaction in setting the pace and having a margin to turn round and talk from. Its effect is that the friend is perpetually straining to catch up, and the pace thus steadily accelerates till both are practically racing. Then one gives up, and both lag, until the game starts again. The habit is often unconscious, but it is extraordinarily irritating on a long tramp, or to a tired companion.

A third breach of manners, all too common, is passing ahead in the line of march. Over most broken country, glacier, snow or rough hillsides, men naturally fall into single file. Cattle tracks or man tracks are rarely wide enough for two abreast, and if it is a question of selecting a line, it saves reduplication of the effort to leave the task to one and to drop in behind him. There are few inexperienced walkers who do not take advantage of the slightest error in the choice of route on the first man's part, to break off and pass him on the shorter line. In doing so, they take the responsibility of taking all the rest who follow off the line also. On an ordinary hill walk, when the going is all free and easy, this is excusable, – no one is compelled to follow another longer than suits him; as also the case when the first man is obviously mistaken, and to cut his line is a distinct saving of effort for those who follow. But, done as by one of a line of men either tired or with a big day before them, where one has been taking the extra burden of route-selecting for the rest, it is a serious breach of mountain manners. The gain is probably only a yard or two, and the front man may justly resent having been left the labour of choosing the route at a hundred points, only to have advantage taken of his single doubtful choice in order to displace him. He either runs ahead to regain his place, and the rhythm of the party is broken in a silly competition none the less irritating that it is rarely acknowledged in words, or he plods behind with a slight sense of injury.

A more debatable occasion, where the same point comes into prominence, is on the ascent of steep slopes or open hillsides. An experienced front man will probably take these on a zigzag. To a less experienced walker, and to all beginners of energy and leg muscle, it is generally a temptation to cut the zigzags on the direct line, and so pass ahead. This is bad walking, but there is the most excuse for it that on such slopes men rarely do follow each other exactly, and most of the party will probably be preferring each to take his zigzag at the most comfortable angle to himself. The best rule of manners to remember is that while every man is free to choose any line and pace he likes on such places, yet, if one man has been definitely leading and choosing the line, the others ought to drop into their places in the line behind him again so soon as the single-file formation is resumed. It is more politic to be considered a well-mannered tramp than to assert one's powers as a limber hill-rusher.

Geoffrey Winthrop Young, *Mountain Craft*

Everest by Divine Command

About three hundred yards above Camp III we found the body of Maurice Wilson, who had attempted to climb Mount Everest alone the previous year and about whom nothing more had been heard. From a diary which we found on his body and from subsequent enquiries we were able to piece together his curious story. He was a man of about thirty-seven and had served in France during the last war. He had developed a theory that if a man were to go without food for three weeks he would reach a stage of semi-consciousness on the borderland of life and death, when his physical mind would establish direct communication with his soul. When he emerged from this state he would be cleansed of all bodily and spiritual ills; he would be as a new-born child but with the benefit of his experience of his previous life, and with greatly increased physical and spiritual strength. Wilson had fanatical faith in his theory. He believed moreover that he had seen a vision in which he had received divine instruction to preach the doctrine to mankind. Somehow the word 'Everest' had featured in the vision, and he thought that it was intended to indicate the means by which he could achieve his purpose. Obviously if he succeeded in reaching the summit of Mount Everest single-handed, the feat would cause no small stir, and his theory would receive wide publicity.

He knew nothing whatever about mountaineering. At the time, however, the Houston Everest Flight was receiving considerable press publicity. Presumably this gave him the idea that if he were to fly a plane as high as he could and crash it on the side of the mountain he would be able to climb the rest of the way to the summit and return on foot. So with this object in view, he learnt to fly, bought a small aeroplane and set out for India. At Cairo he was stopped and turned back by the authorities. But eventually he reached Purnea in India where his machine was confiscated. He went to Darjeeling where he stayed for four months, training himself and making secret preparations for his journey to Mount Everest. He got in touch with some of the Sherpas who had been with us the year before and they agreed to smuggle him through Sikkim and into Tibet. He then covered up his tracks by paying for his room at the hotel six months in advance so that he could keep it locked with his things inside, and gave out that he had been invited by a friend to go on a tiger shoot. It was some time before the authorities discovered that he was missing.

In the meantime, by wearing a disguise and travelling at night he had succeeded in passing through Sikkim and into Tibet. There he travelled more openly, but with practically no baggage and by avoiding the big places he and his three Sherpa companions attracted no attention. When they arrived at Rongbuk he told the abbot of the monastery that he was a member of the 1933 expedition and induced him to hand over a few small items of equipment that we had left there. He had evidently made a good impression upon the old man, who, when we visited the monastery in 1935, talked to us a great deal about him. He left the Sherpas at Rongbuk and started up the glacier alone with the complete conviction that he would reach the summit in three or four days. He had with him a small shaving mirror with which he proposed to heliograph to those at Rongbuk from the summit, so as to provide proof that he had actually reached it. He was used to starving himself and intended to live on a small quantity of rice water. It was early in April and he encountered the usual spring gales on the East Rongbuk glacier. He appears to have reached a point somewhere about Camp II before he was forced to retreat, exhausted.

After the fortnight's rest he set out again, this time with the Sherpas. They reached Camp III and the Sherpas showed him a dump of food which we had left about half a mile beyond, and which contained all kinds of luxuries such as chocolate, Ovaltine, sardines, baked beans and biscuits, with which he was delighted. He left the Sherpas at Camp III and went on alone. He had evidently expected to find intact the steps which we had cut in the slopes below the North Col, and he was bitterly disappointed to find nothing but bare windswept ice and snow. Though he had an ice-axe, he did not know how to use it and could make little headway up the slopes. He camped alone on the rocks near the dump and set out day after day to renew his fruitless attempts to reach the Col. Though he had plenty of food, he was gradually weakened by the severe conditions. This was clear from the entries in his diary, which became shorter and less coherent towards the end. But he would not give up and still clung to his faith in divine inspiration. The last entry was on the 31st of May 1934. He died in his sleep, lying in his small tent. This had been smashed by storms, and all the fragments, except the guy-lines which were attached to boulders, had been swept away.

Eric Shipton, *Upon That Mountain*

CHAPTER 23

◆

Mechanization and Politicization

At the opposite extreme from the British cult of the skilled amateur there grew up in the nineteen-thirties on the Continent an increasing professionalization of mountain climbing, and an increasing reliance on artificial aids. British mountain lovers regarded this as a sinister development, especially because of the links which they saw between mechanized professionalism and Fascist and Nazi ideology.

◆ ◆ ◆

Mechanization and the Cult of Danger

This is an age of mechanization. Our view of the universe and everything in it is more mechanical, more material, than in the early days of mountaineering. The actual instruments used in climbing have recently acquired a peculiar importance which may affect our whole view of the sport. It is curious that until quite lately no implements were used which were not in use in similar but more rudimentary forms hundreds of years ago, before mountains were thought of as anything but obstacles to be passed with the least possible risk.

The rope as a security against danger on a glacier was in use in the sixteenth century. It is mentioned in Simler's book on the Alps, published in 1574. 'The guides tie a rope round them, to which the travellers who follow are attached; the leader sounds, as he goes along, with a pole, and carefully looks for crevasses in the snow, and if he happen by mischance to fall in, his companions on the rope hold him up and pull him out.' . . .

Crampons are mentioned by Strabo as being used in the Caucasus in the wars of Pompey against Mithridates. They were made of hide, shaped like cymbals, and carried sharp points. In the Middle Ages in the Alps the type is a stout sole with three spikes. Saussure mentions crampons made of leather with heel-spikes and attached by straps.

Glissading was well known, and the fashionable winter sports are, like jazz music, an instance of a return to primitive delights practised by savages. Plutarch describes how the Cimbri paraded in front of the enemy by sitting on their shields and tobogganing down steep slopes. The pleasures of both roller-skating and ski-ing were to some extent enjoyed together by the future Emperor Leo the Isaurian when he crossed the snows of the Caucasus on 'cyclopodes', a species of large skates provided with wheels.

The ice-axe is the most original and successful improvement on the old implements, combining, as it does, in handy form the old alpenstock and the peasant's chopping axe. The discovery that ice is easily split by a thin-pointed tool, and is almost unaffected by a cutting edge, made the ascent of ice-slopes possible. Some of the big expeditions of the early sixties, such as the passage of the Eigerjoch and Moming, would have been impossible without something like a modern ice-axe. The glacier has now become an unimportant item of the modern climbing day, which is spent on precipices where the axe, where it is not simply a nuisance, is used as a piton or for cutting steps close to the stomach or the nose. Consequently the handle of the axe has shrunk till its length approximates once more to that of the old chopper and can be stuck in a rucksack with the pointed end protruding. The climber who returns carrying his axe otherwise than in this latest way is liable to be placed among the old fogies.

The great invention with which this mechanical age has endowed the climber is the piton, which varies from a rough, stout peg of iron to an elegant, fragile leaf of steel. It can be adorned with a ring, so that the proudest rock-faces and the most domineering of profiles suffer the degradation foretold by the prophet: 'Behold I will put a ring in thy nose.' This ring opens like the clip at the end of a watch-chain, hence the name *mousqueton* in French, *moschettone* in Italian; in German it is a *Karabiner*. There is no English word for it. It is, in fact, decidedly un-English in name and in nature.

All implements used in mountaineering are essentially utilitarian. In common with all mechanical devices their object is simply to reduce labour and facilitate the achievement of results. Every increase in their use increases the proportion of the purely utilitarian in mountaineering. In the Jungfrau railway we have a proportion which is a hundred per cent; it is the increase of mechanical aids carried to its furthest limit. Any mountain, even in the Himalayas, can be ascended by a sufficient expenditure on mechanical means; but every increase in mechanical equipment affects the ethical value of our contest with the mountain, which has no capacity for increasing its powers of resistance.

Our use of mechanical devices will therefore depend greatly on our aim. If our aim is at all costs to reach the summit, and we measure the value of our success by the speed and ease with which the result is achieved, the ideal climber being like the ideal machine, then the more perfect and complete our mechanical equipment the better. In so far as an aesthetic or moral value is attached to the ascent, the use of mechanical devices cannot help us, and may hinder us. The windows through which the artists and writers of the present day invite us to view these latter values are so distorting that the

modern generation may well be excused for doubting the real existence of any stable abstract values, and for concentrating its attention on what can be measured in mathematical units, speed records, scoring records, height records . . .

The introduction of the piton and the detachable ring has not improved man's natural capacities, but it has allowed places to be climbed which Nature intended should remain untouched by human feet, and it has enabled young men to combine with rock-climbing the love of playing with machinery. To the Teuton it has given to rock-climbing the essential character of a 'sport'. This word 'sport' had been known and understood in Britain for many generations; even the modern passion for records and results induced by the dominance in our life of the machine has not succeeded in obscuring the basic idea in regard to sport, that it must be carried out under fair and loyal conditions. Any deviation from this fairness is not sporting.

The superficial attributes of 'sport', its rivalries, its standardization, and the glorification of results have been adopted with the word itself by other nations of Europe at a time when a mechanized view of life was already established, and it is these superficial attributes that have been accepted as the essential character of sport rather than the idea of it which still remains part of the Englishman's upbringing. To many of the early mountaineers the use of the piton and the fixed rope was anathema . . .

Munich, being near the Bavarian Alps, has given its name to the most famous of the new schools of climbing, which have been described as the 'sporting/heroic/arithmetic' type. It is a necessity of this school that climbing prowess should be capable of accurate measurement. For this purpose it has established six grades of difficulty, ranging from 'easy' to 'quite exceptionally difficult'. This grading is becoming common in the Dolomites and in the Julian Alps, and is beginning to spread towards the west in the Italian Alps . . .

It is easy to see the ludicrous side of this development of 'artificial aids'. Let us not forget that the material view of life, with the disillusionment on the spiritual side that accompanies it, often leaves the contemplative view of life a rather drab affair, from which escape is possible by absorption in rapid or violent action and in an emotional excitement akin to intoxication. And on the higher grade climbs the temporary escape from the 'wretchedness of humanity' must be very complete. If you can imagine yourself on the path cut out of the solid rock called the Steinerne Rinne, which runs along the base of the most arduous climbs of the Wilde Kaiser, you will get a glimpse of an expert party at work. The cost of pitons and ropes is still borne by the climbers themselves, and there is no turnstile yet to defray the expenses of the show. You will find a restaurant on the shelf, and can sip your beer as you watch or drink to the health – which is often in jeopardy – of the party literally 'hanging on' far above you. The cliffs are about a thousand feet high.

A party of two starts for the Fiechtl-Weinberger route, one of the dearly beloved 'direct' routes leading almost in a straight line to the north peak of the Predigstuhl. Provisions and warm clothes hardly enter into the equipment of an expert cragsman. *Kletterschuhe* of course, a couple of long ropes, a liberal supply of pitons and clasp-rings, and couple of hammers. Two caves close to one another in the face of the cliff indicate the way, which lies just to the left of them. An overhanging crack with some good holds is a nice mild beginning; then comes a small, slanting crack of about twenty feet leading to the famous overhang. Some parties have a way of removing their pitons after use, and have been known to remove those left by previous parties. A certain amount of hammering may be done here, and the leader ties on both ropes, the object of this being to ease the work of the leader by letting the second man help to haul him up the overhang on the rope passed through a ring clasped to a piton slightly above and to one side. On one occasion the actual godfather of the climb spent half an hour struggling to pass the overhang and had to give it up. For these sixth-grade tests a man must not only be an expert rock gymnast, he must be feeling perfectly fit and in the right mood! The second man was keen to try but the leader discouraged the suggestion on the ground that it would be even more difficult for him to come up second.

Next day this crack is climbed in a few minutes, the balcony of the hut and the Steinerne Rinne itself being black with spectators. Whether the effect of being watched by many pairs of wondering eyes is to give increased confidence or to diminish caution is an interesting point. Now comes the overhang. Numerous pitons give excellent security, but it is an awkward place, only possible by a delicate adjustment of the feet against a concavity in the rock to maintain the balances, while the body is raised on the bulge, and by getting some help from a very thin crack that rises vertically above it. One of the most brilliant of the experts spent one and a half hours at the place.

A still greater effort is needed for the crack that follows! It is holdless and too narrow to get into. The only grip obtainable is on some smooth, rib-like irregularities in the rock running parallel to the crack. There is no place where it is possible to relax the effort. It is described as 'one of those places where the only salvation lies in continuous movement. One reaches the top with the hands more dead than alive and the heart racing.'

The rest is comparatively easy, a traverse on the face, followed by a succession of vertical cracks and ribs and a long chimney at the end. And when they get back they are welcomed with mugs of beer held out by admirers in the watching crowd. Supper is all ready for them, and they eat it surrounded by a wondering crowd, 'as elephants are watched eating at the Zoo.' . . .

Now, in regard to the use of pitons, it has been said: 'If you cut a step in ice to secure a hold, why not a hold cut out of or hammered into the rock?' Well, the extent of the difference depends on the way you look at mountains. If you regard them, as most men who have spent some time alone with them regard them, as something more than a mere lump of matter, as things that have a sort of personality of their own, ready to give you the things that you prize most; if, in fact, you feel towards them anything of what Kim's lama felt, that 'Who goes to the Hills, goes to his mother', then there is something altogether abhorrent in this method of getting your own way by driving in nails. If you wrestle with a friend, the whole essence of the thing is spoiled if you use sharp claws to get a hold. Ice is but a sort of grease the mountain puts upon his body to make him more elusive; its removal is no violation of any sporting instinct; loose stones, too, are but portions of his scaly skin that are dead; the piton must be driven into the living rock to make it fast. This attitude may appear fanciful; it is the simple truth as I look at it . . .

It is no exaggeration to say that the methods recently introduced into modern climbing, and the utter recklessness that sacrifices all regard for safety to the satisfaction of personal achievement, have disgusted many mountaineers whose record is sufficient proof of their love of adventure, their skill and courage, and their intense love of every sort of mountaineering that does not contain a lie in the soul.

R.G.L. Irving, *The Romance of Mountaineering*

Death on the Eigerwand

Climbing is fundamentally neither a standardised nor a competitive sport, but in recent years, along with its other developments, it has had a tendency to be so. One of the concomitants – part cause, part effect – has been an elaborate system of grading ascents, which originated in the Alps in the 1920s and has since spread over most of the world. By this method, climbs of all descriptions are ranked according to their degree of difficulty, beginning with a First Degree for an easy walk-up and culminating in a Sixth, which has been aptly defined as 'an ascent recognised as impossible until someone does it without being killed'. Inherently, perhaps, there is nothing wrong with such a system; at least it helps a climber in the selection of his route and lets him know roughly what he may expect. But it was soon perverted to the purposes of competition, and by the thirties the Alps were full of glory-seeking young climbers who looked down with contempt on anything less than a certified Super-Sixth. The Eigerwand, the north wall of the Grandes Jorasses, the north and west faces of the Matterhorn, and various of the rock-pinnacles in the Dolomites achieved a notorious celebrity as 'impossible' ascents, and it was on them in particular that the new order of Alpine cragsmen concentrated and struggled – and often died.

Aiding and abetting this suicidal insanity was a rising tide of nationalism. To be sure, mountaineering, since its earliest days, has suffered from ugly and senseless rivalries (witness the stories of Mont Blanc and the Matterhorn), but the jingoistic fervour that developed in the decade before the Second World War touched new heights of absurdity. Inevitably it was the Germans and Italians who carried it to its furthest extreme. Aflame with the hero-philosophy of Nazi-Fascism and egged on by flag-wavers and tub-thumpers at home, brown and black-shirted young climbers began vying with one another in what they conceived to be feats of courage and skill. All or nothing was their watchword – victory or death. No risk was too great, no foolhardiness to be condemned, so long as their exploits brought kudos to *Vaterland* or *patria*.

As a result of all this, Alpine mountaineering – at least in its more 'expert' phases – became an activity with scarcely any relationship to the usual concept of sport. Competition was everything: competition literally to the death. Each year saw scores of new attempts at 'record climbs', hundreds of reckless youngsters clinging to precipices and cliff-faces which a centipede could scarcely have surmounted, much less a man. The Alps had once been looked upon as a playground; then as a laboratory. Now they had become a battlefield. Seldom has there been an unhappier example of how hysterical and perverted nationalism can infect even the most unpolitical of human activities.

One glimpse of this 'all-or-nothing' type of climbing is more than enough. The time is mid-July of 1936; the scene the mile-high precipice of the Eigerwand – the Wall of the Ogre – that rises close by the Jungfrau in the heart of the Bernese Oberland . . .

For years the Eigerwand had been famous throughout Europe as one of the few great unclaimed 'prizes' of the Alps. Many parties of dare-devil climbers – most of them Germans – had tried to force a way up its appalling pitches of rock and ice; but none had succeeded, and almost every venture had ended in the death of one or more participants. Still the suicidal attempts went on – 'victory or annihilation'; 'for *Führer* and *Vaterland*.' (Hitler himself announced that gold medals would be awarded to the first scalers of the Eigerwand, in conjunction with the Berlin Olympic Games of 1936.) And on the morning of July 20th crowds of sightseers again thronged the terrace of the Kleine Scheidegg Hotel, in the valley below, staring upwards through the telescopes. For yet another assault was under way.

High on the mountain wall the figures of the climbers could be seen, clinging to the rock like minute black insects. There were four of them – two Bavarians and two Austrians – all of them young, all with records of many sensational climbs behind them, all resolved to win fame and glory by accomplishing 'the most difficult ascent in the Alps'. By the time the telescopes picked them up on the morning of the twentieth they had already been on the precipice for two full days. Hour after hour they had inched their way upwards, digging fingers and toes into tiny crevices, driving pitons where no crevices existed at all, dangling in space at rope's end as they struggled with vertical cliffs and bulging overhangs. The first night they spent standing upright, lashed to a rock-wall with pitons and rope. On the second a storm swooped down, and the whole mountainside around them was sheathed in a whirling fury of ice and snow. The watchers below gave them up as lost, but at day-break they were still alive – still able to move. And the third day began.

Throughout the morning they crept on and by noon were almost within a thousand feet of their goal. There, however, their good luck ended. Storm and cold and the savage, perpendicular wall must at last have taken their toll of the climbers' strength, for they were seen to remain motionless for a long time and then begin to descend. But their downward progress did not last long either, and presently they were motionless again – four infinitesimal specks transfixed against the wall. Apparently they were unable to move either up or down.

A council of war was held in the valley below, and four guides set out as a rescue party. Following the tracks of the Jungfrau railway, which bores through the rock of the Eiger, they came out on the precipice through an opening in the tunnel wall and began working their way across it towards the point where the climbers were trapped. Soon they were near enough to see the four of them clearly. They were clinging to the merest wrinkles in the ice-coated rock face, one above the other, tied together and supported by a mass of ropes and pitons. Their clothing was in tatters and their faces scarcely recognizable from the effects of exposure and exhaustion. Above them was a sheer, almost holdless wall, down which they had somehow managed to lower themselves. Below was an overhanging precipice and an abyss of blue space.

Slowly, with deliberation and care, the rescue party drew nearer, but while they were still some distance away the inevitable happened. The uppermost of the four Germans lost his hold and toppled backwards into thin air, arms and legs twisting grotesquely. The coils of the rope, spinning down after him, caught the next man around the neck, almost wrenching his head from his shoulders, while a third, still lower, was struck by the falling body of his companion. Then the rope went taut and snapped. The first man plummeted on for four thousand feet to the valley below; the second and third stayed motionless where they had fallen, half lying half hanging from the ropes and pitons. In five seconds it was all over. And one man was left alive.

Still the horrified guides kept on. Hacking their way diagonally across a sixty degree ice-slope, they at last reached a point only a few yards away from the sole survivor – a Bavarian soldier named Kurz. But before they could begin the delicate work of rescue another storm bore down upon the mountain, and they were forced to beat a retreat. Kurz was left to spend his third night on the precipice, his body suspended over space and tied to the corpses of two of his companions.

The next morning, miraculously, he was still alive, but so weak that he was scarcely able to speak or move. Again the guides began the grim work of reaching him and this time succeeded in establishing themselves on a narrow ledge some one hundred feet below his position. Farther, however, they could not go. The stretch that still separated them from Kurz was an ice-glazed overhang, and to have ventured up so much as a step on to it would have been obvious suicide. They called up to Kurz to cut himself loose from the bodies of his companions. This he did, using the point of his ice-axe; then, summoning his last reserves of strength, he knotted several ropes together and lowered them to the guides. He was so feeble by this time that these two operations took him three hours.

On the ropes dangling from above the guides sent up a specially devised sling. As there was no possible way of their reaching him, it was up to Kurz to lower himself on to it – if he had the strength left. Slowly and patiently he wrapped the coils about his body, leaned out into space, started down. The men below could hear his hoarse breathing and see his boot-nails scraping weakly against the rock. In a few moments he was so close that one of the guides, balancing on the others' shoulders, could almost touch his feet.

Then suddenly the rope sling jammed and Kurz's downward progress ceased. For a desperate, straining moment he clung with fingers and toes to the ice-smooth bulge of the overhang; but the last of his strength was gone. His ice-axe dropped from his hand and went spinning downwards. An instant later he himself swung out from the mountain wall into space. And hanging here at rope's end, he died.

This miserable disaster was only one among many of similar nature that occurred in the Alps in pre-war years. The Eigerwand was finally climbed in the summer of 1938, and those other famous 'impossibles', the north wall of the Grandes Jorasses and the northern and western faces of the Matterhorn, also yielded at last to climbers with more luck than sense. For each success, however, there were many failures and many lives lost; and, far from being deterred by the endless list of catastrophes, there appeared to be an ever-growing supply of young men eager to devise still more spectacular and gruesome ways of killing themselves. The coming of war had at least one good effect, in that it put pretty much of an end to this sort of lunatic extreme in mountaineering. True, there are still plenty of accidents in the Alps. 'Impossible' ascents are still attempted, and occasionally made. But at least a measure of sanity has been restored; the hordes of stormtrooper heroes have disappeared, and the mountains are being given back again to those who understand and love them.

James Ramsey Ullman, *The Age of Mountaineering*

CHAPTER 24

—◆—

Failure on Everest

Between 1921 and 1938 seven expeditions attempted to reach the summit of Mount Everest in the Himalayas, the highest point on earth. Each expedition failed, though each expedition could boast of splendid feats of mountain heroism and gallantry. In the 1922 expedition the two climbers Mallory and Irvine disappeared not far below the summit; their bodies have never been recovered. Of those who returned the two climbers who reached the highest point were Eric Shipton and Frank Smythe, in 1933. Here is Shipton's story of their ascent to the topmost camp, Camp VI, up to the day on which they were forced to turn back.

◆ ◆ ◆

Camp Six

We arrived at Rongbuk on April 16th. The next morning was occupied with the ceremony of receiving the blessing of the Abbot of the Rongbuk Monastery. This old man was a great character. He was then close on seventy years of ages, he had a tremendous sense of humour and he took a kindly interest in our project. The blessing ceremony consisted in each of us bowing before the Abbot in turn, receiving a sharp tap on the head from his mace and repeating after him 'Om Mani Padmi Hum' (Hail, the jewel in the Lotus). Most of us had to repeat the formula several times before we got it right, to the great amusement of the Abbot. We were each given a little packet of pills to take when we felt in need of spiritual sustenance. The Sherpas conducted themselves with far greater dignity and *savoir-faire* than we did. The same afternoon we went four miles farther up the valley where we established the Base Camp, which was to be our haven of rest, our coveted metropolis, for nearly three months.

The Rongbuk valley is a grim and desolate place, a waste of stones shut in from all pleasant prospects, flanked by shapeless, disintegrating walls of rock. Its upper end is dominated by the huge mass of Everest. Seen from the top of the surrounding peaks, this northern face of the mountain has a fine simplicity of design and a certain grandeur, though even then it cannot compare with the magnificent architecture of the eastern and southern aspects. But from the Base Camp it appears stunted and deformed, a mere continuation of the graceless forms about it . . .

The establishment of the lower camps was a leisurely business. In the first place we were in no hurry, because the severity of the conditions would forbid operations on the mountain for several weeks; secondly, slow progress was necessary for our acclimatisation, and thirdly, we had so much stuff to transport up the glacier that even with our vast army of porters (forty-six more joined us later from Sola Khombu which brought our total strength up to about one hundred and seventy), many relays were necessary to establish each camp. The distances between these were fairly even, and it took about three or four hours of very easy going to go up from one to the next, and about half that time coming down. The porters carried 40 lbs each; we carried nothing, the theory being that we must conserve our energy for higher up. Though it is a debatable point, there is certainly something in this argument. At high altitudes (in my opinion about 21,000 feet) the wastage of muscle tissue is so rapid that it is well to start with a fairly large reserve of flesh. A man highly trained in the athletic sense is liable to be worn down much more quickly than one less finely drawn . . .

The work of carrying loads up from the Base Camp began on April 19th and on May 2nd we established and occupied Camp III in the upper basin of the East Rongbuk glacier at a height of 21,000 feet. We were now in full view of the North Col. At last we were confronted with a real mountaineering proposition which would require some concentration of energy and skill. The prospect was a good one. Pleasant and immensely interesting though the journey had been, most of us I imagine had been keyed up by the anticipation of the toughest climbing of our lives. So far it had all been make-believe, and it was difficult to avoid the question: 'When are we going to be called upon to do a job of work; when will we have something really to bite on?'

The eastern slopes of the North Col are composed of steep broken glacier and rise about 1,500 feet from the level ice below to the crest of the Col. As the glacier is moving slowly downwards the slopes present a different appearance from year to year. Our task then was to find a way up them, to make a ladder of large safe steps and to fix ropes to serve as hand rails over all the difficult sections, so that it would be possible for laden porters to pass up and down with ease and safety.

We started the work almost at once. It was about an hour's walk from Camp III to the foot of the steep slopes below the Col. The ice of the upper basin had been swept clear of snow by the wind. It was rather like walking on an ice-skating rink and required some little practice to avoid sitting down heavily. But fortunately the slopes above were composed of hard snow, for it would have been a tremendously laborious task to cut steps all the way up in hard ice, and also very difficult to fix the ropes. As it was, it was very hard work. Even at that height any physical exertion left one gasping for breath. We took turns of about twenty minutes each at cutting the steps. Even that seemed an eternity and it was a great relief to be told that the time was up. We climbed about a third of the way up to the Col on the first day.

There followed days of storm and wind which rendered work impossible. Below, we had experienced fairly severe conditions, but Camp III was much more exposed to the weather, which deteriorated a good deal during the fortnight after our arrival there. I gathered from the Sherpas who had been with the 1924 expedition that the conditions were very similar to those experienced in that year . . .

As soon as there was a lull in the wind, we resumed work on the slopes below the Col. We found that the steps we had already cut had been swept away, and that not a trace of them remained. So as to take advantage of brief periods of fine weather we put a camp (IIIA) at the foot of the slopes. This was a bleak and comfortless spot, and even more exposed to the wind than Camp III, which was situated on rocks close under the cliffs of the North Peak. The new camp was pitched on hard, smooth ice on which it was difficult to anchor the tents. One night, during a particularly violent storm, one of them broke loose from its moorings causing a certain amount of excitement. But the new position was a great help, and from it we were able to make progress. But our advance was very slow, and as we set out day after day I began to wonder if we should ever reach the Col. The most difficult part was about half way up. This consisted of an ice wall about 20 feet high, topped by a very steep ice slope. We had a lot of fun getting up it, and succeeded largely owing to a fine lead by Smythe. We hung a rope ladder down it for subsequent use.

At last, by 15th May, the road of steps and fixed ropes was complete, and we established Camp IV on an ice ledge, some 20 feet wide, about 200 feet below the crest of the Col. The ledge was formed by the lower lip of a great crevasse, the upper lip of which, 40 feet above, almost overhung the ledge. The camp was well sheltered and quite comfortable, the only disadvantage being the danger of small snow avalanches falling from above.

For the next four days the storm was continuous, and we could do nothing but lie in our sleeping bags. Nor was any communication possible with the camps below. But on the evening of the 19th, the wind dropped and Smythe and I climbed up the last 200 feet. Apart from the ice wall this was by far the steepest part of the North Col slopes. When we reached the narrow crest of the Col we were met by a most glorious view to the west, over range after range of giant peaks, draped by dark cloud banners, wild and shattered by the gale. The mighty scene was partly lit by an angry red glow, and rose from a misty shadow-lake of deep indigo that often appears among high mountains in the evening after a storm . . .

We were very comfortable at Camp IV. Cooking and breathing soon produced a pleasant fug in the tents: we had large double eiderdown sleeping-bags, and our snow beds were soon made to conform with the shapes of our bodies. The crevasse provided a convenient latrine, though it required a strong effort of will to emerge from the tent. It was only at the upper camps that the cold compelled us to use a bed-pan in the form of a biscuit box. So long as we did not have to do anything, the time passed pleasantly enough. Lethargy of mind and body was the chief trial. Once one got going it was not so bad, but the prospect of toil was hateful. At the higher camps, of course, this lethargy increased tenfold.

Eating, however, was the serious problem, and one which, to my mind, did not receive nearly enough attention. This was entirely the fault of the individual, for we had more than enough food and its quality and variety could not have been better. The trouble is that at such an altitude the appetite is jaded, and unless a man forces himself to eat regular and sufficient meals he does not consume anything like enough to maintain his strength. Melting a saucepan full of snow for water and bringing it to the boil took so long that people tended to delude themselves that they had eaten a hearty meal. Over and over again I saw men starting for a long and exhausting day's work on the mountain with only a cup of cocoa and a biscuit or two inside them; the cold and the wind discouraged eating during the climb, and they were generally too tired to eat anything much when they returned. This state of affairs contributed largely towards the rapid physical deterioration of the party . . .

Weather conditions now appeared to have reached that state of comparative quiet that we had expected just before the arrival of the monsoon. Wireless messages received at the Base Camp spoke of an exceptionally early monsoon in Ceylon and its rapid spread over India. This news was confirmed by the appearance of great banks of cloud from the south which, however, were still far below us. Obviously the critical moment had arrived. On the 22nd of May, Birnie, Boustead, Greene and Wyn Harris, with twenty porters carrying 12 lbs each, established Camp V at 25,700 feet. The plan was for these four climbers and eight of the porters to stop the night at Camp V and to carry Camp VI as high as possible on the following day; Birnie and Boustead would then return to Camp V with the porters, while Wyn Harris and Greene would stop at Camp VI and attempt to climb the mountain by the 'ridge route'. Meanwhile Smythe and I would follow up to Camp V on the 23rd, and make our attempt on the summit on the 25th, choosing our route in the light of the experiences of the first pair. Greene unfortunately strained his heart during the climb to Camp V, and his place was taken by Wager who had accompanied the party for exercise.

It was hard to believe that the time for the supreme test had arrived. Waiting at the North Col on the 22nd of May, I felt as I imagine an athlete must feel just before the boat-race, Marathon or boxing contest for which he has been training for months. It was difficult to keep one's mind from the nagging questions, 'Will the weather hold long enough to give us a decent chance?' 'How will I react to the extreme exhaustion that must inevitably accompany the final effort?' 'What is the climbing really like on that upper part?' 'For all our previous optimism, is it, in fact, possible to climb or even to live at 29,000 feet?' Three more days, seventy-two hours!

It was a great relief when, the next morning, the moment to start arrived. We had the whole day before us, and there was no need to hurry. The basis of all mountaineering is the conservation of energy by the three fundamental principles – rhythmic movement, balance, and precise placing of the feet. As far as possible, steps should be short so that upward motion appears as a gentle sway from the hips rather than a strong thrust by thigh muscles. It is better to use a small nail-hold at a convenient distance than a large foot-hold involving a long stride. If a long stride is necessary, the balance must be adjusted by lateral pressure by the hand or ice-axe. A practised mountaineer is, of course, in the habit of observing these principles even on the simplest ground; his ability to maintain them on difficult and complicated terrain determines in large measure his quality as a climber. Nowhere is perfection of technique so important as at high altitudes where the slightest effort takes heavy toll of the climber's reserves of strength; nowhere is it more difficult to achieve.

Above the North Col we were met by a strong wind, which increased in violence as we climbed. I have no idea what the temperature was. On the glacier below a minimum of 20 deg. F. was observed. I doubt if we experienced less than that on the upper part of the mountain. Judged by winter temperatures in the Arctic or Antarctic, such cold is not considered severe. But at great altitudes it is a very different matter. Due to lack of oxygen, the various functions of heart, lungs, and circulation are most inefficient, lost heat is difficult to restore, and there is danger of frost-bite even at freezing point, particularly when there is a wind blowing: one has constantly to watch for its symptoms. If a foot loses feeling it is wise to stop to remove one's boot and bang and rub it to life again. This is one of the greatest difficulties we have had in dealing with the Sherpas at high altitudes; it was most difficult to induce them to take these precautions.

We were not altogether surprised, when at about four o'clock we reached Camp V, to find that the whole party was still there. Though by now the wind had dropped, it had been even more fierce at Camp V then it had been below, and it had been impossible to move up the ridge. There was no room for two more at Camp V, and, though we offered to go down again, it was decided that Smythe and I should change places with Wyn Harris and Wager, in the hope of being able to push on up the mountain the next day . . .

All that night and most of the next day a blizzard raged, and it was impossible to move either up or down. Fine snow, driven in through the thin canvas of the tent, covered everything inside and filtered in through the opening of our sleeping-bags. Being on the crest of a ridge we received the full force of the gale. There was a continuous and mighty roar, and it seemed that the tents could not possibly stand up to such a hammering. At one point one of the guy ropes of our tent broke loose. Smythe struggled outside to deal with the situation, while I had the soft job of acting as ballast inside to hold the tent down. Smythe was only out for a couple of minutes, but when he returned we spent hours rubbing and thumping his limbs to restore the circulation.

On the evening of the 24th the wind dropped and there was a great calm. We opened the tent flap and looked out. Such cloud as there was, was far below us. The magnificence of the view penetrated even my jaded brain. The summit, greatly foreshortened, seemed close above it. Smythe and I discussed seriously whether it would not be better after all to make our attempt from Camp V. We were still fairly active, and all this delay at high altitudes was certainly doing us no good. Anyway, there was no need to decide yet; we could start out with Birnie and Boustead and the porters who would be going up to establish Camp VI, and judge our condition then. That we could have discussed such a hopeless proposition shows how we were feeling.

But while we were preparing to start next morning, the gale began to blow again. Standing outside the tents the icy wind made us feel supremely helpless and foolish. The others had spent three nights at Camp V; already the Sherpas were nearly exhausted by the storm, and some of them were frostbitten. Had the weather been calm it is doubtful if they would have been able to go far; any advance under the present conditions was out of the question. Nor could we ask the porters to stay at Camp V yet another day and night, even if we had been willing to do so ourselves. There was nothing for it but to retreat to the North Col. It was a bitter blow, for all the time we were losing strength, and none of us could hope to be really fit for another attempt. At least, that is how it appeared to me.

In the meantime a good deal of snow had fallen on the North Col, and Camp IV was in danger of being buried by a snow avalanche. The following day, the 26th of May, was spent moving the tents and stores to the crest of the Col, while Ruttledge, Greene, Crawford and Brocklebank escorted the exhausted porters down to Camp III . . .

On the 28th of May, Birnie, Longland, Wager and Wyn Harris went up to Camp V, with the eight porters. Smythe and I followed on the 29th. This time there was less wind than there had been before. We reached Camp V after five hours' climbing, and we were relieved to find that things had gone according to plan. Birnie was there in sole occupation. For the next few days his was the thankless job of remaining at Camp V in support of the parties attempting the summit. During the afternoon the gale returned with something of its old violence, and we were much relieved when Longland and the porters arrived from above. They had fought a tremendous struggle with the blizzard during the last two hours. Two of the porters were almost exhausted, and Longland had a difficult job in getting them down. Poor, gallant Kipa was in a bad way. It was already clear that he was out of his mind. For a long time he remained firmly convinced that he was dead. In consequence it was most difficult to persuade him to move, for, as he argued with perfect logic, dead men could not walk, even down hill. Even when, after several weeks it dawned on him that he was, in fact, alive, he still clung to his original hypothesis and attributed his phenomenal recovery to Greene's magic. Such temporary madness or hallucination was by no means confined to the porters.

Longland brought us the splendid news that Camp VI had been established at 27,400 feet; 600 feet higher than it had been placed in 1924, and only 1,600 feet below the summit. This was a magnificent achievement on the part of the porters and those that were leading them. Their feat gave us a fine chance of climbing the mountain. Wyn Harris and Wager were now at Camp VI, and would start the next morning on their attempt to reach the summit.

By now the force of the gale had slackened, and after we had provided them with a mug of tea each, Longland and six of the porters went on down to the North Col. The other two porters stayed the night with us.

The next morning was beautifully fine. Not a breath of wind disturbed the stillness, no cloud obscured a single detail of the vast panorama beneath us. To the east was a fantastic tangle of ice and jagged rock, each fold a mighty peak, now dwarfed to insignificance; to the north the desert ranges of Tibet, calm and soft, stretched away into the violet distance. The sun was well up before Smythe and I left Camp V. In spite of a fairly good night I felt far from well. I was suffering from slight diarrhoea which accentuated the weakness due to the physical deterioration that was now becoming only too apparent. Every movement was a great effort, and I found myself counting each step and wondering when I could decently suggest a halt. At first the climbing was fairly difficult over a series of outward sloping buttresses, but after a while it became easier. We followed the ridge until, in a little hollow, we found the remains of the 1924 Camp VI – a few broken and bleached tent poles with some tattered wisps of canvas clinging to them. From there we traversed diagonally across the face of the mountain, climbing slowly up towards the Yellow Band . . . Longland had described the position of Camp VI, and as we approached we had no difficulty in spotting it – a little dark patch against the yellow limestone.

Before reaching the foot of the Yellow Band we had a prolonged struggle, first with a short ice slope which required step-cutting, then in powder snow into which we sank to our knees. I thought we would never get through it.

That was followed by 200 feet of difficult rock climbing, each sloping ledge laden with snow. I found this less unpleasant; to have a technical difficulty to grapple with, which required delicate balance rather than dull plodding, was somehow stimulating. All the same, we were both very thankful when we crawled into the tiny tent that was Camp VI. I believe it was somewhere about one o'clock.

Camp VI was no luxury establishment. A tiny recess at the head of a gully and some loose stones had enabled the others to build a rough platform, perhaps three feet wide, on which to pitch the tent. The platform sloped downwards, and one side of the tent hung over the edge, forming a pocket. But at least it provided somewhere to lie down. After a rest we set about the task of melting a saucepan of snow. At the other camps we had used Primus stoves, but these do not work above a certain altitude, and at Camp VI we used little tins of solid fuel known as Tommy Cookers. Even these were most inefficient at that height, and it took us an hour to provide two miserable cups of tepid water slightly coloured with tea. Then we brewed some more against the return of Wager and Wyn Harris.

They arrived about the middle of the afternoon, showing every evidence of the tremendous effort they had made. They had tried to reach the ridge just below the Second Step but had met a continuous line of overhanging rock, so they had traversed along below the Black Band, and had reached the Great Couloir. This they had managed to cross, but had found the rocks on the other side laden with powder snow, which about 12.30 had forced them to abandon the struggle. How far this decision had been induced by sheer exhaustion and how much by the difficulty of the ground, on which the slightest slip must have been fatal to both, it is difficult to determine. Wager has since told me that he has found it impossible to assess the real position in which they found themselves. At that altitude mental processes are so sluggish and inefficient that it is most difficult to retain a clear memory of what has actually occurred. In any case their decision was absolutely right; there was not the slightest chance of their reaching the summit and to have persisted much farther would most probably have involved them in disaster. They would undoubtedly have got farther had it not been their primary task to examine the Second Step, which had cost them valuable time.

Just below the crest of the north-east ridge they had found an ice-axe. This can only have belonged to Mallory or Irvine and throws some small light upon their fate. It seems probable that they fell from the place where the axe was found. It may be that one of them slipped, the other put down his axe to brace himself against the jerk of the rope, but was dragged down. Certainly the axe cannot have fallen, for had that happened, there was nothing to prevent it from bounding down at least to the foot of the Yellow Band.

I had gone so badly that day that I offered to change places with one of the others, and let him try again with Smythe. In this I was actuated by no unselfish motive. But they had both had more than enough. Wager was gasping for breath in a most alarming manner and Wyn looked terribly tired. So after a short rest and a cup of our home-brewed nectar they went on down to Camp V.

That night and the one which followed were by far the worst that I spent on the mountain. I had the lower berth and kept on rolling off the ledge into the pocket formed by the tent floor. Smythe spent the time rolling on top of me. From sheer self-preservation, to prevent myself from being suffocated, I had to kick him with my knee or jab him with my elbow. This I did over and over again, hoping vaguely that the action would not reveal the temper which was undoubtedly behind the blows. I did not sleep at all and I do not think Smythe fared much better. Several hours before dawn we gave up the unequal struggle and started to prepare for the climb.

But before it was properly light snow started to fall, and presently a strong wind was driving the flakes against the side of the tent. It was no use thinking of starting in those conditions, and there was nothing for it but to resign ourselves to spending the day at Camp VI. I think we both realised then that our slender chance of reaching the summit had now vanished. In the first place, the snow that was now falling would, at the lowest estimate, increase the difficulties enormously; secondly, our physical deterioration due to lack of oxygen, sleep and appetite must now be very rapid. Indeed, we were worried, so far as we were capable of worrying about anything, by the question of how long it was possible to live at 27,400 feet. Would the danger line be apparent? Or would one suddenly find oneself incapable of moving? Or perhaps just die in one's sleep? Nobody had ever tried the experiment of a prolonged sojourn at such an altitude.

It was a dreary day. The next night was a repetition of the first, tossing, kicking, panting. At about three o'clock in the morning we started melting some snow, to make a brew of something – Café-au-Lait I believe it was called, though everything tasted much the same. Thawing our boots was the longest job; they were like lumps of rock. We had intended taking them to bed with us to keep them soft, but, like so many good resolutions made below, this had not been done. But by holding them over candle flames we managed to make the uppers sufficiently pliable, and, with a tremendous effort, to force our feet, already encased in four or five pairs of socks, into them. For the rest we each wore two pairs of long woollen pants, seven sweaters and a loosely-fitting windproof with a hood that went over a balaclava helmet. Our hands were protected by one pair of thick woollen mits covered with a pair of sheep-skin gauntlets. I felt about as suitably equipped for delicate rock climbing as a fully rigged deep-sea diver for dancing a tango. It was quiet outside and we waited for the dawn.

It must have been about 7.30 when we started. It was a fine morning, though bitterly cold. I had a stomach ache and felt as weak as a kitten. We started climbing diagonally up towards the head of the Great Couloir, taking the lead in turns of about a quarter of an hour each. The ground was not exactly difficult nor particularly steep. But it was rather like being on the tiles of a roof; one had to rely largely on the friction of boot-nails on the shelving ledges. A slip might have been difficult to check. The more exposed parts of the Yellow Band had been swept clear of snow by the wind, but in the little gullies and cracks there were deep deposits of powder snow which obscured all foothold. We were not climbing quickly, but our progress was steady and fast enough. After about two hours I began to feel sick and it appeared to me that I was approaching the end of my tether. In such a condition I would certainly have been no use to Smythe in an emergency; also it was a firm rule among us that one simply must not go on until one collapsed altogether, as that would have placed one's companion in a most awkward position. So I decided to stop and let Smythe go on alone.

By now it was fairly warm in the sun. I sat down and watched Smythe making his way slowly along the slabs and wondered if I might follow him at my own pace. But then it occurred to me that, seeing me coming, he might wait for me, so I reluctantly gave up the idea, and after waiting a little longer started back to Camp VI.

It was about 1.30 when Smythe returned. He had reached the Great Couloir, but had found masses of new snow on the rocks beyond and had been compelled to return from much the same place that the previous party had reached. The height at this point was estimated at 28,100 feet.

Eric Shipton, *Upon That Mountain*

CHAPTER 25

◆

The Modern Mountain Muse

Twentieth-century poets have not been inspired by mountains in the same way as those of the nineteenth century; and most twentieth-century mountaineers who have written poems have failed to match their skill in verse with their skill in climbing. The classicist A.D. Godley occasionally applied his gifts as a comic poet to his avocation of mountain-climbing. Freya Stark, initiated in the love of mountains, like so many other people, by the scholar and critic W.P. Ker, was climbing with him when he died in 1923, and commemorated his death in the poem printed below. W.H. Auden, with Christopher Isherwood, wrote a play about mountaineering, *The Ascent of F6*, but it is difficult to anthologize, and he is represented here by a shorter, later poem. Michael Roberts, poet, critic and mountaineer, included one poem of his own in his influential *Faber Book of Modern Verse*. Gary Snyder's poem recalls John Muir, author of *The Mountains of California*. Wilfred Noyce's poem probably holds the record for altitude of composition: it was written at 21,000 feet on 23 May 1953, at Camp IV on Mount Everest.

◆ ◆ ◆

'Switzerland'

In the steamy, stuffy Midlands 'neath an English summer sky,
When the holidays are nearing with the closing of July,
And experienced Alpine stagers and impetuous recruits
Are renewing with the season their continual disputes –
      Those inveterate disputes
      On the newest Alpine routes –
And inspecting the condition of their mountaineering boots:

You may stifle your reflections, you may banish them afar,
You may try to draw a solace from the thought of 'Nächstes Jahr' –
But your heart is with those climbers, and you'll feverishly yearn
To be crossing of the Channel with your luggage labelled 'Bern',

        Leaving England far astern
        With a ticket through to Bern
And regarding your profession with a lordly unconcern!

They will lie beside the torrent, just as you were wont to do
With the woodland green around them and a snowfield shining through:
They will tread the higher pastures, where celestial breezes blow,
While the valley lies in shadow and the peaks are all aglow –
        Where the airs of heaven blow
        'Twixt the pine woods and the snow,
And the shades of evening deepen in the valley far below:

They will scale the mountain strongholds that in days of old you won,
They will plod behind a lantern ere the rising of the sun,
On a 'grat' or in a chimney, on the steep and dizzy slope,
For a foothold or a handhold they will diligently grope –
        On the rocky, icy slope
        (Where we'll charitably hope
'Tis assistance only Moral that they're getting from a rope);

They will dine on mule and marmot, and on mutton made of goats,
They will face the various horrors of Helvetian table-d'hôtes:
But whate'er the paths that lead them, and the food whereon they fare,
They will taste the joy of living, as you only taste it there,
        As you taste it Only There
        In the higher, purer air,
Unapproachable by worries and oblivious quite of care!

Place me somewhere in the Valais, 'mid the mountains west of Binn
West of Binn and east of Savoy, in a decent kind of inn,
With a peak or two for climbing, and a glacier to explore, –
Any mountains will content me, though they've all been climbed before –
        Yes! I care not any more
        Though they've all been done before
And the names they keep in bottles may be numbered by the score!

Though the hand of time be heavy: though your ancient comrades fail:
Though the mountains you ascended be accessible by rail:
Though your nerve begin to weaken, and you're gouty grown and fat,
And prefer to walk in places that are reasonably flat –
        Though you grow so very fat
        That you climb the Gorner Grat
Or perhaps the Little Scheideck – and are rather proud of that:
        Yet I hope that till you die
        You will annually sigh
For a vision of the Valais with the coming of July

For the Oberland or Valais, and the higher, purer air
And the true delight of living, as you taste it only there!

A.D. Godley

'The Mountains of Wales'

Cader and Snowdon and Lliwedd and Glyder
    What, after all, are formations like these?
Stratified rocks (if you come to consider)
    Placed at an angle of x-ty degrees!
Why should a person provided with reason
    Batter his bones and endanger his skin,
Trying in vain to revert for a season
    Back to the ways of his simian kin?

Answer, O climbers of buttress and gully
    Writhing in chimneys and wading in snows
You who have breasted the crags of Cwm Dyli
    You who have clung to the Parson his Nose
Looked from the peak to the limitless distance,
    Mountain and sea in the rain and the sun
Tasted the intimate joy of existence
    Labour accomplished and victory won:

This be your thought as you turn from the summit
    Gripping the rocks as you gingerly go
There, where the cliff with the drop of a plummet
    Dips to the scree and the valley below –
Men with a mind on a rational basis
    Walk on a road (as I'm sure that they should);
    Yours are the truly delectable places
Yours is the spice of the Ultimate Good.

A.D. Godley

'W.P.K.'

On your good rest we laid the mountain flowers –
Rose-frilled dianthus and the dark bluebell,
And yellow lilies fresh with Alpine showers
And every name your love remembers well:-
Secretly, in your cell,
Their wild and tender fragrance will recall

The happiness of our adventurous morns,
While Rosa's shining horns
Receive the night and sunrise, and the fall
Of her loud streams is steady to your ear –
Rough mountain voice to soothe the mountaineer.

Here in the meadows where the pasturing cows
Turn their slow necks and move the collar bell
Your love will ever dwell
Beneath the lime-trees' shade whose flowering boughs
Greeted us with the daylight long ago
Beside the pilgrims way, the path we know.

The seasons in their sequence mild shall bring
Silence in winter and the shining snow,
Dumb voice of cataracts frozen – then the spring,
Quick thaw and sudden ecstasy – and lo!
Summer again when our wild roses blow,
And in their sober row,
Black gowns and kerchiefs bright,
The villagers to Mass or Vespers wend,
Or gather harvest in the clear sweet air –
Or, till night-shadows blend,
The hills and heavens, must rake the flower-strewn hay;
All this was your delight,
And happiness to watch upon your way.

The sun is all about you yet, most dear.
In earliest radiance our hearts rise to you.
In the small brook's awakening voice we hear
Echoes of words, a memory to pursue.
Nor shall the granite ranges ever wear
Their coat of dawn, their earliest cloak of flame
But as a written signal, even your name
Glittering on Time and Space, who art beyond:
As on that day when we upon the hill
Kept through the hours our vigil sad and fond
And spake with you, and knew your heart was still.

Freya Stark

'Mountains, for Hedwig Petzold'

I know a retired dentist who only paints mountains,
But the Masters seldom care

That much, who sketch them in beyond a holy face
    Or a highly dangerous chair;
While a normal eye perceives them as a wall
Between worse and better, like a child, scolded in France,
Who wishes he were crying on the Italian side of the Alps:
    Caesar does not rejoice when high ground
        Makes a darker map,
    Nor does Madam. Why should they? A serious being
        Cries out for a gap.

And it is curious how often in steep places
    You meet someone short who frowns,
A type you catch beheading daisies with a stick:
    Small crooks flourish in big towns,
    But perfect monsters – remember Dracula –
Are bred on crags in castles; those unsmiling parties,
Clumping off at dawn in the gear of their mystery
    For points up, are a bit alarming:
        They have the balance, nerve,
    And habit of the Spiritual, but what God
        Does their Order serve?

A civil man is a citizen. Am I
    To see in the Lake District, then,
Another bourgeois invention like the piano?
    Well, I won't. How can I, when
I wish I stood now on a platform at Penrith
Zurich, or any junction at which you leave the express
For a local that swerves off soon into a cutting? Soon
    Tunnels begin, red farms disappear,
        Hedges turn to walls,
Cows become sheep, you smell peat or pinewood, you hear
    Your first waterfalls,

And what looked like a wall turns out to be a world
    With measurements of its own
And a style of gossip. To manage the Flesh
    When angels of ice and stone
Stand over her day and night who make it so plain
They detest any kind of growth, does not encourage
Euphemisms for the effort: here wayside crucifixes
    Bear witness to a physical outrage,
        And serenades too
    Stick to bare fact: 'O my girl has a goitre,
        I've a hole in my shoe!'

Dour. Still, a fine refuge. That boy behind his goats
   Has the round skull of a clan
That fled with bronze before a tougher metal.
   And that quiet old gentleman
With a cheap room at the Black Eagle used to own
Three papers but is not received in Society now:
These farms can always see a panting government coming;
   I'm nordic myself, but even so
     I'd much rather stay
Where the nearest person who could have me hung is
   Some ridges away.

To be sitting in privacy, like a cat
   On the warm roof of a loft,
Where the high-spirited son of some gloomy tarn,
   Comes sprinting down through a green croft,
Bright with flowers laid out in exquisite splodges
Like a Chinese poem, while, near enough, a real darling
Is cooking a delicious lunch, would keep me happy for
   What? Five minutes? For an uncatlike
     Creature who has gone wrong
Five minutes on even the nicest mountain
   Is awfully long.

                   W.H. Auden, from 'Bucolics'

'Rocky Acres'

This is a wild land, country of my choice,
   With a harsh craggy mountain, moors ample and bare
Seldom in these acres is heard any voice
   But voice of cold water that runs here and there
   Through rocks and lank heather growing without care.
No mice in the heath run nor no birds cry
For fear of the dark speck that floats in the sky.

He soars and he hovers, rocking on his wings,
   He scans his wide parish with a sharp eye
He catches the trembling of small hidden things,
   He tears them in pieces, dropping from the sky:
   Tenderness and pity the land will deny
Where life is but nourished from water and rock,
A hardy adventure, full of fear and shock.

Time has never journeyed to this lost land,
  Crakeberries and heather bloom out of date,
The rocks jut, the streams flow singing on either hand,
  Careless if the season be early or late.
  The skies wander overhead, now blue, now slate:
Winter would be known by his cold cutting snow
If June did not borrow his armour also.

Yet this is my country beloved by me best,
  The first land that rose from Chaos and the Flood,
Nursing no fat valleys for comfort and rest,
  Trampled by no hard hooves, stained with no blood.
  Bold immortal country whose hill-tops have stood
Strongholds for the proud gods when on earth they go,
Terror for fat burghers in far plains below.

Robert Graves

'St Gervais'

Coming out of the mountains of a summer evening
travelling alone;
coming out of the mountains
singing

Coming among men and limousines,
and elegant tall women, and hotels,
with private decorative gardens,
coming among dust.

After the distant cowbells, bringing
memory of mule-tracks, slithering snow,
wild pansies, and the sudden
loose clatterings of rocks

I remembered Sunday evenings, church bells, and cinemas
and clumsy trams
searching interminable streets
for quiet slums, the slums where I
remembering St. Gervais and the gorges, linger, bringing
in the worn shell of air, the pines,
the white-cloud-vision of Mont Blanc, and up
beyond Les Contamines the seven shrines.

Michael Roberts

John Muir on Mount Ritter

After scanning its face again and again,
I begin to scale it, picking my holds
With intense caution. About half-way
To the top, I was suddenly brought to
A dead stop, with arms outspread
Clinging close to the face of the rock
Unable to move hand or foot
Either up or down. My doom
Appeared fixed. I MUST fall.
There would be a moment of
Bewilderment, and then,
A lifeless rumble down the cliff
To the glacier below.
My mind seemed to fill with a
Stifling smoke. This terrible eclipse
Lasted only a moment, when life blazed
Forth again with preternatural clearness.
I seemed suddenly to become possessed
Of a new sense. My trembling muscles
Became firm again, every rift and flaw in
The rock was seen as through a microscope,
My limbs moved with a positiveness and precision
With which I seemed to have
Nothing at all to do.

Gary Snyder, 'Burning'

'Breathless'

Heart aches,
lungs pant
dry air
sorry, scant.
Legs lift –
Why at all?
Loose drift,
heavy fall.
Prod the snow
easiest way;
a flat step
is holiday.

Look up
far stone
many miles
far, alone.
Grind breath
once more then on;
don't look up
till journey's done.
Must look up,
glasses dim.
Wrench of hand,
faltering limb
Pause one step,
breath swings back;
swallow once,
throat gone slack.
Go on
to far stone;
don't look up
count steps done.
One step,
one heart-beat,
stone no nearer
dragging feet.
Heart aches,
lungs pant
dry air
sorry, scant.

Wilfred Noyce

CHAPTER 26

◆

The Mountains of Childhood

During the period between the two World Wars mountain walking and climbing in Britain became a widely popular sport, and extended to whole families, including children. The two extracts in this chapter illustrate this, one in the case of the Lake District, the other in Wales.

Arthur Ransome's stories for children are mainly about sailing in the Lakes; but in *Swallowdale* there is an account of an ascent of Coniston Old Man by the two girls, Nancy and Peggy Blackett ('The Amazons'), who live with their widowed mother at the foot of the mountain, and the four Walkers, John, Susan, Titty, and Roger, ('The Swallows'), children of a naval officer on holiday near Coniston. In the children's fantasy the mountain is Kanchenjunga, a fearsome Himalayan peak, third highest in the world, not ascended until 1955.

The climb of the Swallows and Amazons is fictional, and even in reality Coniston Old Man is no great peak to conquer. But in the nineteen-thirties the children of some families were learning to do real rock climbs which would test the skill and courage of adults. Wilfred Noyce describes how he began to climb when eight years old and by the age of seventeen was doing climbs rated 'Difficult' and 'Severe'.

◆ ◆ ◆

The Ascent of Kanchenjunga

One reason why the Amazons found it hard to make good owl calls was that they had very little breath. They had pulled hard all the way up the river, and then had had to climb the steep gorge to the top of the woods. Not even guides can run uphill and make good owl calls at the same time, and the Amazons, after all, were more pirates than guides, and knew more about sailing than about climbing mountains. Still, for the moment, they were being guides, and Captain Nancy, besides her knapsack, had a huge coil of rope slung on her shoulder for easy carrying. She took it off as she came into the camp and threw herself panting on the ground.

'Where's Peggy?' said Susan.

'Just coming. We raced from the bottom.'

'Would you like some tea?' said Susan . . .

Nancy held the mug upside down and let the last dregs of the tea hiss on the embers of the fire. 'What about going on?' she said, and was going to put the mug as it was in one of the knapsacks, but Susan took it in time to save that, and washed it out in the beck and dried it so that wet sugar should not trickle out of it into places where it was not wanted. The four sleeping-bags, neatly rolled up, were packed between two rocks with everything else that was not being taken to the top. Nothing but food was being taken, besides, of course, the telescope, the compass, and the huge bottle of lemonade, nectar, or grog, that Peggy had carried up from the valley.

'How do we fasten the rope?' asked Roger again.

'We fasten it to all of us,' said Nancy.

'Then we mustn't pull different ways,' said Roger.

'Nobody exactly pulls,' said Nancy. 'It's so that nobody falls over a precipice. There are six of us. If one tumbles, the other five hang on so that the one who tumbles doesn't tumble far.'

'Are there any precipices?' asked Roger.

'Dozens,' said Titty, 'and if there aren't we can easily make some.'

'There really are plenty,' said Peggy.

'We shan't go by the path,' said Nancy. 'When we come to a rock we'll go over it.'

'Let's begin,' said Roger. 'Who goes first? Can I?'

'No,' said John. 'The rope isn't a painter for you to jump ashore with. We must have somebody big in front. It ought to be Nancy. I'll take the other end.'

'We must make loops in it,' said Nancy. 'Six loops, big enough to stick our heads and shoulders through.'

It was done. There were about five yards between each loop. Nancy hung the first loop on herself. Mate Susan took the next, and after her came Able-Seaman Titty, Boy Roger, Mate Peggy, and Captain John.

'Now then,' said Nancy, 'everybody ready?'

'We ought really to have ice-axes,' said Titty.

Nancy heard her. 'I thought of that,' she said, 'but they'd get horribly in the way. Worse than the rope. Hands and feet are better, especially on the rocks.'

The long procession moved off. Just at first the rope made it difficult to talk. This was because when anyone wanted to talk to the one in front he hurried on and tripped over loose rope, while at the same time he stretched the rope taut behind him and so gave a disturbing jerk to someone else. By the time they had learnt to talk without hurrying forward or hanging back they were climbing slopes so steep that nobody wanted to talk at all. There were things to shout, such as 'Don't touch this rock. It's a loose one', but mostly it was grim, straight-ahead, silent climbing.

At the start they had been scrambling up beside the tiny mountain beck that was now all that was left to remind them of the river far down below them in the valley. But as soon as they had come to a place from which they had had a clear view of the summit, Nancy, the leader, had turned directly towards it, and within a minute or two everybody had learnt how useful it is on a mountain to have four legs instead of two. Sometimes Nancy turned to left or right to avoid loose screes, but when she came to a rock that could be climbed, she climbed it, and all the rest of the explorers climbed it after her.

'The really tough bit's still to come,' she said cheerfully.

The tough bit came when nobody expected it, and the explorers were very glad they had a rope in spite of its being such a bother from the talking point of view. They had come to a steep face of rock, not really very difficult, because there were cracks running across it which made good footholds and handholds, but not a good place to tumble down, because there was nothing to stop you and there were a lot of loose stones at the bottom of it. Nancy had gone up it easily enough, and Susan after her. Titty was just crawling over the edge at the top of it, and Peggy and John were waiting at the bottom ready to start, when suddenly Roger, who was about half-way up, shouted out 'Look! Look! Wild goats!'

If he had done no more than shout all would have been well, but he tried to point at the same time. His other hand slipped. He swung round. His feet lost their places on the narrow ledges, and the word 'goats' ended in a squeak. The rope tautened with a jerk and pulled Titty back half over the edge. Susan and even Nancy herself were almost jerked off their feet on the grassy slope above the rock. It was lucky that they had moved on from the edge and had the rope almost stretched between them.

Roger dangled against the face of the rock, about four feet from the bottom, scrabbling like a spider at the end of his silk thread. Titty had grabbed a clump of heather and was being held where she was by Susan and Nancy who were now hanging on to the rope as hard as they could, and had dug their feet into the slope.

'Pull, pull!' called Titty.

'It's all right, Roger,' said John. 'Let me have hold of your feet and I'll put them in the good places. Stop kicking.'

The scrabbling stopped, and Roger felt his feet being planted from below.

'Now then, start climbing again, or you'll be bringing Titty down on top of you.'

The moment Roger began to climb, he took his weight off the rope and Nancy and Susan pulling together found the weight suddenly less. Titty came head first over the edge and was up on the grass above the rock.

'Keep on pulling', she panted, 'or he may go flop again. But don't pull too hard.' She crawled on as well as she could. She had had much the worst of it, and had scratched her elbows and knees slipping back over the edge of the rock.

Roger's voice came cheerfully from below.

'Did you see the goats?'

'Never mind goats,' called Susan from above. 'Is he hurt?'

'Only another scrape,' said Roger, 'but *did* you see the goats? There they are again.'

'Don't point!' shouted John, just in time.

'I must,' said Roger. But he didn't. 'There! There! You'll see them again in a minute. There they go. Right up by the top.'

The topmost peak of Kanchenjunga was directly above the explorers. But to the right of it, as they looked up, the huge shoulders of the mountain, lower than the peak itself but high in the sky above them, swept round to the north, and it was up there, almost behind the explorers, that Roger, looking over his shoulder as he climbed, had seen things moving on the grey stone slopes under the top of the crags. Up and up they were going, now close under the skyline. Just as John and Peggy caught sight of them they crossed the skyline, tiny, dark things, goats cut out of black cardboard against the pale blue of the morning sky.

'I see them,' called Titty.

'Five,' said John.

'There's one more,' said Roger.

A moment later they were gone.

'Well, I'm glad we've seen them,' said Roger.

'Get on up to the top of the rock,' said John. 'And don't look for any more. If it hadn't been for Titty and the others hanging on to the rope you might have broken your leg.'

'And no stretcher to carry me on.'

Roger hurried up with his climbing and was soon on the grass slope above the rock, being looked over by Susan. Neither she nor Nancy had seen the wild goats, so naturally they thought more about the accident.

'Shiver my timbers,' said Nancy, 'but that was a narrow go. We really ought to have waited at the top, taking in rope hand over hand so he couldn't slip. But you can't allow for everything. Who would have thought of his seeing goats just at that moment? If they were goats. Probably sheep.'

'They were goats all right,' said Peggy, climbing up. 'We all saw them.'

'All right,' said Nancy. 'Goats. But not such goats as some people I know. What about you, Able-Seaman? Are you hurt too?'

Titty had been trying to lick the blood off her right elbow, but had found that she could not reach it, and anyway it wasn't really bleeding enough to matter.

'Lucky it was Roger who fell and not John,' said Nancy. 'Not so heavy, for one thing, and if it had been John, what would have become of the grog?'

They were more careful after that, and there were no more accidents. The last few yards up to the top of the peak were easy going. The explorers met and crossed the rough path that they might have followed from the bottom and then, with the cairn that marked the summit now in full view before them, they wriggled out of the loops in the rope and raced for it. John and Nancy reached the cairn together. Roger and Titty came next. Mate Susan had stopped to coil the rope and Mate Peggy had waited to help her carry it.

All this time the explorers had been climbing up the northern side of the peak of Kanchenjunga. The huge shoulder of the mountain had shut out from them everything that there was to the west. As they climbed, other hills in the distance seemed to be climbing too, and when they looked back into the valley they had left, it seemed so small that they could hardly believe that there had been room to row about along that bright thread in the meadows that they knew was the river. But it was not until the last rush to the top, not until they were actually standing by the cairn that marked the highest point of Kanchenjunga, that they could see what lay beyond the mountain.

Then indeed they knew that they were on the roof of the world.

Far, far away, beyond range after range of low hills, the land ended and the sea began, the real sea, blue water stretching on and on until it met the sky. There were white specks of sailing ships, coasting schooners, probably, and little black plumes of smoke showed steamers on their way to Ireland or on their way back or working up or down between Liverpool and the Clyde. And forty miles away or more there was a short dark line on the blue field of the sea. 'Due west from here,' said John, looking at the compass in his hand. 'It's the Isle of Man.'

'Look back the other way,' said Peggy.

'You can see right into Scotland,' said Nancy. 'Those hills over there are the other side of the Solway Firth.'

'And there's Scawfell, and Skiddaw, and that's Helvellyn, and the pointed one's Ill Bell, and there's High Street, where the Ancient Britons had a road along the top of the mountains.'

'Where's Carlisle?' asked Titty. 'It must be somewhere over there.'

'How do you know?' asked Nancy.

' "And the red glare on Skiddaw roused the burghers of Carlisle". Probably in those days they didn't have blinds in bedroom windows.'

'We know that one, too,' said Peggy. 'But not all of it. It's worse than "Casabianca".'

'I like it because of the beacons,' said Titty.

John and Roger had no eyes for mountains while they could see blue water and ships, however far away.

'If we went on and on, beyond the Isle of Man, what would we come to?' asked Roger.

'Ireland, I think,' said John, 'and then probably America . . .'

'And if we still went on?'

'Then there'd be the Pacific and China.'

'And then?'

John thought for a minute. 'There'd be all Asia and then all Europe and then there'd be the North Sea and then we'd be coming up the other side of those hills.' He looked back towards the hills beyond Rio and the hills beyond them, and the hills beyond them again, stretching away, fold upon fold, into the east.

'Then we'd have gone all round the world.'

'Of course.'

'Let's.'

'We will some day. Daddy's done it.'

'So has Uncle Jim,' said Peggy.

'Of course, you couldn't see round, however high you were,' said Roger.

'You wouldn't want to,' said Titty. 'Much better fun not knowing what was coming next.'

'Well, up here you're properly on the roof.' Nancy threw herself down on the warm ground. 'What about that nectar? Oh, I say, I've forgotten all about it and let you carry it all the way up.'

'That's all right.' John brought the big bottle out of his knapsack, and the mug began to make its rounds with lemonade rather warm after its journey, while Susan and Peggy were cutting up the bunloaf and opening the last of the pemmican tins, and Nancy emptied out the doughnuts.

'I wonder whether anybody's ever had dinner on the top of Kanchenjunga before?' said Titty, when she had eaten her share of pemmican and was finishing off with a doughnut.

'They must have done, when they built the cairn,' said Peggy. 'Think of the time it must have taken to build up all those stones.'

'Perhaps it didn't take any time,' said Titty. 'Perhaps some tribe or other had won a victory, and everybody brought one stone and put it there.'

'But they'd have a feast after that,' said Roger. 'Can I climb up the cairn?'

'No,' said Susan. 'You've had one tumble already, and there aren't thousands of us to build the cairn up again if you go and bring it down.'

'It's very well built.'

'That just shows the people who built it didn't want ship's boys to pull it down.'

'I'll be very careful.'

'Have an apple.'

'May I lean against the cairn?'

'Anything you like so long as you don't start climbing on it.'

Roger sat down with his back against the cairn, so as to be less tempted to climb it. It seemed a pity not to and so be a few feet higher even than the top of Kanchenjunga. He would climb it, he thought, next year or perhaps the year after. In the meantime . . . He looked down towards Swallowdale somewhere on the moors so far below, tried to see Wild Cat Island, but could not be sure if he had, watched a steamer moving at the low end of the lake, looked out to sea and then, when he had eaten his apple, rolled over and began feeling the stones at the foot of the cairn. Was it so very well built, after all? . . . 'Look, look! What's this?'

In his hand was a small round brass box with the head of an old lady stamped on the lid of it. Framing the head of the old lady were big printed letters: 'QUEEN OF ENGLAND EMPRESS OF INDIA DIAMOND JUBILEE 1897.' Roger had found a loose stone at the foot of the cairn, had pulled it out, and seen the little brass box hidden behind it.

'She must be Queen Victoria,' said John. 'She came before Edward the Seventh.'

'There's something inside,' said Roger, shaking the box.

'Let's open it,' said Nancy.

'I'll open it,' said Roger, and he did. Inside was a folded bit of paper and a farthing with the head of Queen Victoria on it.

'Take care,' said Titty. 'It may be a treasure chart. It may be a deadly secret. It may crumble at a touch. They often do.'

But the paper was strong enough. Roger let Nancy unfold it. She opened it, began reading it aloud, and then stopped. Peggy took it and read it aloud, while the others looked at it over her shoulder. It was written in black pencil that had scored deeply into the paper:

> August the 2nd. 1901.
> We climbed the Matterhorn.
> Molly Turner.
> J. Turner.
> Bob Blackett.

'That's mother and Uncle Jim,' said Peggy in a queer voice.

'Who is Bob Blackett?' asked Susan.

'He was father,' said Nancy.

Nobody said anything for a minute, and then Titty, looking at the paper, said 'So that was what they called it. Well, it's Kanchenjunga now. It's no good changing it now we've climbed it.'

'That was thirty years ago,' said John . . .

'Why did they put the farthing in it?' wondered Roger.

'Let's put it all back,' said Titty hurriedly. 'They meant it to stay for a thousand years . . .'

'Has anybody got a bit of paper?' said Nancy suddenly.

Nobody had, but Titty had a stump of pencil. Nancy took it and wrote firmly on the back of the paper on which her father and mother and uncle had set forth their triumph of thirty years before:

Aug. 11. 1931
We climbed Kanchenjunga.

'Now,' she said, 'we all sign here', and she wrote her name. 'You next, Captain John. Then the two mates, and then the able-seaman and the ship's boy.'

Everybody signed. Then Nancy folded up the paper, put it back in the box with the farthing, and gave it to Roger.

'You found it,' she said. 'You put it back, and then perhaps in another thirty years . . .' She broke off, but presently laughed. 'Shiver my timbers,' she said, 'but I wish we had a George the Fifth farthing.'

'I've got a new halfpenny,' said Roger.

'Can you spare it?'

'I'll give you another if you can't,' said John, 'when we get back to the camp.'

Roger dug out his halfpenny. The box was closed and pushed far back into the hole at the foot of the cairn. Roger wedged the loose stone firmly in its place.

'Nobody'd ever guess there was anything there,' said Roger. 'I wouldn't have found it if the stone hadn't worked loose.'

'And now perhaps it won't be found for ages and ages till people wear quite different sorts of clothes,' said Titty. 'Perhaps it'll be more explorers just like us. I wonder how big Captain Flint was then?'

'I wonder if they had a clear day for it,' said Peggy.

'And saw the Isle of Man,' said Roger.

They looked out to sea.

'Hullo,' said John. 'We can't see it any more.'

'I saw it a minute ago,' said Titty.

'There must be a fog out at sea,' said John. 'What luck that we came up early while it was still so clear.'

'Come along,' said Nancy suddenly. 'Remember we've got to get down to Watersmeet and then to Beckfoot and then sail to Horseshoe Cove and carry our tent up to Swallowdale. We ought to be starting.'

'Where's the rope?' said Roger.

'I'll carry the rope,' said Nancy. 'We used it all right coming up. I don't see why we shouldn't use the path going down. It'll be lots quicker.'

A minute or two later, after a last look round from the top of the world, the six explorers, who had climbed Kanchenjunga as Kanchenjunga should be climbed, were hurrying down the mountain at a good jog-trot.

Arthur Ransome, *Swallowdale*

Welsh Beginning

To begin, then, in the early days, along paths described so often and so competently: to begin with a cottage in North Wales. There, at Ffestiniog, they said my grandfather had stepped out of the train on a blank and misty morning, sniffed the air, and announced that 'this is the place'. It could be blank; it was usually misty; but the white walls of our cottage of Bryn Hyfryd welcomed us the more through the mist; and the hills no less, on the rare occasions when they showed far and smiling faces to us, peeping over the Bala moors. The faces and shapes of those Ffestiniog mountains came, in fact, when we were small, to present very distinct and individual outlines. Each summit from each angle had its own quality. Moelwyn smiled at us from Ffestiniog, but frowned when you saw him from Harlech and the Portmadoc sea direction; which was strange, because he actually appeared his real height from there, and not smaller than his younger brother. Moelwyn Bach ('the lesser') looked higher from Ffestiniog, on which side he frowned, but smiled at Harlech way over a row of jutty rocks that represented his teeth. The other hills had their own characteristics: Manod, 'the plum-pudding', Moel yr Hydd, 'the jelly', and even, later, the queenly Snowdon with her airy hut crown.

Our holiday imagination played with the buttresses and outcrops of special importance. At the very first it had been the immediate streams and hayfields that attracted our young attention. The Moelwyns loomed, but as a background. A daily anxiety over weather meant a rush to our parents' bedroom, first thing, to see whether they were 'out of cloud'. Hence gradually a longing to climb the shapes that beckoned insistently from every angle; to see whether the skyline edges were as steep as they looked; to follow the line of white quartz that pointed like an arrow straight up the face of Manod from the lake at its foot; to discover whether these things were the same when we got to them.

At eight I was allowed up Manod, a little over 2,000 feet. We had no other special hobby that might distract us; thence perhaps we were the more ready to be friendly with the mountain features themselves. We collected caterpillars, yes. We made models boats and we worshipped swords and knives and aeroplanes. But, when we saw Moelwyn, there was no attraction on his sides, butterfly or bird or flower, to compete with the soaring rock edge of 'Little Finger Crag', and no fish in the streams that could tempt us to picnic away from those brown summit grass slopes . . . The black cave in the face of Moelwyn Bach, which had lured from afar for many years, proved in the end a depressing mossy hole. But 'the crags' which Moelwyn extended like fingers gave a fine afternoon's traverse, and the shiny 'teeth' of Moel yr Hydd a rock climb from which I breathed thankfully for escape. Then came our older cousins – Nigel Kirkus first, then Guy – bitten with the rock-climbing madness. They spared a holiday to come with us and guide our feet on more educated scrambles. The idea of climbing rocks for themselves came thus slowly. We would try to find energetic patches on the north ridge of Tryfan, or in the 'valley of the slaboids', which we named in honour of the plodgy tramp back. Guy talked, and well; he was also a person to admire, for his own feats and for his admiration of the feats of Colin, the eldest. To Guy, rock climbing was natural and great because Colin climbed. And to us it must be all the greater . . . I came to long more and more for the first 'real' rock climb, for the introduction into the sport by the high-grade expert.

It came in the Easter holiday of 1934, under the leadership of Guy. The boots had been brought very specially according to Colin's specifications; the bus ride from Bettws y Coed, gateway to the mountains (and why were the inhabitants so unconscious of their dignity as gate-keepers) had left me on the steps of Ogwen Cottage. It is set in the hollow of black cliffs that group themselves round the gloomy name of the legendary Idwal. To the climber it mattered not at all that the cottage looked bleak and Mrs Jones a little dragonish. I did not know that the reputation of Ogwen Cottage as the climbing centre of the district lingered long after the great climbers had left it. The mutton seemed fair enough, and Mrs Jones was prepared to dry 'the Boots'. 'The Boots' had become the centre of my life. I ran out after supper to practise them, found that they were not so supremely gluey in contact with rock as I had hoped, and reckoned myself deceived and discomfited. The nail-makers were cheats. But the next morning came Guy, tramping easily beside a shepherd from Helyg, and we left for Tryfan and real rock climbing. We passed the Milestone Buttress ('the brightest jewel in Ogwen's crown' had said a guide-book) because it was too crowded; Easter had decked its worn slabs with a varied and colourful humanity. We tramped, for the first climb and the first of many times, up the Heather Terraces.

I am still not certain what it is that makes Tryfan the most lovable mountain in the world – partly the symmetry of it seen from the east, three heathery buttresses rising from the rough horizontal break of the terrace into three separate summits; and of these the central and highest crowned by the twin monolithic blocks, Adam and Eve, a relation far too strange surely for Nature of herself to have been its parent. Partly I have loved the rough feel of Tryfan's rock, and the mountain is rocky on every side. There is comfort in the friendly grey grip of it, and in the huge excrescences and incuts that top its squared grooves. Maybe it is not suitable to beginners, to agile persons who can jump and grab and know that their strong arms will find something. The Idwal slabs, smoother and more delicate, are a fitter gymnasium in which to learn balance and footwork. But it would be hard to deny the pleasurable mountain feel of Tryfan to a very beginner, or the joy of emerging by a rock route at its summit. I found the first grooves of the North Buttress desperately strugglesome, scratched smooth, as they were, by nailed boots. But each ledge provided its friendly bollard and resting-place, and perhaps a bilberry couch. Rocks at an easy angle, the rope above, panorama incomparable towards the lower uplands – here was felicity. That day we climbed North Buttress and the Gashed Crag route on the South Buttress. One 'Moderately Difficult' and one 'Difficult'. I read their history in the evening. A slippery slab above the Gashed Crag I could not climb, but found 'the Boots' scrabbling in a hot determination not to leave me stranded like a fish on a line; it was, after all, only standard 'Difficult' . . .

The next holiday was to be with Colin, now recovered from the Ben Nevis accident in which he was badly injured and Maurice Linnell killed. We stayed at Idwal Youth Hostel; the first evening I walked up to meet him on his way back from the cliffs. Lean, nervous, tattered, a cigarette in a long holder streaming a smoke behind him, he said very little until he came to suggest, with a glint, the Monolith Crack for after supper. The crack held for a long time the reputation of being the hardest climb in North Wales. The Abrahams themselves called it more difficult than the Devil's Kitchen, if not quite so dangerous. The main pitch is a thin rift cut deep into the small Gribin rock face. The Abrahams, who were large of build, had been forced to climb it on the outside, with great difficulty. We, said Colin, get right in now and wriggle up. We left before dusk and roped at the foot. There followed something like this, of thoughtful monologue:

'Roped all right, this first pitch easy. Now Colin's inside and up the long crack. Looks difficult . . . but once inside said to be easier . . . and safer. My turn. Pushed in, difficult. Then to get up. Whole thing smooth, "worn smooth" they say. A foot jammed across, heave up, the thing comes out. Back below, where we started, no breath, sweating pig-like. Body twist, the knees grating the sides, trousers too thin. That graze will be painful later, don't feel it now. Fingers scrabble; one on a ledge, get the other on, pull up, even the hair seems to stick. No matter how bloody later, let's get there now . . . Thank God I'm up; I've been praying long enough.'

Wilfred Noyce, *Men and Mountains*

CHAPTER 27

—◆—

Mountains Domestic

After the Second World War more people than ever before took holidays in the mountains of Great Britain, whether to climb or to walk. W.H. Murray has a unique gift for the description of the physical acrobatics of rock-climbing, and in the passage below records an ascent of Cir Mhor in Arran, by the Rosa Pinnacle, which he made with Norman Tennent and his wife Mona in 1949. For those who are less athletic, but who love mountains and fells, A. Wainwright's detailed Lakeland guides have an unsurpassed appeal. His description of Skiddaw leaves no doubt of his own preference for fell-walking over rock-climbing.

◆ ◆ ◆

The Perfect Rock Climb

The buttress had narrowed, and might henceforth be more aptly called a ridge. Sixty feet above, it whipped up again. The edge overhung and looked unclimbable. Reconnaissance showed that we might turn it to the right or left by long traverses, though it was not clear by what means we should arrive back at the crest. If we went left I guessed that we might now arrive at the Lay-back Crack which was, Hamilton had sworn, an experience not to be missed. Therefore we made the left traverse – a walk on rolling slabs for a hundred feet or more – while the ridge continued to rise on our right. Our soothing slabs at length upended in a great wave against a greater vertical wall, which barred the ridge. In the angle between this wall and the flank of the ridge we saw a long crack. It was the only breach, and lay on a tilt from left to right. Underneath the crack a similarly tilting slab gave Tennent and me footing. I would not call it a good stance. None the less it gave a flake-belay at knee-level. Tennent could tie on, lean back on the light rope, and say honestly that he was safe, perjuriously that he *felt* safe.

Our climb back to the crest looked about sixty feet. I was alarmed at the prospect of having to make all that height by the lay-back technique: it is most exhausting. When a thin crack divides right-angled walls, which are holdless, one may grasp the edge of the crack (which must be sharp), place the flat of the feet against the opposing wall, then lean back on the hands and walk up. The pull of the hands against the push of the feet masters gravity. This difficult technique is made easier for a man short in the leg, but for a long-legged animal like me few things are more tiring. He is doubled up and straining all the time.

What the top part of the pitch was like I could not properly see on account of a sun-shaft streaming across the ridge straight into my eyes. So blinding was the stream that I was doubtful of seeing the holds even when I got to them. Although usually leader, Tennent is also the complete second. He produced a white sun-hat and clapped it on my head. I pulled down the brim and started. By lay-back technique I made no more height than two feet. I stepped down and looked again. It seemed that one did not start with a lay-back. I tried instead a rounded foothold on the left wall, and then took the lay-back position a foot higher than before. I moved up successfully, shifting the hands a few inches, then the feet a few inches, then the hands, until at ten feet I saw an excellent blunt spike ahead of me which I just managed to grasp with a quick movement. One heave pulled me on to its top. That was the perfectly sited resting-place. I stopped for a while and panted. I was in good training, but lay-backs are not my forte. Whatever happened I swore I would not continue up the crack, for its edge had become rounded. I looked rightwards. Across a wide expanse of wall and slab ran a chain of irregular knobs. I crept out on them for six feet to a point where the chain broke, but continued four feet higher, swinging sharply up. Obviously I had to use the knobs now as handholds instead of footholds. The point of real difficulty was the first step at the break. The right foot had to be planted on a steep slab and trusted for friction-grip, while the body swung over and up to use the higher hand-rail.

I was still unaware whether all would be well. At each move of the circling traverse I feared another break in the chain, feared it especially in the absence of a definite foothold. However, the uncertainty was soon over, because there could be no loitering on that rock. I kept going at top speed, and emerged once more on the sharp crest of the ridge. Just over its edge was a grassy hollow big enough for three bodies to stretch out in comfort – a sun-trap – the perfect archetypal stance.

I fetched up Tennent. I expected Mona to have difficulty, for women are not muscularly as strong as men. The traverse being delicate, any leg-tremble or arm-shake due to muscular exhaustion at the crux would be fatal. But she arrived at the top more speedily than either of us, and by skill distinctly fresher than me. We resolved that this was lunch-time, less because we wanted lunch than because the hollow was made to be lunched on – it appealed to our hearts rather than to our stomachs. The ridge above us overhung in a high nose. On all sides we saw nothing but empty space, into which the crest of our ridge projected like the keel of an upturned boat. It was sunlit space, and sun-washed granite, and the sun's heat smote full upon us. A cool breeze made all that sun endurable. Looking back upon the scene I wonder that we ever prevailed upon ourselves to stir. There we should have lain, I think, until the hills crumbled into dust, satisfied in one part of our nature by sloth and ease, and in another by the liveliness of beauty, had it not been for that third part, which brews energy and would always be stirring up trouble. In a quarter of an hour I was on my feet again.

The route goes to the left of the great overhang by triple chimneys spaced in vertical tiers. The total height may be a hundred feet. The first two gave plenty of muscular work and asked for little skill. The last was the type and epitome of all three. Under Chimney III Tennent belayed me in a right-angled corner between the ridge and an open wall to its left. On this left wall was the chimney. It was only ten feet high, exposed, and overhanging at the top where a big stone was jammed. The ascent was crude work at the top – a pull up on the stone – none the less giving unadulterated joy: it is so safe, yet the body swings free over thin air, the muscles tighten exhilaratingly; the climber within revels in what Tennent derisively reminded me was 'a glorious out-of-balance movement'.

Beyond the barrier the angle eased. We climbed together up gentle slabs to the Terrace below the final tower. The Terrace is a grassy scoop inclining obliquely right to left, by which one may walk off the buttress. Such a dismal detour would be taken by no man in his right senses. Straight ahead soars the rock of the pinnacle. From its sharp *arête* enormous slabs slope down to the left, overlapping each other in tiers. At each overlap is a vertical wall of ten to thirty feet.

We started our first slab at its lower left-hand edge. By a long ladder of tiny cobbles we came in a hundred feet to a vertical chimney splitting the first overlap. The holds were big. So, at each tier, the slabs yielded in the same way – a slender line, usually a crack, giving passage to the next wall. Towards the top we kept to the right-hand *arête*, where our way poised us on the edge of the great eastern cliff. The granite was rough as ever, and having been exposed to the sun since dawn, was hot to the hand. We climbed on ideal rock, on an ideal mountain, in ideal weather – the kind of mountain-day we dream about on raw nights in November – or at midsummer dawns in Glen Rosa. Our dream, after all, had passed not through the gate of ivory but through the gate of horn.

We came out on the topmost point of Rosa Pinnacle aware that something unique had happened to us: we had had the best summer rock-climb of our lives.

W.H. Murray, *Undiscovered Scotland*

Skiddaw

Make no mistake about Skiddaw.

Heed not the disparaging criticisms that have been written from time to time, often by learned men who ought to have known better, about this grand old mountain. It is an easy climb, yes; its slopes are smooth and grassy, yes; it has no frightful precipices, no rugged outcrops, agreed; it offers nothing of interest or entertainment to rock-gymnasts, agreed. If these are failings, they must be conceded. But are they not quite minor failings? Are they failings at all?

Skiddaw is the fourth highest peak in Lakeland and but little lower than the highest, Scafell Pike. It is the oldest mountain in the district, according to the evidence of its rocks, definitely not the most impressive in appearance, but certainly one of the noblest. The summit is buttressed magnificently by a circle of lesser heights, all of them members of the Skiddaw family, the whole forming a splendid and complete example of the structure of mountains, especially well seen from all directions because of its isolation. Its lines are smooth, its curves graceful; but because the slopes are steep elsewhere, the quick build-up of the massif from valley levels to central summit is appreciated at a glance - and it should be an appreciative glance, for such massive strength and such beauty of outline rarely go together . . . Here on Skiddaw they do.

Geographically, too, the mountain is of great importance, its main ridge forming the watershed between the Derwent and the Eden. This feature emphasises Skiddaw's supremacy over the rest of the northern fells, for, although situated in the south-west corner of the group, the waters from its eastern slopes cut through the middle of this outlying barrier to augment the drainage from the Pennines - and not even the neighbouring Blencathra, much more handily placed to the east, has been able to accomplish this feat. Engineers have noticed this enterprise on the part of Skiddaw and are planning to impound its eastern flow in a reservoir at Calder Head.

Skiddaw has special interests for geologists. It is apparent, even to unobservant walkers, that the stones covering the summit and exposed in eroded gullies and valleys are very different in character from those seen in the central parts of the district: the latter are of volcanic origin, those on Skiddaw are marine deposits and consist in the main of soft shale or slate which splits readily into thin wafers and soon decays and crumbles when exposed to the atmosphere; hence it has no commercial value.

Skiddaw was formed long before the volcanos of central Lakeland became active; later it overlooked a vast glacier system, a world of ice. Some volcanic boulders are found along the lower southern slopes of the Skiddaw group: these rocks have been identified with those of the cliffs enclosing St John's in the Vale, having been carried along and deposited here when the glaciers retreated and scoured the flanks of Skiddaw on their passage to the frozen sea.

Skiddaw displays a quite different appearance to each of the four points of the compass. The southern aspect is a very familiar sight to visitors, being an unrestricted view from Derwentwater, the Borrowdale fells and most of the higher summits of Lakeland. There is a classical quality about this view from the south. Skiddaw and its outliers rise magnificently across the wide Vale of Keswick in a beautifully symmetrical arrangement, as if posed for a family photograph. The old man himself is the central figure at the back of the group, with his five older children in a line before him (the favourite son, Little Man, being placed nearest) and the two younger children at the front. (Finicky readers who dispute this analogy because no mother of the brood is included in the picture (this is admitted, all the characters being masculine except sweet little Latrigg) are proffered the explanation that Skiddaw is a widower, the old lady having perished in the Ice Age – she couldn't stand the cold).

The western aspect is best known to Bassenthwaite folk, who enjoy a secret delight few others have discovered – the glorious sunset colourings of the mountain, winter and summer alike: a beauty that brings people to their doors in rapt admiration. There is little beauty of outline, though, Skiddaw here appearing at its most massive, a great arc high in the sky, and the only shapeliness in the scene from the west is provided by the graceful cone of Ullock Pike and the curving ridge beyond. Two deep valleys, long shadowy recesses in the mountain, are conspicuous features.

Skiddaw, northwards, faces the unfrequented Uldale Fells, and not many regular visitors to Lakeland would recognise it in an uncaptioned photograph taken from this side. The northern aspect is truly impressive nonetheless; not quite so overpowering as when viewed from Bassenthwaite to the west, but having now a greater majesty and dignity. The summit ridge is seen end-on and appears as a neat pyramid overtopping the sprawling mass of Broad End, below which is the remarkable combe of Dead Crags. All waters coming down this side of Skiddaw, as those on the south and west, in due course reach the Derwent.

The east slopes of the mountain, collectively known as Skiddaw Forest, dominate the vast upland basin of Calder Head, a scene more suggestive of a Scottish glen than of Lakeland, a place incredibly wild and desolate and bare, its loneliness accentuated by the solitary dwellings of Skiddaw House, yet strongly appealing and, in certain lights, often strangely beautiful. In this great hollow the waters unite to form the River Calder, an important feeder of the Eden. Skiddaw is least impressive from the east because there is much less fall on this side. The scene is in view, although not intimately, from Blencathra.

This, then, is Skiddaw, a giant in stature. But an affable and friendly giant.

And a benevolent one. Keswick people have an inborn affection for Skiddaw, and it is well earned. The mountain makes a great contribution to the scenic beauty of this most attractively-situated town, shelters it from northerly gales, supplies it with pure water, feeds its sheep and provides a recreation ground for its visitors. Throughout the centuries Skiddaw's beacon has warned of the town's troubles and alarms – 'the red glare on Skiddaw roused the burghers of Carlisle' – and today shares in its rejoicings.

Skiddaw's critics have passed on, or will soon pass on. Their span of life is short. Skiddaw has stood there in supreme majesty, the sole witness to the creation of Lakeland, for millions of years and will be there to the end of time, continuing to give service and pleasure to insignificant and unimportant mortals.

Let us at least be grateful.

A. Wainwright, *The Northern Fells*

CHAPTER 28

❥

Descent from Annapurna

Annapurna proved one of the most difficult of the Himalayan peaks to climb. Its conquest in 1950 by a French group led by Maurice Herzog was one of the great post-war climbing achievements; its summit was at that time the highest point yet reached by climbers. But the triumph was bought at a terrible price: though every member of the expedition returned alive, the leader, by the end of the expedition, had lost all his toes and fingers through frostbite. What follows is his own account of the descent from the summit.

◆ ◆ ◆

Mission Accomplished

> A fierce and savage wind tore at us.
> We were on top of Annapurna! 8075 metres, 26,493 feet.
> Our hearts overflowed with an unspeakable happiness.
> 'If only the others could know . . .'
> If only everyone could know!

The summit was a corniced crest of ice, and the precipices on the far side, which plunged vertically down beneath us, were terrifying, unfathomable. There could be few other mountains in the world like this. Clouds floated half way down, concealing the gentle, fertile valley of Pokhara, 23,000 feet below. Above us there was nothing!

Our mission was accomplished. But at the same time we had accomplished something infinitely greater. How wonderful life would now become! What an inconceivable experience it is to attain one's ideal and, at the very same moment, to fulfil oneself. I was stirred to the depths of my being. Never had I felt happiness like this – so intense and yet so pure. That brown rock, the highest of them all, that ridge of ice – were these the goals of a lifetime? Or were they, rather, the limits of man's pride?

'Well, what about going down?'

Lachenal shook me. What were his own feelings? Did he simply think he had finished another climb, as in the Alps? Did he think one could just go down again like that, with nothing more to it?

'One minute, I must take some photographs.'

'Hurry up!'

I fumbled feverishly in my sack, pulled out the camera, took out the little French flag which was right at the bottom and the pennants . . . It was impossible to build a cairn; there were no stones and everything was frozen. Lachenal stamped his feet; he felt them freezing. I felt mine freezing too, but paid little attention. The highest mountain to be climbed by man lay under our feet! The names of our predecessors on these heights chased each other through my mind: Mummery, Mallory and Irvine, Bauer, Welzenbach, Tilman, Shipton. How many of them were dead – how many had found on these mountains what, to them, was the finest end of all . . .

Pictures passed through my mind – the Chamonix valley, where I had spent the most marvellous moments of my childhood, Mont Blanc, which so tremendously impressed me! I was a child when I first saw 'the Mont Blanc people' coming home, and to me there was a queer look about them; a strange light shone in their eyes.

'Come on, straight down,' called Lachenal.

He had already done up his sack and started going down. I took out my little pocket aneroid: 8,500 metres. I smiled. I swallowed a little condensed milk and left the tube behind – the only trace of our passage. I did up my sack, put on my gloves and my glasses, seized my ice-axe; one look round and I, too, hurried down the slope. Before disappearing into the couloir I gave one last look at the summit which would henceforth be all our joy and our consolation.

Lachenal was already far below; he had reached the foot of the couloir. I hurried down in his tracks. I went as fast as I could, but it was dangerous going. At every step one had to take care that the snow did not break away beneath one's weight. Lachenal, going faster than I thought he was capable of, was now on the long traverse. It was my turn to cross the area of mixed rock and snow. At last I reached the foot of the rock-band. I had hurried and I was out of breath. I undid my sack. What had I been going to do? I could not say.

'My gloves!'

Before I had time to bend over, I saw them slide and roll. They went further and further straight down the slope. I remained where I was, quite stunned. I watched them rolling down slowly, with no appearance of stopping. The movement of those gloves was engraved in my sight as something ineluctable, irremediable, against which I was powerless. The consequences might be most serious. What was I to do?

'Quickly, down to Camp V.'

Rébuffat and Terray should be there. My concern dissolved like magic. I now had a fixed objective again: to reach the camp. Never for a minute did it occur to me to use as gloves the socks which I always carry in reserve for just such a mishap as this.

On I went, trying to catch up with Lachenal. It had been two o'clock when we reached the summit; we had started out at six in the morning; but I had to admit that I had lost all sense of time. I felt as if I were running, whereas in actual fact I was walking normally, perhaps rather slowly, and I had to keep stopping to get my breath. The sky was now covered with clouds, everything had become grey and dirty-looking. An icy wind sprang up, boding no good. We must push on! But where was Lachenal? I spotted him a couple of hundred yards away, looking as if he was never going to stop. And I had thought he was in indifferent form!

The clouds grew thicker and came right down over us; the wind blew stronger, but I did not suffer from the cold. Perhaps the descent had restored my circulation. Should I be able to find the tents in the mist? I watched the rib ending in the beak-like point which overlooked the camp. It was gradually swallowed up by the clouds, but I was able to make out the spearhead rib lower down. If the mist should thicken I would make straight for that rib and follow it down, and in this way I should be bound to come upon the tent.

Lachenal disappeared from time to time, and then the mist was so thick that I lost sight of him altogether. I kept going at the same speed, as fast as my breathing would allow.

The slope was now steeper; a few patches of bare ice followed the smooth stretches of snow. A good sign – I was nearing the camp. How difficult to find one's way in thick mist! I kept the course which I had set by the steepest angle of the slope. The ground was broken; with my crampons I went straight down walls of bare ice. There were some patches ahead – a few more steps. It was the camp all right, but there were *two* tents.

So Rébuffat and Terray had come up. What a mercy! I should be able to tell them that we had been successful, that we were returning from the top. How thrilled they would be!

I got there, dropping down from above. The platform had been extended, and the two tents were facing each other. I tripped over one of the guy-ropes of the first tent; there was movement inside – they had heard me. Rébuffat and Terray put their heads out.

'We've made it. We're back from Annapurna!'

Rébuffat and Terray received the great news with excitement and delight.

'But what about Biscante?' asked Terray anxiously.

'He won't be long. He was just in front of me! What a day – started out at six this morning – didn't stop . . . got up at last.'

Words failed me. I had so much to say. The sight of familiar faces dispelled the strange feeling that I had experienced since morning, and I became, once more, just a mountaineer.

Terray, who was speechless with delight, wrung my hands. Then the smile vanished from his face: 'Maurice – your hands!' There was an uneasy silence. I had forgotten that I had lost my gloves: my fingers were violet and white, and hard as wood. The other two stared at them in dismay – they realized the full seriousness of the injury. But still blissfully floating on a sea of joy remote from reality, I leant over towards Terray and said confidentially, 'You're in such splendid form, and you've done so marvellously, it's absolutely tragic you didn't come up there with us!'

'What I did was for the Expedition, my dear Maurice, and anyway you've got up, and that's a victory for the whole lot of us.'

I nearly burst with happiness. How could I tell him all that his answer meant to me? . . .

'Hi! Help! Help!'

'Biscante!' exclaimed the others.

Still half intoxicated and remote from reality, I had heard nothing. Terray felt a chill at his heart, and his thoughts flew to his partner on so many unforgettable climbs; together they had so often skirted death, and won so many splendid victories. Putting his head out, and seeing Lachenal clinging to the slope a hundred yards lower down, he dressed in frantic haste.

Out he went. But the slope was bare now; Lachenal had disappeared. Terray was horribly startled, and could only utter unintelligible cries. It was a ghastly moment for him. A violent wind sent the mist tearing by. Under the stress of emotion Terray had not realized how it falsified distances.

'Biscante! Biscante!'

He had spotted him, through a rift in the mist, lying on the slope much lower down than he had thought. Terray set his teeth, and glissaded down like a madman. How would he stop? How would he be able to brake, without crampons, on the wind-hardened snow? But Terray was a first-class skier, and with a jump turn he stopped beside Lachenal, who was concussed after his tremendous fall. In a state of collapse, with no ice-axe, balaclava, or gloves, and only one crampon, he gazed vacantly round him.

'My feet are frost-bitten. Take me down . . . take me down, so that Oudot can see to me.'

'It can't be done,' explained Terray regretfully. 'Can't you see we're in the middle of a storm . . . It'll be dark soon.'

But Lachenal was obsessed with the fear of amputation. With a gesture of despair he tore the axe out of Terray's hands and tried to force his way down, but soon saw the futility of his action, and resolved to climb up to the camp. While Terray cut steps without stopping, Lachenal, ravaged and exhausted as he was, dragged himself along on all fours.

Meanwhile, I had gone into Rébuffat's tent. He was appalled at the sight of my hands and, as rather incoherently I told him what we had done, he took a piece of rope and began flicking my fingers. Then he took off my boots, with great difficulty, for my feet were swollen, and beat my feet and rubbed me. We soon heard Terray giving Lachenal the same treatment in the other tent . . .

Outside the storm howled and the snow was still falling. The mist grew thicker and darkness came. As on the previous night we had to cling to the poles to prevent the tents being carried away by the wind. The only two air-mattresses were given to Lachenal and myself while Terray and Rébuffat both sat on ropes, rucksacks and provisions to keep themselves well off the snow. They rubbed, slapped, and beat us with a rope; sometimes the blows fell on the living flesh, and howls arose from both tents. Rébuffat per-severed; it was essential to continue, painful as it was. Gradually life returned to my feet as well as to my hands, and circulation started again. It was the same with Lachenal.

Now Terray summoned up the energy to prepare some hot drinks. He called to Rébuffat that he would pass him a mug, so two hands stretched out towards each other between the two tents and were instantly covered with snow. The liquid was boiling though at scarcely more than 60 degrees Centigrade. I swallowed it greedily and felt infinitely better.

The night was absolute hell. Frightful onslaughts of wind battered us incessantly, while the never-ceasing snow piled up on the tents . . .

As the night wore on the snow lay heavier on the tent, and once again I had the frightful feeling of being slowly and silently asphyxiated. Occa-sionally in an access of revolt I tried, with all the strength of which I was capable, to push off with both forearms the mass that was crushing me. These fearful exertions left me gasping for breath and I fell back into the same state as before. It was much worse than the previous night.

'Hi! Gaston! Gaston!'

I recognized Terray's voice.

'Time to be off!'

I heard the sounds without grasping their meaning. Was it light already? I was not in the least surprised that the other two had given up all thought of going to the top, and I did not at all grasp the measure of their sacrifice.

Outside the storm redoubled in violence. The tent shook and the fabric flapped alarmingly. It had usually been fine in the mornings: did this mean the monsoon was upon us? We knew it was not far off – could this be its first onslaught?

'Gaston! Are you ready?' Terray asked again.

'One minute,' answered Rébuffat. He did not have an easy job: he had to put my boots on and do everything to get me ready: I let myself be handled like a baby. In the other tent Terray finished dressing Lachenal, whose feet were still swollen and would not fit into his boots. So Terray gave him his own, which were bigger. To get Lachenal's on his own feet he had to make some slits in them. As a precaution he put a sleeping bag and some food into his sack, and shouted to us to do the same. Were his words lost in the storm? Or were we too intent on leaving this hellish place to listen to his instructions?

Lachenal and Terray were already outside.

'We're going down!' they shouted.

Then Rébuffat tied me on to the rope and we went out. There were only two ice-axes for the four of us, so Rébuffat and Terray took them as a matter of course. For a moment, as we left the two tents of Camp V, I felt childishly ashamed at abandoning all our good equipment.

Already the first rope seemed a long way down below us. We were blinded by the squalls of snow and we could not hear each other a yard away. We had both put on our *cagoules*, for it was very cold. The snow was apt to slide, and the rope often came in useful.

Ahead of us the other two were losing no time. Lachenal went first and, safeguarded by Terray, he forced the pace in his anxiety to get down. There were no tracks to show us the way, but it was engraved on all our minds – straight down the slope for 400 yards then traverse to the left for 150 to 200 yards to get to Camp IV. The snow was thinning and the wind less violent. Was it going to clear? We hardly dared to hope so. A wall of seracs brought us up short.

'It's to the left,' I said, 'I remember it perfectly.'

Somebody else thought it was to the right. We started going down again. The wind had dropped completely, but the snow fell in big flakes. The mist was thick, and, not to lose each other, we walked in line: I was third and I could barely see Lachenal, who was first. It was impossible to recognize any of the pitches. We were all experienced enough mountaineers to know that even on familiar ground it is easy enough to make mistakes in such weather – distances are deceptive, one cannot tell whether one is going up or down. We kept colliding with hummocks which we had taken for hollows. The mist, the falling snowflakes, the carpet of snow, all merged into the same whitish tone and confused our vision. The towering outlines of the seracs took on fantastic shapes and seemed to move slowly round us . . .

Were we too high or too low? No one could tell. Perhaps we had better try slanting over to the left! The snow was in a bad state, but we did not seem to realize the danger. We were forced to admit that we were not on the right route, so we retraced our steps and climbed up above the serac which overhung us – no doubt, we reflected, we should be on the right level now. With Rébuffat leading, we went back over the way which had cost us such an effort. I followed him jerkily, saying nothing, and determined to go on to the end. If Rébuffat had fallen I could never have held him . . .

Terray, when his turn came, charged madly ahead. He was like a force of nature: at all costs he would break down these prison walls that penned us in. His physical strength was exceptional, his will-power no less remarkable. Lachenal gave him considerable trouble. Perhaps he was not quite in his right mind. He said it was no use going on; we must dig a hole in the snow and wait for fine weather. He swore at Terray and called him a madman. Nobody but Terray would have been capable of dealing with him – he just tugged sharply on the rope and Lachenal was forced to follow.

We were well and truly lost . . .

Perhaps if we called, someone would hear us? Lachenal gave the signal, but snow absorbs sound, and his shout seemed to carry only a few yards. All four of us called out together: 'One . . . two . . . three . . . help!'

We got the impression that our united shout carried a long way, so we began again: 'One . . . two . . . three . . . help!' Not a sound in reply!

Now and again Terray took off his boots and rubbed his feet; the sight of our frost-bitten limbs had made him aware of the danger and he had the strength of mind to do something about it. Like Lachenal, he was haunted by the idea of amputation. For me, it was too late: my feet and hands, already affected from yesterday, were beginning to freeze up again.

We had eaten nothing since the day before, and we had been on the go the whole time, but man's resources of energy in face of death are inexhaustible. When the end seems imminent, there still remain reserves, though it needs tremendous willpower to call them up.

Time passed, but we had no idea of it. Night was approaching, and we were terrified, though none of us uttered a complaint. Rébuffat and I found a way we thought we remembered, but were brought to a halt by the extreme steepness of the slope – the mist turned it into a vertical wall. We were to find, next day, that at that moment we had been almost on top of the camp, and that the wall was the very one that sheltered the tents which would have been our salvation.

'We must find a crevasse.'

'We can't stay here all night!'

'A hole – it's the only thing.'

'We'll all die in it.'

Night had suddenly fallen and it was essential to come to a decision without wasting another minute; if we remained on the slope, we should be dead before morning. We should have to bivouac. What the conditions would be like, we could guess, for we all knew what it meant to bivouac above 23,000 feet.

With his axe Terray began to dig a hole. Lachenal went over to a snow-filled crevasse a few yards further on, then suddenly let out a yell and disappeared before our eyes. We stood helpless: would we, or rather would Terray and Rébuffat, have enough strength for all the manoeuvres with the rope that would be needed to get him out? The crevasse was completely blocked up save for the one little hole where Lachenal had fallen through.

'Hi! Lachenal!' called Terray.

A voice, muffled by many thicknesses of ice and snow, came up to us. It was impossible to make out what it was saying.

'Hi! Lachenal!'

Terray jerked the rope violently; this time we could hear.

'I'm here!'

'Anything broken?'

'No! It'll do for the night! Come along.'

This shelter was heaven-sent. None of us would have had the strength to dig a hole big enough to protect the lot of us from the wind. Without hesitation Terray let himself drop into the crevasse, and a loud 'Come on!' told us he had arrived safely. In my turn I let myself go: it was a proper toboggan slide. I shot down a sort of twisting tunnel, very steep, and about 30 feet long. I came out at great speed into the opening beyond and was literally hurled to the bottom of the crevasse. We let Rébuffat know he could come by giving a tug on the rope.

The intense cold of this minute grotto shrivelled us up, the enclosing walls of ice were damp and the floor a carpet of fresh snow; by huddling together there was just room for the four of us. Icicles hung from the ceiling and we broke some of them off to make more head room and kept little bits to suck – it was a long time since we had had anything to drink.

That was our shelter for the night. At least we should be protected from the wind, and the temperature would remain fairly even, though the damp was extremely unpleasant. We settled ourselves in the dark as best we could. As always in a bivouac, we took off our boots; without this precaution the constriction would cause immediate frost-bite. Terray unrolled the sleeping-bag which he had had the foresight to bring, and settled himself in relative comfort. We put on everything warm that we had, and to avoid contact with the snow I sat on the cine-camera. We huddled close up to each other, in search for a hypothetical position in which the warmth of all bodies could be combined without loss, but we could not keep still for a second.

We did not open our mouths – signs were less of an effort than words. Every man withdrew into himself and took refuge in his own inner world. Terray massaged Lachenal's feet; Rébuffat felt his feet freezing too, but he had sufficient strength to rub them himself. I remained motionless, unseeing. My feet and hands went on freezing, but what could be done? I attempted to forget suffering, to forget the passing of time, trying not to feel the devouring and numbing cold which insidiously gained upon us . . .

Terray generously tried to give me part of his sleeping-bag. He had understood the seriousness of my condition, and knew why it was that I said nothing and remained quite passive; he realized that I had abandoned all hope for myself. He massaged me for nearly two hours; his feet, too, might have frozen, but he did not appear to give the matter a thought. I found new courage simply in contemplating his unselfishness; he was doing so much to help me that it would have been ungrateful of me not to go on struggling to live. Though my heart was like a lump of ice itself, I was astonished to feel no pain. Everything material about me seemed to have dropped away. I seemed to be quite clear in my thoughts and yet I floated in a kind of peaceful happiness. There was still a breath of life in me, but it dwindled steadily as the hours went by. Terray's massage no longer had any effect upon me. All was over, I thought. Was not this cavern the most beautiful grave I could hope for? Death caused me no grief, no regret – I smiled at the thought.

After hours of torpor, a voice mumbled 'Daylight!' This made some impression on the others. I only felt surprised – I had not thought that daylight would penetrate so far down.

'Too early to start,' said Rébuffat.

A ghastly light spread through our grotto and we could just vaguely make out the shapes of each other's heads. A queer noise from a long way off came down to us – a sort of prolonged hiss. The noise increased. Suddenly I was buried, blinded, smothered beneath an avalanche of new snow. The icy snow spread over the cavern, finding its way through every gap in our clothing. I ducked my head between my knees and covered myself with both arms. The snow flowed on and on. There was a silence. We were not completely buried, but there was snow everywhere. We got up, taking care not to bang our heads against the ceiling of ice, and tried to shake ourselves. We were all in stockinged feet in the snow. The first thing to do was to find our boots.

Rébuffat and Terray began to search, and realized at once that they were blind. Yesterday they had taken off their glasses to lead us down and now they were paying for it. Lachenal was the first to lay hands upon a pair of boots. He tried to put them on, but they were Rébuffat's. Rébuffat tried to climb up the shoot down which we had come yesterday, and which the avalanche had followed in its turn.

'Hi, Gaston! What's the weather like?' called up Terray.

'Can't see a thing. It's blowing hard.'

We were still groping for our things. Terray found his boots and put them on awkwardly, unable to see what he was doing. Lachenal helped him, but he was all on edge and fearfully impatient, in striking contrast to my immobility. Terray then went up the icy channel, puffing and blowing, and at last reached the outer world. He was met by terrible gusts of wind that cut right through him and lashed his face.

'Bad weather,' he said to himself, 'this time it's the end. We're lost . . . we'll never come through.'

At the bottom of the crevasse there were still two of us looking for our boots. Lachenal poked fiercely with an ice-axe. I was calmer and tried to proceed more rationally. We extracted crampons and an axe in turn from the snow, but still no boots.

Well – so this cavern was to be our last resting-place! There was very little room – we were bent double and got in each other's way. Lachenal decided to go out without his boots. He called out frantically, hauled himself up on the rope, trying to get a hold or to wriggle his way up, digging his toes into the snow walls. Terray from outside pulled as hard as he could: I watched him go; he gathered speed and disappeared.

When he emerged from the opening, he saw the sky was clear and blue, and he began to run like a madman, shrieking. 'It's fine, it's fine!'

I set to work to search the cave. The boots *had* to be found, or Lachenal and I were done for. On all fours, with nothing on my hands or feet, I raked the snow, stirring it round this way and that, hoping every second to come upon something hard. I was no longer capable of thinking – I reacted like an animal fighting for its life.

I found one boot! The other was tied to it – a pair! Having ransacked the whole cave I at last found the other pair. But in spite of all my efforts I could not find the camera, and gave up in despair. There was no question of putting my boots on – my hands were like lumps of wood and I could hold nothing in my fingers; my feet were very swollen – I should never be able to get boots on them. I twisted the rope round the boots as well as I could and called up the shoot:

'Lionel . . . boots!'

There was no answer, but he must have heard, for with a jerk the precious boots shot up. Soon after the rope came down again. My turn. I wound the rope round me; I could not pull it tight, so I made a whole series of little knots. Their combined strength, I hoped, would be enough to hold me. I had no strength to shout again; I gave a great tug on the rope, and Terray understood . . .

Somehow or other I succeeded in working my way up, while Terray pulled so hard he nearly choked me. I began to see more distinctly and so knew that I must be nearing the opening. Often I fell back, but I clung on and wedged myself in as best I could. My heart was bursting and I was forced to rest. A fresh wave of energy enabled me to crawl to the top. I pulled myself out by clutching Terray's legs; *he* was just about all in and I was in the last stages of exhaustion. Terray was close to me and I whispered: 'Lionel . . . I'm dying!'

He supported me and helped me away from the crevasse. Lachenal and Rébuffat were sitting in the snow a few yards away. The instant Lionel let go of me I sank down and dragged myself along on all fours.

The weather was perfect. Quantities of snow had fallen the day before and the mountains were resplendent. Never had I seen them look so beautiful – our last day would be magnificent.

Rébuffat and Terray were completely blind; as he came along with me Terray knocked into things and I had to direct him. Rébuffat, too, could not move a step without guidance. It was terrifying to be blind when there was danger all round. Lachenal's frozen feet affected his nervous system. His behaviour was disquieting – he was possessed by the most fantastic idea:

'I tell you we must go down . . . down there . . .'

'You've nothing on your feet!'

'Don't worry about that.'

'You're off your head! The way is not there . . . it's to the left!'

He was already standing up; he wanted to go straight down to the bottom of the glacier. Terray held him back, made him sit down, and though he couldn't see, helped put his boots on.

Behind them I was living in my own private dream. I knew the end was near, but it was the end that all mountaineers wish for – an end in keeping with their ruling passion. I was consciously grateful to the mountains for being so beautiful for me that day, and as awed by their silence as if I had been in church. I was in no pain, and had no worry. My utter calmness was alarming. Terray came staggering towards me, and I told him: 'It's all over for me. Go on . . . you have a chance . . . you must take it . . . over to the left . . . that's the way.'

I felt better after telling him that. But Terray would have none of it: 'We'll help you. If we get away, so will you.'

At this moment Lachenal shouted: 'Help! Help!'

Obviously he didn't know what he was doing . . . Or did he? He was the only one of the four of us who could see Camp II down below. Perhaps his calls would be heard. They were shouts of despair, reminding me tragically of some climbers lost in the Mont Blanc massif whom I had endeavoured to save. Now it was our turn. The impression was vivid: we were lost.

I joined in with the others. 'One . . . two . . . three . . . *Help*! One . . . two . . . three . . . *Help*!' We tried to shout all together, but without much success; our voices could not have carried more than ten feet. The noise I made was more of a whisper than a shout. Terray insisted that I should put my boots on, but my hands were dead. Neither Rébuffat nor Terray, who were unable to see, could help much, so I said to Lachenal: 'Come and help me put my boots on.'

'Don't be silly, we must go down!'

And off he went once again in the wrong direction, straight down. I was not in the least angry with him: he had been sorely tried by the altitude and by everything he had gone through.

Terray resolutely got out his knife, and with fumbling hands split the uppers of my boots back and front. Split in two like this I could get them on, but it was not easy and I had to make several attempts. I lost heart – what was the use of it all anyway since I was going to stay where I was?

But Terray pulled violently and finally he succeeded. He laced up my now gigantic boots, missing out half the hooks. I was ready now. But how was I going to walk with my stiff joints?

'To the left, Lionel!'

'You're crazy, Maurice,' said Lachenal, 'it's to the right, straight down.'

Terray did not know what to think of these conflicting views. He had not given up, like me: he was going to fight; but what, at the moment, could be do? The three of them discussed which way to go.

I remained sitting in the snow. Gradually my mind lost grip – why should I struggle? I would just let myself drift. I saw pictures of shady slopes, peaceful paths, there was a scent of resin. It was pleasant – I was going to die in my own mountains. My body had no feeling – everything was frozen.

'Aah . . . aah!'

Was it a groan or a call? I gathered my strength for one cry: 'They're coming!' The others heard me and shouted for joy. What a miraculous apparition! 'Schatz . . . It's Schatz!'

Barely 200 yards away Marcel Schatz, waist-deep in snow, was coming slowly towards us like a boat over the surface of the slope. I found this vision of a strong and invincible deliverer inexpressibly moving. I expected everything of him. The shock was violent, and quite shattered me. Death clutched at me and I gave myself up.

When I came to again the wish to live returned and I experienced a violent revulsion of feeling. All was not lost! As Schatz came nearer my eyes never left him for a second – twenty yards – ten yards – he came straight towards me. Why? Without a word he leant over me, held me close, hugged me, and his warm breath revived me.

I could not make the slightest movement – I was like marble. My heart was overwhelmed by such tremendous feeling and yet my eyes remained dry.

'Well done, Maurice. It's marvellous!'

Maurice Herzog, *Annapurna*

CHAPTER 29

◆

The Summit of the World

After so many unsuccessful attempts, Mount Everest was finally climbed in 1953 by a British expedition led by Sir John Hunt. The two climbers who actually reached the summit were the New Zealander Edmund Hillary and the Sherpa Norgay Tenzing. Hillary's account of the final stage of the climb makes a fitting ending to this book.

◆ ◆ ◆

Triumph on Everest

At 6.30 a.m. we crawled slowly out of the tent and stood on our little ledge. Already the upper part of the mountain was bathed in sunlight. It looked warm and inviting, but our ledge was dark and cold. We lifted our oxygen on to our backs and slowly connected up the tubes to our face-masks. My 30-lb load seemed to crush me downwards and stifled all enthusiasm, but when I turned on the oxygen and breathed it deeply, the burden seemed to lighten and the old urge to get to grips with the mountain came back. We strapped on our crampons and tied on our nylon rope; grasped our ice-axes and were ready to go.

I looked at the way ahead. From our tent very steep slopes covered with deep powder snow led up to a prominent snow shoulder on the South-east ridge about a hundred feet above our heads. The slopes were in the shade and breaking trail was going to be cold work. Still a little worried about my boots, I asked Tenzing to lead off. Always willing to do his share, and more than his share if necessary, Tenzing scrambled past me and tackled the slope. With powerful thrusts of his legs he forced his way up in knee-deep snow. I gathered in the rope and followed along behind him.

We were climbing out over the tremendous South face of the mountain, and below us snow chutes and rock ribs plummeted thousands of feet down to the Western Cwm. Starting in the morning straight on to exposed climbing is always trying for the nerves, and this was no exception. In imagination I could feel my heavy load dragging me backwards down the great slopes below; I seemed clumsy and unstable and my breath was hurried and uneven. But Tenzing was pursuing an irresistible course up the slope, and

I didn't have time to think too much. My muscles soon warmed up to their work, my nerves relaxed, and I dropped into the old climbing rhythm and followed steadily up his tracks. As we gained a little height we moved into the rays of the sun, and although we could feel no appreciable warmth, we were greatly encouraged by its presence. Taking no rests, Tenzing ploughed his way up through the deep snow and led out on to the snow shoulder. We were now at a height of 28,000 feet. Towering directly above our heads was the South Summit – steep and formidable. And to the right were the enormous cornices of the summit ridge. We still had a long way to go.

Ahead of us the ridge was sharp and narrow, but rose at an easy angle. I felt warm and strong now, so took over the lead. First I investigated the ridge with my ice-axe. On the sharp crest of the ridge and on the right-hand side loose powder snow was lying dangerously over hard ice. Any attempt to climb on this would only produce an unpleasant slide down towards the Kangshung glacier. But the left-hand slope was better – it was still rather steep, but it had a firm surface of wind-blown powder snow into which our crampons would bite readily.

Taking every care, I moved along on to the left-hand side of the ridge. Everything seemed perfectly safe. With increased confidence, I took another step. Next moment I was almost thrown off balance as the wind-crust suddenly gave way and I sank through it up to my knee. It took me a little while to regain my breath. Then I gradually pulled my leg out of the hole. I was almost upright again when the wind-crust under the other foot gave way and I sank back with both legs enveloped in soft, loose snow to the knees. It was the mountaineer's curse – breakable crust. I forced my way along. Sometimes for a few careful steps I was on the surface, but usually the crust would break at the critical moment and I'd be up to my knees again. Though it was tiring and exasperating work, I felt I had plenty of strength in reserve. For half an hour I continued on in this uncomfortable fashion, with the violent balancing movements I was having to make completely destroying rhythm and breath. It was a great relief when the snow conditions improved and I was able to stay on the surface. I still kept down on the steep slopes on the left of the ridge, but plunged ahead and climbed steadily upwards. I came over a small crest and saw in front of me a tiny hollow on the ridge. And in this hollow lay two oxygen bottles almost completely covered with snow. It was Evans' and Bourdillon's dump.

I rushed forward into the hollow and knelt beside them. Wrenching one of the bottles out of its frozen bed I wiped the snow off its dial – it showed a thousand-pounds pressure – it was nearly a third full of oxygen. I checked the other. It was the same. This was great news. It meant that the oxygen we were carrying on our backs only had to get us back to these bottles instead of right down to the South Col. It gave us more than another hour of endurance. I explained this to Tenzing through my oxygen mask. I don't think he understood, but he realised I was pleased about something and nodded enthusiastically.

I led off again. I knew there was plenty of hard work ahead and Tenzing could save his energies for that. The ridge climbed on upwards rather more steeply now, and then broadened out and shot up at a sharp angle to the foot of the enormous slope running up to the South Summit. I crossed over on to the right-hand side of the ridge and found the snow was firm there. I started chipping a long line of steps up to the foot of the great slope. Here we stamped out a platform for ourselves and I checked our oxygen. Everything seemed to be going well. I had a little more oxygen left than Tenzing, which meant I was obtaining a slightly lower flow rate from my set, but it wasn't enough to matter and there was nothing I could do about it, anyway.

Ahead of us was a really formidable problem, and I stood in my steps and looked at it. Rising from our feet was an enormous slope slanting steeply down on to the precipitous East face of Everest and climbing up with appalling steepness to the South Summit of the mountain 400 feet above us. The left-hand side of the slope was a most unsavoury mixture of steep loose rock and snow, which my New Zealand training immediately regarded with grave suspicion, but which in actual fact the rock-climbing Britons, Evans and Bourdillon, had ascended in much trepidation when on the first assault. The only other route was up the snow itself and still faintly discernible here and there were traces of the track made by the first assault party, who had come down it in preference to their line of ascent up the rocks. The snow route it was for us! There looked to be some tough work ahead, and as Tenzing had been taking it easy for a while I hard-heartedly waved him through. With his first six steps I realised that the work was going to be much harder than I had thought. His first two steps were on top of the snow, the third was up to his ankles, and by the sixth he was up to his hips. But almost lying against the steep slope, he drove himself onwards, ploughing a track directly upwards. Even following in his steps was hard work, for the loose snow refused to pack into safe steps. After a long and valiant spell he was plainly in need of a rest, so I took over.

Immediately I realised that we were on dangerous ground. On this very steep slope the snow was soft and deep with little coherence. My ice-axe shaft sank into it without any support and we had no sort of a belay. The only factor that made it at all possible to progress was a thin crust of frozen snow which tied the whole slope together. But this crust was a poor support. I was forcing my way upwards, plunging deep steps through it, when suddenly with a dull breaking noise an area of crust all around me about six feet in diameter broke off into large sections and slid with me back through three or four steps. And then I stopped; but the crust, gathering speed, slithered on out of sight. It was a nasty shock. My whole training told me that the slope was exceedingly dangerous, but at the same time I was saying to myself: 'Ed, my boy, this is Everest – you've got to push it a bit harder!' My solar plexus was tight with fear as I ploughed on. Half-way up I stopped, exhausted. I could look down 10,000 feet between my legs, and I have never felt more insecure. Anxiously I waved Tenzing up to me.

'What do you think of it, Tenzing?' And the immediate response, 'Very bad, very dangerous!' 'Do you think we should go on?' and there came the familiar reply that never helped you much but never let you down: 'Just as you wish!' I waved him on to take a turn at leading. Changing the lead much more frequently now, we made our unhappy way upwards, sometimes sliding back and wiping out half a dozen steps, and never feeling confident that at any moment the whole slope might not avalanche. In the hope of some sort of a belay we traversed a little towards the rocks, but found no help in their smooth, holdless surfaces. We plunged on upwards. And then I noticed that, a little above us, the left-hand rock ridge turned into snow and the snow looked firm and safe. Laboriously and carefully we climbed across some steep rock, and I sank my ice-axe shaft into the snow of the ridge. It went in firm and hard. The pleasure of this safe belay after all the uncertainty below was like a reprieve to a condemned man. Strength flowed into my limbs, and I could feel my tense nerves and muscles relaxing. I swung my ice-axe at the slope and started chipping a line of steps upwards – it was very steep, but seemed so gloriously safe. Tenzing, an inexpert but enthusiastic step cutter, took a turn and chopped a haphazard line of steps up another pitch. We were making fast time now and the slope was starting to ease off. Tenzing gallantly waved me through, and with a growing feeling of excitement I cramponed up some firm slopes to the rounded top of the South Summit. It was only 9 a.m.

With intense interest I looked at the vital ridge leading to the summit – the ridge about which Evans and Bourdillon had made such gloomy forecasts. At first glance it was an exceedingly impressive and indeed a frightening sight. In the narrow crest of this ridge, the basic rock of the mountain had a thin capping of snow and ice – ice that reached out over the East face in enormous cornices, overhanging and treacherous, and only waiting for the careless foot of the mountaineer to break off and crash 10,000 feet to the Kangshung glacier. And from the cornices the snow dropped steeply to the left to merge with the enormous rock bluffs which towered 8,000 feet above the Western Cwm. It was impressive all right! But as I looked my fears started to lift a little. Surely I could see a route there? For this snow slope on the left, although very steep and exposed, was practically continuous for the first half of the ridge, although in places the great cornices reached hungrily across. If we could make a route along that snow slope, we could go quite a distance at least.

With a feeling almost of relief, I set to work with my ice-axe and cut a platform for myself just down off the top of the South Summit. Tenzing did the same, and then we removed our oxygen sets and sat down. The day was still remarkably fine, and we felt no discomfort through our thick layers of clothing from either wind or cold. We had a drink out of Tenzing's water bottle and then I checked our oxygen supplies. Tenzing's bottle was practically exhausted, but mine still had a little in it. As well as this, we each had a full bottle. I decided that the difficulties ahead would demand as light a weight on our backs as possible so determined to use only the full bottles. I removed Tenzing's empty bottle and my nearly empty one and laid them in the snow. With particular care I connected up our last bottles and tested to see that they were working efficiently. The needles on the dials were steady on 3,300 lb. per square inch pressure – they were very full bottles holding just over 800 litres of oxygen each. At three litres a minute we consumed 180 litres an hour, and this meant a total endurance of nearly four and a half hours. This didn't seem much for the problems ahead, but I was determined if necessary to cut down to two litres a minute for the homeward trip.

I was greatly encouraged to find how, even at 28,700 feet and with no oxygen, I could work out slowly but clearly the problems of mental arithmetic that the oxygen supply demanded. A correct answer was imperative – any mistake could well mean a trip with no return. But we had no time to waste. I stood up and took a series of photographs in every direction, then thrust my camera back to its warm home inside my clothing. I heaved my now pleasantly light oxygen load on to my back and connected up my tubes. I did the same for Tenzing, and we were ready to go. I asked Tenzing to belay me and then, with a growing air of excitement, I cut a broad and safe line of steps down to the snow saddle below the South Summit. I wanted an easy route when we came back up here weak and tired. Tenzing came down the steps and joined me, and then belayed once again.

I moved along on the steep snow slope on the left side of the ridge. With the first blow of my ice-axe my excitement increased. The snow – to my astonishment – was crystalline and hard. A couple of rhythmical blows of the ice-axe produced a step that was big enough even for our oversize high-altitude boots. But best of all the steps were strong and safe. A little conscious of the great drops beneath me, I chipped a line of steps for the full length of the rope – forty feet – and then forced the shaft of my ice-axe firmly into the snow. It made a fine belay and I looped the rope around it. I waved to Tenzing to join me, and as he moved slowly and carefully along the steps I took in the rope. When he reached me, he thrust his ice-axe into the snow and protected me with a good tight rope as I went on cutting steps. It was exhilarating work – the summit ridge of Everest, the crisp snow and the smooth easy blows of the ice-axe all combined to make me feel a greater sense of power than I had ever felt at great altitudes before. I went on cutting for rope length after rope length.

We were now approaching a point where one of the great cornices was encroaching on to our slope. We'd have to go down to the rocks to avoid it. I cut a line of steps steeply down the slope to a small ledge on top of the rocks. There wasn't much room, but it made a reasonably safe stance. I waved to Tenzing to join me. As he came down to me I realised there was something wrong with him. I had been so absorbed in the technical problems of the ridge that I hadn't thought much about Tenzing, except for a vague feeling that he seemed to move along the steps with unnecessary slowness. But now it was quite obvious that he was not only moving extremely slowly, but he was breathing quickly and with difficulty and was in considerable distress. I immediately suspected his oxygen set and helped him down on to the ledge so that I could examine it. The first thing I noticed was that from the outlet of his face-mask there were hanging some long icicles. I looked at it more closely and found that the outlet tube – about two inches in diameter – was almost completely blocked up with ice. This was preventing Tenzing from exhaling freely and must have made it extremely unpleasant for him. Fortunately the outlet tube was made of rubber and by manipulating this with my hand I was able to release all the ice and let it fall out. The valves started operating and Tenzing was given immediate relief. Just as a check I examined my own set and found that it, too, had partly frozen up in the outlet tube, but not sufficiently to have affected me a great deal. I removed the ice out of it without a great deal of trouble. Automatically I looked at our pressure gauges – just over 2,900 lb. (2,900 lb. was just over 700 litres; 180 into 700 was about 4) – we had nearly four hours' endurance left. That meant we weren't going badly.

I looked at the route ahead. This next piece wasn't going to be easy. Our rock ledge was perched right on top of the enormous bluff running down into the Western Cwm. In fact, almost under my feet, I could see the dirty patch on the floor of the Cwm which I knew was Camp IV. In a sudden urge to escape our isolation I waved and shouted, and then as suddenly stopped as I realised my foolishness. Against the vast expanse of Everest 8,000 feet above them, we'd be quite invisible to the best binoculars. I turned back to the problem ahead. The rock was far too steep to attempt to drop down and go around this pitch. The only thing to do was to try to shuffle along the ledge and cut handholds in the bulging ice that was trying to push me off it. Held on a tight rope by Tenzing, I cut a few handholds and then thrust my ice-axe as hard as I could into the solid snow and ice. Using this to take my weight I moved quickly along the ledge. It proved easier than I had anticipated. A few more handholds, another quick swing across them, and I was able to cut a line of steps up on to a safe slope and chop out a roomy terrace from which to belay Tenzing as he climbed up to me.

We were now fast approaching the most formidable obstacle on the ridge – a great rock step. This step had always been visible in aerial photographs, and in 1951 on the Everest Reconnaissance we had seen it quite clearly with glasses from Thyangboche. We had always thought of it as the obstacle on the ridge which could well spell defeat. I cut a line of steps across the last snow slope, and then commenced traversing over a steep rock slab that led to the foot of the great step. The holds were small and hard to see, and I brushed my snow glasses away from my eyes. Immediately I was blinded by a bitter wind sweeping across the ridge and laden with particles of ice. I hastily replaced my glasses and blinked away the ice and tears until I could see again. But it made me realise how efficient was our clothing in protecting us from the rigours of even a fine day at 29,000 feet. Still half blinded, I climbed across the slab, and then dropped down into a tiny snow hollow at the foot of the step. And here Tenzing joined me.

I looked anxiously up at the rocks. Planted squarely across the ridge in a vertical bluff, they looked extremely difficult, and I knew that our strength and ability to climb steep rock at this altitude would be severely limited. I examined the route out to the left. By dropping fifty or a hundred feet over steep slabs, we might be able to get round the bottom of the bluff, but there was no indication that we'd be able to climb back on to the ridge again. And to lose any height now might be fatal. Search as I could, I was unable to see an easy route up to the step, or, in fact, any route at all. Finally, in desperation I examined the right-hand end of the bluff. Attached to this and overhanging the precipitous East face was a large cornice. This cornice, in preparation for its inevitable crash down the mountainside, had started to lose its grip on the rock and a long narrow vertical crack had been formed between the rock and the ice. The crack was large enough to take the human frame, and though it offered little security, it was at least a route. I quickly made up my mind – Tenzing had an excellent belay and we must be near the top – it was worth a try.

Before attempting the pitch, I produced my camera once again. I had no confidence that I would be able to climb this crack, and with a surge of competitive pride which unfortunately afflicts even mountaineers, I determined to have proof that at least we had reached a good deal higher than the South Summit. I took a few photographs and then made another rapid check of the oxygen – 2,550 lb. pressure (2,550 from 3,300 leaves 750. 750 over 3,300 is about two-ninths. Two-ninths off 800 litres leaves about 600 litres. 600 divided by 180 is nearly 3½.) Three and a half hours to go. I examined Tenzing's belay to make sure it was a good one and then slowly crawled inside the crack.

In front of me was the rock wall, vertical but with a few promising holds. Behind me was the ice-wall of the cornice, glittering and hard but cracked here and there. I took a hold on the rock in iron and then jammed one of my crampons hard into the ice behind. Leaning back with my oxygen set on the ice, I slowly levered myself upwards. Searching feverishly with my spare boot, I found a tiny ledge on the rock and took some of the weight off my other leg. Leaning back on the cornice, I fought to regain my breath. Constantly at the back of my mind was the fear that the cornice might break off, and my nerves were taut with suspense. But slowly I forced my way up – wriggling and jambing and using every little hold. In one place I managed to force my ice-axe into a crack in the ice, and this gave me the necessary purchase to get over a holdless stretch. And then I found a solid foothold in a hollow in the ice, and next moment I was reaching over the top of the rock and pulling myself to safety. The rope came tight – its forty feet had been barely enough.

I lay on the little rock ledge panting furiously. Gradually it dawned on me that I was up the step, and I felt a glow of pride and determination that completely subdued my temporary feelings of weakness. For the first time on the whole expedition I really knew I was going to get to the top. 'It will have to be pretty tough to stop us now' was my thought. But I couldn't entirely ignore the feeling of astonishment and wonder that I'd been able to get up such a difficulty at 29,000 feet even with oxygen.

When I was breathing more evenly I stood up and, leaning over the edge, waved to Tenzing to come up. He moved into the crack and I gathered in the rope and took some of his weight. Then he, in turn, commenced to struggle and jam and force his way up until I was able to pull him to safety – gasping for breath. We rested for a moment. Above us the ridge continued on as before – enormous overhanging cornices on the right and steep snow sloped on the left running down to the rock bluffs. But the angle of the snow slopes was easing off. I went on chipping a line of steps, but thought it safe enough for us to move together in order to save time. The ridge rose up in a great series of snake-like undulations which bore away to the right, each one concealing the next. I had no idea where the top was. I'd cut a line of steps around the side of one undulation and another would come into view. We were getting desperately tired now and Tenzing was going very slowly. I'd been cutting steps for almost two hours, and my back and arms were starting to tire. I tried cramponing along the slope without cutting steps, but my feet slipped uncomfortably down the slope. I went on cutting. We seemed to have been going for a very long time and my confidence was fast evaporating. Bump followed bump with maddening regularity. A patch of shingle barred our way, and I climbed dully up it and started cutting steps around another bump. And then I realised that this was the last bump, for ahead of me the ridge dropped steeply away in a great corniced curve, and out in the distance I could see the pastel shades and fleecy clouds of the highlands of Tibet.

To my right a slender snow ridge climbed up to a snowy dome about forty feet above our heads. But all the way along the ridge the thought had haunted me that the summit might be the crest of a cornice. It was too late to take risks now. I asked Tenzing to belay me strongly, and I started cutting a cautious line of steps up the ridge. Peering from side to side, and thrusting with my ice-axe, I tried to discover a possible cornice, but everything seemed solid and firm. I waved Tenzing up to me. A few more whacks of the ice-axe, a few very weary steps, and we were on the summit of Everest.

Edmund Hillary, *High Adventure*

Glossary

◆

Aiguille – a pointed peak or needle of rock

Alpenstock – long iron-tipped staff to assist in mountain walking

Arête – a ridge

Arroyo – a gully

Belay – v. To secure a rope by hitching it over a projection or passing it round one's body. – n. a spike of rock etc. used to belay

Bergschrund – a crevasse separating a glacier from the snow slopes above it

Bivouac – a temporary overnight resting place

Cairn – a pile of stones to mark a summit

Chimney – a narrow vertical cleft in a wall of rock

Col – a mountain pass

Couloir – a narrow mountain gully

Crampons – metal frames with spikes attached, worn under boots for walking on ice or snow

Crevasse – a deep open crack in a glacier

Glacis – sloping defensive wall

Gneiss – rock formed by layers of minerals

Moraine – an area covered by rock and debris carried down by a glacier

Névé – a high snow field above a glacier

Pitch – a short, steep section of a rock-climb

Sérac – an ice-tower on a glacier caused by crevasses crossing

Talus – debris at the foot of a cliff

Traverse – to cross a mountain horizontally or diagonally

Sources and Acknowledgements

◆

CHAPTER 1: 'The Abode of the Gods' from Homer, *Odyssey*, trans. A.D. Murray, Loeb Classics, 1919; 'Olympus Explored' from Sir John Mandeville, *Travels*, ed. J.O. Helliwell, Early English Text Society, 1883; 'Olympus Etherialized' and 'Zeus on Mount Ida' from *Poems of Alexander Pope*, ed. Maynard Mack, Methuen, 1967; 'In the Footsteps of Moses' from *The Pilgrimage of St Silvia to the Holy Places*, trans. J.H. Bernard, Palestine Pilgrims' Text Society, London, 1891; 'Moses the Mountaineer' from John Ruskin, *Modern Painters*, Vol. 5, ed. Cook & Wedderburn, George Allen, 1905.

CHAPTER 2: 'The Battle of Thermopylae' from Herodotus, *Histories*, trans. A.D. Godley, Loeb Classics, 1922; 'Hannibal Crosses the Alps' from Livy, *Histories*, trans. B.O. Foster, Loeb Classics, 1919; 'The Massacre at Roncesvalles' from *Hilaire Belloc*, ed. W.N. Roughead, Mercury Books, 1962. Reprinted by permission of Peters Fraser & Dunlop Group Ltd.

CHAPTER 3: 'St Basil's Retreat' from St Basil, *Letters*, trans. Deferrari, Loeb Classics, 1926; 'St Benedict at Subiaco' and 'The Foundation of the Grande Chartreuse' from *Butler's Lives of the Saints*, ed. Husenbeth, Nemo, 1866; 'St Francis on La Verna' from *The Little Flowers of Saint Francis*, trans. T.W. Arnold, Dent, 1898.

CHAPTER 4: 'On the Road to Cathay' from Marco Polo, *The Travels*, trans. R. Latham, Penguin, 1958. Reprinted by permission of Penguin Books Ltd; 'An Ascent in Provence' from Francis Gribble, *Early Mountaineers*, T. Fisher Unwin, 1899; 'Tall Stories from the Caucasus' from Sir John Mandeville, *Travels*, Early English Text Society, as above.

CHAPTER 5: 'The Ascent of the Inaccessible' from Francis Gribble, *Early Mountaineers*, as above; 'On the Slopes of Mount Carmel' from *The Complete Works of St John of the Cross*, trans. E. Allison Peers, Burns Oates, 1935. Reprinted by permission of Burns & Oates Ltd; 'Shakespeare and Mountains' from John Ruskin, *Modern Painters*, as above; 'Evelyn Crossing the Simplon' from John Evelyn, *Diary*, ed. E. de Beer, O.U.P., 1959.

CHAPTER 6: 'The Death of Empedocles' from Diogenes Laertius, trans. A. Hicks, Loeb Classics, 1970; 'Vesuvius in Eruption' from Pliny the

Younger, *Letters*, trans. V. Melmoth and W.M. Hutchinson, Loeb Classics, 1921; 'Evelyn on Vesuvius' from John Evelyn, *Diary*, as above.

CHAPTER 7: 'Nature's Extravagancies' from John Dennis, *Miscellanies in Verse and Prose*, 1693; 'Winter Crossings of the Alps' from George Berkeley, *Collected Works*, Vol. VIII, ed. A.A. Luce, Nelson, 1957. Reprinted by permission of Thomas Nelson and Sons Ltd; 'Rousseau Entertains Himself' from Jean Jacques Rousseau, *Confessions*, trans. J.M. Cohen, Penguin, 1953. Reprinted by permission of Penguin Books Ltd; 'Pregnant with Religion and Poetry' from *Letters of Thomas Gray*, ed. Toynbee, O.U.P., 1935; 'The Glaciers of Savoy' from C.E. Mathews, *Annals of Mont Blanc*, Fisher Unwin, 1898; 'Barbarism and Beauty' from *The Letters of David Hume*, ed. J.T.T. Greig, O.U.P., 1932. Reprinted by permission of Oxford University Press; 'Gray in Borrowdale, 1769' from Thomas Gray, *Journal in the Lakes*, ed. E. Gosse, Macmillan, 1884; 'Johnson in the Highlands' and 'Boswell on the Same Road' from *Johnson and Boswell, a Journey to the Western Isles*, ed. R.W. Chapman, O.U.P., 1924.

CHAPTER 8: 'Balmat's Dream Come True' from C.E. Mathews, *Annals of Mont Blanc*, as above.

CHAPTER 9: 'Wordsworth on Snowdon' and 'The Crossing of the Alps' from William Wordsworth, *The Prelude*, ed. J.C. Maxwell, Penguin, 1971; 'Coleridge's Descent from Broad Crag' from Kathleen Coburn, *Inquiring Spirit*, Routledge and Kegan Paul, 1951. Reprinted by permission of Kathleen Coburn; 'To Joanna' and 'On the Summit of Helvellyn' from *The Poetical Works of William Wordsworth*, ed. T. Hutchinson, O.U.P., 1911; 'The Bonfire on Skiddaw' from R. Southey, *Selected Letters*, ed. M.H. Fitzgerald, O.U.P., 1912.

CHAPTER 10: 'With Shelley in Chamonix' from *Journals of Mary Shelley*, ed. Paula R. Feldman & Diana Scott-Kilvert, O.U.P., 1987. Reprinted by permission of Oxford University Press; 'Mont Blanc' from *Shelley's Poetical Works*, ed. T. Hutchinson, O.U.P., 1970; 'The Monster on the Montanvert' from Mary Shelley, *Frankenstein*, Penguin, 1985; 'A Journal for Augusta' from *Lord Byron, Letters & Papers*, ed. Marchand, Belknap Press, 1976. Reprinted by permission of John Murray (Publishers) Ltd; 'Keats on Ben Nevis' from *Letters of John Keats*, ed. Maurice B. Forman, O.U.P., 1935. Reprinted by permission of Oxford University Press.

CHAPTER 11: 'The Passage of the Cordillera' from Charles Darwin, *The Voyage of the Beagle*, ed. H.E.L. Mellersh, Heron Books, 1968; 'The Motion of the Glaciers' from John Ruskin, *Modern Painters*, as above; 'How many Degrees Below Freezing?' from John Tyndall, *The Glaciers of the Alps*, Dent, 1906.

CHAPTER 12: 'The Fiancée of Mont Blanc' from C.E. Mathews, *Annals of Mont Blanc*, as above; 'Suggestions for Alpine Travellers' from *Peaks, Passes and Glaciers*, ed. J. Ball, Longman, 1859; 'The First Ascent of the Weisshorn' from John Tyndall, *Mountaineering in 1861*, Dent, 1906.

CHAPTER 13: 'A Garden of Eden in Sicily' from John Henry Newman, *Letters*, Vol. III, ed. I.T. Ker and T. Gornall, O.U.P., 1979. Reprinted by permission of Oxford University Press; 'The Economist in the Alps' from W. Bagehot, *Works*, ed. N. St John-Stevas, 1965; 'The Mountain Glory' from John Ruskin, *Modern Painters*, as above; 'A Reading Party in Scotland' from *Poems of Arthur Hugh Clough*, ed. F.L. Mulhauser, O.U.P., 1974.

CHAPTER 14: 'Travellers at the Great St Bernard' from Charles Dickens, *Little Dorrit*, ed. L. Trilling, O.U.P., 1953; 'A Palace of the Kings of France' from *Matthew Arnold*, ed. M. Allott and R.H. Super, O.U.P., 1986; 'Ruskin's Rebuke to the Hermits' from John Ruskin, *Praeterita*, ed. K. Clark, O.U.P., 1949; 'Gloomy Blackclad Men' from Edmund Lear, *Selected Letters*, ed. Vivien Noakes, O.U.P., 1988. Reprinted by permission of Watson, Little Ltd.

CHAPTER 15: 'Triumph and Tragedy' from Edward Whymper, *Scrambles in the Alps*, John Murray, 1871; 'The Italian Angle' from G. Rey, *The Matterhorn*, Blackwell, 1946; 'Zermatt' from Thomas Hardy, *Complete Poetical Works*, ed. Hynes, O.U.P., 1982.

CHAPTER 16: 'The Mountain Gloom' from John Ruskin, *Modern Painters*, as above; 'The Lady Bountiful' from Augustus Hare, *The Story of My Life*, Century, 1984; 'The Guides of Chamonix' from C.E. Mathews, *Annals of Mont Blanc*, as above; 'A Guide on the Schreckhorn' from Leslie Stephen, *The Playground of Europe*, Longman, 1894; 'Advice for the Novice Traveller' and 'Alpine Advertisements' from E. Whymper, *Guide to Zermatt and the Matterhorn*, John Murray, 1897.

CHAPTER 17: 'The American and his Dog' from W.A.B. Coolidge, *Alpine Studies*, Longman, 1912; 'A Lady's Life in the Rocky Mountains' from Isabella Bird Bishop, *This Grand Beyond*, Century, 1984; 'Mountain-sickness on Chimborazo' from E. Whymper, *Travels Among the Great Andes of the Equator*, John Murray, 1892.

CHAPTER 18: 'Newman in Ashes' from John Henry Newman, *Letters*, Vol. III, as above. Reprinted by permission of Oxford University Press; 'Songs of Callicles' from Matthew Arnold, as above; 'A Virginian on Vesuvius' from Mark Twain, *The Innocents Abroad*, Century, 1988; 'The Ascent of Cotopaxi' from E. Whymper, *Travels among the Great Andes of the Equator*, as above; 'The Spoils of the Volcanoes' from E. Whymper, *A Guide to Zermatt and the Matterhorn*, as above.

CHAPTER 19: 'Love is of the Valley' from *The Works of Alfred Lord Tennyson*, Macmillan, 1915; 'The Desecration of the Alps' from John Ruskin, *Sesame and Lilies*, George Allen, 1907; 'The Repentant Climber' from *The Oxford Book of Local Verse*, ed. J. Holloway, O.U.P., 1987; 'Mountaineers vs Mountain Lovers' from Arnold Lunn, *The Alps*, Williams and Norgate, 1914. Reprinted by permission of Peter Lunn.

CHAPTER 20: 'Experimental Faith' from Leslie Stephen, *The Playground of Europe*, as above; 'The True Mountaineer is a Wanderer' from A.F. Mummery, *My Climbs in the Alps and Caucasus*, T. Fisher Unwin, 1908; 'Beyond Platonic Love' from G. Rey, *The Matterhorn*, as above; 'Alpine Mysticism and Cold Philosophy' from Arnold Lunn, *Mountain Jubilee*, Eyre and Spottiswoode, 1943. Reprinted by permission of Peter Lunn.

CHAPTER 21: ' "In attempting to pass the corner I slipped and fell" ' from E. Whymper, *Scrambles in the Alps*, as above; 'The Death of Carrel' from E. Whymper, *Guide to Zermatt and the Matterhorn*, as above; 'The Golden Moments before the Fall' from Arnold Lunn, *The Mountains of Youth*, Eyre and Spottiswoode, 1925. Reprinted by permission of Peter Lunn; 'Death by Misadventure?' from F.S. Smythe, *Over Welsh Hills*, A & C Black, 1941. Reprinted by permission of Nona, Countess of Essex.

CHAPTER 22: 'A Night Adventure in the Dolomites' from F.S. Smythe, *Climbs and Ski Runs*, Blackwood, 1929. Reprinted by permission of Nona, Countess of Essex; 'Management and Leadership on the Mountains' from Geoffrey Winthrop Young, *Mountain Craft*, Methuen 1920. Reprinted by permission of William Heinemann Ltd; 'Everest by Divine Command' from Eric Shipton, *Upon That Mountain*, Hodder & Stoughton, 1943. Reprinted by permission of the Executors of the Estate of Eric Shipton.

CHAPTER 23: 'Mechanization and the Cult of Danger' from R.G.L. Irving, *The Romance of Mountaineering*, Dent, 1935. Reprinted by permission of J.M. Dent Ltd; 'Death on the Eigerwand' from James Ramsey Ullman, *The Age of Mountaineering*, Collins, 1956. Reprinted by permission of Harper Collins Ltd.

CHAPTER 24: 'Camp Six' is from Eric Shipton, *Upon That Mountain*, as above. Reprinted by permission of the Executors of the Estate of Eric Shipton.

CHAPTER 25: 'Switzerland' and 'The Mountains of Wales' are reprinted from A.D. Godley, *Fifty Poems*, ed. C.L. Graves and C.R.L. Fletcher, O.U.P., 1927; 'W.P.K' from Freya Stark, *Traveller's Prelude*, John Murray, 1950. Reprinted by permission of John Murray (Publishers) Ltd; 'Mountains' from W.H. Auden, *Selected Poems*, Penguin, 1958. Reprinted by permission of Faber & Faber Ltd; 'Rocky Acres' from Robert Graves, *Collected*

Poems, A.P. Watt & Son, 1947. Reprinted by permission of A.P. Watt Ltd on behalf of the Trustees of the Robert Graves Copyright Trust; 'St Gervais' from Michael Roberts, *The Faber Book of Modern Verse*, Faber, 1936. Reprinted by permission of Faber & Faber Ltd; 'John Muir on Mount Ritter' from Gary Snyder, *Myths and Texts*, Corinth Books, 1960. Reprinted by permission of New Directions Publishing Corporation; 'Breathless' from Wilfred Noyce, *Poems*, Heinemann, 1960. Reprinted by permission of William Heinemann Ltd.

CHAPTER 26: 'The Ascent of Kanchenjunga' from Arthur Ransome, *Swallowdale*, Jonathan Cape, 1931. Reprinted by permission of the Executors of the Estate of Arthur Ransome and Jonathan Cape Ltd; 'Welsh Beginning' from Wilfred Noyce, *Men and Mountains*, Geoffrey Bles, 1949. Reprinted by permission of Harper Collins Ltd.

CHAPTER 27: 'The Perfect Rock Climb' is reprinted from W.H. Murray, *Undiscovered Scotland*, Dent, 1951. Reprinted by permission of J.M. Dent Ltd; 'Skiddaw' from A. Wainwright, *The Northern Fells*, Westmoreland Gazette Ltd. n.d. Reprinted by permission of the Westmoreland Gazette.

CHAPTER 28: 'Mission Accomplished' is reprinted from M. Herzog, *Annapurna*, trans. Nea Morin and Janet Adam Smith, Jonathan Cape, 1952. Reprinted by permission of Jonathan Cape Ltd.

CHAPTER 29: 'Triumph on Everest' from E. Hillary, *High Adventure*, Hodder & Stoughton, 1955. Reprinted by permission of Hodder & Stoughton Ltd.

Index

◆